Praise for
# Act Natural

"Traig mocks contemporary and historical parenting advice with usually spot-on dark humor. . . . The upside of reading *Act Natural* is that you feel better about whatever nonsense your children have committed, which is the point."

—*Wall Street Journal*

"In *Act Natural*, her informative deep dive into Western caretaking, Traig investigates the history of parenting manuals, nutrition, children's literature, and more to show that, in the end, no one really knows the right way to raise a child. We're all just doing the best we can."

—*Real Simple*

"This is the best parenting book I've read in a very long time. I recommended it to everyone I could. . . . After reading through this cultural history of parenting, I feel so much better about many of my parenting choices."

—Book Riot

"With a dry wit, and brutal honesty about her own parenting experience, Traig weaves personal anecdotes throughout this thoroughly researched, incredibly interesting read. . . . Completely refreshing. Much like parenting itself, *Act Natural* will teach readers something new in one moment and make them laugh out loud the next."

—*Booklist* (starred review)

# Act Natural

## ALSO BY JENNIFER TRAIG

*Devil in the Details: Scenes from an Obsessive Girlhood*

*Well Enough Alone: A Cultural History of My Hypochondria*

# Act Natural

A Cultural History
of Misadventures
in Parenting

## JENNIFER TRAIG

ecco
*An Imprint of HarperCollinsPublishers*

ACT NATURAL. Copyright © 2019 by Jennifer Traig. All rights reserved. Printed in the United States of America. No part of this book may be used or reproduced in any manner whatsoever without written permission except in the case of brief quotations embodied in critical articles and reviews. For information, address HarperCollins Publishers, 195 Broadway, New York, NY 10007.

HarperCollins books may be purchased for educational, business, or sales promotional use. For information, please email the Special Markets Department at SPsales@harpercollins.com.

A hardcover edition of this book was published in 2019 by Ecco, an imprint of HarperCollins Publishers.

FIRST ECCO PAPERBACK EDITION PUBLISHED 2020.

Designed by Michelle Crowe

Library of Congress Cataloging-in-Publication Data has been applied for.

ISBN 978-0-06-246981-6

20 21 22 23 24   LSC   10 9 8 7 6 5 4 3 2

Rob, Rachel, Sam, with love

# Contents

## Introduction

# Act Natural

Though we think of having children as the most natural thing in the world, actually becoming a parent has taught me that there's nothing natural about it, and to pretend otherwise leads only to trouble. A short time ago I followed my natural impulse to nap on the rug while my young son followed his to deface, in hot pink marker, the floor, the wall, the velvet couch, a lamp, an electrical socket, and a coffee-table book lengthily inscribed by a former first lady. Had we been at home, this would have been irritating, but we were staying at someone else's house, so it was mortifying.

"Sam was being Sam," I explained helplessly when my husband came to survey the wreckage. "It's just his nature."

"Did you fall asleep?"

"That's *my* nature."

"This mess is on you two," Rob answered, shaking his head. "Let's not drag nature into it."

And while I thought it might be nice if Rob had fought *his* nature to be right about this particular matter, we both knew he was. From the cocktail of chemicals that brought our two children into the world to the countless perverse decisions we've made every day since, the only role nature has played is scapegoat.

But that's never how it feels. In the moment, everything we do seems like the logical, instinctual, natural response. Sam cries, and we pick him up. His older sister, Rachel, asks us to intervene in their fight, and we do.

At the store, one or the other will lick a package of something he or she desperately wants, and after making sure no one's looking, we will place it back on the shelf. Normal, logical, appropriate. It doesn't even feel like a decision, just the only thing a sane person would do. Act natural.

But really, of course, that's all it is—an act, a performance of a script that was written a long time ago. And when recently I started to examine the hundreds of parental actions I take every day, I realized that I have no idea why I do any of them, or whether I should or shouldn't. I just go along with the received wisdom, without asking where I received it from, or whether it's even wise. Dr. Spock's famous line "You know more than you think you do" had it almost right—as a parent I know what to do most of the time, but I don't think about why I do it, or if it's such a good idea after all.

As is true in many houses with small children, questions are asked all the time in ours, but these are seldom about big-picture matters. Why is there yogurt on the TV? Why are my car keys in the trash? Where's the front doorknob? Who let a squirrel in the house?

Much of what we do, in fact, other parents would never consider. The things we take for granted as normal and natural strike parents in other parts of the world as absurd and dangerous, as wrong as letting your toddler play with a machete, which, by the way, some Congolese parents do. And as horrified as we are by their methods, they are by ours. Playing with knives is one thing, but putting your child to sleep alone? That's child abuse.

Which is where this book comes from, a curiosity about what parents actually did throughout history, what they do now in other parts of the world, and why, here and now, we do what we do.

Here and now, most of us rely on rules and a general idea of what constitutes good parenting as defined by developed-world, middle-class Westerners. This is the parenting tradition I've inherited, and thus the one I focus on, though it's by no means the only or the best. It is certainly worth interrogating, which is in part what this book is trying to do.

Because the tradition does and should raise a lot of questions. Why do we teach our children what sounds animals make before we teach them the sounds people do? Why do we encourage them to crawl, when it doesn't help them learn to walk? Why do we read them stories about homicidal stepparents? Why do we sing them soothing songs about fatal accidents and incurable diseases? Why do we beg them to eat? Why do we give them time-outs, and why do we think this changes anything? Why do they know the toy keys are not the real keys, and why do they think the real keys are better? Why do we let other people take care of them? Why do we take care of them ourselves? Was it always this hard, and is it this hard everywhere else?

The short answer to that last question is: probably. Even the Buddha named his son "Burden," and by the way, he left the family a week after the birth. You can hardly expect the less enlightened of us to do any better. Biology certainly doesn't. As sociobiologist Robert Trivers argued in a landmark paper, the ideal pairing, from an evolutionary perspective, is children who ask for too much coupled with parents who won't meet all their demands. This way, both parent and child survive. Their selfish/withholding genes pass on, and the hard work continues.

It is—let's be clear—very, very hard. Freud called child-rearing one of the three "impossible professions" (the other two: governing nations and psychoanalysis). To do even a half-assed job is a Sisyphean task. Children get away with things no adult would. They defecate in the living room; they assault us with impunity. In a single week one summer, I was smacked, punched, scratched, and bitten; my ears were boxed, my hair was pulled, and my glasses were thrown across a parking lot. I was slapped across the face *with a foot*.

With children, the most basic human activities are fraught. A couple of years ago my husband and son stumbled out of a restaurant bathroom, both looking traumatized. "Did he pee his pants?" I asked. "He peed his *daddy*," Rob answered. "He peed all over me. He peed on *his own face*."

It's all so hard, but what choice do we have? The modern practice known as natural parenting appealed until I realized it does not in fact mean "do nothing," and requires as many if not more interventions than unnatural parenting does. No parent really wants nature alone to take its course, though parents have often turned to nature when faced with a crisis of confidence. This is a little like asking the house cat for contractor recommendations, and is generally just as helpful. When nature alone has served as parent, as in the case of the feral children who occasionally turn up in history, things haven't turned out so well, unless you were hoping for a chronically masturbating child with no language skills or table manners.

Since I'm hoping for a bit more, the past few years have been a lot of work. Much of what children subject us to—sleep deprivation, extreme noise, stress positions, physical abuse, use of bodily fluids as weapons—fits the technical definition of torture. Most of our parenting actions are taken simply because they've broken us down. We are too tired to question the custom, too weary to fight, too worn out to spend the next two hours— okay, four—playing Mozart musical chairs and not watching eight consecutive episodes of *Caillou*. Why is my forehead bruised? What's this on the carpet? Who wants to watch episodes nine and ten?

It is so difficult that despite Trivers's argument I can't help but think it used to be easier, or the species simply wouldn't have continued. Oh, sure, caveman parents had to fight off mastodons and appease the bear god, but they didn't have to worry about competitive preschools. Medieval parents never had to fish a smoking banana out of a heating grate, never had to pull over when their toddler figured out how to open the door of a moving car. They never had, as I did the other day, to scrub grease stains off the upholstered dining room chairs after my son decided to spray them all with PAM. They did not bother with time-outs, they did not agonize over self-esteem, and if only because they didn't have indoor plumbing, they didn't have children who routinely confused the toilet with the bathtub, climbing feetfirst into the former and relieving themselves in the latter. Why are your socks wet? Why are you making that face? Why is the bathwater opaque?

And the most troubling question of all: Why do we think any of this matters? The best research indicates that little of it actually does. Above a certain threshold, it makes no difference how you treat your kids. You can spend their entire childhood reading them Plato, supervising violin practice, and carefully cultivating their self-image, but the steaming cauldron of seventh-grade homeroom is ultimately going to have more of an impact on them than you are.

Which is not to say that you're not ruining their lives, the minor missteps snowballing into lifelong grievances and injuries. My husband and I play this game all the time, wondering what mistakes we're making now will surface in group therapy when our kids are in college. Then, of course, there are all the things we're doing that are unwittingly killing them that we won't even realize are dangerous for another twenty years, just as our parents blithely drove us around unbuckled in smoke-filled cars. My own mother, a nurse married to a chest surgeon, smoked so often while nursing me that my father termed the tableau "Madonna and Cigarette." Maybe our equivalent will be the phthalates in their bottles or the carcinogenic flame retardants so omnipresent they show up in cord blood. Maybe, by some great irony, it will be the naturally produced aflatoxins lurking in the organic produce we all thought was best.

But really: smoking while nursing?

Still, who am I to judge? Because the other thing parenting has taught me is that you can't see what you're doing while you're doing it. Smoke, I guess, gets in your eyes. It's all just so hard to navigate, and even when you think you have a plan, you don't; you just make it up as you go, and it will be all wrong, but also not that important. As this book documents, people have done crazy, crazy things to their children throughout history and the species continued all the same. Our children will survive and go on to have their own children. They'll receive the received wisdom, and they'll pass it on. They will make their little changes to the script, just as we did, and the act will continue, naturally.

But all that's a long way off. By then we'll have a cure for the organic-beet-induced tumors, and hormone transfusions will let us live long enough to meet our grandchildren, even though they won't be born until their parents are in their sixties. A baby translator will allow us to know what they're actually crying about, making it that much easier. But it will still be very, very hard, because as much as we evolve, that probably won't change.

Old-fashioned names will once again be in vogue, and I'll hold Ichabod LeBron Traig-Mickey-Shapiro-Johannsen to my chest, breathing in the ineffable scent of his downy head. Then my daughter will remind me that I'm supposed to hold the child upside down, the way everyone does now because of the polar reversal, and will I please put the ozone mask back over his face. This will wake him up and he'll start crying, and because I'm the grandmother, and I can, I'll hand him back to his mother.

Together they'll settle into the ionic glider. She'll rock him in the serene glow of the cold fusion lamp, on and on, their eyes getting heavy. Sleepily she'll pat his back, giving the baby what comfort she can, while the monitor of the baby translator reads "More, more, more."

# 1

# **Look Busy**

## *On Outsourcing*

There is some debate about when the practice of parenting originated, but the word itself only came into common usage about forty years ago, which I guess means parenting was invented after I was. Like many nouns that became verbs and changed history for the worse—*jam, trip, streak*—this happened in the 1970s. Before that, children weren't parented, but reared, which did not require much anxious philosophical examination. You loved them; you did your best to make sure they didn't die; but you didn't give a lot of thought to optimizing their cognitive development or nourishing their self-esteem. If they kept a handful of their teeth and lived to thirty-two, you'd done your job. Maybe you taught them a few psalms or how to write their name in the dirt. Any parental efforts beyond that just weren't, in seventies parlance, anyone's jam.

This is presuming the parents were the ones making the efforts in the first place. Often they weren't. A big part of the reason it wasn't called *parenting* is that for much of history, parents did so little of it. A cast of wet nurses, dry nurses, tutors, servants, slaves, clergy, older siblings, other relatives, and apprentice masters did the day-to-day labor. Sometimes this was because it was necessary for economic survival, sometimes because it was fashionable, sometimes (always) because children are just so much work. The history of parenting is, in large part, a history of trying to get out of it.

IT TURNS OUT there are very good reasons for this. It's how we evolved. To repeat evolutionary biologist Robert Trivers's famous argument, the genes that got passed on were the ones that demanded more than parents can provide. We overcome this inequality by making other people do as much of the work as possible. From the perspective of species survival, the best strategy for a parent is the same as the one for a bad employee: do as little as you can get away with. Look busy, and let someone else do the real work.

The practice of dumping the kids on someone else is called allo-parenting, and it's as old as people are. My own perceptions of caveman parenting are based mostly on *The Flintstones*, from which I conclude that prehistoric parents were well-meaning but a little irresponsible, letting their children do things like juggle boulders and play with saber-toothed house cats, not to mention smoking in front of them. But people who study the Stone Age for a living confirm that early humans were actually pretty good parents who kept their kids and themselves alive by outsourc-ing as much child-rearing as they could. Evolutionary biologist and all-around genius person Sarah Blaffer Hrdy suggests that it's what allowed us to become people in the first place: "Without alloparents, there never would have been a human species."

Although alloparenting is common in many animals (flamingos, bottle-nose dolphins, bison, killer whales, bees, and pronghorn antelopes all form what are essentially daycare centers), it's not seen much in other primates, most of whom are far more likely to eat a neighbor's infant than babysit him. Once our hominin ancestors began sharing the parenting duties with one another, they could retain enough resources to evolve the big brains and complex social relationships that let them leapfrog over other primates to become *Homo sapiens*. And once humans became humans, they contin-ued thinking up ways to avoid being around their children.

One of the oldest methods is the same as the one I use on broken vacuum cleaners and soiled recliners, which is to surreptitiously unload them on someone else's street in the middle of the night, then pretend I don't know anything about it. With furniture this is called *illegal dumping*, but with children it's known as *exposing*, and by classical times, it was routine. In ancient Rome an estimated 20 to 40 percent of all infants were exposed, suggesting that a majority of families exposed at least one child. Romans actually expressed surprise when a woman did not expose any of her children, and were baffled that some other cultures didn't engage in the practice at all. When Plutarch famously wrote, "mothers ought to bring up and nurse their own children," he meant *some* of them. Because you'd have to be crazy to keep them all.

Infant abandonment was common in both reality and myth, and was such a frequent part of city founders' origin stories that historian James Boswell calls them "founding foundlings." Famous exposed heroes include Oedipus, Poseidon, Paris, Jupiter, Jupiter's twin sons, Cybele, Ion (founder of the Ionians), Cyrus (founder of the Persian empire), and Remus and Romulus (founders of Rome). Seeing how well these guys turned out, it's not surprising that abandoning parents expressed no shame. Exposing your children was perfectly legal (as was selling them or, for that matter, killing them). Plato and Aristotle both recommended disposing of babies who showed any sign of defect, as did the Greek physician Soranus, who titled a chapter of his first-century childbirth and parenting book "How to Recognize the Newborn That Is Worth Rearing."

Children were deemed not worth it for any number of reasons: because their parents were too poor to feed them or too rich to imperil the estate; because the child's paternity was questioned, or because it was female; or even because the parents wanted to register a political statement, as Romans reportedly did on a number of occasions, as when Caligula died or Nero murdered his mother. That time, a baby was exposed with a sign reading I WILL NOT RAISE YOU, LEST YOU CUT YOUR MOTHER'S THROAT. Girls faced grimmer odds. Hilarion's letter to his wife circa 1 BCE expresses the typical sentiment: "If it is a boy keep it, if a girl discard it."*

---

\* The preference for boys holds true across all eras and cultures wherever infanticide is practiced. Though illegal, sex-selective abortion continues today, most notably in

Generally, the rich wanted nothing to do with the infants they abandoned—who might lay claim to an inheritance—but the poor would take pains to see them again. As for the middle class, they sometimes exposed a child if they couldn't afford a good enough school, giving them up, as Plutarch writes, "so as not to see them corrupted by a mediocre education that would leave them unfit for rank and quality." Imagine the awkward reunion should they meet again: "Sorry we abandoned you on a dung heap, but we knew we'd never be able to pay for Stanford, and isn't being eaten by wild dogs preferable to a state school?"

As to what happened to the infants, there were a number of fates. Some died of neglect or were eaten by animals. Some were taken and raised by slave traders or brothel owners (Romans being enthusiastic supporters of both slavery and underage prostitution); and some were adopted. Adoption, like abandonment, was a common part of Roman life. The practice was not limited to babies or even children; adults were sometimes adopted, too. Adoptions were done for a number of reasons besides, you know, actually wanting a child: to form alliances, to continue a family name, or even just to rankle your own biological children. Another awkward conversation: "Since all of you have been such great disappointments to me, I'm bringing Chad here onto the team. I think we can all admire the work he's been doing on his quads. Naturally, I'm leaving him the house."

Horrifyingly, young children were also adopted as pets. We treat our dogs like children; Romans were known to do the opposite. They sometimes took on a pet child, usually a slave or a foundling, which they kept for entertainment and amusement purposes, or, more disturbingly, sexual ones.

I guess they just had a different idea of family. The word *family* is in fact derived from the Latin word for "servant." Things weren't much more comfortably domestic in ancient Greece, where there wasn't a word for family at all. The closest was *oikos*, which actually means "house," and besides parents and children, residents of the house could include

---

Asia. In eighteenth- and nineteenth-century China sex-selective infanticide was so common that wagons were dispatched on regular routes to pick up the bodies of all the unwanted girls (Sarah Blaffer Hrdy, *Mother Nature*, 320–22).

extended family members as well as enslaved household staff. (To contemporary Americans, Oikos means yogurt, and given the quantities of it that have been smeared on my walls and floorboards, I suppose it's holding my house together as much as any familial bond.) As for the exposed infants, most simply died. The historical record suggests that Romans and Greeks did not lose a lot of sleep over this, nor did their Norse, Celtic, and Germanic contemporaries. Infant death was a part of life in the ancient world, and parents let their children die from neglect or from actual homicide for a host of reasons. These ranged from desperation to simple convenience to "the gods made me do it." Ancient texts make multiple references to child sacrifice, though there's some question as to how often it actually occurred.* It does seem worth noting that the references are almost always to what *other* cultures do, not *us*, because of course *we're better than that*.

The other usually mentioned is that of the Carthaginians, who, if ancient Greek sources are to be believed, offered up a child when asking the gods for a particularly big request, like a new chariot or a promotion at work, which I guess makes it less a "sacrifice" than a "transaction." The Carthaginian practice even gets a mention in the Bible, where it's said to occur at a *tophet*. (Depending on your interpretation, this translates roughly either to "roasting place" or "drum circle," both equally disturbing as far as I'm concerned.)

Other children died for more mundane reasons, like their parents' abject inability to support them. It should be noted, however, that historically the wealthy were no less likely to kill their children. Under certain circumstances, they were actually more apt to.† Monarchs, in particular,

---

* Whether or not the Carthaginians actually sacrificed their children is the subject of much heated debate in archaeological circles and the pages of their scholarly journal, *Antiquity*. In the December 2014 volume, Oxford archaeologist Josephine Quinn sets out to settle the matter once and for all, asserting, on some pretty solid evidence, that they certainly did.

† Here, too, girls get the short and fatal end of the stick. When the parents are doing well, it's the girls who are more likely to be offed. While for poorer families, girls are a hardworking asset, for the rich, they're a costly liability. Nineteenth-century English colonials socializing with India's elite were often puzzled by the lack of women, and horrified when they learned the reason. High-caste clans like the Jhareja

resorted to the practice, including Ivan the Terrible, Peter the Great, Constantine, Korean King Yeongjo, King Philip II of Spain, and Daenerys Targaryen.* In Carthage, child sacrifice was carried out only by the wealthy; the cremation required for the ceremony was expensive. (The wealthy who were attached to their own offspring but still wanted to experience the excitement of a child sacrifice could purchase a child to kill, and it appears that some did.)

By early Christian times, people were becoming a bit squeamish about killing innocent children. But since they were also squeamish about raising yet another child when they were already stretched to the absolute limit, this presented a conflict. To resolve it, parents came up with a number of ways to reconcile their distaste for infanticide with their need not to let yet one more mouth bring the whole family down. The first was to decide that the baby wasn't actually a baby. It was, instead, a "changeling," the offspring of a demon, elf, fairy, or troll who'd been left in the baby's place. Its nonhuman nature was proved by criteria like being sickly or too thin or crying too much. Since it was not human, it could be left in the woods to die without breaking any commandments. (Though not without breaking any laws; cases involving the death or abuse of children purported to be changelings occasionally came to court in Europe and America, up until the end of the nineteenth century.)

In parts of France, sick babies were sometimes left in the woods as part of a rite involving St. Guinefort, a thirteenth-century greyhound-cum-patron saint of infants.† After throwing the child around and dunk-

---

Rajputs and Bedi Sikhs (also called the Kuri Mar—"daughter destroyers") sometimes killed their daughters. Because girls were expected to marry up, females born at the top of the caste system had nowhere to go but down, and families killed them off rather than suffer this dishonor (Sarah Blaffer Hrdy, *Mother Nature*, 326).

* Not really infanticide, since the child was not yet born. But I think we can all agree that the Mother of Dragons probably would not make a very reliable Mother of Toddlers.

† Yes, a dog saint. It should be noted, however, that Guinefort was only locally venerated, and though Guinefort worship continued up until the 1930s, it was actively discouraged by the Catholic Church. There are, to my knowledge, no officially canonized animals, though St. Christopher was often depicted with a dog's head instead of a human one due to a translation mix-up, the Latin term *Cananeus* (Canaanite) being mistaken for *canineus* (canine).

ing it in cold water, parents would leave it in the dark forest, asking St. Guinefort to replace it with a healthy infant. Whether or not this worked, it certainly provided a convenient cover story when the parents themselves replaced the child with a healthier abandoned one and passed it off as their own.

Parents who wanted to dispatch their babies but didn't want to have to go outside could "accidentally" fall asleep on top of them. Sometimes, of course, this really was a tragic accident. Occasionally, however—perhaps a quarter of the time—it was not, and *overlaying* became a euphemism for infanticide. The frequency with which it occurred eventually led to the invention of the *arcutio*, a contraption that pinned the child under a sort of croquet hoop and was supposed to prevent acciden-tal smothering. Although it didn't work at all—either for saving babies or for lawn sports—wet nurses in Italy were required to use them or face excommunication.

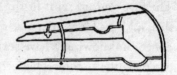

*Arcutio.* The cutouts on the sides are for the nurse to park her breast on.

EXPOSURE AND SMOTHERING ARE, of course, unfathomable choices to the modern parent. Losing a child is an unimaginably painful ordeal for any parent, and the fact that it was more common and more deliberate in the ancient world makes it no less horrifying. However, losing a child is not what most of these parents thought they were doing. Their choices make more sense when we view them as really, really late-term abortions. One-fifth of all pregnancies end in abortion today; millions more never even occur, thanks to widely available birth control. But before modern medicine, abortions were much safer for the mother when they were per-formed in, say, the tenth month than in any of the previous nine. For many cultures, a child so young wasn't considered a human yet. Abandoning this not-yet-human child meant more resources for the already quite human children they already had. Even today, when women have access to neither contraceptives nor safe abortions nor the resources to raise another child, as is the case in some hunter-gatherer societies, they quietly and reluctantly resort to the infanticidal methods that were practiced for millennia.

Abandonment and infanticide, then, functioned as a very crude form of family planning, allowing parents to subtract children as was convenient. This was especially true in ancient Rome. It is hard not to notice that ancient Roman families were awfully small for people without access to birth control besides the use of underage prostitutes. Child abandonment kept family size down (while also producing more underage prostitutes). It may in fact have been too effective. Eventually the senate saw fit to pass inducements encouraging bigger families, including permission for a mother of three or more to wear a special dress of honor, the *stola*.*

Nonetheless, child abandonment continued well into Christian times. The first-century saint Justin Martyr was troubled by the implications of this, asking "How many fathers, forgetting the children that they abandoned, unknowingly have sexual relations with a son who is a prostitute or a daughter become a harlot?" Which as far as I'm concerned raises some real questions not just about infant abandonment but about how his contemporaries spent their leisure time.

By the seventh and eighth centuries, abandonment had become so widespread that institutions were needed to manage it. Over the next few centuries, foundling hospitals were established in most major European cities. In France, Napoleon arranged for the installation of turntables, which were also used in Italy, permitting parents to deposit their infants anonymously. It was like a reverse drive-through window, only with babies instead of tacos. Like tacos, the windows proved enormously popular, overwhelming the hospitals to such an extent that some windows had to be removed.

Even without the drive-through option, foundling hospitals could not keep up with demand. When things were going well, 10 percent of all infants were abandoned; when things went badly, it rose past 40 percent. At the Ospedale degli Innocenti, Florence's main foundling hospital, administrators had to install a grille across the rotating barrel that served as the baby depository when parents began trying to push their older children through it as well. At one foundling home in Naples, parents greased

---

* If you are wondering what the *stola* looked like, you can see an example on the Statue of Liberty.

larger children to squeeze them through. Grease did not prevent the poor oversize castoffs from getting bones fractured in the rotating mechanism, however, so the opening was made smaller to keep all but the youngest out altogether.

For children large and small another option was oblation, in which the child was handed over as a gift to a religious order. This, too, could be done anonymously, and frequently was, as these children tended to be the illegitimate offspring of priests.*

At foundling homes, parents often included notes and trinkets to identify their offspring, hoping to reclaim them when things improved. Most would not get the chance. The limited number of wet nurses and copious number of diseases at most foundling homes did not do much for the residents' long-term survival. Oblation was safer, but more permanent: once children were handed over, there were no take-backs, and they'd stay in the order their entire lives. They would, however, live, something that was unlikely at the founding homes, where mortality rates were typically in the 70 to 90 percent range. In Brescia, so many infants died at the local foundling home that townspeople suggested carving a more honest motto over its gate: "Here children are killed at public expense."

It was a desperate decision, but one that even today parents are sometimes overwhelmed enough to make. In 2008, with infanticide rates climbing, Nebraska passed a "safe haven" law, allowing parents to abandon unwanted children at designated drop-off points. The aim was to save newborns, but lawmakers had failed to specify a cutoff age. Centers were overwhelmed by cast-off tweens and teens; apparently older children make parents more desperate than babies do. One father dropped off his entire family of nine, aged one to seventeen. Other parents drove from out of state to unload their kids. When the state legislature called an emergency session to rewrite the law, parents raced to Nebraska before it went into effect. In one case that made national news, a woman sped 1,200 miles from the rural California county I grew up in to drop off

---

* Interestingly, some of the more involved fathers of the fifteenth and sixteenth centuries were popes, Alexander VI in particular (John Merriman, *A History of Modern Europe: From the Renaissance to the Present* [New York: W. W. Norton, 1996], 99).

her fourteen-year-old son. Had my parents had the option—I was not particularly pleasant at that age—I'm not sure they wouldn't have made that drive, too.

Thanks to improved standards of living, the Nebraska foundlings survived, an outcome that was unlikely for children abandoned in the Middle Ages. Still, some of these earlier foundlings lived to have children of their own. The reason we know this is because foundling homes assigned infants surnames that are not uncommon today. These names include Esposito ("exposed"); Colombo ("pigeon," the mascot of the Milanese foundling home); Vondeling ("foundling"); Trouvé or Trovato ("found"); Temple, Iglesias, and Copro ("church" and "dung heap," both frequent drop-off points); Proietti ("castoff"); and Bastardo (less common but unforgettable). In England it became customary to name foundlings after the day and place they were left, which is how there came to be a number of children called "Saturday Cripplegate."

AND WHO'S TO SAY these unfortunates would have done any better with their own families? In the Middle Ages, even if you weren't exposed on a dung heap or dispatched to a foundling home, your odds weren't great. It was not a good time, what with the Crusades, the Black Death, and general misery. French scholar Philippe Ariès famously argued that parental love, and childhood as we know it—a distinct period of life, with charms all its own—simply didn't exist at the time, and wouldn't even begin to until the sixteenth century. Ariès based much of his findings on artwork that depicted children not as children but as small adults. His views held sway for twenty years or so, until other historians pointed out that this was not a particularly accurate approach to history, it being the same approach that might lead a person to believe, for instance, that prehistoric toddlers wore one-shouldered sundresses made of saber-toothed cat hides.

Ariès and his colleagues may have been wrong about some things, but it's true that the Middle Ages was not a good time to be either parent or child. It was best just to put your head down and get through it with as much outside help as you could muster, or enter a religious order and opt out of reproduction altogether. Fourteenth-century poet Eustache Deschamps put it bluntly: "Happy is he who has no children, for babies mean nothing but crying and stench; they give only trouble and anxiety; they have to be clothed, shoed, fed; they are always in danger of falling and hurting themselves; they contract some illness and die; when they grow up, they may go to the bad and be cast into prison. Nothing but cares and sorrows; no happiness compensates us for our anxiety, for the trouble and expenses of their education." Maybe it sounds better in late medieval French.

But Deschamps was right about the danger and illness and death. Many of these occurred because parents weren't watching their children, and unfortunately, alloparents weren't either. The medieval parent who wanted to outsource childcare did not have a lot of reliable options, which meant the unreliable options would have to do. Without modern conveniences, parents had their hands pretty full, and would often leave small children in the care of less-than-optimal babysitters. Bad things could happen to a toddler when she was being watched over by, say, a slightly older toddler, or by a blind neighbor who couldn't really keep an eye on her at all.

Medieval records are full of accounts of the terrible things that happened to youngsters while their caretakers were busy elsewhere. Medieval homes weren't the least bit childproofed, and generally featured an open hearth over which bubbling pots of gruel were suspended. Farm animals wandered in and out. The child might drown or get burned. In a reversal of the usual order of things, he might get eaten by livestock.*

---

\* From medieval English court records, it appears that pigs were a particular nuisance in this department. Though it sounds baffling now, the animal was subjected to a courtroom trial just as a human would be, complete with witness testimony to the animal's conduct, mind-set, and background, all of which was carefully considered by the judge. In one instance, when a sow and her piglets killed a five-year-old boy, the sow was sentenced to death but the piglets were allowed to live; although they were covered in blood, no witnesses had actually seen the piglets attack. Besides, they were still just children and couldn't have known what they were doing. There was some mercy for medieval youth, after all, at least for the animal kind (Jen Girgen, "The Historical and Contemporary Prosecution and Punishment of Animals," *Animal Law Review* 9 [2003]: 97–133).

*Portrait of Swaddled Twins: The Early-Deceased Children of Jacob de Graeff and Aeltge Boelens*, artist unknown, 1617

To compensate for the low levels of supervision, infants were essentially bubble-wrapped, bundled into swaddling so tight and thorough they could be (and sometimes were) thrown like a football from room to room. They were also occasionally hung from hooks, like purses in a bathroom stall. More often the swaddled bundle was strapped into a cradle as though readying for a space shuttle launch. But even this didn't guarantee safety, due to the ill-advised practice of placing the cradle near the open fire. Nearly a third of the infant deaths in medieval England were caused when the baby was burned in its cradle. Sometimes it was ignited by sparks, and sometimes it was nosed in by the aforementioned pigs. Even if the baby stayed out of the hearth, he might be strangled by his restraints.

When the child became upright, a host of new dangers opened up. As soon as he was old enough to stand, he was parked in a standing stool or walking stool. These were seatless contraptions that forced the child to stand and functioned as stocks, or babysitters, or in some cases, as when they rolled down stairs, death machines.

It was not a good time. There aren't very reliable statistics, but if we ballpark it from patchy death records, you had about a fifty-fifty chance of making it to your seventh birthday, at which point you'd probably be turned out to serve as a menial apprentice. There would be no cake.

In the fifteenth and sixteenth centuries things got a little bit better, if only because there was, thanks to increased sugar production, more cake. There was also more money, and once families could afford it, they began hiring others to take over the more unpleasant aspects of raising children. This of course had always been an option, but was now more possible and more widely done.

**THESE RENAISSANCE YEARS,** historians tell us, are when the concept of the nuclear family first emerged, but it seems these nuclear particles often repelled one another. In many families it was considered a good idea for the mommy and daddy particles to spend a great deal of time away from the squalling infant particle. Montaigne's pronouncement on his children was typical: "I have not willingly suffered them to be brought up near me." Many agreed. If you played your cards right, you wouldn't have to see your children until age seven, and not much of them after that, leaving you free to, well, play cards.

The shunting-off began immediately at birth thanks to an elaborate, far-flung wet-nursing network that thrived across Europe for hundreds of years. Many historical phenomena puzzle me (powdered wigs, eunuchry, the enthusiasm for public executions), but nothing leaves me quite as slack-jawed as this one. The wet-nursing industry was a complex racket whose closest modern analogue is probably eBay, a multifaceted regional distribution system with a lot of middlemen between baby and breast and very little oversight.\*

It seems strange that anyone would consent to this frankly dangerous and bizarre system, but in France especially, most parents did. Out of the 21,000 infants born in Paris in 1780, a full 17,000 were put out to country wet nurses (only 700 would be nursed by their own mothers, with the remaining 3,000 or so placed in nursery homes or with in-home nurses). It was simply the natural order of things: the farmer takes a wife, the wife takes a child, the child takes a nurse. Hi-ho, the derry-o, let's go play whist.

The process began with a *recomendaresse*, an agent from a private or public bureau, who would find a peasant wet nurse for the expected infant. Once the infant was born, it was picked up by the *meneur*—a man the parents had never seen—whose job it was to transport the infant to the wet nurse, whom the parents had also never seen, and who would be solely responsible for the child for the next two to five years. Sometimes the wet nurse might be waiting in the meneur's cart, to nurse the child en

---

\*  By the twentieth century, wet-nursing had died out, but the demand for breast milk continues, at least in some esoteric and frankly weird corners, where it goes for as much as $2.50 an ounce. Body builders, for example, sometimes seek it out for its nutritional profile.

route. Often, however, the infant was simply loaded into one of the many baby baskets on the meneur's horse for a long, bumpy ride. I can't help but contrast this to my own children's entry into the larger world, an ordeal that required a great deal of paperwork and proof of a properly installed car seat before the hospital would release them, and imagine how the staff might have reacted had we tried to send the children off with a hobo on a pack mule, insisting that everything was *just fine*.

After the babies were picked up, there followed a long journey to the wet nurse's home in the remote country. Along the way, they might pass meneurs taking children in the opposite direction. These were infants whose rural families were abandoning them to urban foundling homes, and used the same transport service. These children did not have it quite as good as the outbound nurslings; the only sustenance they would receive en route would be from a wine-soaked rag. If a baby fell out along the way, its basket would be filled with a new charge in the next town, as the foundling homes paid the meneur per child delivered. When the public eventually became scandalized by the high mortality rate, a law was passed requiring meneurs to carry their charges in straw-lined wagons with a wet nurse on board.

As for the babies headed to rural wet nurses, they were in for a rough ride, too. Like the inbound foundlings, they were sometimes lost on the trip. Should the child actually make it to its destination, it would then be placed with its wet nurse, who may or may not, in fact, be wet (and may in fact be prepubescent). Prospective nurses sometimes borrowed babies and passed them off as their own as proof that they were lactating. Lacking milk, they instead fed their charges with pap, a mixture of liquid and starch, a practice that did not bode well for their survival.

The wet-nursing system didn't bode so well in general, with mortality rates doubling for infants wet-nursed away from home. Children died from malnutrition or neglect or even syphilis, contracted from a nurse who contracted it from a sailor.* Some thought wet-nursing was essen-

---

* But probably neglect. Tellingly, most of the deaths occurred during the summer and fall, harvest time, when the wet nurses were too preoccupied with farm chores to pay as much attention to their charges (Susan Allport, *A Natural History of Parenting*, 197).

tially a culturally permissible form of infanticide, and *angelmaker* became a widely used slang term for wet nurse in England, France, and Germany.

Now we expect to get fired for killing a child. But then it didn't even prevent the family from hiring you again for the next one. And there probably would be a next one; because the birth mother wasn't breastfeeding, she became fertile faster and could conceive in fairly short order.

As with real estate and retail, location was everything. Survival rates were generally higher the closer the child was to home, but so were expenses, a real concern for the many middle- and lower-class mothers who used wet nurses when they had to get back to work themselves. Even at reduced rates, they couldn't always afford it. When parents defaulted on the wet nurse's payments, as 10 percent of them did, the baby was sent not to the family but to a foundling home.

At the bottom of this (literal) trickle-down economy were, of course, the wet nurses themselves, and the uncomfortable question of what happened to their own infants. Families preferred that the milk supply be undivided, so if the nurse's own child was still alive, and still nursing, it would need to find another breast. In that case, the nurse would send her own offspring to an even poorer wet nurse even farther out in the country, leaving her own breast free to nurse at a higher rate. As to what happened to the very poorest nurses' own offspring, I don't think we really need to ask.

WHEN ALL WENT WELL and the nursling survived, he was returned to the family after weaning, some time between the ages of two and five or, if the family was in no rush, as late as seven.* But this did not have to mean his parents would start spending time with him. There were lots of options for parents who wanted to off-load their offspring. He could be deposited in the care of servants and tutors, or be sent to live somewhere else entirely, as many children of all classes were.

In England, this usually meant sending your child to live with another

---

\* In ancient Rome, the child often wasn't returned until puberty, with the wet nurse serving as caregiver as well as instructor until then.

family, which makes an excellent premise for an MTV show but a rather disconcerting premise for a life. Upper-class children were sent off to develop their manners, while lower-class children were sent off to work. This was often done around the time the child was entering adolescence, or just when they start to be *reallllly* annoying. The trade-off, of course, was that someone else's annoying child would come live with *you*. It was a strange system, and other countries were baffled and dismayed by it. William Penn remarked that the English "do with their children as they do with their souls, put them out at livery for so much a year." One Italian visitor observed:

> The want of affection in the English is strongly manifested toward their children; for after having kept them at home till they arrive at the age of 7 or 9 years at the utmost, they put them out, both males and females, to hard service in the houses of other people, binding them generally for another 7 or 9 years. And these are called apprentices, and during that time they perform all the most menial offices; and few are born who are exempted from this fate, for every one, however rich he may be, sends away his children into the houses of others, whilst he, in return, receives those of strangers into his own. And on inquiring their reason for this severity, they answered that they did it in order that their children might learn better manners. But I, for my part, believe that they do it because they like to enjoy all their comforts themselves, and that they are better served by strangers than they would be by their own children. Besides which the English being great epicures, and very avaricious by nature, indulge in the most delicate fare themselves and give their household the coarsest bread, and beer, and cold meat baked on Sunday for the week. . . . That if they had their own children at home, they would be obliged to give them the same food they made use of for themselves.

Given the reputation of English cuisine, this reasoning seems unlikely. Whatever the cause, however, the practice became quite common. These exchanges were widely done from the Middle Ages on, eventually evolving into the regulated apprenticeship system that would stay in place for hundreds of years. Thus, instead of just learning social niceties, youth might acquire useful workplace skills, like how to make and style a periwig.

They might also learn some harder lessons. Apprentice masters, who were paid by the parents for the child's training and board, were not always benevolent. They were supposed to act in loco parentis, but in some cases were simply loco. Henry Timbrell may have been one of the worst. Abandoning his career as a preacher and religious instructor, he began taking in boys strictly for money. He tried to rid himself of two of his charges by exposing them to smallpox. When that failed, he decided to castrate them and sell them to the opera. Coming upon them while they slept, he managed to relieve the boys of three of their four testicles, for which he was fined 13s4d.

Upper-class families had other outsourcing options. Boarding schools have existed since early medieval times and made an ideal choice for well-off parents who wanted their sons to learn the classics while being brutally traumatized by upperclassmen. These could be rough places. Medieval schoolboys tended to be heavy drinkers; they were also armed. It's not entirely surprising that the combination of alcohol, weapons, and under-supervised adolescent boys might prove volatile, and it did. Mutinies and riots broke out. Fights were common and occasionally fatal.

For hundreds of years, the brutality was institutionalized into a practice called—in a term that will rattle modern ears—*fagging*. Fagging was a system that gave younger students (fags) as servants to older students (fag masters, and you should know that this is killing me). Typically the fag's duties entailed activities like bootblacking and errands but could also include being on the receiving end of sexual abuse, nonsexual abuse, beatings, and torture. Roald Dahl's fag duties included warming his fag master's toilet seat.

Boarding schools for girls came along sometime later, and if they were less violent, they were also far less challenging. Instead of Latin and Greek, girls learned sewing, singing, and the fine art of complimenting from instructors with few if any qualifications. Mrs. Devis's esteemed London school included lessons on disembarking; students rehearsed getting in and out of a practice carriage without exposing their ankles.

Of course, not all children were packed off to learn or to work or to live somewhere else. But even those who stayed home didn't see much of their parents, who were busy with other concerns. This was very much the case among the nobility. One of the best-documented examples is provided by Louis XIII, whose physician, Jean Héroard, recorded every development in the young king's life from birth until age twenty-seven. Héroard describes how the toddler king was raised primarily by his governess, with infrequent parental contact, at a children's court. Héroard's notes also reveal that like many children, Louis XIII enjoyed dropping his pants to amuse his courtiers, though he did it in the royal chambers and not, as my son did, in Pinkberry.

Héroard's account is surprisingly bawdy. A lot of attention is paid to the—for lack of a better phrase—crown jewels. Upon his engagement—at age three—to the Infanta of Spain, Louis responded to the question "Where is the Infanta's darling?" by patting his business. The text also records what is perhaps the most mortifying wedding night in history, which took place when Louis married at fourteen. After courtiers told him racy stories to get him in the mood, his mother escorted him to the bridal bed. (According to some accounts, he was carried forcibly; Louis's heterosexuality, it should be mentioned, is the matter of some debate.) There he was tucked in with his wife to perform an act that did not occur but was nonetheless "witnessed" by two nurses and "verified," via stains, by his mother the next morning.[*]

AS A KING, Louis undoubtedly benefited from a unique upbringing, but it was typical of families with money in that the parents did almost zero child-rearing themselves. Oh, sure, they attended the occasional wedding night, but most of the time it was a hands-off relationship, leaving parents plenty of time to go to wig fittings and pianoforte concerts.

Children from all social classes just did not spend that much time with their parents. Parents with the means paid others to do the grunt

---

[*] It is not entirely surprising that Louis refused to do so much as eat with his wife for the next six months.

work. Parents without the means were too busy doing the grunt work. And even if they had the time and the means, it's unlikely they'd have the inclination. Parents saw *producing* children as their job, and rearing them as someone else's: the wet nurse, or the governess, the tutor, or the apprentice master, the slave or the servant or the older siblings.* Even parents who were their children's primary caregivers weren't that hands-on, instead relying on restraints like swaddling and standing stools for much of the day-to-day supervision.

Most parents did not parent; the verb, and the concept, did not exist. Unlike us, they probably did not feel much guilt about it, much as my mail carrier doesn't feel guilty for not mowing my lawn. It's simply not his job, no matter how much I try to convince him it is.

With the Enlightenment, however, the parental guilt trip finally arrived, thanks to John Locke and Jean-Jacques Rousseau. These two will be discussed at length in a later chapter, but for now I'll just mention that they're the ones who introduced the West to the revolutionary idea that parents should raise their own children. I'll also mention that Locke didn't have any kids, and that Rousseau had five, all of whom were abandoned to foundling homes, where, it's presumed, they died.

Locke, true to his name, was the more rule-bound of the two. In his 1693 treatise *Some Thoughts Concerning Education* Locke argued that parents hold "regal authority" over their children, and they're not to delegate too much of it. Writing a few decades later, Rousseau was a little more relaxed. In his view, children are like plants, and the parents' role is simply to nurture their natural growth. But like Locke, he thought the parents—and not the gardener—ought to do it. Apparently this did not apply to Rousseau himself.

That said, both he and Locke had a point. Parents and children were missing out on a lot by more or less ignoring each other. And the technologies that let them do this—off-site wet-nursing, rigid swaddling, stocks-like standing stools, and widespread neglect—weren't doing anyone much good.

---

* To be fair, the production line was always in production; since they weren't breast-feeding or using particularly effective birth control, women were almost continually pregnant, and all that babymaking and gestating did take up a fair amount of energy. The men, though—they don't have that excuse.

We also need to consider what they meant when they encouraged parents to raise their children themselves. The presence of tutors, governesses, and servants—even if Locke distrusted them, and he did—was assumed. (Locke was particularly uptight about letting kids hit the sauce with the help, "[t]here being nothing that lays a surer foundation of mischief, both to body and mind, than children's being used to *strong drink*; especially, to drink in private, *with the servants*.") And though Rousseau's *Émile* opens with a fiery rebuke of parents who neglect their duties, the book itself depicts Émile's interactions with his tutor, not his parents, who don't appear in the text at all. Locke and Rousseau were simply urging parents to become more interested and involved. They should *direct* the child-rearing, but they don't actually have to *do* it.

LOCKE AND ROUSSEAU'S IDEAS would prove wildly influential, and over the next couple of centuries more and more European parents would begin expressing interest in the little souls they'd brought into the world, even if they didn't do much of the day-to-day work. In the up-and-coming territory of America, however, parents were doing the day-to-day, day after day after day. Due to a combination of circumstances, religious beliefs, and a general propensity toward masochism, Puritan parents spent far more time with their children than anyone else had for most of Western history.

Puritans took child-rearing *very* seriously, devoting much of their time and thought to the subject. They cornered the contemporary market on advice manuals and established parenting philosophies that remain influential today. In bumper sticker form, that philosophy was: Life sucks and then you die. It was essential, therefore, that you be spiritually prepared. Unlike Locke, who considered children a blank slate, Puritans believed that children were born inherently evil (in Benjamin Wadsworth's words, "filthy, guilty, odious, abominable . . . both by nature and practice"). Their very souls were at stake, and it was the parents' obligation to save them through education and discipline.* Breaking with tradition, they

---

* To ensure that they did so, families were visited regularly by a tithingman, a caseworker of sorts who functioned as the fun police. His other job was to watch pa-

would do much of it themselves. Raising pious, moral children was far too important to outsource to the help.

It was also too important to outsource to the mother, as women were thought to be too untrustworthy to be responsible for much more than nursing. Thus it was that for the first and only time in human history, men were primarily responsible for the child-rearing. This included not just the religious instruction and moral development, but the feeding, recreation, and middle-of-the-night rocking against their bony breasts. The practice would continue into the early nineteenth century. Cotton Mather, John Adams, James Madison, and Thomas Jefferson fondly recalled their fathers' ministrations, mentioning their mothers rarely if at all. The founding fathers, as it happens, really were founded by fathers.*

Despite their reputation as stern taskmasters, Puritan fathers weren't generally abusive, at least not physically. Discipline was achieved not by frequent beating, or, as in my house, yelling empty threats while hiding in the bathroom and eating cookies, but by constantly reminding children that they could die, unsaved, at any minute. Thanks to a healthier environment, they were less *likely* to die than their European counterparts, but were reminded of their mortality far more often. This pronouncement from Cotton Mather was typical: "Go into the Burying-Place, CHILDREN; you will there see *Graves* as short as your selves. Yea, you may be at *Play* one Hour; *Dead, Dead* the next." Yayyyyy.

Healthier though they were, the *Dead* may actually have been more likely than the *Play*. In the Massachusetts Bay Colony, children's play was in fact illegal. And it wasn't enough just to work—they had to multitask. A law passed in 1642 demanded that children who had the easy jobs, like watching the cattle, "bee set to some other implement withal, as spinning upon the rock, knitting, weveing tape, etc." In case you're wondering, it was also illegal to complain.

Because the parents were expected to work constantly themselves, some form of childcare was required for the youngest children, though

---

rishioners in church, using a long rod to jab anyone who talked, slept, whispered, giggled, or even smiled, though I'm guessing they didn't have much occasion to.
* And slaves and servants, who did no shortage of the grunt work.

"care" might not be exactly what they got. This need was met by the dame school, which sounds like a vamp camp run by Barbara Stanwyck but was actually an informal neighborhood daycare center. In keeping with the Puritan law and spirit, the dame school was not much fun. It was usually held in the home of a neighborhood woman who kept up her own household chores during the school day, sometimes compelling the children to join in. Multitasking all around, they'd learn the alphabet, numbers, and prayers as they did.

Though some children were sent out to other families between the ages of seven and twelve, the Puritans didn't employ the wholesale system of teenage musical chairs that was practiced in England. There was plenty of space to keep them at home, and few places to send them to; and besides, Puritan teenagers were not the wild adolescents their whoring, boozing English counterparts were. Their wildness was mostly confined to accusing people of witchcraft.[*]

But, you know, young goodmen will be young goodmen, and there were occasional problems. Children who disrespected their parents were subject to civic punishments that included the death penalty. Perhaps because obedience was so thoroughly drummed into them, charges of disrespecting one's parents were rarely brought. As for the death penalty, it was never actually handed down for filial disrespect. The few times it was even considered, lenience always prevailed, as in the case of Edward Bumpus, who was ultimately sentenced to a comparatively lax public whipping instead, because, as the record notes, "he was crasey brained."[†]

---

[*]   Though this may in fact have been caused by drugs. Some scholars have suggested that the Salem witch mania was caused by eating rye contaminated with ergot, a fungus whose consumption can cause seizures and hallucinations—and which is used in the manufacture of LSD. This is unlikely, but interesting. And as for the whoring: well, if I'm honest, there was some of that, too. The Puritan out-of-wedlock birthrate was a full 30 percent, fairly typical for a culture that prizes virtue but fruitfulness just a bit more, and looks the other way when necessary (David F. Lancy, *The Anthropology of Childhood*, 65).

[†]   The other instance was John Porter's epic potty-mouthed tantrum of 1655, in which he called his father a "shittabed," and his mother a "shithouse" and a "pisshouse." He was, notably, thirty-one at the time. Porter also beat the family servants and tried to burn down the family home, kill the cattle, and stab his brother. For this he was sentenced to stand on the gallows (but not actually hang) for an hour, receive

Edward got off easy in another sense. Bumpus isn't great, but it could have been a lot worse, and Edward is just fine. The worst form of abuse the Puritans laid on their children might have been their names. Puritans took naming seriously and favored names that, they felt, would set the child on the path of righteousness. Coupled with their disproportionately goofy surnames, this was a recipe for hilarity. Witness: Humiliation Scratcher, Kill-Sin Pimple, Faint-Not Blatcher, Hope-Still Peedle, More-Fruit Fowler, and—that's what she said—Experience Clap.

Except for the naming, the Puritans weren't really bad parents. They were very concerned with their children's development and well-being; they just had what to us looks like a screwed-up way of achieving that. It looked pretty screwed-up to their children, too. When Puritan children were abducted by local Native American tribes, they often refused to return to their families after their ransom was paid, and were brought back kicking and screaming or not at all. The Native Americans—who, unlike the Puritans, alloparented—gave children far more freedom. Children were nurtured and treated kindly, and weren't forced to work. No wonder they didn't want to go back. Also, presumably, they preferred the name Sleeping Deer to Fly-Fornication.*

**WEIRD NAMES** and paternal involvement aside, it's hard not to notice that Puritan parenting isn't all that different from the kind we practice today. Historian C. John Sommerville calls the Puritans "the first modern parents"; anthropologist David Lancy, a little more pointedly, describes them as "the first anxious parents." Either way, their legacy is clear. The Puritans simultaneously established two American traditions: (1) making

a beating, and do jail time. Porter escaped before any of the punishments were meted out (Elizabeth Pleck, *Domestic Tyranny* [Champaign, IL: University of Illinois Press, 2004], 26).

* A real name. Fly-Fornication Bull didn't quite live up to her name; she was impregnated by a yeoman named, of course, Goodman Woodman. The worst names of all were chosen by a family already saddled with the gay-porn last name of Barebone. They named one son Jesus-Christ-Came-into-the-World-to-Save, and another If-Christ-Had-Not-Died-for-Thee-Thou-Hadst-Been-Damned. The latter went by Nicholas.

child-rearing an all-consuming DIY activity, and (2) ruining things for everyone. Before, benign neglect was the norm. Now you had to either obsess over your children or feel guilty for failing to.

Things would play out a little differently if you lived in the American South, where alloparenting was the norm, but in a deeply sinister way. Because enslaved women were encouraged to have children, but not given time to care for them, communal childcare was necessary. (As one enslaved woman recalled, it seemed like your children belonged to everybody "but you"). On larger plantations, the children were watched in a nursery, while on smaller ones, they were supervised somewhat by older children or the elderly, leaving their mothers "free" to do other chores, such as nurse and raise the white children of the owner.

Enslaved children would be given small chores of their own until they joined the full-time workforce sometime between the ages of eight and twelve. Before then, however, they would actually have some time to play, and perhaps the most horrifying detail of all is that they would play auction, "in which a young child would pretend to be an auctioneer at a slave sale while others played the roles of slaves crying and begging not to be sold or traded." In another game, "master and slave," "one child would wield a simulated whip as an owner or overseer while the others would do his or her bidding." Add to this the fact that black and white plantation children often played *together*, and you get a pretty disturbing visual image as well as a crime against humanity whose repercussions continue today.

Meanwhile, this system left better-off slaveholding families of the day free to spend their energy on more frivolous activities, like supervising (if not actually doing) the raising of their own children and complaining about how hard it was. By the Victorian era, this shift was occurring in Europe as well, most likely due to the lingering impact of Locke and Rousseau, coupled with the changes brought about by the Industrial Revolution. More and more, books preached that parents should raise their children themselves; and more and more, this advice was directed at women, who were apparently trustworthy enough to take the job on now that men had lost interest. This was the legacy of the Locke/Rousseau revolution: "Parents, raise your own children" became *"Mothers,* you do it; Daddy has to work."

Of course, the upside of Daddy's long hours was that there was enough money to hire help, and despite the increasing pressure on mothers to spend time with their children, it's clear many of them were outsourcing a lot of the job. *Mrs. Beeton's Book of Household Management*, which was widely used throughout the English-speaking world, gives an idea of how common this was: its chapter on child-rearing[*] begins by addressing the mother's natural squeamishness at letting someone from a lower social class care for her child. It then goes on to lay down not what the mother is to do herself, but what she's to instruct the staff.[†]

Having help left mothers the time and energy to obsess over their children, if not actually to *tend* to them. Obsess they did, for this was an era devoted to the idea of children. Let me emphasize that: the *idea* of children. Not actual children, who are filthy and disgusting and, if left to their own devices, will happily spend the morning splashing in last night's chamber pot. The *idea* of children, perfect specimens in starched white pinafores that stay spotless as they play games like cock-a-hoop, while never once shouting, "You said *cock*-a-hoop." Worst of all, children were expected to dress the part. Thanks to the popularity of *Little Lord Fauntleroy,* sons were a particular target, and spent much of the era enduring velveteen suits and long curling sessions for their hair.

Children were becoming, in Viviana Zelizer's famous phrase, "economically worthless but emotionally priceless." In 1874, for the first time, children are kidnapped for ransom.[‡] Before that, such a thing would have been unthinkable—you want me to pay to get the child *back*? Kidnapping wasn't even criminalized in the UK until 1814, though it was commonly done, especially to poorer children dragged away to staff the Industrial Revolution. Until then, while it was illegal to steal objects, it was perfectly legal to steal children. When they were charged at all, kidnappers could be

---

[*] Note that the subject merits a single chapter out of the book's forty-four. In contrast, the care and cooking of the common hog gets two.

[†] Probably a good thing, at least in the case of Mrs. Beeton herself. Despite her matronly name, she wrote the book in her early twenties, dying, at age twenty-eight, from puerperal fever after the birth of her fourth child. Her children, then, would be raised entirely by others—but at least it could be by her own instructions.

[‡] As discussed earlier, some Native American tribes also ransomed—but those weren't kidnappings so much as abductions, and were done to adults and children alike.

charged only with theft—for the clothes the children were wearing when they were snatched.

Children's increase in value was partly a function of supply and demand. Between 1870 and 1920, the birthrate in England was halved. It decreased in America as well, where Dr. Nathan Allen blamed the decreasing birthrate and the resulting "degeneracy" on women's increasing access to education and distaste for housework.

Having fewer children meant fewer children to watch, but it also meant fewer children to do the watching. No longer could the day-to-day minding be outsourced to older siblings. If parents needed help, they'd have to hire it. If the help under consideration had children of her own, arrangements had to be made so she'd be free to watch the little lords and ladies of others.

The least fortunate children joined their parents in the workforce when they were as young as three, negating the need for childcare, as they were essentially no longer children and weren't receiving any care. Children too young to work were dispatched to "baby farms,"* rural boarding homes where working-class children were fostered for pay. Some homes were perfectly fine, but others lived up to the charge by the Society for the Prevention of Cruelty to Children† that these were "concerns by means of which persons, usually of disreputable character, eke out a living by taking two, or three, or four babies to board . . . They feed them on sour milk, and give them paregoric to keep them quiet, until they die."

Panic over the latter led to reforms in 1872 and 1908. This, coupled with coincident societal changes, soon meant mom would be saddled with more and more. Texts like Hilary Pepler's *His Majesty* (1905) urged mothers to take on all child-rearing tasks, forgoing a nurse altogether or using someone else only for jobs like the laundry. (Here I will note that Pepler had no children at the time; and also, he was a dude.)

---

* The term was pejorative and gave rise to dark jokes about not planting the babies too deep or they wouldn't grow. In the worst cases, they didn't, when their caretakers neglected them horribly and overdosed them with opiates, a crime for which several earned a death sentence.

† Created, in case you're wondering, sixty-seven years after the Society for the Prevention of Cruelty to Animals.

The twentieth century was declared the Century of the Child, and in Ellen Key's book of the same name, she exhorted mothers to "be as entirely and simply taken up with the child as the child himself is absorbed by his life." This, from a forward-thinking feminist. Reformer Jane Addams took a similar tack, supporting a proposal for "mothers' pensions" that would allow mothers to stay at home over the nascent daycare movement. A few others had alternate ideas. Charlotte Perkins Gilman, for instance, promoted a compelling if unrealistic plan for women who were actually good at mothering to watch twenty children at a time, leaving other mothers free to work.*

But Gilman lost. This left the mother at home with several children, no TV or modern conveniences of any kind, many hours to fill, and a high bar to reach. For now, after a couple of centuries of believing that children were born either bad or blank, children were presumed to be born *good*. It was the mother's job to protect them from any corrupting forces, to preserve them in a suffocating innocence for as long as possible. To make matters worse, the tools that might have helped her do that, or at least to keep the children in one place—heavy swaddling and standing stools—had fallen out of favor.

Perhaps unsurprisingly, it was around now that there was a great big uptick in drug use, primarily in the form of patent medicines, but also in the form of cocaine. "Since the invention of vaccination and the discovery of general anaesthesia . . . no more wonderful and simple secret has been filched from nature's healing stores than that revealed through the recent discovery of the local anaesthetic, cocaine," Dr. J. Herbert Claiborne, Jr., wrote in *Babyhood* magazine. It had no downside, he said, except for cost.

Readers' interest was piqued. "The question we are all asking with great interest is, Cannot cocaine be used to relieve the pain of babies when they are getting their teeth?" one mother writes in. Another wonders, "What is the best means of applying it to the mucous membrane of the nostril?" Her apparently unrelated follow-up question: "How much sleep

---

* This is something CPG essentially did herself, with suboptimal results, when she sent her toddler daughter across the country to be raised by her ex-husband and his second wife. Gilman fretted over the decision for the rest of her life, and her daughter remained resentful.

should be expected of a fifteen-month-old baby during the day?" After applying cocaine to the mucous membrane of his nostril? I'd say none. Besides, isn't cocaine the last thing you'd want to give a baby? They're already far too energetic and self-absorbed.

You want to give the baby opiates, is what you want to do. And these indeed proved very popular. Not only do they knock the children out, they constipate them, which is a boon for the parent who just can't face a diaper today. The other boon, of course, is the opiates themselves, which were also marketed for the mothers' use. One for you, one for me. It seems apt that the Victorian mother was known as the Angel in the House; much of the time, she was in the clouds.

It wasn't long before this became a problem. Soon the same magazines that carried ads for opiate-spiked patent syrups were carrying ads for detox doctors. As for the syrups themselves, many now claimed to be opiate-free, but remained popular, as they still contained no shortage of booze.

BY THE EARLY 1900S, the dreamy, druggy Victorian indulgences were being replaced by a sobering dose of twentieth-century scientific parenting. The charge was led by Luther Emmett Holt, whose influential book *The Care and Feeding of Children* aimed to bring scientific practice and objectivity to the business of child-rearing—as well as plenty of outside assistance. Raising children would now be a hands-off affair, and even these hands needn't belong to the parents: Holt assumes you'll be hiring help. The book is explicitly addressed to mothers *and* nurses, and presumes the nurse, not the mother, is the one who'll be carrying out most of these instructions. The mother is to oversee the nursery as she might a lab, delegating the actual pipetting and centrifuging to the research assistants.

A couple of decades later, the new psychological field of behaviorism would take things even further. Now, child-rearing would be outsourced to science itself. Behaviorism was founded by John B. Watson, a deeply disturbed psychologist who aimed to take parents out of the picture altogether, arguing that parents were the *least* qualified for the job of raising children, as they tended toward oversentimentalization. He wrote that it was a serious question in his mind "whether there should be individual homes for children—or even whether children should know their own parents. There are undoubtedly much more scientific ways of bringing up children which will probably mean finer and happier children." Better the child should be taken away from the mother in the third or fourth week and tended to by nurses, with limited parental contact. If the mother can't afford to hire a nurse, she should pretend she is one herself: "she must look upon herself while performing the functions of a nurse as a professional woman and not as a sentimentalist masquerading under the name of 'Mother.'" Best of all would be to raise the child in a lab with no parental contact whatsoever. Watson declared, "I shall never be satisfied until I have a laboratory in which I can bring up children from birth to three or four years of age under constant observation."

If this wasn't an option, then children should be raised in a series of foster homes or by a rotating cast of caretakers. These should be changed every week to ensure that the child doesn't grow too attached to, and therefore dependent on, anyone. Which—given that this is exactly, literally, what children are: *dependents*—was some terrible advice and a perfect recipe for producing messed-up kids.

It did, including the kids of the behaviorists themselves. Three of Watson's children attempted suicide, and one succeeded. As for the children of Watson's behaviorist successor B. F. Skinner, they turned out fine, despite rumors to the contrary. Skinner did not, as is popularly believed, raise his daughter Deborah in a "Skinner box," a contraption he devised to condition rats to perform certain tasks. He did, however, design for her a large, temperature-controlled crib, enclosed in glass, that was supposed to encourage movement while simplifying cleanup for mothers. When readers expressed interest in acquiring their own, he tried to get a manufacturer to make them. These were eventually produced under the name Heir Conditioner—I'm not making that up—but were shoddily made, without Skinner's input, and sold only a thousand units.

BY THE 1940S, behaviorist principles had segued into a panic about "overmothering." Books like Edward Strecker's *Their Mothers' Sons* argued that overinvolved mothers were creating a generation of psychological cripples, like the 1,825,000 men he claimed were unfit for military duty due to psychiatric conditions. Philip Wylie went even further in *Generation of Vipers*, blaming "the woman who has failed in the elementary mother function of weaning her offspring emotionally as well as physically."*

This was truly nasty trash talk, and as for the behaviorists, they were wildly, demonstrably wrong. Still, there's something to be said for a cultural climate that

The Skinner crib *(Courtesy B. F. Skinner Foundation)*

suggests parents, and children, might benefit from a little time apart and a little outside help. And indeed, it was around this time that the United States, for the only time in its history, offered universal childcare.

Until then there'd been very few daycare centers, and for black families, there'd been next to none. Most daycare programs, nursery schools, and kindergartens admitted only whites. In 1930, there were only forty daycare centers for black children in the entire country—even though far more black mothers than white mothers worked.

The new universal childcare program began as a WPA venture, primarily to create jobs for daycare staff; that this also meant children would receive badly needed workday care was just a side benefit. (It was also a limited one. Childcare was available to parents only while they looked for work; once they found a job and actually needed childcare, the child was kicked out.)

With the arrival of World War II, however, the program was resurrected

---

* Given Wylie's disdain for the mother-child bond, it's interesting that his own daughter, Karen Wylie Pryor, would go on to write the "breastfeeding bible," *Nursing Your Baby*. A busy woman with diverse interests, she also invented the "click" training method for training animals, and is discussed in chapter 9.

and enlarged. Now there would be more separation and more outside childcare, whether people liked it or not. Fathers went overseas; mothers went to work; and kids went to a greatly expanded daycare network thanks to funds granted by the Lanham Act. This miraculous piece of legislation would support 3,000 federal daycare centers for 600,000 kids.

In reality, it fell short of a miracle. Many centers were inconvenient and overcrowded, expensive and inadequate. One was deadly, a firetrap in which sixteen children burned to death. But some sound downright paradisiacal. The daycare centers for the shipbuilding Kaiser Company operated twenty-four hours a day, six days a week, fifty-two weeks a year, and sent families home with a ready-made dinner. Childcare centers in Baltimore provided hot dinners to go plus a host of other amenities: they would do a mother's grocery shopping for her, take her children to any necessary appointments, and do the family laundry. Where it worked, the program was enormously popular and beneficial, though it's possible that no one but the participants knew this; a study showing how much it actually benefited participating families wasn't done until 2013. In any case, the dream would be short-lived,* with centers closing in 1946.

It was at this point, of course, that babies started booming. Meanwhile, there were fewer people to outsource care to. Federally funded daycare was out, and with families now moving around much more, it was less likely that relatives would be able to pitch in. Nannies had become a thing of the past, and the patchwork private daycare system, inadequate as it is, was a thing of the future. This just left mom, who had good reason to be less than thrilled with this arrangement. Thanks to the growing influence of Freud and psychoanalysis, there was increasing pressure on mothers not to screw things up. Because if anything went wrong, she would now be to blame.

Of that, there would be plenty. Within a few years the neglected child would plant the seeds of his revenge, in the form of John Bowlby and his attachment theory. Attachment theory holds that primates (including humans) are hardwired from birth to form a strong attachment

---

* In America, anyway. There are still subsidized full-service childcare programs in much of Europe, childcare paradise.

to their mother or mother substitute. Infants who do not form secure attachments—because the mother isn't reliably present or emotionally available—are prone to a host of problems, including mental illness, delinquency, and a lifelong feeling of resentment. Worst of all, Bowlby argued, this damage is irreversible.

It's hard not to read attachment theory as a direct reaction to Bowlby's own upbringing at the hired hands of nurses, nannies, and boarding schools. (Indeed, his son, Sir Richard Bowlby, characterized aspects of the theory as "straight autobiography.") As was typical of the time, Bowlby spent very little time with his parents: an hour a day with his mother, an hour a week with his father. Any more, it was felt, would spoil a child (and would certainly spoil a parent's social life). But Bowlby's later research showed the opposite: that secure, independent children are produced when they've had lots of contact with their parents or a consistent caregiver.

As for the parent's social life—well, that was about to take a blow. Over the years to come, parents would become afraid to outsource too much of the childcare lest their children turn into psychopathic deviants. Their dread was underscored by images from experiments done by Harry Harlow—which had partly inspired Bowlby's work in the first place—in which rhesus monkeys, deprived of their own mothers, clung desperately to crude substitutes made from wire and cloth, even when the mummy dummy was rigged to abusively puff air at them. I find the pictures unbearable, because, apparently, I'm much more disturbed by sad monkeys than widespread infanticide. Even more devastating is another one of Bowlby's sources, psychoanalyst's René Spitz's 1947 documentary about children separated from their mothers in a Mexican foundling home, *Grief: A Peril in Infancy*. Spitz's scientific methods were shaky but his aim was true, brutally driving home the message that parents and children should be together.

The question was *how* together. Bowlby called for "continuous" care, and some people took this literally (perhaps because he also called for "constant attention day and night, seven days a week and 365 days a year"). But Bowlby was not in fact promoting skin-to-skin contact from birth to age eighteen. In 1958 he tried to clarify his position with a pamphlet entitled "Can I Leave My Baby?" The short answer: yes. As long as it's with the same trusted person. And hopefully just because you want to go out and get your nails done and not, say, so you can do something frivolous like try to work full-time, because what job is more important than the one you already have?*

While Bowlby did make the point (which more recent science has backed up) that a child needs frequent ongoing attention from one† reliable caregiver, he agreed that this caregiver needn't always be the mother. He even endorsed boarding schools for older children. Although Bowlby was traumatized by his own packing off at a young age—he later declared, "I wouldn't send a dog away to boarding school at age seven"—he felt it was perfectly appropriate for a child over eight. It was good, he wrote, for kids to get away from the tensions of home, and the absence could make the parent's heart grow fonder as well: "by relieving the parents of the children for part of the year, it will be possible for some of them to develop more favorable attitudes toward their children during the remainder."

Parents who needed a little chemical help to develop that favorable attitude could turn to pharmaceuticals. As in the Victorian era—the last time mothers were encouraged to do all the child-rearing themselves— drugs again became a popular at-home activity. Enter Miltown and Valium, aka mother's little helper.‡ For children, there was mother's little

---

* In Bowlby's own home, there was plenty of outside help from nurseries and au pairs, as his wife wrote in her anonymous column for *Nursery World* magazine. Ursula Bowlby described herself as her own "head nurse" and urged mothers to take charge—but not to take on all the work themselves (Katherine Holden, *Nanny Knows Best: The History of the British Nanny* [Stroud, Gloucestershire: The History Press, 2013]).

† Or better yet, more. Some research suggests that the ideal number of securely attached caregivers is actually three (Marinus van Ijzendoorn, Abraham Sagi, and Mirjam W. E. Lambermon, "The Multiple Caretaker Paradox: Data from Holland and Israel," *New Directions for Child and Adolescent Development* 57 [Fall 1992]: 5–24).

‡ The association with mothers is not entirely fair, as Andrea Tone points out in her book *The Age of Anxiety: A History of America's Turbulent Affair with Tranquilizers* (New York: Basic Books, 2008). Sure, mothers took them, but so did lots of other people; by 1956, they were used by one out of every twenty Americans. Tranquil-

knockout drug, Nembutal, also available in suppository form if Junior had a problem swallowing pills.* I'm not sure it's such a good idea to give your child heavy barbiturates, but I guess it's nice to share a hobby.

NOT EVERYONE THOUGHT all this togetherness was such a good thing, however, and as the sixties turned into the seventies, attachment theory faced a backlash, mostly from feminists and their allies, who argued for more outside childcare. One of the greatest champions of outsourcing childcare was Bruno Bettelheim, who might have had more influence if he weren't, as Dr. Spock himself noted, a "[v]ery frightening" figure who "scared the hell out of people."

A Holocaust survivor with a heavy accent, a stern manner, and some outlandish ideas, Bettelheim gave people the creeps, and after his suicide in 1990, we'd learn there was good reason: his credentials were faked, as were his positive results; former patients and employees came forward to say he beat them and touched them inappropriately. But some of his ideas were tremendously forward-thinking and sympathetic. In articles like the boldly titled "Why Working Mothers Have Happier Children," he admitted that full-time child-rearing could be boring and unfulfilling, and that mothers were unfairly blamed when things went wrong.† It was time, he

---

izers were especially popular with businessmen and entertainers. Uncle Miltie was reportedly such a fan that he wanted to change his name to Miltown Berle.

* Weirdly, according to the Giancana brothers' book *Double Cross* (New York: Skyhorse Publishing, 2016), a Nembutal suppository is what Mafia hit men used to kill Marilyn Monroe. True or not, it's maybe not such a good thing to give a child, nor is phenobarbital, which my mother reports our neighbors used to knock out their overactive kids forty-five years ago. Phenobarbital was in fact what Nazis used, in suppository form or mixed in formula or cocoa, to exterminate disabled children. Lung failure would result, and the death would be recorded as pneumonia (John Donvan and Caren Zucker, *In a Different Key: The Story of Autism*, 318).

† Ironically, Bettelheim hurled some of the worst blame himself at the mothers of autistic children, writing that "the precipitating factor in infantile autism is the parent's wish that his child should not exist." He compared these mothers to witches and SS guards, and prescribed a "parentectomy" to treat the child's condition (Bruno Bettelheim, *The Empty Fortress: Infantile Autism and the Birth of the Self* [New York: Free Press, 1967], 125).

declared, for a new model: "Some of our psychologists and psychiatrists—and those social scientists whom they unduly influence—will have to stop viewing the Victorian woman as the ideal female type, as the only mother who does not cheat her children out of motherlove."

Even the expert who coined the term *parenting* agreed that parents needn't do all the work themselves. This was Fitzhugh Dodson, whose 1970s advice book *How to Parent* introduced the word as a verb. He wrote, "I'm going to define this new verb as a dictionary might define it: *to parent*—'to use, with tender loving care, all the information science has accumulated about child psychology in order to raise happy and intelligent human beings.'" Dodson continues: "This verb does *not* describe the simple biological act of giving birth to a child. And it does *not* describe the raising of that child by the usual trial and error methods. The raising of a child is a complex and difficult proposition."

All the more reason to hire help, then, and mercifully, Dodson endorses this idea. In his 1977 book *How to Discipline with Love* he devotes an entire chapter to "The Working Mother" and the need for childcare, claiming that "it should be obvious that neither a mother nor a father can find *all* of his other fulfillment through parenting . . . It is completely normal to want to get away from your children from time to time. And this is a perfectly valid reason (among others) for wanting to take a job outside the home."

But who would watch the kids? The sixties and seventies left families scrambling. The grandparents probably did not live nearby, and daycare options were few (in 1974–75, 1.6 percent of children attended daycare; in 2011, 23 percent did). Vicki Breitbart addressed the conundrum in her 1974 omnibus, *The Day Care Book*, coming up with some creative and very seventies solutions, including communes and group marriage.

Help came from surprising corners. When female Black Panthers complained that a lack of childcare was preventing their full participation in the party, the organization opened several daycare centers around the country. These would be explicitly alloparental, with children raised in a group, by the group. In Spanish Harlem, the Young Lords, a militant Puerto Rican group, got daycare centers operating out of local churches.

Panther Cubs, West Berkeley Day Care Center, 1971
(Courtesy itsabouttimebpp.com)

Over the next decade, daycare would expand, and with it, panicked concern about its safety. Anxiety was fanned by the absurd McMartin Preschool trial, in which seven staffers were charged with 321 counts of molesting forty-eight children in satanic rituals conducted in tunnels beneath the school. The trial lasted seven years, cost $15 million, resulted in no convictions, and set a new standard for prosecutorial misconduct.

As it happens, those years coincided with my own brief time as a daycare staffer. As I recall, there was no Satan worship and the only object of abuse was the copier, which came in for some mistreatment after my sister and I figured out it could be used to copy not just memos but our own heads. When I wasn't in the Xerox portrait studio I spent my time honing the skills that would serve me well when I had my own children—hiding in the supply closet and self-soothing with dry cereal. Look busy.

When John Bowlby discouraged mothers from working outside the home, the primary reason he gave was not that the separation was so bad for the kids, but because "it is very difficult to get people to look after other people's children." His point was well illustrated by the fact that I, a teenager who spent as much of my day as possible with my head in a copier, held the job. There just wasn't much competition for it. Childcare is hard, exhausting, and boring, and while there are plenty of jobs that require you to clean up human poop, this is the only one where you also have to praise its author for making such a nice one. The pay is bad, and no one would do it if they weren't impelled by some other reason than, say, the fact that your mother is the office manager and is threatening to make you pay for your own frozen yogurt if you do not spend at least part of the summer helping her out at work.

And as it turns out, there *is* another reason. The species simply wouldn't continue if alloparents didn't pitch in, but the job is hard enough that survival alone, or even survival plus frozen yogurt, isn't enough to motivate assistants. Helpers *are* motivated by cuteness, however. As Sarah Blaffer Hrdy points out, human children, like those of many other species, evolved to attract caregivers with their downy hair, big eyes, and fat cheeks. I made $4.50 an hour and was bored senseless, but even I, who am dead inside, couldn't help but be charmed by a three-year-old boy in a princess dress coming in hard for a hug.

BY THE TIME I left in the early nineties, there were more daycare centers than ever before and more concerns that this might not be a good thing. Parents were beginning to worry that even daycare centers that didn't employ me could do harm, by separating the child from the parent for any time at all. Boundaries that somehow held through the sixties, seventies, and eighties dissolved as attachment theory morphed into attachment parenting. Bonding quickly became bondage, and attached became attached at the hip. It had taken a full generation for Bowlby's revenge to arrive, but the clinging chickens had come home to roost.

There are various theories as to why. This generation of parents had grown up with working mothers and widespread divorce, and their attraction to attachment parenting may have been in part a resentful attempt to raise their own children differently. Forty percent of Generation X children were latchkey kids; a 2004 study calls them "one of the least parented, least nurtured generations in U.S. history." As Judith Warner points out, they'd also grown up with pictures of Harry Harlow's sad monkeys in their abnormal psych books, and I'm telling you, those pictures stay with you.

Or maybe it was just because William and Martha Sears arrived on the scene. In the same era that Hillary Clinton was arguing that it takes a village to raise a child, the Searses were saying that it takes a sling and a family bed. Their philosophy, it should be noted, was based not on the science, flawed though it may be, of attachment theory, but on the ideas of a childless part-time model who "discovered" attachment parenting while in Venezuela on a diamond-hunting expedition with an actual Italian count.

The model in question was Jean Liedloff, who laid down her ideas in the seventies bestseller *The Continuum Concept.* As a child development expert qualification, "part-time model on a diamond-hunting expedition with an actual Italian count" pretty much demands ridicule. Still, I have to admit, both the author and the book are charming: thoughtful, self-aware, and engaging, and generations of readers became devoted fans.

Jean Liedloff and pet monkey
(*Courtesy* New York Times/*Redux*)

Susan Douglas and Meredith Michaels sum up the Sears philosophy: "Reattach your baby to your body the moment she is born and keep her there pretty much until she goes to college." A brief reading of the Sears's back catalog will confirm that Douglas and Michaels have a point. But even the Searses allow for outsourcing, preferably in an attachment-friendly setting, and preferably for a good reason. *The Baby Book* devotes a whole chapter to the topic of "Working and Parenting," with strategies for securing good outside care. As Martha herself reminds her husband, "If I hadn't worked while you were an intern, we wouldn't be sitting here right now."

The amount of time we spend with our children is determined by so many factors: financial, legal, cultural, circumstantial. To have any say in the matter is an enormous luxury. Whether by choice or not, the majority of American families today use some form of childcare.

And most people feel bad about this. In a 2003 Pew poll, 72 percent of respondents felt that children spend too much time in daycare. At the same time, even though parents work more hours, we're actually spending more time with our children now than we have at any time in recent history. Between their paid caregivers and their parents, kids are getting an *awful* lot of attention. We're providing our children with more nurturing than children have ever had. The mystery is why we feel so much worse.

For so much of history, parents did not raise their children and did not feel guilt. This was partly because they were too busy feeling, say, *plague*, but also because they did not face blame. As Hrdy points out, previous generations blamed mothers only for things like failing to produce a boy, or failing to produce any child at all. But once the child was born, any bad outcomes would be blamed on something else: witchcraft, a curse, divine will, fate. The culprit was never insufficient hugs or too many hours at Happy Time Tot Center.

As for the blame for the blame, that goes in large part to Freud and his colleagues. Though we've dismissed most of Freud's assertions, this aspect continues to reverberate. We think: And *yet* . . . Even though studies undertaken to prove that outside care is bad for children have in fact proved the opposite. Even though outsourcing care is exactly what we've evolved to do.

We still feel bad. And this may be because we've *also* evolved to feel guilt and to use blame to produce it in others. Some evolutionary psychologists have argued that guilt is a spur that pricks us into tending our children more. They also argue that this is a feeling that children (and men) have evolved to *promote*, as it gets children what they want and dads some time off. Which is exactly what T. Berry Brazelton, for one, does when he calls guilt an "important motivator": "Women should allow themselves to feel anxious and guilty about leaving their children—those feelings will press them to find the best substitute care."

Or to say screw it and figure out something else. And this in fact is what we've done in my house. Because substitute care manages to be both criminally underpaid and obscenely expensive, we can afford only a limited number of daycare hours every week. Because this number is far less than the number of hours my husband and I need to work (and, if I'm honest, to shop online and watch YouTube in peace), our family has had to come up with alternative solutions.

Most of the techniques used in the past are out, and by now the children are too big to dispatch to a wet nurse or straitjacket with swaddling. It's no longer legal to expose them on a hillside or give them to a brothel. The foundling homes have all closed. Our relatives are thousands of miles away, and there's no kerchiefed hag or especially alert pig in the thatched hut next door to watch them while their father and I tend to the blacksmithing.

But there is TV, and in the end, this is the substitute caregiver we always turn to. In our home we do not emphasize attachment parenting but connection of another kind: the entertaining tether of premium cable. It is expensive, but given how much our children watch, it's far less than the hourly rate we would pay a human to keep them occupied. And when concerned outsiders recite the data showing how very bad it is for our children to have this much screen time, my husband and I tune them out, a skill we both learned as children when our own mothers, stuck at home without adequate childcare themselves, relied on the very same sitter.

Then, of course, the faces were different. Now Disney and Nick offer a steady rotation of scrubbed and sassy tweens, but forty years ago there wasn't much children's programming, and besides, our mothers were in charge of the remote. TV offered them a break, a chance to watch *All My Children* instead of all theirs. And so, with no daycare for me to go to, my mother and I would pass the morning in Pine Valley, letting the cast's dissatisfactions distract us from our own.

In Texas, my four-year-old future husband was doing the exact same thing. Like me, he would come to view the blow-dried, chiseled characters as friendly aunts and uncles, alloparents of a sort. Many of the shows have gone off the air, but the actors are still around, and from time to time we'll spot one in a made-for-TV movie or in a life insurance ad. We'll shout, "It's Cliff!!!!" happy to see the long-lost loved one who stepped in when our own parents were too worn out, letting the species continue for one more generation.

So we stop what we're doing and settle in to watch the rest of the show. Just for a bit, while we refold laundry, pretend to answer email, look busy. We ignore the apocalypse taking place in the playroom, the lunch we still haven't made, the shouts and the whines and the crashes, because we have other things to do. The children won't die if they don't get their juice for thirty more minutes, and this show, like our kids, won't watch itself.

# 2

# The Second Coming

## *On Childbirth*

I n the spring of 2011, I was pregnant with my second child and there was a small chance I was carrying the messiah. A fringe religious group was predicting the world would end the same week my son was due, and it certainly seemed like the end times were nigh. As the days ticked down, the horsemen of the apocalypse lined up. Four days out, I landed in the ER when half my face suddenly became paralyzed, making it impossible to chew, see, hear, or speak normally, and I couldn't feel my hands. The good news was that it was a palsy, not a stroke. The bad: I would have to wear a patch over the eye that would not shut, making me a nine-month-pregnant pirate. The next day our toddler daughter's dislocated elbow sent us back to urgent care, where we learned she also had a double ear infection. The day after that my husband herniated a disk and found himself unable to walk or stand. When we arrived at the hospital for the birth, both of us in wheelchairs, I half expected to find the wheels in flames, with chariots and seraphim trailing behind.

Compared to how childbirth could go throughout most of history, however, we were actually doing pretty well. Though the fringe group's rapture would not arrive, for us it was an age of miracles. To have a baby in the twenty-first century is a blessing previous generations couldn't imagine.* There are anesthetics and antibiotics. Should something go wrong, brilliant people and equipment are on hand to ensure both mother and baby live. After you deliver, you're given marvelously comfortable free underwear that's as large and airy as a mosquito net.

All of which is not to say that modern birth is easy, just that you're more likely to survive. Even with drugs and the full force of modern medicine behind you, birth is typically a grueling process. Radical feminist Shulamith Firestone likened it to "shitting a pumpkin." Jessica Mitford's more reserved mother Lady Redesdale said it's "like an orange being stuffed up your nostril." Something big has to pass through something small, and this is going to cause a great deal of pain.

A hundred years ago obstetricians held that "Nature has provided a certain degree of postpartum amnesia," erasing the pain of childbirth so we'd be willing to go through it again. We still don't really know if that's true. The few studies that have examined mothers' memories of childbirth pain have either been fairly inconclusive or shown that any minimizing effect is small. Which makes our willingness to have more than one a miracle in itself: the second coming. Because we do remember how hard it was, but we do it again anyway.

What's unclear is why is it's so hard in the first place. Until recently the usual explanation has been something known as the obstetrical dilemma hypothesis, which blames the evolutionary conflict caused by our species' insistence on walking upright. Walking is a skill that is supposed to require both big brains and narrow pelvises, which constitutes quite a problem when the former has to emerge from the latter. The obstetrical dilemma hypothesis explains both why birth is difficult and why babies are so helpless. Compared to most species, humans are born terrifically premature, while their heads are still small enough to squeeze, albeit terribly uncomfortably, through the narrow hominid pelvis.

Humans give birth to infants so immature they're called exterogestate fetuses, requiring nine to twelve months of development outside the

---

* In the developed world, at least, and even there, with notable and shameful exceptions, like the higher maternal mortality rate for women of color.

womb to be as advanced as chimpanzees are at birth. Human brains must quadruple in size after birth (those of most other primates only double). The term for this is *altricial*; the opposite is *precocial*. Precocial animals, which include most large mammals, are born able to hold on to their parents, eat, and walk shortly after birth. Squirrel monkey babies actually help deliver themselves; once they're halfway out, they use their arms to pull out the rest of their body.

The obstetrical dilemma hypothesis provides a good excuse for human babies' comparative uselessness, but recent research suggests it might be missing the mark. It turns out you can walk just fine with a wider pelvis (as some early hominins, who likely had much less painful births, did). Instead, anthropologist Holly Dunsworth has proposed an energetics of gestation and growth (EGG) hypothesis, which argues that it's not the mother's pelvis but the baby's energy needs that are the issue. We give birth when the baby's metabolic requirements are just about to outstrip what the mother's body can provide. The baby is, essentially, a guest who gets eighty-sixed from the all-you-can-eat buffet after eating it all. The bouncer doesn't measure the doorway first. As far as evolution is concerned, ejection doesn't have to be comfortable or easy as long as it's possible. If there are some dings and scratches, that's fine. Time to go. Don't let the door hit you on the way out.

The problem, of course, is that the door *does* hit the baby, and you wouldn't believe what the baby does to the door. Birth is a tight squeeze in the best of circumstances. In the worst, it's an impossible one. And in the developed world, worst is pretty common. Sitting in chairs rather than squatting has made our pelvises tighter and our diets have made babies bigger. Human babies' brains may be comparatively small, but on the whole, babies are enormous. Relative to their mother's size, human newborns are three times bigger than newborn gorillas. With some frequency, they get stuck.

The clinical name for this is *dystocia due to cephalopelvic disproportion*, a fact I learned firsthand with my first delivery, when after thirty-eight hours of labor (and a failed epidural) my daughter hadn't gone anywhere. Interventions had succeeded in making the contractions unbearably intense, but not in advancing her toward the exit. Eventually the ordeal ended in an emergency C-section under general anesthesia for me, and a trip to the NICU for her.

Within a few hours we were both fine, and one of us was eating French toast sticks. A few generations earlier, however, we would have both died. Human birth is so difficult that it's made us the only species that needs help to get through it, a phenomenon anthropologist Wenda Trevathan calls obligate midwifery.* Some evolutionary biologists have theorized that this is the reason human labor and delivery are more likely to take place at night; a woman delivering in the afternoon, when her clan was dispersed gathering food, might find herself alone without help.†

In contrast, most animals get through delivery quickly and easily, as if it were no more than a minor interruption in their day. Fifteen minutes after a wildebeest gives birth, both she and her child are off and running. A typical howler monkey birth lasts about two minutes. Polar bears take longer, but can sleep through both the birth and the first three months of parenthood. Cubs emerge during hibernation and nurse without waking their mothers until spring. Those cubs, by the way, are born smaller than human babies, while the mothers typically weigh 500 pounds.

The only animal whose labor is more difficult than ours is the hyena, whose birth process is an abject horror beyond imagining. Female hyenas essentially give birth to a four-pound baby *through a penis*. During pregnancy, a hyena's testosterone levels rise dramatically, enlarging the clitoris until it becomes a pseudo penis measuring up to seven inches long. Cubs are born through a tiny tube at the center, which is as easy and comfortable as it sounds. Labor is slow and painful and frequently fatal.

---

* We are not, however, the only species that *accepts* help. Dolphins, in particular, have occasionally been observed assisting each other deliver (Trevathan, *Human Birth*, 108). From time to time there are also reports of dolphins helping deliver *humans*, a practice promoted by a few fringe folks in Hawaii and Russia. But as Penn and Teller documented in their series *Bullshit!*, while a few women have considered having dolphin midwives, none have actually gone through with it, and the whole thing seems to be little more than myth.

† While obligate midwifery is unique to humans, laboring at night isn't. It's common among most diurnal mammals. If the baby's not born by morning, some animals will actually pause labor and begin again at nightfall. Among nocturnal animals, conversely, it's more common to labor during the day. In both cases, it's possible that these are evolutionary adaptations that let mothers avoid predators.

The hyena birth canal (which, again, passes through *a penis*) is unusually long and makes a 180-degree turn. Sixty percent of the time, a first-time mother's offspring will die; they suffocate. The mother has an 18 percent chance of dying herself. If the mother survives, it will likely be with a ruptured clitoris. Hyenas give birth to litters, not singles, and every one of the infants is born with teeth and claws, which they sometimes use to attack and kill their siblings should they actually survive the birth. Hyena pregnancies can even be dangerous for other hyenas. The elevated levels of testosterone make expectant mothers extremely aggressive, and they frequently lash out at males.

HUMAN MATERNAL MORTALITY RATES are better, but they weren't always. Whether maternal mortality rates were high in previous generations depends on whether you view the glass as half full or half dying from entirely preventable conditions. It's hard to pinpoint exact figures, but European records from 1400 to 1800 suggest a maternal death rate of 1 to 3 percent. This is much higher than the .015 percent for American mothers now, but still less than today's .04 percent mortality rate for *tonsillectomies.* Of course, the 1 to 3 percent risk applied per birth, and given an average of five births, this could add up to a 4 to 10 percent chance over a woman's life.

That meant that pretty much everyone would know a woman who died in childbirth. (If those figures held today, three of the kids in my son's kindergarten class would be motherless.) It was a fate that befell queens as well as commoners, though few received a monument as impressive as Mumtaz Mahal, whose death delivering her twelfth was commemorated by the Taj Mahal. Childbirth killed the notorious Lucrezia Borgia, two of Henry VIII's eight wives, and the first Pilgrim to give birth in Plymouth.

Which is all to say that the maternal mortality rate was high, sure, but still not the 30 to 50 percent I would have guessed from watching BBC period dramas. The period dramas are right about one thing, however: a hundred years ago, you had a fairly decent chance of dying in childbirth, even if you were rich and fancy. In fact, being rich and fancy made it even more likely. As the nineteenth century turned, women of means began to have their babies delivered by doctors, often in hospitals, rather than by midwives, at home, a change that brought a one-two punch of incompetence and disease. Maternal mortality rates, which had been declining, suddenly reversed direction. Doctors and hospitals were to blame.

Maternity hospitals were particularly dangerous. These were known as lying-in hospitals, but dying-in seems more apt, given their astronomical maternal mortality rates. The deaths were largely due to overcrowding—in some hospitals, up to six women shared a single bed—and medical practices that quickly spread disease. This was a fact I tried to bear in mind that apocalyptic morning in May, when I wheeled into a hospital under construction that was so overloaded with delivering mothers I got the last room; the next to arrive, they told me, would be laboring in the elevator.

An elevator would have been only slightly worse than the room I got, which was a single-sized double in the pediatric oncology unit with a bathroom shared by six. Because my bed was closest to the door, you had to pass by it to reach the other patient, a postpartum Amish woman with a very large family, all present, who spent the entire time shouting into the landline. I have no idea who she could have been calling, as presumably no one she knew had a phone. I did learn, however, that Pennsylvania Dutch sounds a lot like Yiddish, especially when yelled.

A century ago, it would not have seemed at all strange that there were a dozen people crowded into my hospital room. That my son was one of them, however, would have. Until recently it was thought the baby belonged in the nursery, away from his exhausted mother and her germs. Instead, the child joined a heap of babies in the nursery, where he might get mixed up and sent home with the wrong family. Hospitals didn't begin tagging babies with name bands until the 1930s and '40s. Previously, their faces had served as their only ID. Mothers and nurses assumed they'd remember which baby was theirs, but they didn't always, and DNA testing is now revealing how often babies went home with strangers.

As for rooming-in, that wasn't introduced until Arnold Gesell and Frances Ilg coined the term in 1943, and initially it was implemented not because it facilitated bonding but because hospital space was scarce during World War II. (Later, bonding research done by John Bowlby and others spurred more widespread use of the practice. Still, it didn't become standard practice to keep your newborn in the room with you for several decades. In the 1970s I spent the better part of my first week of life in the nursery so my mother could nap.)

My own postpartum stay, several decades after that, was not as recuperative. Still, my primary worry was how many Amish children had to see me in my giant mesh underwear, not whether or not I'd leave there alive. This was very much a concern for previous generations, and the odds weren't good. In England, maternal mortality rates at lying-in hospitals could be as much as ten times higher than the national average. In America, where there was far less medical regulation, they were even worse. By the 1920s, America had become perhaps the most dangerous First World country to give birth in, with a maternal mortality rate nearly three times that of other nations.

Though the death rates increased in the nineteenth and twentieth centuries, lying-in hospitals had always been dangerous, a last resort used almost exclusively by the poor. There, patients were treated to a mandatory 500-hour stay that included not just subpar medical care and rampant contagion, but also spiritual lectures and moral condescension. Presuming, I suppose, that patients would mistake it for a casino, the British Lying-In Hospital posted rules that forbid patients to play cards or dice, smoke, swear, or drink gin. Even tea was off-limits. Rude behavior or vermin would get you kicked out, as would not actually being pregnant. Why women would fake a pregnancy to get a stay in an uptight asylum with high mortality rates, I don't know, but I suppose it tells you something about the Georgian-era idea of R&R.

**AS THE TWENTIETH CENTURY APPROACHED,** hospitals were being used more frequently by women of means, who saw them as more hygienic and scientific. These women also began rejecting midwives in favor of doctors, an unfortunate choice, as doctors were spectacularly unqualified. Deliveries were performed by general practitioners rather than obstetricians, because obstetricians didn't officially exist. Obstetrics didn't become a field of its own until the early twentieth century. The term itself, coined in 1828, comes from Latin and means "to stand before."[*] As many scholars have observed, that's about all these early doctors did, when they weren't actively causing harm with unnecessary or dangerous interventions.

Doctors had little to no training in obstetrics, and what training they had was likely useless. At medical schools, obstetrics was "a despised subject" worthy of hacks and illiterate country women, not men of science. A 1912 report out of Johns Hopkins noted that 30 percent of obstetric professors were not in fact obstetricians, but general practitioners with no extra training or interest in the subject who'd taken the job simply because it had been offered. The obstetric education medical students did receive wasn't particularly useful. At the University of Pennsylvania in the mid-1800s, obstetrics professor William Dewees considered direct examination of a woman's genitals unthinkable, and instructed his students to perform their internal exams *without looking*. Medical students might graduate from a top medical school having witnessed only a single birth. Until the mid-1800s, they were not permitted to witness any at all. When James Platt White, the first professor of obstetrics at the University of Buffalo, had his medical students examine a laboring woman in 1850, scandal ensued, eventually resulting in a libel trial and White's expulsion from the American Medical Association. Depressingly, it wasn't just the obstetricians who were underqualified—it was everyone. By 1900, Johns Hopkins was the only American med school that required incoming students to have a college degree, and many didn't even require a high school diploma.

This did not prevent new doctors from delivering babies, just from doing so knowledgeably or well. Irvine Loudon describes nineteenth-century obstetric education as "a system which might have been designed to maximize maternal mortality." It was, he writes, a curriculum based on "the carelessness, the impatience, the scorn of proper standards of antisepsis, and the numerous instances of clumsy, dangerous, and unnecessary interference in the birth process." Doctors made frequent internal

---

[*] To be fair, the coiners weren't really suggesting the only thing obstetricians did was stand around. They were actually referencing *obstetrix*, the Latin word for *midwife*, which also comes from the Latin verb meaning "to stand before."

examinations with hands that had been washed perfunctorily if at all, used unsterile lubricant and tools, and performed aggressive interventions that did more harm than good.

The most tragic and common result was childbed fever. Also called puerperal fever, or puerperal septicemia, this was an incredibly awful way for a new mother to die, arriving right after an enormously happy event. It came on quickly and could be terribly painful. As Alexander Gordon described it, it was "so excruciating that the miserable patients described their torture to be as great, or greater than, what they suffered during labour."

Gordon, a Scottish physician, wrote a 1795 treatise on the subject which argued—correctly—that puerperal fever was a contagious condition spread by midwives and doctors. Previously, it was believed to be caused by rotten breast milk (physicians doing autopsies mistook the pus it produced for milk); or by the wearing of corsets so tight they forced poop into the uterus or bloodstream. Others blamed bad air. In 1877 the president of the American Gynecological Society would blame it on bad character, noting that the disease typically spread in lying-in hospitals, where unwed mothers were more common. Their shame and anxiety, he said, made them more susceptible to the disease.

This was, of course, totally, totally wrong. Writing almost a hundred years earlier, Gordon had gotten it totally, totally right. What he got wrong was the treatment: heavy bloodletting. Understandably, patients weren't crazy about this, especially since the condition had previously been treated with alcoholic cordials. This, coupled with Gordon's admission that he himself had unknowingly infected patients, soon brought an end to his obstetrical career.

In the United States, the first to argue that puerperal fever was contagious was Oliver Wendell Holmes, Sr. In an 1843 paper, Holmes made the clear and convincing case that caregivers spread the disease, although he did not yet know how. His argument fell not so much on deaf ears as defiantly ignorant ones. Doctors were incensed by the charge, none more so than Charles Meigs, a medical professor known as "the dean of American midwifery" and the country's leading expert in obstetrics. Meigs was unbearably patronizing and sexist, teaching his students that woman

"has a head almost too small for intellect and just big enough for love."[*]
He also famously argued that laboring women should never be given pain
relief, and that doctors had no business trying to "contravene" the suffering that "Divinity has ordained," especially when anesthesia might not be
safe. He asked, "What sufficient motive have I to risk the death of one in
a thousand in a questionable attempt to abrogate one of the general conditions of man?"

Meigs was, however, happy to risk the death of one in, say, five hundred, if it meant he didn't have to wash his hands.[†] Holmes argued that
physicians must be vigilant about hygiene to protect their patients. Meigs
strongly disagreed, replying that a doctor is a gentleman, "and a gentleman's hands are clean."

Perhaps Meigs's definition of clean was different than ours; in any
case, contemporary reports suggest a standard of hygiene so low that I
wouldn't want a doctor to make me a sandwich, never mind a mother. A
Maine doctor recalled that until 1870, medical students balked at washing
up before treating laboring women, even if they'd come straight from an
autopsy: "What is the use of washing one's hands before making a vaginal
examination? Will they not be just as dirty after it?" Dirtier, probably—
but that's not the point. *The point is you wash the dead person's deadly germs*

---

* In the same lecture, Meigs elaborates: "*It is easy to perceive that her intellectual force
is different from that of her master and lord.* I say her master and lord; and it is
true to say so, since even in that society she is still in a manner in bonds, and the
manacles of custom, of politics, or of *bienséance* not yet struck from her hands. She
has nowhere been admitted to the political rights, franchises and powers that man
arrogates to man alone. The Crown, when it rests on the brow of a woman, is always
a political accident, grievous and deprecable; and even then, where woman reigns,
man governs" (*Females and Their Diseases*, 40). At the time this was published—in
1848—Queen Victoria was the most powerful person in the world, eleven years
into her highly successful sixty-three-year reign.

† I am not being entirely fair here. Although Meigs rejected the idea that doctors bore
any responsibility for transmitting puerperal fever, he did urge his colleagues to
take all good antiseptic precautions, including washing their hands and changing
their clothes. And while it sometimes seemed like he had more sympathy for the
doctors whose careers were ruined when they lost enormous numbers of patients to
the disease than for the patients themselves, he did regard puerperal fever as a terrible tragedy and went to lengths to prevent and treat it. STILL A PATRONIZING
CHAUVINIST, THOUGH.

*off before you touch the lady in labor.* In Europe, the chances the doctor's hands would be carrying some dead person's germs were high, as autopsies were required by law. Washing, however, was not.

Widespread acceptance of the germ theory was still a decade or so off, and doctors truly did not know how disease was spread. Still, they did some things that just seem objectively careless now. Edinburgh physician William Campbell may take the cake. At the 1821 autopsy of a puerperal fever victim, he removed the pelvic organs to bring to class. Defying all common sense, he transported them in his pocket. Call me uptight, but I just don't think it's appropriate to transport a septic uterus in your sport-coat. And if you do, by all means *change before you deliver another baby.* Campbell did not: "The same evening, without changing my clothes, I attended the delivery of a poor woman in the Canongate; she died. Next morning I went in the same clothes to assist some of my pupils who were engaged with a woman in Bridewell, whom I delivered by forceps; she died."

Of course she did, and lots of other women did as well. The next cru-sader who tried to put a stop to things was the Austrian physician Ignaz Semmelweis, whose research in the 1840s clearly showed that caregivers spread the disease. He insisted his staff wash with chlorinated lime and reduced the unit's puerperal fever rate by 90 percent. But like Gordon and Holmes, Semmelweis was ridiculed and ignored. He died shortly there-after, disgraced, in an insane asylum.[*]

Over the next half century or so thousands more women would die from puerperal fever until the germ theory finally took hold and everyone realized the only way to prevent it was to use the same standard of antisep-tic precautions used for general surgery. Still, most didn't, because it was a pain and they didn't want to. Instead of washing, they might just wipe their hands on a towel; instead of sterilizing an instrument, they would pass it through a bar of soap. This accomplished nothing, and women continued to die.

---

[*] Semmelweis actually died from septicemia himself, the result of a beating by asylum guards two weeks after he arrived there. As for what got him sent to the asylum in the first place, it was likely Alzheimer's, not insanity caused by being right about puerperal fever when everyone said he was wrong. *But still.*

What finally began to turn things around, in part, was a 1917 study conducted by physician Grace Meigs, ironically the great-granddaughter of Charles Meigs, who'd argued so forcefully against doctors' responsibility for puerperal contagion. Apparently, Grace's head was big enough not only for love but for revolutionary public health research. Her report brought attention to what might be the cause of the egregious maternal mortality rates in the United States. Doctors and hospitals began to clean up their acts, albeit slowly. It took two more reports on the still shockingly high maternal mortality rates, one by the New York Academy of Medicine in 1933, and another by the White House, to really light a fire. By then sulfa drugs and penicillin were on their way, and these finally put the brakes on puerperal fever for good.

BUT WHILE MORTALITY was dropping fantastically—it would go down by 90 percent between the 1930s and 1950s, to one in two thousand births—newborn mortality remained shockingly high at one in thirty. By now there were antibiotics, proper medical training, and rigorous hospital standards. Why were so many babies still dying?

The answer turned out to be straightforward: obstetricians were ignoring them. The typical delivering doctor gave the baby a quick look and a cursory pat and turned his attention back to the mother, leaving the child to live or die on its own. There seemed little point in doing otherwise, when there was no standard way to evaluate newborns and little expectation they could be helped if help was needed.

Enter the Apgar test, conceived in 1949 by a clever anesthesiologist named Virginia Apgar. This is the evaluation performed one minute after birth and five minutes later, in which signs like the baby's appearance, pulse, and breathing are rated. Apgar dashed off her idea over a meal in the cafeteria. The innovation that would save countless lives over the coming decades was originally scrawled on the back of a card that urged "Please Bus Your Trays."

Her idea was astoundingly simple. Babies were assigned from zero to two points in each of five areas that a colleague would later give a mnemonic acronym to in tribute: appearance, pulse, grimace, activity, and respiration.* The test took one to two seconds, cost nothing, and required no complicated equipment or training.

From the start, the Apgar test wrought a sea change. First, it got medical staff to actually examine the baby, letting them see what was wrong and required intervention, as well as what was right, suggesting that the infant might be viable if the intervention was done. A child with compromised respiration but a detectable heartbeat now received oxygen and attention instead of a shoulder shrug, and was far more likely to live.

Introducing scores also made birth competitive, a huge inducement for the type-A personalities that tend to staff a delivery room. When caregivers noticed that small interventions like providing oxygen or even warmth could raise the five-minute Apgar score from a 2 or a 3 to a 7 or an 8, they started intervening. Then they started developing new equipment to aid in these interventions, like infant heart monitors and baby-sized CPR tools. Neonatal intensive care units (NICUs), which had never existed before, began to open. A whole new field of neonatology resulted, and infant mortality plummeted.

Assigning numbers to the birth process also introduced a data set that let doctors and researchers view bigger trends. They could see what generally helped the birth process along and what stressed babies out—for instance, anesthesia. Apgar had suspected that babies born under anesthesia were more likely to experience respiratory distress, and her newly invented score quickly showed she was right.

Seventy years later, when my daughter was born in a C-section under general anesthesia, she earned the sort of Apgar score that gets you whisked off to the NICU. The anesthesia was a major factor in her rock-bottom score, but by now, the staff knew to expect this and what to do. After a couple of hours in the NICU, she was perfectly healthy, and unlike the generations of mothers who came before me, I was too. I had been spared the death in childbirth that was more or less guaranteed before

---

\* The Apgar test is used around the world, and the acronym works in the Romance languages as well as in German. More recently, in the United States, some have begun using the alternate mnemonic "How Ready Is This Child" (heart rate, respiration effort, irritability, tone, and color). As a fan of Virginia, I prefer APGAR, though I do like the fact that HRITC makes irritability a vital sign.

C-sections resolved stalled labors, and before doctors figured out the need to wash their stupid hands.

IF IT'S EASY to blame men for the abysmal maternity mortality rates that plagued previous generations, it's because they were in fact to blame. While there were certainly inept midwives, they did not kill on the industrial scale that these overconfident, undertrained men did. Many were no more qualified than my hairdresser. Weirdly, had my children been born three hundred years earlier, that's exactly who would have delivered them. Seventeenth-century deliveries were often performed by barber-surgeons, the only individuals legally permitted to use forceps. This was a controversial development not because of the new equipment—which could kill both mother and child—but because of the barber-surgeons' gender.

The birth process has generated no lack of debate, but few subjects have been more contentious than the presence of men in the birthing chamber. For most of history, men were excluded entirely, and those who tried to sneak in met with severe consequences. In 1522, a Hamburg doctor named Wertt tried to gain some obstetric experience by furtively attending births dressed as a woman. When he was caught, he was burned at the stake.

Men's exclusion did not, however, prevent them from holding themselves experts on the process. Although men did not experience or even witness birth, they felt perfectly qualified to lecture on the subject. Many of the earliest books on obstetrics and gynecology were written by monks, who presumably know less about female reproductive anatomy than anyone on the planet. They did know Greek and Latin, however, and since most medieval texts on the subject came directly from classical sources— medicine having advanced not at all in the intervening millennium—they were the ones who got the job. And though they had no familiarity with feminine hygiene, I think we can agree that anyone who feels qualified to hold forth on something he has no actual knowledge of can, rather accurately, be called a douche.

The most famous of these books is probably *De Secretis Mulierum* (*Women's Secrets*), a late medieval text compiled by anonymous monks.

Even by the standards of the day, the authors' conception of female anatomy is fanciful. The text declares that menses is not blood but excess food; asks if said menses comes out the anus; and suggests that urine comes from the vagina. Its grasp on male anatomy is shaky, too. Male readers are warned that if they consume sage on which a cat has ejaculated—which is a *really* weird hypothetical—they will become pregnant with kittens. The esophagus would have to serve as the birth canal, and the father would need to vomit them out.

No surprise that women were perfectly happy to keep this dubious expertise out of the birthing chamber, which remained an all-female space for thousands of years. Around the sixteenth century, that began to change, however, as barber-surgeons and medical men started to muscle their way in. One of the first was Ambroise Paré, barber-surgeon to the French court, who brought a number of new twists to the birth process.* Whether they helped the mother or child is unclear, but they certainly made things easier for the practitioner. Paré pioneered induction techniques for stalled labor and the sewing of perineal tears. His most lasting innovation was his least helpful one: he convinced women to deliver lying down, in bed, rather than squatting, on a stool. This made things much harder for the mother (try pooping while lying down and you get the idea), but helped the caregiver quite a bit. For whatever reason,† this remains the norm. The name given to male birth attendants reflects the shift: they were called *accoucheurs*, from an Old French verb that meant "put to bed." Childbirth became *accouchement* in French, and in English, "lying-in." Paré was followed by a number of influential accoucheurs, who came up with extremely French techniques like cleansing perineal sutures with red wine.

---

* Paré opened a school for midwives and wrote a number of books on the subject, the most intriguing of which is *Of Monsters and Marvels*, which details all the ways a mother can produce horrific birth defects by sitting the wrong way, eating the wrong food, seeing the wrong thing, or thinking the wrong thought. I'm also partial to Paré's earlier work *Ten Books of Surgery with the Magazine of the Instruments Necessary for It*, because it has a chapter titled "On the Hot Pisses."

† The reason is mostly epidurals, which make squatting difficult or impossible. Note, however, that women no longer lie flat on their backs, but instead in what is called the *lithotomy position*, originally prescribed for the removal of kidney stones.

That male birth attendants first appeared in France is not surprising. French births tended to have an open-door policy, at least when the mother was a royal.* Witnesses were actually required at the birth of blood princesses to ensure the infant was not a changeling. (This was the reason that the queen's bedroom in royal residences was so large—to accommodate an audience of hundreds.) The practice culminated most famously at Versailles, when the birth of Marie Antoinette's first child nearly erupted into Altamont. After twelve hours of labor—before an audience—the accoucheur announced that the child was emerging. The overflow crowd of commoners rushed into the room and almost caused a stampede. More aggressive visitors climbed on top of the furniture to get a glimpse of the proceedings, but it's unlikely that they saw much. European accoucheurs typically draped the mother with a sheet (sometimes tying one end around their own neck to make a tent) so that even *they* couldn't see what was going on, and had to figure things out by touch.

After the suffocating crush nearly killed her, Marie Antoinette put a stop to amphitheater births, but the presence of men in the birth chamber continued and spread throughout Europe as a whole new cadre of male midwives charged in.† In England the market was quickly cornered by the famous Chamberlens, inventors of the forceps, whose domination began in the seventeenth century and continued for five generations. They went to great lengths to keep their precious invention secret. Bystanders were forced out of the birth chamber, and the mother was blindfolded and draped with a sheet. Lest the sound give anything away, an assistant let loose with various sound effects, including bells and shouts.

The theatrical production was a little much, but the Chamberlens were on to something. Their forceps worked. For most of history, a stuck child would have to be gruesomely dissected out, and obstructed labor was

---

* The practice of open births is not, however, unique to French royalty. It is still practiced by the Agta people of the Philippines. Births are public affairs that anyone may attend, and the audience is permitted to shout instructions to mother and midwife (Jared Diamond, *The World Until Yesterday: What Can We Learn from Traditional Societies?* [New York: Viking, 2012], 176–77).

† There still are male midwives today, but very, very few. In the United States, .6 percent of licensed nurse-midwives are men. In the UK, the number is half that.

usually a death sentence for both child and mother. The mother might be saved if the child was removed—horribly—in pieces in a procedure known as a craniotomy. Over the centuries, a number of tools were invented to aid in this task, ranging from the holy water syringe that allowed the doomed baby to be baptized in utero to more gruesome implements. These included the fairly simple hook called a crotchet as well as more complicated contraptions like the cephalotribe and basiotribe, which featured a fetal skull perforator and a hand crank for easier operation. It was never, however, easy. Because vaginal perforations were common, craniotomies were also fatal for the mother up to half the time.

The invention of the Chamberlens' forceps meant that a stuck child could be guided out gently, with spoons, rather than piecemeal, with knives. At the time, 1.5 percent of mothers died in childbirth, but 10 percent of infants did. Forceps changed that. It was a huge innovation, and the Chamberlens would be heroes if they hadn't also been greedy exploiters. Their fees were astronomical—the equivalent of $10,000 in today's money—meaning only the very rich could use their services. They refused to share their design, and as a result, thousands of less fortunate women and infants would die.

WHEN THE DESIGN finally leaked out, after a hundred years, the forceps were revealed to be not much more than big metal salad tongs. Others copied and tweaked the model and went into the midwifery business for themselves. Over the next few centuries medical men would force out more and more midwives, wresting their clientele away with forceps and fearmongering.

The best known of these was the Scotsman William Smellie. It's hard to imagine that there was a time when the top obstetrician in Great Britain was a giant dress-wearing man named Dr. Smellie who delivered babies blindly under a sheet, but in the eighteenth century this was in fact the case. Smellie is considered a founding father of obstetrics,* and he

---

* Note, however, the lack of founding *mothers*. It is hard not to notice how androcentric the origins of obstetrics and gynecology are. Even the vocabulary came

certainly contributed a good deal to the field. He viewed birth as a natural process and generally advocated letting it take its course. His classification of the stages of a normal delivery is still used today. He refined the shape and application of forceps, developed a number of obstetrical tools, and even better, exercised restraint in using them. And though he sometimes, deservedly, invited their ire, Smellie was generally pro-midwives and often worked closely with them.

On the other hand, he occasionally had some funny ideas. There was, for instance, the dress. Smellie attended births in a woman's gown and nightcap for reasons that remain un-clear. Perhaps he was trying to make his patients feel more comfortable; perhaps the gown let him conceal his tools; or perhaps it was just because a smart frock makes everyone feel better. In any case, it was something. One of his detractors described him as having "the delicate fist of a great horse godmother of a he-midwife, however softened his figure might be by his . . . night-gown of flowered calico, or his cap . . . tied with pink and silver ribbons." William Douglas called him a "raw-bon'd, large handed Man" no more fit for midwifery "than a Plough-man is for a Dancing-Master."

Caricature of a man-midwife assumed to be William Smellie, 1793 *(Courtesy Wellcome Library)*

Thanks to Smellie, having a male birth attendant of dubious competence was no longer just a privilege of the rich, but available to those of more modest circumstances. Smellie treated the lower classes himself, and trained nearly a thousand male midwives to do so as well. At his

---

from men. Sixteenth-century anatomist Gabriele Fallopio named both the placenta (which means "cake") and the vagina (which means "sheath"); and the Fallopian tubes were named *for* him (Fallopio himself called them *uteri tuba*). Kegels take their name from gynecologist Arnold Kegel. As restitution I propose women get to rename all the male bits, and I'll start the list with *abzugs*.

eighteenth-century equivalent of the Learning Annex, Smellie offered a full series of lectures on male midwifery for the bargain price of three guineas.* William Douglas complained that as a result of Smellie's low tuition fees "there are now more men-Midwives than streets in London." Students were charged an additional fee to attend a birth. For an extra five shillings (about $25 today), the student could perform the delivery himself.

Smellie's births were a hot ticket. In one instance, in 1748, the twenty-eight student spectators—most of them army and navy vets from the recent Austrian War of Succession—so crowded the mother's bedroom it erupted into a near riot and caused a distracted Smellie to break the child's leg.

When poor laboring women weren't available, Smellie's students trained on a mannequin of his own design constructed from bones and leather, with beer substituting for amniotic fluid. Smellie also practiced on pregnant corpses, which has caused some to wonder if he was up to no good. A 2010 journal article accused him of being a serial murderer or, at least, of asking far too few questions about the provenance of his study cadavers. The charge is based mostly on the observation that Smellie somehow managed to get ahold of more dead pregnant bodies than you'd come across if you weren't, say, actively commissioning them. But there's not a lot of hard proof to go on, and the accusation is widely disputed.

In any case, for better or for worse, Smellie did a great deal to advance the cause of men in the birthing chamber. By the early twentieth century, men, now in the form of physicians, had mostly forced the midwives out. The only man who would *not* be allowed at the birth was, ironically, the father, who in many states was barred by law. Hospitals worried about safety (much was made of fathers' likeliness to faint†) as well as propriety.

---

* About $340 today. Male midwives could easily earn this back after three deliveries, as a guinea was the lowest going rate at the time (Helen King, *Midwifery, Obstetrics and the Rise of Gynaecology: The Uses of a Sixteenth-Century Compendium* [Burlington, VT: Ashgate Publishing, 2007], 81).

† This almost never happened, but occasionally it did. In a freak and horrifically tragic 2005 case, a California father passed out while supporting his wife through an epidural. He hit his head on a piece of equipment, and the resulting brain hemorrhage was fatal.

One doctor dissuaded fathers by comparing birth to using the bathroom: "You wouldn't want to watch your wife defecating, would you?" Which, given the mechanics of birth, they might get to see as well.

In 1960, four years before fathers were legally permitted in the delivery room, police had to come when a California father chained himself to his wife's side. In 1964 a New Jersey man who refused to leave his laboring wife found himself charged with disorderly conduct and was fined $150. It was only in the 1980s that fathers' presence started to become the norm. Although my father was himself a physician at the hospital where I was born in the 1970s, he wasn't allowed to attend my birth either, and passed the event napping in the residents' lounge.

THOUGH SAFER THAN at any point in previous history, hospital births certainly left a lot to be desired. Still, there weren't many alternatives. Ina May Gaskin's home-birthing manifesto *Spiritual Midwifery* wouldn't be published until 1977. In the meantime, women could turn only to Patricia Cloyd Carter's wacky *Come Gently, Sweet Lucina,* self-published in 1957. The book was among the first to advocate free-birthing, the practice of giving birth without medical assistance. In many ways it was far ahead of its time, arguing against enemas, episiotomies, and pubic shaving, and calling for a number of practices that have since become the norm, like rooming-in and skin-to-skin contact. In other ways it was just straight-up nuts.

Today PDFs of the book are circulated among free-birthers, who presumably do not embrace Carter's advice in its entirety, given her stance on smoking during gestation (pro), drinking during delivery (pro), and race-mixing (con). Perhaps like the author herself, the book is deeply eccentric and more than a little irresponsible while still being breezy, funny, and utterly charming. While I would not have wanted Carter in the birthing room, I can't help but think she would have been fun to grab a drink with (which, come to think of it, is exactly what she did in the birthing room).*

---

\* In tone and charm, though not in craziness, it reminded me of the parenting book with my favorite title ever, *Didn't I Feed You Yesterday?*, by architect and *Project*

Carter, the wife of a real estate agent and retired army general thirty years her senior, decided childbirth should be a DIY affair after some pretty horrible experiences birthing her first three in a hospital. (In a mix-up, her daughter was given to another mother for two days following the birth; as if that weren't traumatizing enough, the poor infant picked up a case of impetigo and got her eyebrows scalded off by a carelessly placed sterilizer.) The next six babies were delivered by Carter herself alone at home.

In *Come Gently* she shares how she does it. Carter's methods consist pretty exclusively of drinking and keeping the child's birth weight down by any means necessary. To this end, she recommends heavy smoking, laxative abuse, appetite suppressant pills, and strict dieting. She exhorts: "They, (the general run of experts) hold that a 24-pound weight gain is *normal.* . . . Therefore, I try to lose weight. Not having time between pregnancies to get really plump, I seldom manage to lose more than a few pounds, but lose I do. I weighed 107 pounds when this last child was conceived. Two days before her birth I weighed 109 pounds. A few hours after her birth I was up town and weighed on the same scales in the general's office. They registered 103 pounds. So, tho I had not eaten for two days, it is plain that I gained nothing. Only the uterus gained. I lost."

If you must eat while pregnant, Carter insists that you avoid foods with calcium, as a baby with weak bones will be easier to deliver. Where you *do* want bones is in your girdle: "I am for a STRAIGHT UP-AND-DOWN GIRDLE as much as possible so as to restrict the baby's romping ground. . . . it should also be BONED, B-O-N-E-D. Boned up and down the front. This will really stop that little rascal." In Carter's bizarre logic, it may also save him. She insists: "THE GIRDLE IS A MATTER OF LIFE AND DEATH. In addition to helping obtain a safe lie, it also helps to obtain a safe weight in the baby. More so, even than diet. It helps keep the contents of the womb at the bare minimum. I don't know how it does it, unless it is the restricted space, but the tighter the girdle, the smaller the baby."

The pregnant mother, then, is to keep it high and tight (preferably

---

*Runway* contestant Laura Bennett. Like Carter, Bennett is a glamorous southern woman who married an older man and gave birth to an army, and is also someone I wouldn't mind drinking with.

on high, flimsy heels), with one important exception: she should let her lady business go to—well, seed. After Carter tore during her first birth—which she blamed on her unbelievably firm, unyielding muscle tone—she decided a flabby downtown was in order. "Now I see how unfit I can get. How soft and yielding. I am for a lazy, no account, po white trashy perineum."

As for a po white trashy father, this is recommended only if you are white yourself. Carter was a progressive activist for both civil and women's rights, but she wasn't a scientist, and in her book she puts forth the mistaken idea that a biracial conception can result in a potentially fatal mismatch between the mother's pelvis and the baby's head. Having noticed that African American women die in childbirth at much higher rates than whites, she concludes, rather bizarrely, that this must be due not to egregiously subpar health care but to black women's unusually narrow hips. She argues that it's only humane to keep white men away from black women, lest delivering big-headed biracial babies kill them.

Whatever your race, once labor begins, Carter encourages heavy drinking, favoring whiskey highballs herself. You won't get drunk, she promises, because the uterus is going to use the liquor for energy. Science doesn't back her up here, but if nothing else, the booze seems to have made her a relaxed and cordial hostess. The reporter she invited to witness one birth wrote: "She showed absolutely no signs of fear or concern. In fact, about 10 minutes before the baby was born, she interrupted our conversation about the best ways of preparing Italian spaghetti to apply some fresh makeup to her face. Mrs. Carter wanted to be looking neat and pretty, and indeed she did, when the baby came."

Five minutes before, with highball . . . *(Courtesy* Daytona Beach News-Journal*)*

. . . and ten minutes after, with cigarette
(*Courtesy* Daytona Beach News-Journal)

After the baby's out, Carter more or less leaves you to your own devices, aside from an assurance that parenting is an easy undertaking that
won't ruin or drastically change your life. It is, she says, a racket, and
claims that she actually spends most of her time relaxing in her rocking
chair. You know, like any mother of nine. In actuality, this assurance itself
seems to have been the racket; Carter kept busy. In addition to founding
an early free-birthing group, the League of Liberated Women, and publishing a newsletter, *The Wellborn Wag,* she wrote poetry, started a free
library open to all races in Jim Crow Florida, was an activist for women's
education and equal rights, opened her house to the needy, worked in her
husband's realty office (at least once, the same day she gave birth), and
oversaw her home. One article about her feats titled "Halts Chores for
Hour, Gives Birth to Child Unaided" noted that immediately after giving
birth she went back to dusting furniture and preparing lunch; she gave the
housemaid, who was too excited to work, the afternoon off.

SIXTY YEARS LATER, free-birthing and home-birthing have become
more common, but medicated births remain the norm. About two-thirds
of American women ask for an epidural, a far more effective option than
pretty much everything that came before. Previous methods were a good
deal less dependable, and were frequently denied altogether. Though pain

relief for laboring women has existed for thousands of years, it often wasn't given on the grounds that pain in birth is biblically mandated. Eve travailed in childbirth, so Yvette and Lavinia and Nancy would, too. Here I'll just point out that the Bible also mandates presenting a sin offering of a lamb and a dove to the priest at the tent of meeting after the child is born, but somehow everyone was comfortable with skipping that particular requirement. Labor pains, meanwhile, were mandatory.

There are plenty of good reasons to forgo pain meds should you choose to, but the Bible isn't one of them.* Although this was one of the primary arguments against the practice for more than a thousand years, it's not historically accurate. Even in biblical times, laboring women sought and received relief. Ancient Israelite women used hashish to ease pain and speed labor, a fact confirmed in 1993 when archaeologists discovered the body of a young teen who died in childbirth with seven empty bottles of the stuff. Ancient Chinese and Indian women used opium, and in Persia, they hit the booze. Egyptian women turned to wine, beer, and fenugreek. Mayans used jimsonweed, which contains the same powerful compound used to induce twilight sleep. Several ancient writers discuss drugs used during childbirth, including Plato and Hippocrates, who recommends willow bark (basically aspirin). Aristotle mentions dittany, an herb found primarily on Crete and in *Harry Potter*, where it's used to treat Harry's snakebite.

Ancient Greek women used opium, henbane, and white mandrake, though some scholars believed these were reserved for complicated births. And this may well be true for most ancient substances and most ancient women. The poor hashish-using teen, for instance, was in the throes of an obstructed labor she wouldn't live through. Surviving records are few, and we really don't know. We do know, however, that drugs have been used in births in one form or another for millennia. Eve may have gone without analgesics, but the following generations quickly found ways to take the edge off. If pain in childbirth is natural, so is the impulse to do something

---

* Also, it's not actually biblically mandated; "pain" is probably a mistranslation. In the original Hebrew the word is *etzev*, and it's the same word used in the next verse commanding Adam to work for his food, where it's translated not as "pain" but as "toil." In modern Hebrew, it means "sadness."

Detail of women hitting the pitcher in Albrecht Dürer's *The Birth of the Virgin*, 1511

about it; and as long as women have experienced the former, they've given into the latter.

By the Middle Ages, when things got a lot less fun in general, women were relying more on prayer and amulets than drugs to get them through labor. Only one medieval midwifery book (notably the *Trotula*, which was at least partially authored by a woman) advocates the use of opiates. Labor wasn't all psalms and suffering, though, because the mother was drinking throughout. Laboring women were served caudle, a boozy nog that was supposed to keep their strength up.

Births could, in fact, turn into pretty lively hen parties. It's where we got the term *gossip*, a contraction honoring the attending women's status as divine sisters, lending a hand to a lady in need. They were also hosting a social event. Food and drink in great quantities would be brought in, always including a "groaning cake" and a "groaning cheese," which, in some places, it was the custom to hollow out and pass the baby through for luck, because what is more lucky than being surrounded by Jarlsberg? "Groaning beer" washed it all down. When necessary, the parish would provide or subsidize the alcohol, which could include wine, cider, brandy, and aqua vitae (the medieval equivalent of Everclear).

Asking for anything more than prayers and a pint, however, could get you in a good deal of trouble. In 1591, Eufame MacLayne, a Scottish lady of rank, requested a mixture of something* to ease her difficult labor with twins. She survived, only to be burned at the stake on the orders of King

---

\* What that something was remains unclear. Some sources indicate that it was pain-killing herbs; others, perhaps to shore up the witchcraft claims, say it was made from the fingers, toes, and knees of exhumed corpses. The former seems both more effective and more *possible*, so I'd go with that.

James VI for trying to avoid her biblically mandated travails.* MacLayne's twins were taken by the bailiff and her midwife was also killed, for practicing witchcraft. In 1521 the Hamburg physician Dr. Viethes provided pain relief to a desperate woman in labor; he, too, was executed.

Interestingly, a few centuries later, a London chemist would get in no trouble whatsoever when he theorized that women could minimize Eve's curse by recommitting her crime. An 1841 pamphlet by a "Mr. Rowbotham" recommended a fruit diet that, he said, produced a pliant baby that could be delivered without pain. After his own wife followed the plan, the midwife raved, "A more easy labor I never witnessed . . . ! The child, a boy, was finely proportioned and exceedingly soft, his bones resembling gristle."

Mostly, however, mothers would stick to the prayers and the liquor. By the Elizabethan era, as A. Lynn Martin observes, booze in labor was such a given that *Twelfth Night* uses the analogy "like aqua vitae with a midwife." When Charles Dickens created the dipsomaniac midwife Sarah Gamp in 1843, the stereotype still held.

In the eighteenth and nineteenth centuries people would become a little more open-minded, and opiates, more available. Still, they weren't used much in childbirth.† Long after opiates were used to treat such conditions as "afternoon," they were typically withheld from women experiencing the worst pain of their lives. This was largely for practical reasons: until the invention of the hypodermic syringe in 1853, opium was administered

---

\* This, by the way, is the same King James who would commission the namesake English Bible in 1604. Interestingly, the King James Version is one of the few that translates Genesis 3:16 as "in sorrow shall you bring forth children" rather than "in pain." Not that it did MacLayne any good.

† Which is not to say they weren't used at all. William Smellie recalled treating a woman another man-midwife had so overloaded with opium that labor had to be delayed until she woke back up. Hugh Chamberlen prescribed the use of opium, and the records of a number of eighteenth-century American doctors—including William Shippen, Jr., the most prominent midwifery professor of the day—show that opium and laudanum were used when needed (William Smellie, *A Collection of Preternatural Cases and Observations in Midwifery,* vol. 3 [London, 1764]; 537–41; Adrian Wilson, *The Making of Man-Midwifery: Childbirth in England, 1660–1770* [Cambridge, MA: Harvard University Press, 1995], 68; Judith Walzer Leavitt, *Brought to Bed: Childbearing in America, 1750–1950* [New York: Oxford University Press, 1986], 39–44).

orally, and laboring women tended to throw up. An alternative was needed. In 1847 a prominent Scottish professor of midwifery, James Simpson, decided to experiment with inhaled chloroform, trying it on himself first. When he woke on the floor, he figured he'd found his substance. Four days later he used it on the laboring wife of one of his colleagues. She was so pleased she named the baby Anaesthesia.

Simpson became a great champion of chloroform, promoting it in pamphlets and lectures. It quickly caught on. Doctors began using it for surgery, but hesitated to use it for labor. A great deal of debate ensued. Chloroform, like ether and opium, had a significant number of side effects, and there were plenty of good reasons to avoid them. The reason given with troubling frequency, however, wasn't danger but virtue. What was safe and responsible in surgery was dangerous and sinful in childbirth. No one suggested that accepting anesthesia during your amputation made you a fallen person. Accepting anesthesia during your labor, however, was suspect. This was partly because chloroform was rumored to heighten sensuality and loosen inhibitions, and there were fears that chloroformed mothers would try to molest the medical staff. (Why anyone would think a mother might find labor a convenient time to get it on, I can't imagine, but there it is.)

Given that no one got worked up about the use of anesthesia outside the delivery room, it's hard not to view the double standard as misogynistic repression, as punishment, as discomfort with how the baby came to be in the first place transformed into actual discomfort for the mother. Meanwhile, no one felt the need to stomp on the father's junk, which was just as responsible for the baby's existence as the mother's.*

Some obstetricians argued that pain was crucial because it helped the mother bond with her child. In fact, bonding is helped not by pain but by oxytocin, which floods the mother's system at birth and for a period afterward. I can testify to its effects. I became desperately attached not only to my daughter but also to the socks I wore to the hospital, which for the next

---

* The Mexican Huichol tribe did something similar, however. To allow the father to experience the laboring mother's pain, his testicles were tied with a string, which the mother tugged on during contractions (Cassidy, *Birth*, 201).

year I would continue to regard with tender fondness. And when we had to move out of the house we lived in when the children were newborns, I mourned the loss like a death.

In Great Britain, the religious issue should have been largely settled in 1854 when the head of the Church of England and Defender of the Faith herself, Queen Victoria, used chloroform while having her eighth child. Privately, she called it "delightful beyond measure." No official statement was made, but rumors began to spread. When medical leaders were scandalized—in part because its safety had not been established—court physicians denied it had been used at all. Still, word got out, and must have had a normalizing effect. When Victoria used it again with her ninth, four years later, the court could admit it, as it was no longer so controversial.

Chloroform was not, however, universally safe. There were no established standards for its use, and doctors tended to come up with their own dosing schedules. Some of them were clearly bad at math. By the time the Royal Medical and Chirurgical Society of London undertook a study of chloroform's effects in 1863, 123 deaths had already been attributed to it.

Doctors also didn't know how safe anesthetics were for the child, and debated whether or not they crossed the placenta (they do). The sleepy babies with ether breath should have been the tip-off, but promoters like Simpson apparently didn't pick up on the signs and continued advocating their largely unchecked use. Still, there weren't a lot of great alternatives. Injections of morphine became available by the 1860s, but this carried risks for mother and baby, too.

EVERYTHING HAS A DOWNSIDE; everything has side effects. Hoping to minimize the cons and maximize the pros, early twentieth-century doctors in Freiburg, Germany, decided to combine two labor anesthetics, morphine and scopolamine, naming the resulting mix *Dämmerschlaf.* In the United States, it was called twilight sleep, and it promised total oblivion. You'd settle in for a nice rest, and when you came to, a nurse would hand you your bathed and bundled newborn. *Danke schoen*, darling, *danke schoen.*

The reality was a little messier. Twilight sleep didn't make birth pain-less; it just erased your memory of the pain. While it was going on, how-ever, hoo-boy. Doctors stuffed women's ears with gauze so they wouldn't be woken by their own screams. (The women's shouts were reportedly so loud they were sometimes heard down the street.) Scopolamine could cause hallucinations, and mothers thrashed and behaved unpredictably. To mini-mize the damage, their arms were restrained and the walls were padded.

But mothers remembered none of this and clamored for the treat-ment. Frances Carmody was so eager that she traveled to Germany for the delivery of her child with her obstetrician in tow. Delighted with the results, she opened a twilight sleep hospital in Brooklyn on her return, and devoted herself to promoting the procedure.

Besides the horror show of the birth itself, twilight sleep had some pretty nasty side effects. It produced babies who were groggy and had poor respiration. It also increased the mother's risk of bleeding out. This, in fact, is precisely what happened to Frances Carmody when she died delivering her next child in 1915. Maybe twilight sleep made American women forget this painful event, too, because heavy anesthesia grew only more popular, and remained so into the 1970s.

By the 1980s, the epidural was the method of choice. The epidural as delivered today is generally safe and effective for mother and child, though it took a while to get there. Beta versions were being used as far back as the late nineteenth century and were a good deal less predictable, as was the research that produced them. In one of the stranger examples, German doctor Karl August Bier, having already used spinal anesthesia in surgery six times, decided to conduct further research with his assis-tant Dr. Hildebrandt one night in 1898. They injected cocaine into each other's backs, Bier much more successfully than Hildebrandt, who spilled both the cocaine and a good deal of Bier's cerebrospinal fluid. Bier then proceeded to test the numbness of Hildebrandt's lower half—and the lim-its of their professional relationship[*]—by taking a hammer to his shin,

---

[*] The relationship would not, in fact, survive. Hildebrandt later turned on Bier in favor of one of Bier's rivals. Although this was not the direct result of the night of anesthetized torture, it surely didn't help.

pushing a needle down to his femur, burning his leg with a cigar, yanking out his pubic hair, and crushing his testicles. The next day both men would suffer severe spinal headaches, but in the meantime, wrote Bier, "we proceeded without feeling any symptoms to dine and drink wine and smoke cigars."

By 1909, German physicians were using both epidurals and a similar technique, the caudal block, for labor pain. But these continued to carry a good deal of risk, and worked only about half the time. Enter Dr. John Bonica, a Sicilian American anesthesiologist and professional wrestler. After working his way through medical school performing as the Masked Marvel, Bonica was left with chronic pain that inspired him to pioneer a host of new treatments, and after his wife nearly died in labor from a clumsy dose of inhaled ether (and Bonica saved her life by shoving the intern out of the way and clearing her airway himself), he devoted himself to developing safer obstetric pain relief. The result was an epidural that numbed the lower half but left the mother alert. Although Bonica used this quite successfully with his own wife in the 1940s, it would take another thirty years to really catch on.

Other physicians worked on pain management methods that required no medication at all. Unsurprisingly, they were men. The first of these was Grantly Dick-Read. Despite the fact that his name is basically a synonym for mansplaining, Dick-Read was to some degree coming from a good place. In *Natural Childbirth* and his 1942 follow-up, *Childbirth Without Fear*, he offered an appealing alternative to the harsh interventionist practices that had become the norm. He argued that the mother should be conscious and sentient during delivery, and that the doctor's role was to support her. He advocated for prenatal education, relaxation techniques that included yoga and breathing exercises, rooming-in, breastfeeding, and the father's presence in the birth room.

Unfortunately, Dick-Read's theories were based on little more than his imagination, and many of them were wrong, not to mention racist, eugenicist, and paternalistic. He insisted that having a baby should be no more painful than having a bowel movement. Labor pain, he said, was caused not by physical effort of forcing a human through an orifice that is normally the circumference of a dime, but by fear and tension. This, it seems to me, is getting it backward. Reducing fear and tension can certainly help—but they're still not the cause. Having been through the experience myself, I'd say fear and tension are a pretty natural response to DEFCON 1 level agony; and will also point out that sleeping women, who are so relaxed they're *asleep*, still have labor pain so bad it wakes them up. It's a little hard to take Dick-Read's argument that the suffering mother has only her own bad attitude to blame, and not, say, the seven-plus pounds of flesh and bone trying to make its way through her pelvis. And that's a *normal* birth. When the baby is excruciatingly mispositioned or enormous, no amount of relaxation will help. (I suspect no amount of relaxation is *possible*.) It's true that childbirth isn't always painful, but when it is—the overwhelming majority of the time—it's not because the mother failed to adequately chill out.

For evidence, Dick-Read pointed to what he called "primitive" women, who, he said, were naturally more relaxed and consequently had easy and painless births. He offered no data to support this (because the data does not in fact exist), instead giving only his own dubious memory of seeing two women "drop a quick one" in the field during his military service. This seems to have inspired Dick-Read's eugenicist and frankly racist mission. Fearing that the birthrate of these "primitive" women, with their quick and painless deliveries, would quickly outpace that of whites, Dick-Read wrote his book encouraging civilized white ladies to do their part. In spite of all this, Dick-Read was so popular that he was sometimes compared to Elvis. Like Elvis, he released a 1957 album: a recording of a woman giving birth while Dick-Read coached her. It sold well and is still available on CD.

Dick-Read offered no scientific evidence to back his claims, which were easily demolished in a 1950 *JAMA* article. By then, a less racist and slightly more scientific alternative was emerging: the Lamaze method, popularized by French obstetrician Fernand Lamaze. In the United States, Lamaze has become synonymous with natural childbirth, and hence the painful kind. But Lamaze's original intent was exactly the opposite. In France, his method is not known as Lamaze but as *l'accouchement sans douleur*—childbirth without pain. At a time when obstetric anesthesia was often ineffective and dangerous, he hoped to give women a safe, comfortable way to navigate birth.

Lamaze was, it must be said, something of a shitheel. Early in his career, when his wife was delivering their first child, he was so put off by her moaning that he bailed on her completely and spent the rest of the night in a bar knocking out two full bottles of wine. In the ensuing years he would cheat on this wife with scores of mistresses, including a Mme. François, whom he installed in their home in the room next to his mother-in-law. Mme. François also ate dinner with the family every other night at his insistence. When this mistress, distraught that Lamaze would not divorce, drowned herself in the Seine, he quickly replaced her with two others, one of whom—an ex-con—was his secretary and chauffeur. He also had a thing for prostitutes, and his only wedding present to his wife, his granddaughter recalled, was "a case of syphilis he had gotten from a whorehouse in Nancy."

On a trip to the Soviet Union in 1951, Lamaze witnessed the widespread use of psychoprophylaxis, the mind-training method pioneered by Ivan Pavlov of dog-drool fame. Psychoprophylaxis gave pregnant women breathing and relaxation techniques to manage their labor pain. Because it was free and because anesthesia was scarce, this became the Soviet Union's official method of obstetric pain treatment.

Blown away by what he saw, Lamaze brought the technique back to France, modifying it somewhat in his 1955 book *Painless Childbirth*. Instead of the Soviets' (somewhat effective) deep breaths, he recommended something he called "little dog breaths" (much less effective). These *hee-hee-hee* breaths, which became Lamaze's trademark, were supposed to speed up birth (they do not) and increase oxygen in the blood (but can do the opposite). They can also produce hyperventilation, and don't form the basis of today's Lamaze practice.

In the United States, the Lamaze method didn't fully fledge, in part because of its communist imprimatur, but it still found some success in the States and abroad. In 1955, Lamaze preceded Dick-Read with a bestselling live childbirth album. Side 1 includes such hits as "Fragments du cours sur 'le mécanisme du travail'" in an eighteen-minute supercut.

Most women, however, stuck with the drugs. This resulted in a rise in induction rates, as the two go hand in hand. If you use one, you're more likely to need the other. But while induction has become much more common, the practice isn't new at all. Caregivers have used a number of methods to bring on or speed up labor since ancient times, with varying degrees of success. Many involved food: women were fed weasels (so the baby would weasel out), eggs (so the mother might lay hers), or nothing (so the baby would look for food on the outside).

Other methods were both ineffectual *and* dangerous. Some killed the baby, some killed the mother, and some managed to kill bystanders. Because violence and fear were thought to prompt labor, humans have used labor induction methods including beating the mother, charging at her with horses, and more recently, shooting guns close by. In one of the stranger instances, related by Martin Luther, birth attendants tried to induce labor not by beating the mother (she was royalty) but by beating men in her presence. Twenty men were subjected to blows, and two died, none of which sped the labor along.

Other methods were dangerous but worked. One of the more potent inductors was ergot, the grain fungus that contains a precursor of LSD and may or may not have been responsible for the mass hysteria of the Salem witch trials.* Ergot has been used since ancient times to bring on contractions, which it (sometimes) does very effectively. It does not do so, however, controllably, and once given, it's not reversible. If the mother gets too much, or if the baby is in the wrong position, contractions can be so strong they rupture the uterus. By the nineteenth century, ergot was mostly used after the baby was already out, to expel the placenta or stop hemorrhaging.

IN THE TWENTIETH CENTURY, a more reliable alternative came along, and it is still the most common induction method today. This is Pitocin, the synthetic version of the hormone oxytocin, which floods the mother's

---

* But probably not. Widespread ergot poisoning might have contributed to the Great Fear at the start of the French Revolution, however.

body during birth and plays a big role in labor, lactation, and bonding. Oxytocin's name comes from the Greek words meaning "swift birth," and some of the more effective ancient induction methods were the ones that naturally produce oxytocin: having sex and stimulating the nipples. I was surprised to learn that oxytocin is also triggered by vomiting, but I suppose this explains why I feel so attached to people I've thrown up on.

Although inductions have been attempted for thousands of years, in the past, they were usually done because the baby was already dead or because the mother was sick. Now they tend to be done for less pressing reasons, which may include the obstetrician's dinner reservations.[*] In theory, they're done only when they're best for mother or baby, but the timing of them makes it pretty clear staffing concerns are a factor as well.

The reason often given for induction is "failure to progress." The diagnosis is a fairly recent invention, as there was no established standard of progress until the 1950s. Emanuel Friedman was an obstetric resident who couldn't get the night off when his own wife went into labor in 1951. To channel his anxiety, he spent his shift calculating how long it took his twenty-five patients to go through each of the three stages of labor, something no one had thought to do before.[†] The result, a bell-shaped graph that became known as the Friedman curve, is the standard timetable that's used to evaluate pretty much every American birth to this day.

Friedman's innovation was huge. His sample size, however, was not. His initial study was done on a small group of women at one hospital in New York. All were white Jews having their first child.[‡]

This small group of women from a very specific background established the standard that's now applied to everyone. This was not what Friedman

---

[*] Or lunch. When my mother was in labor with my sister, her obstetrician encouraged her to have the baby before the staff's Chinese food order arrived. She did, and was rewarded with an egg roll.

[†] The project was actually suggested by the doctor whose revolutionary rubric is also used in all American births today: Virginia Apgar. Apgar had suggested Friedman use his considerable math background to evaluate whether caudal anesthesia slowed labor, leading Friedman to examine how long labor took with and without it (Cassidy, *Birth*, 156).

[‡] Friedman's follow-up study was wider, and included women who'd previously given birth.

had in mind, and more recent studies suggest an updated curve is badly needed. Anesthesia, ethnicity, and previous births are among the many, many factors that can influence labor times, a fact that Friedman himself would not contest. This, in fact, is why Friedman wanted to make the curve in the first place: to show how wide a range of safe labor times there are. Unfortunately, the opposite happened. Now when mothers don't stick to Friedman's curve, they tend to get Pitocin or C-sections, exactly what Friedman hoped to avoid.[*]

I was one of the mothers who got both. An anesthetized white Jew having my first child, I nonetheless fell outside of Friedman's range. Although I didn't particularly enjoy either treatment, I was lucky to have the option. In previous centuries, my failure to progress would have meant my certainty to die. Cesarean sections have existed for thousands of years, but it was only recently that they stopped being fatal. In Caesar's own time, they were performed only on mothers who were already dead. (This is how we know Caesar was born the normal way; his mother lived. The name of the procedure probably derives not from Caesar but from *caesura*, which means "cutting.")

Over the next thousand-plus years C-sections continued to be performed when the mother was dead or nearly dead in a gruesome last-ditch effort to save the child. According to the somewhat dubious written record, the first successful, nonfatal cesarean was performed by Jacob Kufer, a Swiss pig gelder. In 1500, after several days of labor and thirteen midwives failed to deliver his child, he took matters into his own hands. Mother and child lived. In 1794 the first successful C-section in America would be performed under similar circumstances, by a husband in a Virginia log cabin.

In the British empire the first nonfatal cesarean was performed in South Africa in 1826 by James Barry, an army surgeon who after his death was discovered to be a woman.[†] The next recorded successful C-section

---

[*] At Beth Israel, the hospital where Friedman served as obstetric chief of staff, he made sure C-sections weren't overused by keeping close tabs on the progress of every birth, including, as it turns out, my own: I was born there the year after Friedman arrived.

[†] Given that Barry lived before the advent of modern medicine, it goes without say-

on the continent was performed by a Ugandan healer in 1879. Banana wine served as both anesthesia and sterile solution, and mother and child survived.

The cesarean I received was a good deal different. My uterus, unlike that of the Ugandan mother, was not left unstitched; it also wasn't removed entirely (the method preferred by some nineteenth-century physicians). Besides disease and death, I was spared a host of other historical horrors, some of which were discontinued quite recently, like shaving and episiotomies, all of which were thought to prevent infection and injury but actually caused a great deal more. Modern science has also begun to rethink the "once a cesarean, always a cesarean" maxim, though when I was having my second child, I did not rethink it myself. Figuring we were working with the same equipment, we went ahead and scheduled the procedure the week of the end of the world.

And so it was that we rolled into the hospital that portentous spring morning, in the middle of, naturally, Noah-caliber rains. The spinal block was given, the incisions were made, and by nine thirty there was one more person in the world. He was not the Chosen One, but we were still glad he was here, wrapped in a standard-issue pink-and-blue-striped hospital blanket that looked, at least to me, like a tallis.

Though the research on postpartum amnesia is mixed, studies do show evidence of what's known as a halo effect—a tendency to view the pain as less painful, the hardships less hard, when we're grateful and thrilled by the result. In my case, it was literal—thanks to pregnancy complications, my vision would not return to normal for several weeks, and in the meantime everything had a sort of hazy corona, amplified, just a bit, by the Tylenol #3.

My face was still paralyzed, my husband still injured, our toddler still sick and freaked out, and I was still half dressed in a room full of surprisingly loud Amish strangers. Whatever halo effect I might have had ren-

---

ing that this was also before the advent of trans rights. I use the term *woman* here because it's what was used in contemporary reports. Whether Barry was a woman who lived as a man for professional reasons, or was instead what we'd now call *trans*, we can only guess.

dered all that no less annoying. But it was also easier to ignore, distracted by the new arrival, the discomfort and noise receding to the background of a beatific tableau. I was still sore and tired and irritated, but I knew that the big things were fine and would probably stay that way; and the things that weren't would get better.

They did. The torrential rains would stop in a day or two. The paralysis and herniated disk would take longer to resolve, but eventually these would go away as well.

So, too, would the halo effect, when, exhausted by the demands of a newborn and toddler, I would forget to be grateful that we were not killed by evolutionary biology or medical incompetence, that I got to give birth at a time when it was relatively safe and easy. But for now, in this hospital room, I was okay, and so was Sam. It was an age of miracles, and the world, at least for now, would go on.

# 3

# You're Doing It Wrong

*Advice Manuals Through the Ages*

I t's hard to say exactly when the parenting advice industry began, but given human nature it's safe to assume it was around the time the second human couple got pregnant and the first one realized there were now people who knew less about raising children than they did. Suddenly, there were both experts and an audience. Sure, the experts didn't inspire a lot of confidence, as they'd lost their first two infants to predatory birds and the third was currently teething on a wad of hyena droppings, but at least he wasn't crying. Hyena droppings, you say? Let me get a pen.

Over the next several thousand years advice would be passed down, prized, rejected, and revised. Eventually the advice would be recorded, and later still, published and distributed.

A shocking amount of it would be very, very bad, written by people who either had no children or were estranged from them. A surprising quantity was written by monks, celibate bachelors who presumably have less child-rearing experience than pretty much anyone else. Some of the advice would scar children mentally, some physically; and some would actually kill them.*

---

* Even today, there are advice books by parents who might do better with a visit from Child Protective Services than a book contract. The saddest example is probably

Still, you can't really blame bewildered parents for taking whatever advice they can get. Children are baffling, mysterious little machines that are always beeping and breaking. Unlike my printer, which kindly directs me to clear paper jams or add more toner, most of the time they can't even tell you what's wrong. The books, however, can, and the answer is usually simple: It's you. You're doing it wrong. Your incompetence may be due to your inexperience or the mistakes of your own parents; to your gender, your social class, or your nationality; to the bad advice of other experts; or to simple stupidity. Lucky for you there's a cadre of experts who won't let their own lack of knowledge get in the way of telling you what to do.

Unlike past experts, today's tend to be reasonably qualified, if far less entertaining. Although I'm a big fan of advice columns, it turns out I don't much care for advice *books*, especially when the subject is raising healthy, happy children and not organizing my closet. The columns offer schadenfreude; the books, a guilt trip and to-do list, which I ignore on the grounds that the books don't know my life and aren't the boss of me. The actual boss of me—my mother—has a policy of letting me make my own mistakes. In more than forty years, I can recall only two pieces of advice from her: "Don't wear red with pink" and "Never smoke in bed." As for raising her grandchildren, I'm on my own.

And thus like most people, my husband and I reluctantly return to the books. Despite their relative uselessness, advice books have been with us for a very, very long time. The first written texts date back to the first century, and were inscribed on parchment and housed in libraries. Given their format, these generally weren't intended as handy guides for parents, as it was impractical to turn to panel LXIV of the scroll to determine what to do when Agathocles wouldn't eat his stewed goat. They were, instead, by and for physicians, who could impart the contents to their patients. The oldest and best known is probably Soranus's *Gynecology*. As the title indicates, the text mostly concerns lady parts, but there is a full chapter on the care of newborns, which gives us an idea of what was prescribed,

---

*The Fun Starts Here* by Paula Yates, who would later overdose on heroin while her toddler played nearby. Eleven years later Yates's older daughter, Peaches Geldof, would die the exact same way, down to the toddler. The fun, clearly, stopped.

proscribed, and actually done at the time. Mainly because people didn't have a whole lot of alternatives, it was used until the sixteenth century.

Though advice manuals would get much, much weirder over the years, this first one is, for the most part, fairly reasonable. Much of Soranus's advice comes from experienced, practical sources like midwives, so it generally sounds sane and sensible, and he's quick to condemn dangerous practices. This usually means anything non-Greek, like the foreign habit of dipping the baby in cold water, wine, brine, or the urine of "an innocent child" to test the baby's fitness.

What you *should* dip the baby in, says Soranus, is salt. Though it sounds crazy now, this was widely done throughout the ancient world (and in the more rural corners of the world, still is). It's even mentioned in the Bible. Soranus directs you to pat down the baby with fine powdered salt like a cut of corned beef, taking care not to get it in its eyes or nose. If you're dealing with a particularly delicate baby, he says, you may want to mix the salt with olive oil or honey, which is getting very close to a recipe I sometimes use for salad dressing. I don't know how good it is for a baby, but for carrots it's *delicious*.

The Greek Soranus also explains why Roman children's legs are frequently deformed. Contrary to popular belief, he writes, it's not because Roman women have too much sex, or because they have sex while drunk, though they do both. It's because they're *bad mothers*, who aren't as devoted and attentive as their Grecian counterparts are. As for Roman childcare advice, the primary source is Galen, who aims his barbs at the Germans: "Among the Germans, children are not well brought up. But we are not now writing this for the Germans or for any other savage or barbarian people, any more than for bears, boars, lions, or for any of the other wild beasts." While childcare books would change quite a bit down the line, this aspect—faulting other cultures—would remain fairly constant for the next sixteen hundred years. If there's a single theme to the history of childcare advice, it's Other People Are Crazy (it is certainly the theme of this chapter). The Greeks sneered at the Romans, the Romans at the Germans, the Germans at the Romans, and the French at pretty much everyone. And if this impulse is unfortunate, it's also understandable. We need someone to look down on and point fingers at, be it the poor souls the book criticizes or even the book itself. The infuriating instruction manual's purpose isn't to tell us how to program the TV; it's to give us something to blame when we fail to. Without it, after all, we'd have to acknowledge our own inability to do the job.

Once childcare experts stopped hating other cultures on principle, they turned on people closer to home, directing the blame at segments of their own society. Authors faulted the working classes or the upper ones; other experts or amateurs; the help; the previous generation; or, as was the case in the seventeenth and eighteenth centuries, women in general. Occasionally the books were written explicitly to settle scores, either with colleagues, or, as in a few instances, with the author's own parents.[*]

Here it's probably worth pointing out that the original meaning of *advice* was "judgment." And judging, as much as anything, is what advice books allow both the author and the reader to do. They appeal to our basest impulses. We all like to read about the ways other people are doing it wrong, be those people tiger mothers or helicopter parents. Or Finns, their high test scores be damned. I mean, they let their *babies* nap in the *snow*.

**WRITING IN THE FIRST CENTURY,** Soranus could circulate his judgment only so far. But by the late Middle Ages, mechanical reproduction made it possible to spread the judgment farther and faster. Enter the printing press, and with it, a good deal more parenting advice. The print itself, however, was just about the only thing that was new. Medicine and psychology hadn't advanced much since Soranus's time. Medieval parents and advice-givers were working with a limited arsenal. There were no six-month checkups or speech therapy, no antibiotics or after-school enrichment programs. What there was, was prayer.

Medieval childcare books are generally very stern and preachy. They are still fun for the modern reader, however, because early printers used a long *s* that, to the modern eye, looks just like an *f*. Since the books tend to

---

[*] As Peter Stearns points out in *Anxious Parents: A History of Modern Childrearing in America* (New York: NYU Press, 2004), criticizing the previous generation also gives the current generation a good reason to buy a new book.

dwell at length on breastfeeding, you read a lot about getting the fuckling infant to fuckle.

Mostly, however, you read about faving the infant's foul from fin. Medieval parenting advice is concerned not just with the child's life, but with its afterlife. The medieval parent wasn't trying to get her child into Harvard; she was trying to get him into heaven. Much childcare advice was preached, composed, and delivered as sermons. I'm not sure that makes it any less maddening. It can't be any more pleasant to be hectored in a hard medieval church pew than in the comfort of your own hard medieval reading chair. More maddening still is the fact that these works were, by definition, authored by childless men, who though they may be called "Father" most pointedly *weren't*. It's easy to think you know what to do when you've never actually spent any time with a toddler. Fine, Padre, if you know so much, *you* watch the baby and I'll go play in the bell tower.

One of the more prominent preachers was Giovanni Dominici, who, in addition to composing countless sermons, authored a book on raising children, *Regola del governo di cura familiare*. Though Dominici didn't have any of the qualifications you'd expect in a childcare expert such as a medical education or, you know, *his own children*, he did have the necessary xenophobia. Even for a fifteenth-century Italian priest, Dominici was unusually anti-Semitic. He was a driving force behind the Jews' expulsion from Venice, a city from which Dominici himself would be banished a few years later. He then went on to continue his campaign in Florence, even though it didn't actually have any Jews.[*]

Dominici advocates a regimen of toughening beginning when the child is small. The child should treated like "the son of a peasant": denied affection and punished and beaten regularly. He should be dressed in rough clothing, forced to go without food or wine, deprived of a bed and made to sleep in the cold, when he's allowed to sleep at all. When he's older, he should be given strong laxatives so he can get used to feeling sick. Even the paintings on the wall of the family home should make him

---

[*] It should be noted, however, that Dominici was pretty hard on everyone. He was so disliked by Venetian nobility that he was subjected to seven assassination attempts. Even his own monks and nuns found him to be an unpleasant tyrant, openly wishing for his death.

miserable: "It will not be amiss if he should see Jesus and the Baptist, Jesus and the boy Evangelist pictured together; the slaughtered Innocents, so that he may learn the fear of weapons and armed men. Thus it is desirable to bring up little girls in the contemplation of the eleven thousand Virgins as they discourse, pray and suffer."

As for the mother, she doesn't have things much easier. Dominici reminds his female reader that her husband is the master and she is the servant. The wife goes to sleep and gets up at her husband's orders, and he determines what she will wear, eat, say, and do. The book is in fact as much a guide to raising your wife as it is to raising your children. It's probably worth noting that at the time, Italian grooms were typically over thirty while their brides were still teens.

An age gap that was sometimes smaller between mother and child than between husband and wife may be the reason why Dominci seems preoccupied with the importance of making it clear to your children that you love them, but not in *that* way. Fathers must not be lighthearted with their daughters, "lest they may become enamored of masculinity." Mothers shouldn't even smile at their sons. And if you're hiring your newborn son a wet nurse, you'd better make sure she's not young and attractive: "Many such have aroused the fire of passion prematurely, as true accounts relate and, I venture to say, experience proves."

Medieval child-rearing manuals have plenty of passion as it is. Most of them tend to cover the mechanics of conception, and many offer more discussion of positioning than seems strictly necessary. Take, for instance, 1655's *Callipaedia, or, the Art of Getting Beautiful Children*. The short answer, according to the author, is to be good-looking yourself, and French. The long answer is just as xenophobic and much, much steamier.

Written by Claude Quillet, a French physician and abbot, the book is in large part a medieval sex manual. Though less a *Joy of Sex* than a *Dampened Pleasures of Procreative Congress Sanctioned Within Certain Rigid Bounds*, it is still pretty racy, especially for a medieval childcare book, especially for a medieval childcare book by an *abbot*.*

---

* Even stranger than the book itself is the reason Quillet wrote it, which was purely and simply to exact revenge. The original manuscript contained a digression damn-

For a book by a physician, its grasp on physiology is shaky. Like many of his contemporaries, Quillet believed that male infants come from the right ovary, females from the left. Because boys were much preferred ("A female child deceives the father's hopes"), Quillet helpfully suggests sexual positions that will produce the desired male. He advises the would-be father to aim to the mother's right: "From a Left Womb a Female Issue flows, / And from a right a Male, as there it grows. / By Art, when Nature may be here supply'd, / The weaker testicle is firmly ty'd. / That a right Flood may fill the fertile Womb; / Not from the Left the Genial Deluge come."

If the Genial Deluge comes toward the backside, writes Quillet, you're really in trouble. He warns: "What shall we here of Wicked Postures say? / When Lovers with Inverted Dalliance play / Nor take the Joy as Nature bids the Bliss, / But to the Pillow [read: butt] turn the Balmy Kiss. / What Monsters spring from such impure Delights? / What hideous Forms? What foul Hermaphrodites?"

It's hard not to notice that there is a surprising amount of anal sex in medieval childcare manuals (any amount at all being pretty unexpected). It also shows up in *Regola del governo*, when Dominici warns the reader not to give in to her husband's pleas to copulate "like beast or male." As for other kinds of sex, their presence in medieval childcare manuals, though jarring now—especially given that the authors were typically stern ecclesiastical bachelors—made sense at the time. Following Galen, medieval scholars believed that female orgasm was necessary for conception, which required baby-making books to go into some detail as to how to achieve that. Also, readers liked it, and there was no Cinemax.

---

ing one Cardinal Mazarin, whom he blamed for the death of a priest charged with siccing demons on nuns. Quillet, however, knew that this digression wouldn't sell on its own, so he tacked on subjects likely to attract a wider audience: parenting, sex, love, travel, beauty tips, and astrology, making the book the medieval equivalent of *Us* magazine. By the time the book was published, however, Mazarin and Quillet had mended fences; Mazarin granted Quillet an abbacy, and Quillet replaced the smear with some verses praising Mazarin instead; and the book sold very well as hoped. Late medieval abbots: they're just like us! (Beekman, *The Mechanical Baby*, 10).

FOR THE ILLITERATE EXPECTANT PARENT who didn't like poetry, there were pictures, most notably in *The Birth of Mankind: Otherwise Named, The Woman's Book*, which was first published in 1540, and remained a bestseller for a hundred years. Its popularity was largely due to the fact that it was one of the first printed books with illustrations, and certainly the first with illustrations of the female reproductive system. (Interestingly, in surviving copies of the book, this page is often missing, though whether this says something about the fragility of sixteenth-century manuscripts or the scarcity of sixteenth-century pornography, I couldn't say.) As for the other illustrations, they indicate that sixteenth-century fetuses had the proportions of full-grown men and hat hair.

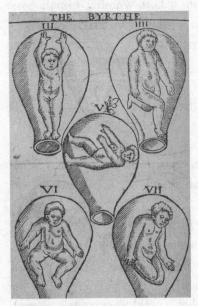

The Birth of Mankind
(Courtesy Wellcome Library)

*The Birth of Mankind* was also one of the first books addressed directly to a lay audience, specifically to women. In deference to this new readership, the book helpfully offers a chapter of beauty tips, including instructions on how "To Take away Hair from Places Where It Is Unseemly" and advice on combating "the Rank Savour of the Armhole." (The answer: eat artichokes.)

This, along with Jane Sharp's *The Midwives Book*, was as close as it got to a Girlfriends' Guide in the Middle Ages. Given the extraordinarily high rates of maternal and infant mortality, you probably didn't want a frank no-nonsense guide anyway. It would basically have to consist of, Listen, girlfriend, chances are you're going to die. What to expect when you're expecting? Expect not to survive childbirth.[*]

---

[*] This might be an exaggeration. In her introduction to Jane Sharp's *The Midwives Book* (New York: Oxford University Press, 1999), Elaine Hobby cites much more

One of the few texts to deal frankly with the issue of mortality was printed in Boston in 1694, and expressed the blunt honesty for which America would later become known. This was the pamphlet *A Present to be Given to Teeming Women*, which was addressed, in equally blunt fashion, to America's "big-bellied women." Along with lots of advice on being humble and pious, it includes a chapter on preparing for your possibly imminent death. Given the odds, this wasn't such a bad idea, but still: what a lousy present.

Most advice books, however, tended to avoid the topic and say the same bland things, all of which had been repeated with minor variations since Soranus's time. Breastfeed or choose a good wet nurse; salt the baby's skin and swaddle it, but not too rigidly; bathe it regularly but not in cold water; teach your children piety; hire good tutors; don't do what the stupid foreigners do; and of course, lay off the anal sex.

**THAT WAS IN THEORY.** In practice, however, much of this advice was ignored until the Enlightenment, when two men came along and enlightened everyone to the fact that they were doing everything wrong. These were John Locke and Jean-Jacques Rousseau. Apparently they were widely read authors a few hundred years before they performed the far more important function of providing names for characters on *Lost*. Locke's and Rousseau's books were hugely influential, and though not intended as such, they were the first phenomenally popular advice books for parents. The fact that these philosophical tomes were dragged into this particular service suggests what a demand there was for the genre, how desperate parents were for some sort of guide. Thus they clung to the closest thing they could find—a philosophical treatise and an allegorical novel—which is a little like raising your children according to the principles of *The Celestine Prophecy*.

Or it would be if *The Celestine Prophecy* were written by one man

---

optimistic figures. In England, at least, a woman had a 10 percent chance of dying in childbirth in her lifetime; on average, she'd go through the childbirth process six to seven times. And her child had an 80 to 85 percent chance of surviving the first few years (xv).

(Locke) who had no children, and another (Rousseau) who had five but gave every single one up to the foundling home. Though this was tantamount to a death sentence for a child, the decision did not appear to cause Rousseau much concern. He gave so little thought to trying to find the children later, as many parents did, that he did not record their birth dates or even their genders. He seems to have been a good dog owner, though.

The bachelor Locke had even less experience with children, but was at least a doctor who sometimes treated them, and was moved by the many questions their overwhelmed parents had for him. His 1693 work *Some Thoughts Concerning Education*, which also included some thoughts on feeding, sleep, and bathing, established the format that advice manuals would continue to use through today, and not just because other authors freely plagiarized his text. For a philosophical treatise, the book offers a great deal of practical preventative hands-on advice for the typical parent of a typical child, not "the sick or crazy." Gone were the flowery verse couplets on conception and the superfluous chapters on hair removal; in were specifics on sleep, feeding, and for the first time, even potty training.

Unlike his *Lost* namesake, Locke does not seem to have had any particular father issues, and much of his advice sounds sensible even now. He advocates a simple diet and lots of fresh air, exercise, and rest. He was an early and influential critic of swaddling, which at the time was rigid, head to toe, and rarely changed, immobilizing the child in its own filth for the better part of each day. Locke does not, however, advocate coddling. He emphasizes the importance of "hardening" children by putting them to sleep on uncomfortable surfaces and rejecting regular mealtimes so they don't learn to expect food. What they should learn to expect is for their feet to be wet and cold. Locke wants you to dunk their feet daily in cold water, and dress them in shoes that are thin and leaky.

To his credit, Locke also did away with the xenophobia that characterized earlier parenting advice. Locke notes with approval the practices of many other cultures, especially if they involve frequent bathing in cold water. He devotes several pages to the virtues of cold water, which he considers quite healthful as long as you're doing something sensible like bathing the baby in it in the middle of winter and not drinking it on a hot day. Because *that*, writes Locke, will make you sick: "drinking cold drink, when they are hot with labour or exercise, brings more people to the grave, or to the brink of it, by fevers, and other diseases, than any thing I know." If the child must drink, he should, of course, be served room-temperature beer.

Seventy years later Rousseau published *Émile, or On Education* and took up where Locke left off, inspiring a revolution in more "natural" parenting that was a decidedly mixed blessing. On the good side, he condemned swaddling, advocated breastfeeding, introduced the idea of developmental stages—a huge innovation—and exhorted parents to raise their children themselves rather than dump them on indifferent hired help. On the bad side, he took the idea of hardening a wee bit too far.

*Émile* is an allegorical novel, not an advice book, and Rousseau's ideas could be intriguing in the abstract. In practice, however, they could be dangerous, and practice is exactly what some parents did. Rousseau may have been speaking metaphorically, at least in part, when he suggested parents wear fright masks and fire pistols near their children's heads to make them less skittish; expose them to spiders to make them less squeamish; and discontinue all formal education and ban all books so that the young'uns might spend all their time scantily clothed outdoors in all weather, but many parents took him at his word. The prince and princess of Württemberg treated *Émile* as gospel, and when they encountered issues that weren't covered in the text, they corresponded directly with Rousseau himself. Over the course of fifty letters Rousseau answered their questions on subjects ranging from crying to teething, even though he maintained that *Émile* should not be read literally or used as a parenting manual, writing to another parent, "I cannot believe that you took the book . . . for a real treatise on education."

Unfortunately for their daughter Sophie, the prince and princess of Württemberg did, subjecting the child to a regime that included baths in an icy fountain and copious naked outdoor time in all weather. Not entirely surprisingly, Sophie died at age eleven. The five daughters of Guillaume-François Roussel, a Swiss banker, were raised according to the same tenets, and made to spend their days nearly naked, foraging for food in the woods. They were spared Sophie's fate when Rousseau himself visited and, horrified to see how they were being treated, ordered their father to let them come inside and put on some clothes.

Despite the miseries they produced, Rousseau's methods became quite fashionable. Subjecting your child to Rousseauian challenges became rather trendy among well-heeled families, the eighteenth-century equivalent of toddler yoga or gluten-free diets. Marie Antoinette was a fan (it was in fact Rousseau, and not she, who said "Let them eat cake," in book 6 of his *Confessions*). True to her reputation, she dabbled; for Marie Antoinette, following Rousseau's philosophies mostly meant getting rid of her corset, not turning her offspring into frostbitten savages.

A few hundred years later, I'm baffled as to why Rousseau became so huge. He was asking parents to make their children miserable and ungovernable, and to oversee much of the child-rearing themselves. It's one thing when the nursemaid has to interact with the young yeti, but quite another when the viscount himself does.

In any case, it wasn't too long before the fervor for Rousseau died out. In part, this was because the subjects died, too; children perished. Parents rolled their infants in the snow, soaked them in icy water, and exposed them to the elements even when the elements were fatal. One father lost five of his children this way, prompting the surgeon John Hunter to ask him if he planned to subject his sixth child to the same methods that had "killed all the rest." And even if Rousseau's methods didn't kill your kid, they didn't exactly prompt him to thrive either. Philosopher David Williams described one Rousseau-raised thirteen-year-old as "a little emaciated figure, his countenance betraying marks of premature decay, or depraved passions; his teeth discoloured, his hearing almost gone." He could not read or write, spoke a language he'd cobbled together himself, and slept on the floor.

**BUT ROUSSEAU HAD PROVED** there was a voracious audience for parenting books, even if the illiterate children his methods produced could not read the books themselves. Far more parenting books followed over the next couple of centuries, and they tended to be a good deal more traditional than Rousseau's. Locke's and Rousseau's books were remarkable in ignoring the child's religious development, which had been the focus of most childcare advice up until then. *Émile* had actually been banned in parts of Europe for its criticism of religion, and in its aftermath, authors returned to their biblical bread and butter. Playing heathen in the woods might have been fun for a while, but that didn't work out so well, so come on, everyone, let's go back to church.

These books also tended to blame the mother for the sorry state of affairs, as if forgetting that it wasn't a mother who suggested we all send our kids out to play naked on the frozen lake with pistols. More and more, childcare books were addressed to women, and their address tended to be rather critical. Even more annoyingly, they took the position that they were just trying to help. Mothers were overwhelmed and needed guidance, and these self-appointed experts were stepping in to provide it. Which is fine, though it might have been more helpful if, for instance, they stopped saying things like "in all cases of dwarfishness or deformity, ninety-nine out of a hundred are owing to the folly, misconduct or neglect of mothers." And by the way, it's probably too late to do anything about it: "No subsequent endeavours can remedy or correct the evils occasioned by a mother's negligence; and the skill of the physician is exerted in vain to mend what she, through ignorance or inattention, may have unfortunately marred."

In his 1825 book *Treatise on the Physical and Medical Treatment of Children,* Pennsylvania professor of midwifery William Dewees thought it unfortunate that women were saddled with educating their children when they clearly weren't up to the task.[*] Dewees suggests the father pitch in, because "the father, from his education and studies, is, for the most part, better qualified." But, he admits, that's never going to happen. Though Puritan fathers did indeed handle much of the childcare, by the nineteenth century, as Dewees notes, any sensible father found this duty "a bore" that "he would feel almost disgraced to perform."

As more and more books addressed mothers, some were even authored by them.[†] Given their experience in the field, their advice tended

---

[*]  If the name is familiar, it's because this is the same genius who told his medical students to perform gynecological exams without looking (see page 50).

[†]  These would have to be shelved separately. The Victorian era was so repressed that etiquette dictated that books by male and female authors not be shelved next to each other unless the authors were married. One wonders if they thought this was how baby books were made. When a mommy book and a daddy book *really* love each

not to be the deranged stuff childless men like Rousseau came up with, for which they had little patience. This passage by the anonymous female author of the 1811 book *The Maternal Physician* is typical: "These gentlemen must pardon me if I think, after all, that a mother is her child's best physician . . . and that none but a mother can tell how to *nurse* an infant as it ought to be nursed."

But as the nineteenth century approached and advice books became more science-minded, the childcare advice industry by and large remained something of a sausage party, with the most influential authors being male. The most influential of these was pediatrician Luther Emmett Holt, and as far as he was concerned, it wasn't much of a party at all. Holt, who referred to the baby as an "it," was the straitlaced corrective to the experimental indulgences of the past. In spite of this, his 1894 book *The Care and Feeding of Children* remained enormously popular for the next fifty years. Dr. Spock himself was raised according to its tenets, and Spock's relative permissiveness was in no small part a reaction to Holt's iron fist. Holt laid down a strictly regimented schedule that was supposed to make life easier for both mother and infant. It was designed to make the child more independent, and it did that, but also, if Spock is any indication, very resentful.

Holt certainly gave the child plenty to resent. He recommended that toilet training begin at one or two months, and suggested soap suppositories to get things started. Other than that, however, Holtian parenting was largely a hands-off affair, with little physical contact: "Infants should be kissed, if at all, upon the cheek or forehead, but the less even of this the better." If it cries, let it.

As for recreation, there was sitting, and there was lying. Playing was discouraged: "Babies under six months old should never be played with, and the less of it at any time the better." Why? Because: "They are made nervous and irritable, sleep badly and suffer from indigestion and in many other respects." I would argue that it was not the playing but the soap-shard enema that made them nervous and irritable, but that's just me.

---

other . . . (Jacques Bonnet, *Phantoms on the Bookshelves* [New York: Overlook Press, 2012], 40).

STILL, HOLT WAS a basket full of hugs compared to the twentieth century's John Watson, a real-life Don Draper figure who had as much business giving parenting advice as Don Draper himself did. An incorrigible womanizer and alcoholic from rural origins, Watson became a Madison Avenue golden boy after being fired from Johns Hopkins—where he was voted Most Handsome Professor—for sexual misconduct, the same charge that would later get him fired from the New School.

Though he did not, apparently, practice it on his more nubile students, Watson, like Holt, preached a hands-off philosophy as far as offspring were concerned. In his popular 1928 book *Psychological Care of Infant and Child*, Watson advised: "There is a sensible way of treating children . . . Let your behavior always be objective and kindly firm. Never hug and kiss them, never let them sit in your lap. If you must, kiss them once on the forehead when they say good night. Shake hands with them in the morning. Give them a pat on the head if they have made an extraordinarily good job of a difficult task. Try it out. In a week's time you will find how easy it is to be perfectly objective with your child and at the same time kindly. You will be utterly ashamed of the mawkish, sentimental way you have been handling it."

These were tenets of behaviorism, the branch of psychology dominant in the 1920s and '30s that Watson founded and described for a lay audience in his popular 1925 book on the subject. Behaviorism held that we are the products of nurture and not nature, and that nurturing should be limited to job training. As Watson argued in his most famous line: "Give me a dozen healthy infants, well-formed, and my own specified world to bring them up in and I'll guarantee to take any one at random and train him to become any type of specialist I might select—doctor, lawyer, artist, merchant-chief and, yes, even beggar-man and thief, regardless of his talents, penchants, tendencies, abilities, vocations, and race of his ancestors."

Watson's objective advice was based on objective science, as determined by his own clinical studies. It appears, however, that these studies were almost certainly bullshit, and definitely cruel. In the most famous one, he conditioned a nine-month-old named Little Albert to fear small animals, and by extension, all fur-bearing creatures, including Santa Claus.

Over the course of several days, Albert had rats, rabbits, and barking dogs dropped on him and shoved in his face, all while being subjected to loud, clanging noises and the rough administrations of Watson and his research assistant.* Even worse was an experiment he proposed at the Manhattan Day Nursery at Teachers College of Columbia University; Watson casually wondered, "Would it not be possible to arrange a table containing interesting but not to be touched objects with electric wires so that an electrical shock is given when the table to be avoided is touched?"

*Now he fears even Santa Claus*

Little Albert with Santa Claus

Even for the days before ethics committees and institutional review boards, Watson's work was shady business† and largely a farce. Little Albert was not the normal, healthy baby Watson claimed, but a profoundly disabled, hydrocephalic child of a wet nurse who worked at the hospital where the experiment took place. As for Watson's other studies, they did not include thousands of babies, as suggested, but "several," all of them also the offspring of hospital wet nurses, and only two of whom were studied in any depth.

Given his desire to traumatize and electrocute children, a hands-off policy was probably a good idea for Watson himself. But for the rest of

---

* This was Rosalie Rayner, who was also his mistress. They later married.
† Watson had a habit of making university officials nervous. He also proposed studies on "sexual hygiene" movies and what became known as the infamous rye whiskey study, which examined how alcohol affects behavior. For this he somehow convinced the president of Johns Hopkins to secure him ten gallons of booze—during Prohibition.

America, it was, perhaps, not so wise to listen to Watson when he said things like, "Parents today are incompetent. Most of them should be indicted for psychological murder," or "Won't you then remember when you are tempted to pet your child that mother love is a dangerous instrument? An instrument which may inflict a never healing wound, a wound which may make infancy unhappy, adolescence a nightmare, an instrument which may wreck your adult son or daughter's vocational future and their chances for marital happiness."

Still, readers ate it up, finding Watson's approach exciting and new. But if the science was new (and wrong), the misogyny (also wrong) was old hat. Watson dedicated *Psychological Care* to "the first mother who brings up a happy child." The average mother, he wrote, is "unquestionably unfitted to bring up her child," and the working mother is even worse, "sharpening her brains when these things are of little importance to her in her emotional life as a woman." Watson also suggested a twenty-year ban on reproducing—except to produce infants for experiments—to give us all time to learn how to raise children properly. Ideally, he wrote, children would be raised in labs or in a series of foster homes, switched every three weeks so they wouldn't form attachments. And if this didn't work, if the child was still "hopelessly insane" or sick, a doctor "would not hesitate to put them to death."

Watson's ideas and advice are usually so outrageously bad that you can't help but wonder if he was kidding, and there's some evidence that his tongue, sharp as it was, was at least partly in cheek. As Ann Hulbert reminds us, satirist H. L. Mencken—who ghostwrote ridiculous child-care advice himself—was a good friend of Watson's, and may have inspired his over-the-top tone. Watson told his colleagues his popular books were just "pot-boilers" written for a paycheck, and that they shouldn't pay them any mind.

But if Watson's approach was a joke, the joke was on us. He was embraced by the intelligentsia, courted by Harvard and Columbia, praised in *The New York Times*, *The New Yorker*, and *The Atlantic Monthly*. In 1957, he was lavishly honored for his contributions to the field by the American Psychological Association; he'd earlier served as its president. (This, even though he'd once argued that thought processes occur not in the brain but in the *larynx*.) Bertrand Russell was an admirer and used Watson's techniques on his own daughter, who, in her later biography of him, wished he'd taken a different approach. And though he later changed course, childcare messiah Benjamin Spock himself used behaviorist methods to raise his first child. Average folks, too, were subjected to Watson's advice, when it found its way into the ubiquitous *Infant Care* advice bulletins put out by the Children's Bureau and sent to millions of American homes.

Watson also deployed his advice in his own home, even in its more outrageous forms. He really did conduct the baffling "jealousy test" he describes in *Behaviorism*, in which he removed his son from all family contact for three months. When they were reunited, Watson promptly got romantic with his wife in front of the child, then pretended to hit her, to see what the boy would do. Watson really did conduct weekly sessions of a family "talk it out club" on the subject of sex, with him doing most of the talking, usually on the importance of sexual endurance. He really did eschew all physical affection, hugging his children only once, when their mother died at age thirty-five (after which the children were packed off to boarding school). Unsurprisingly, his progeny did not turn out well; several attempted and committed suicide.[*]

THE NEXT WAVE of childcare books sought to undo Watson's damages. Among these was the pointedly titled *Babies Are Human Beings* by Mayo pediatrician C. Anderson Aldrich (who would later be Dr. Spock's boss) and his wife, Mary. First published in 1938, the book contains almost nothing a modern parent would object to; it's a thoughtful, practical guide to child-rearing based on the Aldriches' own experiences and solid science. Still, despite, or perhaps because of, all the parenting advice, mothers were feeling addled. Pediatricians reported visits from large numbers of anxious mothers, frantic and confused by experts' conflicting advice, exhausted and worried that they were doing everything wrong.

---

[*] Watson did, however, give us two great things: (1) the coffee break, a concept he invented in his ad work, and (2) beloved seventies actress Mariette Hartley, his granddaughter, who wrote her own book about how much he messed them all up.

They were only further demoralized by the publication of books like Philip Wylie's *Generation of Vipers*, which argued that the overbearing culture of "Momism" was ruining America. Or as Wylie himself put it: "Gentlemen, mom is a jerk."

Into this rumble Benjamin Spock arrived like a calm, bespectacled Fonzie, reminding everyone to just be cool with his enormously popular 1946 book, *The Common Sense Book of Baby and Child Care*. It opened with the now-famous mantra "Trust yourself. You know more than you think you do," then proceeded to dole out the sort of advice parents of the nascent baby boom were eager to hear: Don't worry too much about schedules. Feed them when they're hungry. Put them to bed when they're tired. When they cry, pick them up. Kiss them as much as you like. Trust your instincts. Have fun with your children, and try to enjoy them. Heyyyyyy.

The first true childcare bible, Dr. Spock's book was outsold only by the actual Bible. There are a few reasons for its success, but as Daniel Beekman points out, one of the most important was its simple but revolutionary innovation: a long and thorough index. A parent himself, Spock realized that you don't have time to leaf through hundreds of pages when you're in the middle of a crisis. Instead, the reader could flip to the index and find such detailed specifics as "Allergies, hair-filled mattress" or "Bowel movements, messing with." If Junior is messing with bowel movements, knowing exactly what page you can find a response on is a big plus.

Mostly, however, Spock's success was a matter of tone and timing. His actual approach wasn't much different from other experts'. But Spock's book came out just as the baby boom was beginning. Suddenly there were a lot more customers. These customers also tended to live farther away from their own parents than previous generations. Instead of turning to grandma, then, they had to turn to a book. This particular book turned out to be nicer than grandma, too. Spock offered commonsense advice in a wonderfully encouraging you-can-do-it tone. Instead of Holtian strictness, he encouraged parents to enjoy their children and not worry too much about schedules. He was also honest about how unpleasant the job can actually be. And he related this all with a remarkable, and radical, lack of mansplaining (likely due in no small part to his wife, Jane, who helped compile the book). In a huge departure from nearly everything that came before, Spock did not want to instruct or judge, but to reassure.

As it turns out, this is what we want from an advice manual: not a how-to so much as a high five, a more positive expression of the impulse behind the xenophobia in so many earlier advice manuals. I'm okay, you're okay, but the *Germans* . . .

Being told you're doing okay is a powerful and rare thing. *The New York Times* quoted a friend of Spock's: "The women strain toward him, they're happy, they seem to be saying, 'Tell me more! Tell me again that I'm not so bad!'" That's all most of us really want to hear. Also, that it's okay to let your kid eat pretzels for dinner. At eleven P.M.

A more careful reading reveals that that's not actually what he says. Although Spock was widely considered permissive, the book is not nearly as loosey-goosey as its reputation suggests. Spock was surprised when parents took what was really just an aside—a supposition that it *might*, in some instances, be okay to let young children dictate their own feeding schedule—and applied it to all areas, letting them dictate their own bedtimes and rules as well. In a later edition he set readers straight, clarifying that a kid might know when he wants to eat, but as far as everything else is concerned, "he doesn't know what's good for him."

It's true, however, that Spock's book, unlike most of what came before, was child-centered. This was largely a reflection of the times: as Jennifer Senior reminds us, America was becoming what *Fortune* magazine called a "filiarchy," with children calling the shots. And while Spock's child-centered approach was more easygoing, it wasn't necessarily easier. For the parent, it could be a lot more work, and, depending on your interests, a lot less interesting. Child-centered parenting means that if Betsy wants to play hopscotch, you're playing hopscotch and not your own favorite game, Drinking Gin in Front of the TV. A couple days of this and Holt's prohibition on playing with your children sounds like not such a bad idea after all.

Spock himself acknowledged as much ("The fact is setting aside a chunk of time to be devoted exclusively to companionship with children is a somewhat boring prospect to a lot of good parents"), and in later editions, he handed more power back to mom and dad. In a *Ladies' Home*

*Journal* article entitled "Mothers Need a Break" he urged moms to take exactly that.*

The book's numerous reprints show a steady progression toward stricter, more structured parenting, in large part because that's what readers asked for. It was continually revised to reflect reader response, as well as the times; in his last edition, published in 1998, he advocated veganism.

Even at his strictest, however, Spock never crossed the middle of the road. His relaxed approach was largely a reaction to Holt, and more specifically, to his own mother's use of Holt's parenting advice. The book's most insightful line might be in the dedication: "When a young man writes a book about how to raise children, in a sense it's his reflection on the way his mother raised him." Though not exactly Norma Bates, Mildred Spock was by all accounts more than a little overbearing (a reaction, no doubt, to *her* mother, who was distant). Mildred's strict adherence to Holtian methods meant that Benjamin grew up cowed and anxious with a particular fear of bananas.† (They would not be allowed until he was twelve; and then, only half.)

Frostbite, however, was fine. Holt advocated fresh air, which Mildred took to with Rousseauian fervor. She put her children to bed on an outdoor sleeping porch in all weather, even when it was so cold the urine in the chamber pots froze. Determined the children should spend their days outside as well, Mildred started an open-air school in a family friend's backyard. This was not unpleasant in spring and fall but fairly miserable

---

* Some readers, however, needed a little more than the break he prescribed, and wrote to tell him so. Jane F. Levey shares one such letter: "This is the worst part of the whole thing—being confined with the children without any hope for getting away for awhile. When the tension makes us wild-eyed, when the squabbling drifts to our feet, no matter how often we direct it back to the living room, when the last of grandmother's precious figurines is flushed down the toilet, and the carrots burn while you change bath-training pants—who wouldn't love to take off? . . . Even with those happy outlets you suggest, these frantic moments are frequent and difficult; without them to anticipate, what keeps us sane through the whines? Sometime, will you write an article on 'How Can Mothers of Small Children Keep from Being Driven Crazy Inside the House?' And please, please don't suggest television, spearmint gum, or a long, warm bath for either Mother or the children!" ("Spock, I Love Him," *Colby Quarterly* 36, no.4 [December 2000]: 273–94).

† Holt banned the fruit (see page 140).

in the New Haven winter, when the students bundled felted wool bags over their coats and tried to write with knitted gloves on. Their teacher, optimistically, was called South Wind. To warm up, the class folk-danced to the jeers of the neighborhood kids.

Under the circumstances, it's hard to imagine Ben would develop a surplus of self-esteem, and Mildred guaranteed he did not. When told he was handsome, his mother assured him that wasn't true: "Benny, you are not attractive looking. You just have a pleasant smile." In spite of this, Spock went on to Yale, won an Olympic gold medal in rowing, graduated from medical school, then wrote the bestselling American book of all time. His mother admitted she found the book "sensible."

Readers agreed. Off the page, however, at Benjamin Spock's own home, things were a little messier. In addition to the typical burdens of young children and a frequently absent husband, Spock's wife, Jane, was saddled with a drinking habit and a diagnosis of paranoid schizophrenia that would eventually get her a six-month stint in an asylum. This volatile combination was topped off with a prescription for Miltown, the tranquilizer often pressed into service as mother's little helper. It did not help Jane, and would occasionally result in her loudly trash-talking her husband at cocktail parties.

BY THE SIXTIES and seventies, the party was ending. Though the book continued to be popular and widely used—and others, like the wonderful *How to Raise Children at Home in Your Spare Time* took the same relaxed tack—the backlash had begun. Spock's child-driven, easygoing style of parenting was blamed for the excesses of the era by critics who maintained that the generation "got Spocked when they should have been spanked."

One of these critics was Walter Sackett, Jr., a Florida pediatrician who published *Bringing Up Babies* in 1962. Declaring that "Citizenship begins at birth," Sackett argued that Spockian coddling is a recipe for bolshevism: "If we teach our offspring to expect everything to be provided upon demand, we must admit the possibility of sowing the seeds of socialism. The dictators of our age have utilized early indoctrination well. Hitler, Mussolini, Stalin, and more recently Castro have all taken the malleable child from the home and trained him to look toward the state as the source of all beneficence. Aren't we doing much the same thing, somewhat less efficiently, when we temporarily interpose an over-indulgent parent who provides the answer to every desire during the early formative years?"

The most prominent of the Spocklash books was the one that introduced parenting as a verb, Fitzhugh Dodson's *How to Parent* (1970), a title that sounded so bizarre to contemporary ears that it required a definition. What is this strange verb *to parent*? According to Dodson, a psychologist and minister, it meant combining the latest science and tender loving care. It also meant you didn't pull any punches. The book's *Family Circus*–style isn't-this-fun? cover belied the contents, which included a chapter on applying the principles of animal training to child discipline, and a strong endorsement of spanking. "Some of you may have heard the old saying 'Never spank a child in anger.'" he writes. "I think that is psychologically very poor advice, and I suggest the opposite: 'Never strike a child *except* in anger.'" It's better for the child, he says, but more important, it's better for the parent. "The main purpose of spanking, although most parents don't like to admit it, is to relieve the parent's feelings of frustration. All of us need to do this from time to time when our kids get on our nerves." Parents shouldn't hold back, either; Dodson advocates "the 'pow-wow' type of spanking: your 'pow' followed by his 'Wow'!"[*]

The childcare books of the decade that followed would focus more on the physical dangers that lurked *beyond* mommy's last nerve. This was the era when childproofing first began, and childcare advice books show a growing concern with everything that can kill your child, starting at or even before conception. Faced with the dire selection in 1983, a pregnant advertising copywriter named Heidi Murkoff decided to write the more reassuring advice book she wished she could find herself. This was before reality TV and the Internet, so Murkoff could not spend her pregnancy as I myself did, watching MTV shows about troubled teenagers and shopping

---

[*] On the plus side, Dodson was also among the first to argue that a child's early years are a crucial time for their intellectual development. This was a finding that escaped my own parents, who allowed me to spend my time watching TV instead of attending math enrichment camps. I appreciated the freedom at the time, though now I do sometimes wish I didn't have to take my shoes off to count higher than ten.

for jewelry on Etsy. Instead, she wrote a book proposal, delivering it a couple of hours before going into labor.

The book that resulted, *What to Expect When You're Expecting*, rivaled Spock's success, with 34 million copies sold in the United States alone. It's estimated that 93 percent of American mothers have read it. The book has been translated into thirty languages and spawned an entire library of companion books ranging from *What to Expect Before You're Expecting* through *What to Expect: Babysitter's Handbook*. There is also a spin-off line written for children, whose titles include the alarmingly named *What to Expect When You Use the Potty*.

As for the original, it's now had five editions, each reflecting its time. Although the instantly recognizable patchwork border remained the same, the content and cover continually changed. The cover model grew more and more active with each edition, first changing into pants, then getting out of her rocking chair. When she was eventually depicted standing, in jeans and boots, it made national news.

This was the version I bought, along with a half-dozen other volumes, about an hour after two lines showed up on a stick in the ladies' room at my husband's office. We'd been married a few weeks. I'm not sure What We Were Expecting, but it was not this. And while we were thrilled—at thirty-eight and forty, we knew conception wasn't guaranteed—we were also panicked, and drove immediately to a bookstore.

We bought a stack of books, all that we could carry. There was the Sears, the Mayo, the Brazelton; the feminist one, the illustrated one, and the *What to Expect*, which became my go-to. I liked the question-and-answer format, not because it was catechistic, but because the questions reminded me that other people had far more dangerous things to worry about than I did. I might be doing it wrong, but someone else was doing it high. Their first-trimester drug binge trumped my diet soda habit, and made me feel competent and smug. That is what the good advice books do. They make you feel like you're doing a good job, even if it's simply by reassuring you that someone else is doing a worse one.

Despite the diet sodas, the baby turned out just fine, as all the books assured me she would. As for the bookstore where I got them, that would close within the year. By then, the advice was migrating from books to websites, the advisers shifting from dangerously uninformed doctors and monks to dangerously uninformed sixteen-year-old girls with MySpace accounts. They would become our misspelled, semiliterate resources after we were led to them by the Google searches we did in the early days of parenthood, word salads that sounded like badly translated child-rearing titles themselves: "Baby eat diaper cream dangerous?" "Newborn eight hours TV brain damage?" "Toddler show signs of psychopathy?" "Military school how young?"

In the end, we wouldn't follow their advice; their advice was not what we wanted (especially when it included emoticons). What we wanted was the original kind of advice: judgment. What we wanted was assurance that we were doing okay, or more precisely, that someone else was doing a lot worse. That someone might be an ancient Greek or a medieval peasant, a Florida crackpot or a high school junior on MTV.

It might be me. Given that I use the failings of others to feel better about myself, it's only fair that I let others do the same to me: instead of an advice book, a cautionary tale. This is a service I provide for any number of acquaintances, who can look to my parenting when they're feeling bad about their own. After they give their child the cookie or let them watch the cartoon, they can assuage their guilt by remembering that my kids eat gum for breakfast and watch eight hours of TV a day.

A kid can get away with a lot when no one's paying attention. And for this, let's blame the advice books, too. Because the one thing they did teach me to do was to ignore what I don't like. It might be the assertion that yelling is both damaging and ineffective, that too much screen time is dangerous, that snacking establishes bad habits that last a lifetime. It might be the fact that my children have begun ignoring me back, and that they sometimes try to use the remote to pause real life. I'm not particularly worried. Because when this inevitably results in subpar SAT scores and clinical anxiety, we can buy more advice books and ignore those, too. There are so many ways to do it wrong, and we're just getting started.

# 4

# Nasty, Brutish, and Short

## *The First Three Years*

When Thomas Hobbes called life "nasty, brutish, and short," he was describing life during war, but it applies equally well to life with small children (as well as to the children themselves). Like war, it manages to be both boring and exhausting. Day after day, there's nothing to do and so much to get done.

The first three years present an overwhelming to-do list that starts with holding your head up and ends with reliable diaper-free continence. In a very short time, children must learn to sit, stand, walk, and run. We expect them to acquire a full mouth of teeth and learn where to deploy them (apples: yes; siblings: no). They have to understand and speak at least one language, preferably at a volume that leaves eardrums intact. They need to develop hand-eye coordination, object permanence, and enough cognitive function to distinguish toes from French fries. All this must be accomplished while doubling their height and quintupling their weight. It's an extraordinary workload. No wonder we get a little bit cranky when we don't get our naps.

Given how all-absorbing this agenda is, it's hard to imagine that for most of history these achievements were something parents either gave no thought to or actively discouraged. Even the ones we view as biological inevitabilities vary quite a bit from culture to culture and even more from era to era. For hundreds of years, crawling was thought to be sinful and was skipped entirely. Teething was considered a life-or-death rite of passage, and potty training wasn't considered at all.

When the odds of baby making it to his first birthday are fifty-fifty, I suppose you've got bigger things to worry about, but still, it's surprising how little most of these milestones are mentioned in historical accounts. You rarely read about young Bartholomew taking his first step, about little Hester saying her first word. Today, if you have a Facebook account and friends with young children, you rarely read about anything else. I'm sure it's annoying, but I posted these things, too. It's hard not to get excited when each advance has the promise to change your world, if not *the* world: one small step for Brody, one large step for Brodykind.

Mostly, though, it's small steps, baby steps, which is frustrating for someone like me, who is so impatient that loved ones must remind me, whenever I'm faced with a dessert buffet, that it's a marathon, not a sprint. This haste is a quality that does not serve me well as a parent. Parenthood, after all, is a marathon conducted while sleep-deprived to the point of psychosis, with ten pounds of helplessness strapped to your chest and its sibling clamped like a human binder clip to your leg.

For most of Western history, the first step was acquiring human form. We take this for granted, focusing instead on goals like lifting your head, turning over, crawling, and walking, but for several hundred years the primary task was to acquire a recognizably human body. Throughout Europe, babies were thought to be formless blobs who wouldn't go on to develop human form unless it was forcibly imposed on them, which it would be, daily, in its first stage of life. Acquiring human form was not a biological inevitability, it was believed, but a process that would not occur without extensive interventions. I'm not sure what they thought would happen if you just left the poor thing alone, but I suppose they expected you'd end up with a feral lesser mammal, or perhaps an inanimate object, like a pudding or a bolster pillow.

Beginning immediately after birth and continuing for some time thereafter, caregivers shaped the blob, firming up its skin, stretching its arms into arms, legs into legs, rounding the head, pinching the nose.* Many cultures believed that salt helped the process. The idea was to cure the baby, to stiffen it up and give it some shape like so much beef jerky. To ensure the salted blob retain its form in between molding sessions, it was then wrapped in full-body swaddling that sometimes included splints and corsets, because it's never too early to start worrying about your figure. As directed by the ancient Greek physician Soranus, you should swaddle boys' trunks rigidly and evenly, but with girls, go looser from the waist down, "for in women this form is more becoming."† You had to swaddle your children or they'd grow up deformed, if they grew up at all.

Today there's a lot less wrapping and a good deal more fanfare. We get all worked up about the micro-milestones of the first year: a child lifts his head for the first time to big smiles, rolls over to cheers, sits up to applause, and stands to a standing ovation. Previous generations, however, made little mention of these achievements, in part because swaddling made them unnecessary or prevented them altogether. Even when swaddling fell out of favor, parenting books didn't address steps like rolling, sitting, and standing, suggesting that the things we make such a big deal over were scarcely noticed at all. Soranus has nothing to say about babies lifting their heads or rolling. As for sitting, standing, and walking, they merit three paragraphs altogether, and one of these paragraphs is mainly about the drunken whorishness of Roman women. The other paragraphs simply instruct the parent to place the child against a wall and leave it there to figure the whole business out, bit by bit, on its own.

Swaddling hung around for over a thousand years. It was akin to mummification and, as I've mentioned, a good deal more smelly. Though caregivers were advised to change the swaddling once or more a day, it was cumbersome to do so (it could take up to two hours) and the chore was frequently neglected. Sure, judge, but we all know, and are sometimes

---

\* In some cultures, like the Fulani, this still takes place.

† The ancient Greeks, it seems, liked big butts and they can't deny. As for the boys' business, Soranus warns that you should never lift a male child over four months old onto your shoulders, as this will cause the testicles to draw into the body or dissolve entirely. Personally, I'd fault the rigid swaddling on that one.

married to, parents who pretend not to notice the soiled diaper because it just feels like too much work to put on a new one. Here I will just share that when my husband was confronted with a leaking diaper on his lap, his response was typically to change his *own* pants, leaving the baby in sodden Pampers but wrapping her lower half in a throw blanket to protect the couch, until I came home to change her myself.

Besides encouraging human form, straitjacket swaddling was supposed to keep an infant receiving minimal to no supervision safe, but it sometimes did the opposite. Swaddling kept babies so rigid that a big drooler placed on his back could actually drown in his own saliva. Babies could also die from an infected cut, as both swaddling and diapers were held in place by open straight pins until the invention of the safety pin in 1849. Thus secured from head to toe, the baby was, in effect, a sentient pincushion. Because baby gear required so many pins, a customary newborn gift was a pincushion embroidered with a phrase like WELCOME LITTLE STRANGER. GET YOUR TETANUS SHOT might have been more helpful, but that vaccine wouldn't be invented until the early 1900s.

A baby was viewed as a lump of dough and treated in much the same way. You shaped it and set it aside to rise, but you didn't dandle it in your lap and you certainly didn't read to it. You wouldn't try to stimulate neurological development in a baby any more than you would in a wad of sourdough.* The fact that the brain is the one part of a baby's body that really is elastic and shapable wouldn't be discovered for several hundred more years.

NOW, OF COURSE, the brain is the main focus of our ministrations, which we begin before birth, piping neurologically stimulating classical music into the womb, reading Dostoevsky to a fetus that still has its ves-

---

* Rousseau and his followers were a notable exception, devoting a great deal of attention to children's intellectual development. Rousseau, however, encouraged parents to develop said intellect with some terrifying measures, including fright masks and spiders, making me think they mostly developed a good deal of resentment and neuroses.

tigial tail, and once it's born, playing endless rounds of peekaboo in an effort to teach object permanence. This is the concept, much researched by Jean Piaget, that an object continues to exist even if you can't see it. Children typically figure this out around one or so, as did our daughter, who put her new knowledge to use hiding our credit cards. We quickly learned the concept is somewhat oxymoronic: once discovered by a child, objects rarely remain permanent for long.

Peekaboo itself, however, has been around for a very long time, dating to the 1300s if not earlier. It's one of the few nearly universal childhood games. Across centuries and cultures the rules have remained more or less the same, though the vocabulary changes. In England, it's known as bo-peep or peep-bo; in the Netherlands, *kiekeboe*; France, *cou-cou*; Korea, *gock-um*; and in Japan, *inai inai ba* ("not here, not here, boo"). It seems unlikely that it was played to inspire neurological development, given that it often wasn't played with children at all; surviving references describe grown-ups playing peekaboo with their toes, their creditors, scripture, and the devil. The oldest reference, in fact, is to a tavern wench playing peekaboo with a judging public as she stewed in a stockade in punishment for cheating her customers. I see you!

Aside from playing peekaboo, the closest previous generations got to worrying about the head's contents was the teeth. And about that, they worried a lot. Teething was considered a potentially fatal milestone, and though it's not, the treatments for it could be.* Beginning with Hippocrates, physicians warned that teething could be dangerous, causing fevers, seizures, diarrhea, or death. In the seventeenth century, Queen Anne's physician John Arbuthnot claimed that teething would take the life of one out of every ten children; in 1894, dentist Dr. Marion Thrasher upped that number to one out of every three. To ward off the danger and ease the discomfort, parents fashioned amulets, balms, and teethers from materials including coral, amber, wood lice, donkey hair, opium, stink-

---

* Among the Beng tribe, however, teething could be fatal if the top tooth emerged before the bottom. This was considered a bad omen and meant a family member would die soon. To prevent this (though I guess it actually ensured it), the parents would drown the child. The practice has been outlawed and is no longer done, but belief in the omen continues (DeLoache and Gottlieb, *A World of Babies*, 82).

ing nightshade (a narcotic), honey, salt, an actual frog, rattlesnake bones, and the teeth of wolves, bears, and deer, none of which actually help and several of which are choking hazards.

Teething is, in fact, listed as the cause of death for a good chunk of nineteenth-century London infants. The actual causes of death were likely rickets, epilepsy, scurvy, or the teething "cure" itself. Scurvy was a frequent culprit; because it produces red gums, it was often mistaken for teething

trouble, and because feeding babies fruit and vegetables was thought to be dangerous, scurvy was fairly common. The treatment some doctors prescribed for teething—withholding fruit and vegetables—surely didn't help. Some physicians were even less helpful, prescribing treatments like powdered mercury (which is toxic), bloodletting, blistering, leeching,

*(Courtesy Kunstkammer Georg Laue, Munich/London)*

Fancy children used combination rattle-teethers made from animal fangs and coral. Note that every one of these kids looks like he's about to stab someone.

burning the head, and lancing the gums. Other treatments were merely re-volting, like rubbing the gums with a minnow or rabbit brains, or giving the child a wad of chicken fat to chew on.

In the Middle Ages, teething was thought to be the child's cue to start talking, but parents probably did next to nothing to facilitate this. As Steven Pinker has observed, the practice of deliberately developing children's linguistic abilities is unique to our time and culture; for most others, there was simply no point. Talking to a baby made as much sense as talking to a moccasin.* Though parents probably cooed and clucked, they did not pretend this was a conversation, and they certainly didn't ask if bubba wants his num-nums. The term *baby talk* dates only to 1836, *motherese* to 1970.†

Motherese itself, however, is ancient. Though Western parents didn't put much thought or effort into language lessons, the actual practice of speaking to children in singsongy, exaggerated tones is common to most cultures and dates to prehistoric times. Anthropologists have even hypothesized that motherese was what led to human speech in the first place, as the reassuring grunts mothers made toward their infants gradually morphed into actual words.

This, however, may have been its only contribution to culture. Mother-child speech is rarely mentioned in Western history, and child speech more rarely still. Now we make a big deal about baby's first words, but for several thousand years this event seems to have gone unremarked. If parents ever recorded their children's first words, those records didn't survive. Given how little time many parents spent with their children, it's likely they wouldn't have heard them, but still, the omission is surprising. Speech, after all, is the primary thing that separates us from beasts, something previous generations were obsessed with to the point of banning crawling as too animal-like. It also seems strange that first words weren't

---

* Rousseau, again, is the exception here, and wrote a fair amount about children's linguistic development. And Locke wrote about the linguistic development of older children, noting how easily they learn foreign languages.
† *Child-directed speech* has replaced *baby talk*, *motherese*, and *parentese* as the preferred term, though I myself vastly prefer the term the French use, *mamanaise*, because it sounds like a tasty sandwich spread.

viewed as a sort of omen, given that pretty much everything else was. People read portents into the child's birth date, placenta (amniomancy), and behavior during nursing (mazomancy). Other forms of divination looked to moles, bodily fluids, barley cakes, onion sprouts, fava beans, and poop, but not first words, all of which suggests that previous generations were more likely to find meaning in the contents of a child's diaper than in its speech.

This is not to suggest there was *no* interest in what children had to say. In the past, as in the present, there was a tendency to view children as a link to a lost linguistic history.* Today we look to baby talk for evolutionary clues to the speech of our hominin ancestors, but previous generations sought a "natural" Edenic language, sometimes through rather awful experiments. In one of the more legendary ones, thirteenth-century Holy Roman Emperor Frederick II arranged for six infants to be raised in silence, uncorrupted by language. The idea was that they'd eventually begin to speak the innate language spoken by Adam and Eve; instead, they died. James IV of Scotland conducted a similar experiment two hundred years later, sending two infants and a nonspeaking deaf caretaker to live alone on the island of Inchkeith. These children lived and were said to speak perfect Hebrew, though few believed the claim. Sir Walter Scott argued, "It is more likely they would scream like their dumb nurse, or bleat like the goats and sheep on the island," and despite its guttural elements, that's not what perfect Hebrew sounds like. When the Mughal emperor Akbar the Great repeated the experiment in the sixteenth century, the children simply ended up mute.

Because it was so unethical, language deprivation became known as the "forbidden experiment," and such experiments could never be conducted in an age of institutional review boards and basic human decency. But researchers occasionally found subjects nonetheless, typically terribly

---

* Or the heaven whence they recently came. Steven Pinker notes that this claim is a particular favorite of tabloids, whose headlines have included "Baby Born Talking—Describes Heaven"; "Amazing 2-Headed Baby Is Proof of Reincarnation. One Head Speaks English—The Other Ancient Latin"; and, name-dropping, "Baby Speaks and Says: I'm the Reincarnation of Natalie Wood" (*The Language Instinct*, 23).

neglected children who'd grown up without language before being rescued by authorities. They did not speak an Edenic language because they didn't speak, period. And although intensive therapy would help them acquire other basic skills, none ever learned to speak normally or even close, confirming that language development must be achieved in a certain time window or not at all, and giving parents yet another thing to worry about.

As it turns out, they needn't. There's a window, sure, but it's more a sliding glass door than a transom. Children learn to speak in a wide variety of ways over a wide range of time. The Beng speak with their children because they believe that babies can understand every language; the Ifaluk don't because they believe children can understand none. Strictly speaking, they're both right. As long as children hear language, they learn it, whether or not they're directly addressed, whether or not you routinely point out the doggie or ask who's a big boy. Children left to pick up language on their own, as is still done in many cultures around the world, may progress more slowly, but they catch up fast enough.

What takes longer to learn is volume control. Inside voice develops several years after regular voice, which tends, from the start, to be quite loud. A baby's screams clock in at around a hundred decibels, putting them in the same range as a jet taking off, a level at which hearing damage occurs. Over the next few years babies become more skilled at expressing themselves, but not at controlling the volume at which they do this. The upshot is a years-long period during which everything is shouted regardless of its import or your distance from their voice box.[*]

This has given rise to a whole library of books, including *Little Tiger Is Loud: A Book About Using Your Inside Voice*, *Too Loud Lily*, *Voices Are Not for Yelling*, and a title that sounds more like drag cabaret than a children's story, *Decibella and Her Six-Inch Voice*. With or without the books, most children eventually learn, and remember, to control their volume, but not everyone does; it can be an especially difficult skill for autistic children to master. And some people are just naturally louder, born with vocal cords and resonant

---

[*] Leading many parents to agree with Sir Anthony Gwyn's statement that "A true Britishman feels that children should not be seen either" (Harris, *The Nurture Assumption*, rev. ed. [New York: Free Press, 2009], 190).

heads that function more or less as megaphones. At four and six, my own children continued to speak at a volume that rattled my cochleas and made my eardrums throb, and occasionally prompted my husband to complain that he couldn't hear his own demons.* As for him, he shouted everything in such a loud Texas twang (AH'M ROBERT N' AH'M SEE-YUX!) that his elementary school sent him to speech therapy to learn to speak more quietly. Ostensibly, this was for his benefit—vocal polyps were developing—but I'm sure his teacher and parents appreciated the intervention, too.

WHEN OUR DAUGHTER was about to turn one, a friend told us she'd soon choose between walking and talking, as infants don't have the neurological capacity to master both tasks at the same time. This turns out not to be true—in fact, motor development partially facilitates language development—but no one told our daughter this, so she chose talking.† The language exploded, and the walking went nowhere. We weren't surprised. Due to the unfortunate combination of a big baby tummy on little baby feet, she seemed no more likely to walk than a turnip.

As it turns out, weight does factor into walking, but it's not the weight of the tummy so much as the weight of the brain. You have to reach a certain brain mass before you can do it. All animals walk at the same point of brain development; humans just get there much later than pretty much everyone else. Our daughter got there later than most humans. By the time she finally started walking, around eighteen months, she was already speaking in full paragraphs.

As is common in most modern first-world societies as well as inspirational poster mottoes, before our daughter learned to walk, she learned to crawl. It seemed the natural order of things at the time, but historically

---

* In the wonderful book *The Flame Alphabet*, novelist Ben Marcus imagines a world in which children's speech is toxic to parents, literally killing them with exposure. The scourge begins in Jewish families and soon spreads to everyone else. The book is experimental fiction, but any parent recognizes it as straight-up documentary.

† Steven Pinker suggests that there may be a good reason children acquire language around the time they learn to walk. Once they're mobile, a whole host of new dangers becomes accessible, and the ability to understand their parents' commands is suddenly crucial (*The Language Instinct*, 294–95).

and culturally speaking, it's not at all. We think of crawling as the inevitable precursor to walking, but in fact they draw on completely different skill sets, and for much of history crawling was actively discouraged, if not skipped entirely. In many parts of the world, it still is.

There are a number of reasons for this. A primary one is having nothing suitable for children to crawl *on*. In parts of Turkey, Papua New Guinea, Jamaica, and Bangladesh, children who crawl are exposed to all sorts of health hazards, human feces not least among them, and are firmly discouraged from doing so. This was the case across most of Europe for hundreds of years as well. For centuries floors were typically made of dirt or, even worse, rushes, and were pretty much the last place you'd want to plop down a baby. At the time, crawling was known as creeping, and given all the critters lurking in the rushes, the name seems apt. Erasmus described the floors' sorry state:

> [T]he bottom layer is left undisturbed, sometimes for twenty years, harbouring expectoration, vomiting, the leakage of dogs and men, ale droppings, scraps of fish, and other abominations not fit to be mentioned. Whenever the weather changes a vapour is exhaled, which I consider very detrimental to health. I may add that England is not only everywhere surrounded by sea, but is, in many places, swampy and marshy, intersected by salt rivers, to say nothing of salt provisions, in which the common people take so much delight. I am confident the island would be much more salubrious if the use of rushes were abandoned, and if the rooms were built in such a way as to be exposed to the sky on two or three sides, and all the windows so built as to be opened or closed at once, and so completely closed as not to admit the foul air through chinks; for as it is beneficial to health to admit the air, so it is equally beneficial at times to exclude it.

Rushes were, in short, a pretty fantastic breeding ground for both vermin and disease, and a child was likely to pick up something a lot worse than crawling from them.

Even when the condition of the floors improved, the stigma remained.

Crawling was viewed as unseemly, degrading, and bestial (in Bali, it still is). Creeping about on all fours was for animals, not for people. Two legs good, four legs bad. Medieval children who insisted on crawling were called kittens, and this wasn't a compliment. Crawling was considered so vulgar that it couldn't even be discussed in polite company; it certainly couldn't be *performed*. It wasn't until the nineteenth century that this began to change. Over the course of the century, as floors grew cleaner, carpets more common, and parents more indulgent, more and more children were permitted to crawl. Still, by 1900, less than half ever did.

In the preceding centuries, parents devised a number of ways to keep would-be crawlers off their knees. First was the swaddling, which prevented not only crawling but movement of any kind. Once children were considered human-shaped enough to graduate out of swaddling, around six or nine months, both boys and girls were put in long dresses. Because they made it difficult to crawl, and because parents liked the way they made the baby look more grown-up, dresses were typically a foot longer than the child itself, the infant equivalent of a bridal train. Thus attired, they were parked in a standing stool, a tiny little prison, often made from a hollowed-out tree trunk, that kept the child upright and in one place. Older children might be placed in a walking stool, which was more or less

Children parked in stools that look an awful lot like a hoop skirt . . .

. . . and a witness box

the same thing but on wheels. In a home with an open hearth, or a staircase, this could and did prove extremely dangerous.

Still, parents used them, because anything was better than letting a child crawl. Parents believed that permitting a child to crawl would prevent it from learning to walk. Now we typically believe the opposite—you *have* to crawl to learn how to walk—but we're wrong, too. The skills children acquire through crawling don't transfer to walking at all; it's a completely different activity, so they can't build on what they've learned. Nicholas Day describes the phenomenon: "the development of locomotion isn't at all like someone progressing to fluency in Spanish. It's like someone taking Spanish 101, and then the history of Japanese puppetry, and then multivariable calculus." As a number of what I imagine have been very cute studies have shown, children go from being very talented crawlers to really terrible walkers.

There are, however, children who never learn how to shift from locomoting on four limbs to locomoting on two. This is not because they were permitted to crawl, but because their parents were wayyyy too closely related to each other. In 2004 doctors discovered a Kurdish family in rural Turkey whose members moved around, quite quickly and easily, by "bearwalking" on all fours. The condition is known as Uner Tan syndrome after Turkish evolutionary biologist Üner Tan, who first described it, and is caused by inherited chromosomal mutations resulting in cerebellar impairment. The Kurdish siblings also suffer from mild mental retardation. The quadrupedalism, however, proved treatable; after the family hit the news, they received physical therapy, and like the majority of humans, learned to walk upright.

THE OFT-REPEATED IDEA that the crawling phase is necessary for normal *brain* development is false as well. As hundreds of years of history have demonstrated, you can skip crawling entirely and still grow into a neurologically normal adult. If we don't think so, it's largely the fault of physical therapist Glenn Doman and psychologist Carl Delacato, who in the 1960s and '70s argued that the act of crawling was essential to healthy brain development—and that you could make the brain healthy *by* crawling, rewiring the brain by moving around on all fours. Doman and Delacato developed a technique called *psychomotor patterning*, which they claimed could treat brain injuries, autism, learning disabilities, and mental retardation (even, some suggested, in adults).

The Doman-Delacato technique was based on recapitulation theory, Ernst Haeckel's 1866 idea that every human passes through each stage of evolution personally, from primordial protoplasm to fish to rodent to ape. Though mistaken, recapitulation theory was highly influential before it was disproved in the 1920s. Both Jung and Freud were believers, and it was behind many of Freud's biggest ideas, including Oedipalism. It also seems to have enchanted L. Ron Hubbard, who made recapitulation the basis for the theory of evolution he sets forth in *A History of Man*, a text his biographer Russell Miller described as "possibly the most absurd book ever written." (As critics have noted, Hubbard gets weirdly obsessed with clams.)

Haeckel argued that men were more evolved than women and some races were more evolved than others, which he helpfully ranked from best to worst. His own Germanic Caucasian race, naturally, placed at the top. As for the "lower" races—that is, the nonwhite ones—they were little better than animals. Haeckel wrote, "These lower races (such as the Veddahs or Australian negroes) are psychologically nearer to mammals (apes or dogs) than to civilized Europeans; we must, therefore, assign a totally different value to their lives."

By the time Doman and Delacato came along, recapitulation had been thoroughly discredited and debunked, but they nonetheless made it the cornerstone of their theories. In their recapitulationist formulation, conditions like mental retardation were the result not of genetic mutation but of a failure to pass through the proper order of evolutionary development (amphibious, reptilian, mammalian, etc.). To set things right, patients were put through a crawling regimen four times daily that was designed to rewire and integrate the brain's hemispheres. If the patient was physically unable to do this on his own, a team of assistants would move his limbs for him.

Other Doman-Delacato interventions were far more rigorous. They instructed desperate parents to do things like dip their child's hands in warm and cool water six hundred (six hundred!) times a day, and startle them by banging blocks behind their head every half hour. Then there was the therapy in which a mask was placed over the child's face every fifteen minutes in an effort to increase oxygen flow to the brain. This was supposed to put an end to the child's neurological problems, though I imagine it did little for the parents' mental health.

I DON'T REMEMBER WHEN our daughter began to crawl, but if she was on time, it was somewhere between eight and ten months.* Both the timetable and the canonization of crawling are fairly recent and come to us courtesy of the same person: Arnold Gesell, the Yale psychologist who, beginning in the 1920s, introduced the idea of developmental timetables that remain in place today.

Given how much we obsess about hitting benchmarks according to schedule, it's hard to imagine there was a time we didn't. As Nicholas Day has cleverly pointed out, Gesell came along to change this at a time when time itself was becoming a universal issue. Starting in the mid-nineteenth century, officials undertook the massive project of establishing a world clock and calendar, which had previously been a local matter. In one part of Detroit it might be noon; in another, 12:28. This made things rather complicated, especially when traveling. Until 1875, the American railway system had to deal with seventy-five different local times. There were six different time zones in St. Louis alone, and five in Kansas City. Over the next few decades, however, a single standard time with synchronized time zones was implemented around the world. Weights and measures were standardized as well. That we'd standardize the moments and milestones of childhood, too, was only natural.

That we'd then obsess about whether our own children were hitting those milestones early, on time, or late was only natural, too. If childhood is a marathon, we all want our children to get the best time in their age

---

* For Gesell, babies were supposed to crawl at ten months; more current timetables put it at eight. On average, children start crawling earlier now, as they do most things, probably due to better infant nutrition (Nicholas Day, *Baby Meets World*, 242).

category. And unlike previous generations, we have cognitive milestones to worry about as well as physical ones, thanks to Jean Piaget and his colleagues. While Gesell was formulating his timetables, Piaget was developing his thoughts on object permanence, inspired by watching his young daughter play with—the symbolism is almost too perfect, given how obsessed modern parents are with hitting milestones on time—a pocket watch.* Like Gesell, Piaget gave time frames for each stage of cognitive development. To be fair, neither insisted that these time windows were crucial, and sometimes said exactly the opposite. But parents of small children are *crazy*. By giving time windows at all, Gesell and Piaget provided a peg for parents to hang their anxieties on, a reason to Google, as we did, phrases like "five years old when wipe self?" and "three years sleep deprivation parent die?"

Steering children through early childhood can feel like jet lag that never ends, because that's basically what it is, a years-long stretch of sleep disruptions and torpedoed schedules. Having young children cuts your day and night into three-hour cycles of feeding, burping, and changing; it bisects or trisects each day with naps that must be attempted but won't be achieved. Parenthood makes time contract and expand. The boring game of hide-and-seek is endless; the delicious cuddle is over in the blink of an eye.

It is crazy-making, and in some ways Gesell didn't help at all. In others, he helped enormously. The beautifully static, beautifully standard timelines offered a reminder that all children eventually learn to sleep through the night, feed themselves, walk, and wipe. Gesell's timetables offered something like a bus schedule, and indeed, kids are as reliable as buses, usually arriving late, filthy, and spattered with vomit. Even if it was aspirational, it helped to know it was there. Of course a parent needs a schedule to cling to as the clock melts like a Salvador Dalí painting.

For Gesell, the clock was real and physical. Breaking with many of his colleagues, Gesell believed that stages are innate and biological. His maturational theory of child development posited that children are driven by an

---

* Or possibly just the chain; accounts differ. But the actual watch works much better for my metaphor here, so let's go with that.

internal clock that prompts them to sit around six months, stand around nine months, and be mortified by their parents around 168 months. In his publications he gave target times for pretty much every childhood milestone from rolling over to getting a job. He argued that both behavioral and physical developments were primarily products of nature, not nurture. In doing so, he did parents both a big favor and a huge disservice. It was nice to be informed that junior was flinging his diaper because he was two, and that's just what two-year-olds do. But it was less nice to be reminded that he should have been out of his diapers six months ago.*

Events that made it onto Gesell's timeline became enshrined as developmental milestones; those that didn't became unimportant asides. Such was the fate of *cruising*, when children hold on to furniture as they tentatively take a few steps. Although Gesell seems to have originated the term, he left it off his developmental charts, and thus out of the canon, turning cruising into what one study termed "the Rodney Dangerfield of motor milestones." The term didn't even make it into the *Oxford English Dictionary* until 2011. This probably was why I'd never heard of it and was startled when our pediatrician asked if our daughter was doing it; I'd spent the previous twelve years in San Francisco, where *cruising* has a different meaning entirely.†

When anthropologists began studying childhood development in other parts of the world, the flaws in Gesell's theories became obvious. If stages and milestones are driven by biology, children should reach them at more or less the same point the world over. But they don't. Children in African studies sat, stood, and walked months before the American children in Gesell's studies did, consistently hitting milestones so much ear-

---

* It is worth noting that in removing the guilt from the parent, Gesell also removed the guilt from the *working* parent. Though this follows from Gesell's overarching theory, it probably didn't hurt that his two main collaborators—Frances L. Ilg and Louise Bates Ames—were single mothers, and many of his researchers were working mothers as well. Nice work, ladies (Ann Hulbert, *Raising America*, 167)!

† Like most parents, we thought cruising was helping her learn to walk, but here, too, we were wrong. Even though it looks so much like walking, cruising doesn't help a child learn to walk any more than crawling does, which is not at all. Neither does *scooting*, also left out of Gesell's canon, in which a child drags herself across the rug on her bottom like a dog with an itchy anus.

lier that the phenomenon even acquired a name: African Infant Precocity Syndrome. It also acquired controversy, with researchers disagreeing on its cause and even on whether or not it exists. But most findings suggest that it does and the cause is sociocultural: African children reached milestones earlier because of the way they were held, touched, and encouraged to move. Genetic disposition was ruled out; when African children were raised in a more Western manner, the precocity disappeared.*

But sooner or later, one way or another, just about all children get up and walk. At times, this has been a mixed blessing. (A fourteenth-century French doctor called early childhood "the age of concussion.") In the past, a child who seemed to be on the verge of walking posed considerable safety hazards, and parents were far more likely to safety-proof the child than the house. They weren't terribly likely to do either, but did take a few precautions, like putting beginning walkers in a "falling cap" or "pudding." So named for its resemblance to black pudding, this was a sausage-shaped padded roll that went around the head and was kept in place with a chin strap. Having seen the pictures, I have to wonder if parents used them because they kept children safe or because they looked *hysterical*. They eventually disappeared, but left a linguistic remnant in the term of endearment *puddinhead*.

Parents also relied on leading strings, which were straps sewn to the back shoulders of a child's garment that a parent could use like reins to steer a beginning walker and keep him safely upright; or to tie that begin-

---

* In the United States it's a bit more complicated. On average, African American infants do hit their motor development milestones (holding their head up, standing, walking, etc.) ahead of their white counterparts. The reasons for this aren't well understood, but may include a combination of genetic and environmental factors. Bias must also be taken into account (we know from other studies, for instance, that whites routinely overestimate the ages of black children, especially when they're arresting, arraigning, or shooting them in so-claimed self-defense). So any causation remains unclear, and here be racist dragons, besides. For what it's worth, studies in the United States show that economically disadvantaged young children, whether black or white, develop motor skills faster. And a study in Ireland showed the opposite. Like I said, complicated (Theresa Overfield, *Biological Variation in Health and Illness: Race, Age, and Sex Differences*, 2nd ed. [Boca Raton, FL: CRC Press, 1995], 45; Martin McPhillips and Julie-Anne Jordan-Black, "The Effect of Social Disadvantage on Motor Development in Young Children: A Comparative Study," *Journal of Child Psychology and Psychiatry* 48, no. 12 [December 2007]: 1214–22).

ning walker to a fence post. Parents did both. Leading strings eventually fell out of favor, with critics warning that they could cause deformities, an awkward gait, "habitual indigestion," and "consumptive complaints." Not true, but I will note that leading strings disappeared right around the time flush toilets appeared, and given that the strings trailed quite a ways down the child's back, the timing was certainly fortuitous.

Child with pudding and leading strings.

Pudding caps could be quite decorative. Note that the fancy lady pictured here is actually a boy.

**POTTY TRAINING** has since become a milestone in its own right, which seems a bit odd. Marking milestones is generally a public affair; using the toilet is generally a private one. Celebrating it seems only slightly less awkward, than, say, throwing a party because the dog finally stopped humping the couch or because your seven-year-old conquered that nose-picking habit. While many of us post video of the first time our child smiles, walks, or eats his or her first cupcake, I would hope none of us share images from the first time there's progress in this particular department.

Not that I could blame anyone for wanting to celebrate. Caregivers spend so much time dealing with their infants' output that children and their waste have occasionally become synonymous. In France, newborns were once called *ecrême* (excrement); slightly older children, *merdeux* (turd). Yiddish has *pisher* (pisser), and who among us has not called her beloved child an asshole, a little shit? These, after all, are the parts we spend so much time with.

Potty training is a development that truly changes the whole family's life, opening up a whole new world of daycare options, of outings without cargo holds of Pampers and wipes, of disposable income instead of disposable diapers. There are accidents, sure, but you can go days at a time without seeing anyone's excreta but your own, a miraculous development.*

In any case, toilet training, like the toilet itself, is a fairly recent invention. Diapers have existed since medieval times, but were used only by children who weren't walking yet.† Once they were mobile, both boys and girls wore dresses without undergarments, in houses whose floors were made of dirt or rushes, and could go more or less anywhere they wanted. If they received any potty training at all, it was presumably to aim away from the furniture.

For most of history, adults weren't exactly potty trained either. Members of the Versailles court seem to have been particularly sloppy; one visitor described it as "the receptacle of all humanity's horrors—the passageways, corridors, and courtyards are filled with urine and fecal matter." And it's not like there was no proper place for them to go. The court featured the eighteenth-century equivalent of porta-potties, seated latrines that led to a cesspit. Should these be busy or locked, however, visitors simply did their business outside them, much like my childhood cat did, pointedly and deliberately, when the litter box was not up to her standards.

---

* To make them a little less maddening, my husband encouraged me to view floor accidents as good practice for what life will be like when I finally get the mini horse I'm dying to own.

† Though they date to the Middle Ages, diapers weren't widely used until the 1800s, two hundred long and unfortunate years after the introduction of upholstered furniture. *Diaper* originally referred to the diamond-patterned fabric diapers were made from, but many other items were made from it, too. Sixteenth-century texts occasionally refer to diaper tablecloths, which conjures quite an image for the modern reader.

Potty training isn't even discussed in print until 1693, when Locke devotes quite a bit of space to it in *Some Thoughts Concerning Education* (as critics have noted, the section on toilet training is ten times longer than the section on ethics). By the eighteenth century, toilet training would become fairly widespread, as would frequent use of suppositories and enemas to get things moving predictably.

Today, however, it's a development that develops much later than it used to. Twenty-first-century children hit almost every milestone from crawling to puberty months or years earlier than children a hundred years ago, but on potty training they're way, way behind. In the first half of the twentieth century, most children began before their first birthday and were completely trained by eighteen months. Now most children aren't trained until they are three, and for at least a couple of years are so inconsistent the smart parent makes them sit on pool towels. Pull-ups adorned with either superheroes or fairies come sized to fit children up to 125 pounds, a weight I did not hit until college.

Delayed potty training has a number of causes, but one of the main ones is simple convenience. Before, it was easier to make children's bathroom business their own business as early as possible; now it's easier to delay the battle and let them stew in diapers for three or four or five years. This is in large part due to the diapers themselves. When diapers had to be handwashed and air-dried, they were hardly worth the trouble. They were leaky and inconvenient, not to mention dangerous, given the open straight pins that held them in place. Frequent checks and changes required the attention of an adult who had little to spare. Today in areas where diapers aren't used—like China, India, and elimination communication* enclaves of Silver Lake and Park Slope—children become toilet trained far earlier.

But in the rest of the world we are content to take our sweet time. Busy panicking about hitting the other milestones on time, we apparently let this one slide. And why not? With the arrival of washing machines and, in the 1970s, disposable diapers, there was no rush to get the child on the

---

* For the unfamiliar, this is the practice of forgoing diapers in favor of learning to read your child's "cues," rushing them to a suitable receptacle when they cue that an excretory event is imminent.

potty. Better you should do it right. For decades leading up to that point, botched toilet training was being blamed for everything from homosexuality to World War II. This was largely due to Freud, who raised the stakes immeasurably. Before, if you got it wrong, you might ruin some linens; now you ruined the child's whole *life* and might even make him *gay*. Freud held that potty training was a major psychological milestone and, if done too early or too harshly, would stunt the child in the anal phase, rendering him rigid, uptight, mentally ill, and deviant.

In the 1940s, anthropologists including Margaret Mead and Geoffrey Gorer wondered if Japanese toilet training practices might be to blame for "the overwhelming brutality and sadism of the Japanese at war." Gorer—who served as a national profiler for the U.S. Office of War Information's Foreign Morale Analysis Division—believed that Japanese infants were potty trained before their sphincters were sufficiently developed, causing them to feel and repress rage they would later express by, say, bombing Pearl Harbor. Gorer charged: "'Early and severe' toilet training is the most important single influence in the formation of the adult Japanese character."

Many of Gorer's colleagues agreed, and the theory was widely circulated until later studies pointed out that the Japanese don't in fact toilet train earlier or more aggressively than Americans, and national interests, not bathroom habits, motivated the country's actions in World War II. As for Germany, the Harvard psychologist tapped by the Office of Strategic Services (the forerunner of the CIA) to profile Hitler concluded that strict toilet training may have been to blame there as well, producing a sadistic streak that would result in the extermination of eleven million people. In a similar vein, Freudian psychiatrist Mortimer Ostrow argued that anti-Semitism is a by-product of botched toilet training, in which a revulsion toward filth is displaced onto the Jews. A 1999 study would link it to neo-Nazism as well, blaming the forced communal potty training methods of postwar East Germany for the hate crimes of the 1990s.

Although eventually proved wrong, Freud's theories had a big influence on twentieth-century parenting books, most of which recommended delayed, gentle potty training techniques. As exemplified by Spock, the whole process would be child-directed, proceeding as the child showed readiness. For Spock, signs that the child is ready to start bowel training include taking pleasure in giving gifts and in putting things in containers, though I for one would be afraid to open any present from a child going through this process.

In America, coming as late as it does, potty training is the last milestone of early childhood, the last hurdle of the marathon, and the one that qualifies children for a whole host of new childcare venues. Cue the celebration: by this point, everything Gesell's timetables promised has come true. Children can sit, stand, walk, and wipe, and though they typically refuse to, when push comes to shove, they can brush the teeth whose arrival failed to kill them. There's still a lot to learn, but most of it they'll learn from someone else. The next few years are easy ones, and the endurance course of puberty is still so far off. It will get difficult again, the clock will melt and time will stretch, and then that will all be over, too.

Shortly after Beng babies receive their first enema,[*] their mother ties a string around their neck, to be worn night and day, making a blessing that it should never tear. The day one cord falls off, another is attached. And though I don't care for fiber jewelry, I sort of wish we had this ritual, too. Because the moment the first milestone is passed, the miles start to add up. The formless blob becomes a human, the crawling beast becomes bipedal, the inarticulate cries become words. The baby steps that seemed so tiny and slow become strides, and they all lead away.

When we were still in the worst of it, older parents would sometimes remind me that the days are long but the years are short. They left out the nasty and brutish part, I suppose, because they'd forgotten it. Not remembering how difficult the first few years really are, they'd urge me to treasure them, warning I would miss them when they were gone. At the time it just made me think of the old line about a bad restaurant: the food is terrible—and such small portions.

They were right, though. It's awful, and it goes by way too fast. The clock races and shudders. We were counting the minutes. Where did they go?

---

[*]  "Baby's first enema" is a milestone that does not exist in the Western world, but it's a significant event for the Beng, who use enemas as a mode of toilet training. This first one is a real firecracker: it's made with chili peppers, and is administered the day the baby's umbilical stump falls off, which marks the infant's entry into the world of the living (DeLoache and Gottlieb, *World of Babies*, 68).

# 5

# Tooth and Nail

*Feeding and Fighting*

About three minutes after I became a mother, I started worrying my child wasn't getting enough to eat. We'd just been through a long ordeal, and refreshments seemed in order for both of us. My daughter was looking so thin, and my milk wouldn't come in for a while, so in the meantime, how about a nice snack?

At the time I chalked this anxiety up to being Jewish, but it probably had a lot more to do with modernity. We worry that our children aren't eating enough, but parents in other eras worried more about them eating too much. Until pickiness was invented in the twentieth century, children ate indiscriminately. Until nutritional science was invented around the same time, experts offered parents dubious advice. They warned against letting children eat tomato with dairy, drink cold water with meat, or drink hard liquor with the help. Vegetables were pointless, fruit was dangerous, and beer and wine were perfectly fine, even for newborns. Everyone has an opinion, and one man's meat is another's anaphylactic reaction.

Though children's diets were never the fraught subject they are today, they were occasionally the cause of skirmishes. Sometimes the fights were between parents and children; sometimes between parents and experts;

sometimes between experts and scientific fact. As far back as the first century, experts had lots of ideas about feeding newborns, many conflicting and most of them wrong. The most fundamental of these was the belief, widely held by physicians and scientists including Galen, Hippocrates, and Aristotle, that breast milk was menstrual blood made white by heat, semen, or both. The question was, should the baby drink her parents' menstrual blood and semen, or another couple's? That is, should the mother herself breastfeed, or should a nurse be hired? Since milk was thought to transmit not just nutrition but character, this was a question that could determine the child's entire future.

Moralists like Tacitus, Favorinus, and Plutarch argued strongly for maternal breastfeeding, asking what kind of "unnatural, imperfect" mother would corrupt "the nobility of body and mind of a newly born human being, formed from gifted seeds," with "degenerate" milk from a slave or foreign barbarian who was "dishonest, ugly, unchaste and a wine-bibber" to boot. A couple of thousand years later, Thomas Phaire's 1546 *Boke of Children* would say more or less the same thing, urging parents to choose a nurse "who was no dronkard, vycyous nor sluttysshe, for such corrupte the nature of the chylde."

First-century physicians like Soranus were a little more easygoing, claiming that there were some good reasons to hire a wet nurse, like if the nurse's milk was superior, or if the mother wanted to avoid premature aging. But even if she planned to feed the baby herself, a mother should hire a nurse for the first few days, if not weeks. Soranus, like many others, mistook the antibody-rich colostrum for Cheez Whiz both in texture and nutritional value, insisting that it was bad for babies.[*] Instead, he said, the

---

[*] This belief was common to several ancient cultures, and is also mentioned in Brahminical texts of the second century BCE. In Europe, the belief that colostrum was harmful would persist into the eighteenth century, and in many parts of the world is still believed today. One study of 120 cultures found a full 50 where colostrum was considered dangerous for babies, who were given other substances (including honey) instead (Ian G. Wickes, "A History of Infant Feeding: Part III: Eighteenth and Nineteenth Century Writers," *Archives of Disease in Childhood* 28, no. 140 [1953]: 332–34; and Janice M. Morse, Corinne Jehle, and Diane Gamble, "Initiating Breastfeeding: A World Survey of the Timing of Postpartum Breastfeeding," *International Journal of Nursing Studies* 27, no. 3 [1990]: 303–13).

baby should be fed honey, which actually *is* bad for babies. As for wine-bibbers, Soranus correctly claimed that alcohol passes through breast milk and advised the nurse to lay off the bottle. The baby, however, was free to drink up, so long as the wine was watered down or poured over bread.

But what about the baby who had access to neither wet nurse nor sommelier? He would get animal milk or pap, for which recipes date back to the fifteenth century BCE. Baby bottle prototypes, made from glass, animal horn, and clay, have been around at least four thousand years. These came in a variety of shapes ranging from beaker-like vessels to multi-teated terra-cotta udders. Later versions resembled gravy boats and bananas. These could be made from glass, wood, pottery, or pewter, in which case the child received a dose of lead poisoning as well.

This was not the only problem. Wood, horn, and pewter are all hard, and glass and clay are both hard *and* breakable, making them a poor material for tender baby mouths with little tiny windpipes. Some mothers tried to fashion tips from softer materials, like leather or animal teats, but these were impossible to wash and great carriers of disease. When the rubber nipple was invented in 1845, it was no big improvement. Early versions, made from foully pungent India rubber, were like nursing from a car tire, and didn't stand up to repeated washings besides. It wasn't until the twentieth century that a durable, pleasant, nontoxic nipple finally came along.

Given these options, and the problem of spoilage, it's no surprise that many chose to serve animal milk straight from the tap. This was especially true in foundling homes, where whole herds were employed to feed the charges, who were placed directly at the teat. Though donkeys, sheep, deer, horses, cows, camels, dogs, and pigs were sometimes used, goats were more common and convenient, and were celebrated in an 1816 German book titled *The Goat as the Best and Most Agreeable Wet Nurse*. Goats were considered easier to manage than human wet nurses, though admittedly more likely to take a dump in the crib. On the other hand, they didn't transmit syphilis, and became the favored infant milk source in villages and foundling homes where the disease had become a problem.

This is not to say that the animal wet nurses' sexual and ethical habits weren't as much of a concern as the humans'. Since milk was thought to convey character, it was important that your baby be nursed by an animal of high moral standing. In this reckoning, goats, being the sluts of the barnyard, weren't nearly as desirable as the staid and sober donkeys. Slatternly pigs, naturally, were out of the question.

Most virtuous of all, of course, was the mother herself, and by the eighteenth century physicians and philosophers were encouraging mothers to take this job on themselves. Thanks to an earlier breast reduction, I performed the job very badly. As it turns out, my delivery room anxiety was well placed. I didn't know how to feed my daughter; she didn't know how to eat; and within a few days, she'd lost a dangerous amount of weight. My milk had not come in, and never really would. Despite several lactation consultants and six crazy-making weeks of fruitless pumping every four hours around the clock on a unit that I came to loathe—hooked up to pumps that looked like air horns, with a motor that was just as loud—I never managed to produce much more than two ounces of milk a day, about a tenth of what a newborn requires. As we lacked goats and wet nurses, we opted for formula, whose moral qualifications I did not have to worry about. Perhaps I should have, given that two of its ingredients, soybean oil and taurine, are also the relevant components of Coffee-Mate and Red Bull.* In any case, it did a fine job of keeping our daughter alive, which previous versions didn't always manage to do.

Commercial formulas have been around for about 150 years, since several prominent chemists independently began creating breast milk alternatives for their own feeding-challenged children. The first to become widely available was Justus von Liebig's Soluble Food for Babies. This was a blend of milk, flour, malt, and potassium bicarbonate, which was sold first as a liquid and later as a powder. Others quickly followed. Mostly these were starch-and-sugar blends to be added to milk, making it, essentially, what's left in the bowl after you've eaten all the cereal. Which is delicious, sure, but notably lacking in vitamins, minerals, lipids, proteins,

---

* Though it's a common ingredient in energy drinks—and the inspiration for Red Bull's name—taurine isn't really an upper. It's an amino sulfonic acid, and breast milk has lots of it. Thought to be crucial to neurological development, taurine has been added to infant formulas since 1984, and if there's any link between this and the rise of the X Games, it has not yet been studied.

and amino acids. Children developed scurvy and rickets, or failed to develop at all. The missing essentials would be added in the coming years, sometimes in the form of cod liver oil, which may be healthy but does not taste very good in cereal milk.

By 1882, there were twenty-seven infant formulas on the market. Mothers of a more DIY sensibility made their own according to various recipes they got from magazines or friends. Usually, homemade formula consisted of milk boiled with toasted flour and sugar. When sugar became expensive, doctors recommended corn syrup instead. Late into the twentieth century many American mothers served their babies a cheap formula of evaporated milk and Karo syrup, a nutritional disaster that also makes a fine basis for seven-layer bars.* (L. Ron Hubbard's formula recipe, still in use today, uses homogenized milk and adds barley water.)

Formula, initially a product of hard science, eventually became one of commerce, widely advertised in physician's journals and women's magazines. It was a highly successful campaign. In the early twentieth century, almost 70 percent of women breastfed; by 1950, only 25 percent did, and that number would continue to fall. Companies aggressively sought market share, most criminally when women in developing countries in Asia, Africa, and Latin America were convinced to replace free, healthy breast milk with expensive, less healthy formula. When it was watered down to make it last longer, children died of malnutrition. Other marketing moves weren't fatal, just stupid. In 2010, a chocolate-flavored formula was introduced and then quickly discontinued after a public health outcry. (A bacon-flavored baby formula offered online, with *4 Nutritious Servings of Bacon in Every Scoop!*, was only a hoax.)

FORMULA WAS THE FIRST food designed expressly for children, but many would follow. By the 1920s, harried mothers could buy Clapp's Baby Food in seventeen canned varieties, including every baby's favorite,

---

* Really, though, the bars should be made with sweetened condensed milk. And butterscotch chips.

liver soup.* Over the coming decades the offerings would grow more appealing. Now there are whole aisles devoted to their juice boxes and fruit gummies and viscous products in squeezable pouches. And almost every restaurant features a children's menu whose offerings invariably sound so much better than the adults' that it's only a sense of shame that keeps me from ordering off them.

But these developments are very new. For most of history, children ate what their parents ate, and that's if they were lucky. Often they just got the scraps, and frequently they weren't even allowed at the table to eat them. For centuries it was fairly typical for children to eat the parents' leftovers while standing somewhere off to the side. Siblings often shared a single plate and cup, and, if the family was fancy, a fork.† This is something I often think about while frantically cramming a dinner of rejected grilled cheese crusts into my mouth over the kitchen sink.

If children didn't like their lot, we don't hear much about it. There does not seem to have been much pushback, which is hard for me to imagine, given that I cook at least three and sometimes four different dinners every night out of a fear, and a reality, that if I don't make something they like, they won't eat at all.

As it turns out, this is the worry of our age—and *only* our age. The children of previous generations, it seems, were far less fussy, and the parents' primary concern wasn't that they ate too little, but too much. The phrase *picky eater*‡ didn't enter the lexicon until 1970, and the idea that

---

* Though designed for children, baby food was occasionally marketed to adults as well. In 1953 Beech-Nut published a cookbook to promote its products to all age groups. *Family Fare from Baby Foods: 100 Beech-Nut Recipes for the Entire Family* included recipes like the regrettable "Puree Mongole," a combination of Beech-Nut peas, tomato paste, sherry, curry, and cream (Amy Bentley, *Inventing Baby Food: Taste, Health, and the Industrialization of the American Diet* [Berkeley: University of California Press, 2014], p. 134). And in 1974 Gerber launched Singles by Gerber, a line of gloppy ready-to-eat jarred foods like Chicken Madeira and Beef Burgundy that was aimed at young adults. Unsurprisingly, it tanked.

† More likely they'd use their hands or a knife (knives were used as forks are today, and were viewed as personal property you carried on your person; if you were invited to dinner, you'd eat with your own knife). There was only one fork in all of Massachusetts Bay Colony, owned by Governor John Winthrop.

‡ *Picky* is fairly new, too, dating to 1867.

children would refuse food is very, very recent. Until about a hundred years ago, you almost never find parents or doctors worrying about it.[*] You do, however, find a lot of the opposite: worry that children eat too much. In *Some Thoughts Concerning Education*, Locke wrings his hands over children who insist on being "serv'd out of every dish," a concern that only grew over the next few centuries. By the late eighteenth century, William Buchan was lamenting that "Children in general are over-cloath'd and over-fed . . . To these causes I impute almost all their Diseases." By the nineteenth century, overfeeding was becoming a major concern in mothers' magazines and parenting books; Dr. Andrew Combe called it the "leading error in the rearing of the young." In 1870 *The Mother's Magazine* declared: "Most diseases of the age are produced by overfeeding. We all eat too much for either health or happiness. If a girl eats every three hours in a day, she is digging her own grave."

Victorians were particularly obsessed with the subject and its attendant condition, dyspepsia. In fact, many people probably were eating too much. Victorians typically ate twice as many calories per day as we do. Most were also twice as active as we are, and few Victorians were overweight. But this lifestyle was changing as the Industrial Revolution made work increasingly sedentary. The upshot was a good deal of indigestion, and an even greater deal of books and articles about indigestion.

Overeating was blamed for many childhood conditions, including, counterintuitively, being underweight. *The Mother's Magazine* warned, "The ill-shaped and slender-formed girls of the present period are the result of this cause. They are constantly chewing something—keeping the stomach constantly at work, except during the night; but they will surely learn from headaches, lassitude and general weakness the folly of this practice, when it may be too late to remedy its evil results."

And it was never too early to start limiting intake. In 1890, *Babyhood* magazine opined, "The foundation of the habit of overeating is

---

[*] Though you do occasionally encounter them *complaining* about it. As Linda Pollock documents, parents' diaries from the eighteenth century make some mention of the table-time battle to get kids to eat their damn food (Linda A. Pollock, *Forgotten Children: Parent-Child Relations from 1500 to 1900* [Cambridge: Cambridge University Press, 1983], 110, 157).

laid in childhood, and it is unquestionably true that nearly all persons eat much in excess of what they should. An eminent British physician is quoted as saying, 'one-fourth of what we eat goes to sustain life, while three-fourths goes to imperil it.' While another says that 'most people dig their own graves with their teeth.' To dig the grave of a naturally sound stomach before even the teeth come, is handicapping the little one indeed as he comes up through life's portal." Elsewhere the magazine recommends children follow a simple diet that includes, somehow, oysters.

Now it's pretty much a given that children won't touch the grown-up food, but for centuries, the problem, apparently, was that they couldn't stay away from it. In *The Rearing and Feeding of Children* (1895), Dr. Thomas Dutton cautioned, "Children will eat anything and everything that comes in their way, no matter how injurious it may be, neither do they possess the faculty of knowing when they have had enough." He warned parents not to let children join them at the table, lest they start angling for the parents' food like a dog who thinks he's people. Dr. Leroy Yale agreed, writing, "Nothing can well be worse than the habit of giving 'tastes' of things."

Unrestrained eating imperiled not only their bodies but their souls. In 1839 Reverend Thomas Hopkins Gallaudet maintained that "it ought never be forgotten that *the tendency of their animal nature is to excess*, and that this should be particularly guarded against when they come to the domestic table. Self-control in the use of food is one of the first and most important lessons which they should there be taught, and this in various respects."

American children were considered especially gluttonous, appalling European visitors with their eating habits. An English visitor complained, "As soon as he can sit at the table," the American child "chooses his own food, and as soon as he can speak argues with his parents on the propriety or impropriety of their directions."

In 1855's *Transatlantic Wanderings*, Captain John Oldmixon expressed wonder that American kids "do not die of clarified molasses and gobbling mixtures of rich food long before they become men and women!" Oldmixon recorded "an ordinary dialogue, which may be constantly heard all over the Union," between a parent and a child facing a plate already overloaded with food:

Child.—I want some ham.

Mother.—Well, you ain't no room.

Child.—I want some ham—(louder).

Mother.—I guess you won't like it. (To waiter) Hand the ham up. (Helps the little animal.)

Child.—I want some homany.

Though both boys and girls were warned not to overeat, girls were warned a whole lot more. Girls' books and magazines urged readers to curb their appetites, which, I suppose, they still do, only now the goal is not moral virtue but thigh gap. Stories with titles like "The Little Glutton"* were common, and instructed that "A young lady should be ashamed of exhibiting so lively a pleasure at the sight of anything to eat."

FOR BOTH BOYS AND GIRLS, the problem wasn't just that they ate too much, but that they ate foods unsuitable for their tender age. As Gallaudet wrote, "Children, too, should early be accustomed to see older persons at table using certain articles of food, without feeling that it is hard for them to be deprived of them." Largely due to the Victorian obsession with dyspepsia, by the end of the nineteenth century there was an increasing concern about what foods were appropriate for children's delicate stomachs. This was the beginning of special foods for kids, and though it would eventually lead to chicken nuggets, purple ketchup, and Lunchables, for the first several decades it meant the most bland and textureless

---

* A "Little Glutton" story also appears in an American edition of the horrifying German nightmare-generator, *Der Struwwelpeter* (see pages 243–44). In that iteration, the little glutton gets off easy: stung by bees when she tries to take their honey, she spends the next four weeks in bed, "and ah! Instead of honey, she on medicine was fed." The protagonist of "Augustus Who Wouldn't Eat His Soup"—one of the rare stories about children *refusing* food—meets a far more Struwwelpetery end. Augustus rejects his soup for four days, growing thinner and thinner, and "on the fifth day—he was dead!" Then there's the story of "Little Jacob and How He Became Fat," which (literally) splits the difference. His parents, frantic over his stick-thin frame, beg him to eat. He obliges, growing "as fat as he was thin before," and after putting away a little more, "he burst in two."

foods imaginable. These became known as nursery foods and for years to come would inspire a shudder in all who'd had to endure them. In taste and texture, they were little better than school paste (weirdly, a popular but forbidden snack in my own kindergarten class).

The invention of nursery foods doubled mothers' workload, as they now had to prepare two full menus at every meal, one of flavorless mush and one of actual food. To help these harried moms, the authors of the 1937 book *How to Feed Young Children in the Home* offered advice and recipes for children's foods that would appeal to children and adults alike. I have read it and can report that the chocolate cake and macaroni and cheese I could probably sell, but doubt I'd have many takers for the jellied tomato salad, liver loaf, lima beans baked in milk, fish soufflé, or prune tapioca pudding. All of which gives us a window into how much kids' foods have evolved, or devolved, depending on your particular tastes. As for mine, I will agree that cotton-candy-flavored yogurt pouches are a crime against nature, but on the other hand: codfish balls.

The widely prescribed bland diet of mush was due in no small part to Luther Emmett Holt, whose 1894 book *The Care and Feeding of Children* was the most popular and influential childcare book of its age. *Care and Feeding* is mostly concerned with the latter, with very detailed charts describing what the child should eat and when, all of it unappealing. Typical fare includes such favorites as barley gruel, rice jelly, oat water, stale bread, and something called "beef juice."[*] Children should be fed nothing overstimulating, which includes anything with recognizable color or texture. Food is to be boiled into abject submission: oatmeal should be cooked for no less than three hours, and fruits and vegetables must be stewed, strained, mashed, and sieved. Eggs are permissible if they are poached or soft-boiled, but never fried, and "most omelets are objectionable." Salads should not be served to a child under ten, and fresh produce is to be avoided, especially bananas. When Holt's son, also a physician, gave bananas the okay in the 1926 reprint of the book, it caused a minor controversy among his siblings.

Holt's attitude toward fruit, though baffling now, was nothing new. Locke was a weirdo about fruit, too, writing, "Fruit makes one of the most

---

[*] Actually just broth.

difficult chapters in the government of health, especially that of children."
In part because of its association with Eden, and in part because of the
disgusting market practices of the time, a lot of people were wary of this
particular food group. Often fruit was not all that widely available, and
what did arrive at market was filthy at best, or cleaned in the vendor's own
saliva at worst.* If only because it was so repellent, an apple a day could in
fact keep the doctor away.

Locke does permit some fruit under certain conditions. Berries, cher-
ries, and pears are okay, as long as they are eaten only when ripe, only in
moderation, and never on an empty stomach. As for watermelons, peaches,
plums, and grapes, however, "I think children should be wholly kept from,
as having a very tempting taste, in a very unwholesome juice: so that if
it were possible, they should never so much as see them, or know there
were any such things." Following the polemic against eating fruit, Locke
thoughtfully provides advice on dealing with your child's constipation.

Other contemporaries of Locke thought fruit was fine as long as it was
fermented to, say, thirty proof. Though viewed with horror now (at least in
the United States), alcohol has been commonly given to even the youngest children since ancient times, and was certainly common in Locke's
own time. Locke recommends children avoid hard liquor and wine, but
endorses beer as healthier than water. He was probably right. Beer, which
was fermented and boiled, was far less likely to sicken drinkers than water
of dubious origin. It was also more nutritious and was served to grown-
ups and children alike at every meal, including breakfast. And while it's
fun to imagine all of Europe's children half in the bag for hundreds of
years, this was not actually the case. Their primary drink was small beer,
a very low alcohol brew. Often unfiltered and somewhat chunky, this was
basically liquid bread, and was a primary source of calories and nutrition. It began to fall out of favor only in the seventeenth and eighteenth

---

* In centuries past, giving the wares a tongue bath was commonly practiced by service workers of all types, including the household help, who used their own saliva
to clean the family silverware, a practice whose history remains in the phrase *spit-
polish*. While admittedly dis-*gust*-ing, saliva does have antibacterial properties and
enzymes that make it an ideal cleanser for many items, including old artwork. Fruit,
though: gross.

centuries, when coffee, tea, and chocolate—which offered boiled water plus caffeine—became more common. Still, children didn't stop drinking alcohol entirely. In the United States and the UK, the sale of liquor to children would not become illegal until the late nineteenth century, and that was only the *sale;* in the UK, at least, actual consumption of liquor by minors remained perfectly fine. Even today, it's totally legal to serve alcohol to a British child over five in a private home, as long as you don't charge her for it.*

Meanwhile, fruit remained suspect into the early twentieth century. According to *Babyhood* magazine, many people "regarded fruit in a child's stomach as something quite diabolical." An article promoting fruit for children as healthy still included lots of warnings about how to serve it and when: "Fruits are always 'golden' in the morning and every hour thereafter depreciate in value until night, when they are worse than useless for children—dangerous." Nineteenth-century British court records often attributed childhood fatalities to "death by fruit."

Vegetables weren't considered much better. A lengthy 1890 article on "Vegetables as Food for Young Children" is full of cautions: Carrots are too much for a child's stomach. Lettuce is permitted if dressed only with salt. After age four, tomatoes are okay if stewed but not if served at a meal involving dairy. Most vegetables should not be given to a child younger than three or four. At eighteen months, the only advisable vegetables are potato and rice, which I'm pretty sure isn't a vegetable at all. And, like fruit, vegetables may only be eaten early in the day: "In giving vegetables to children it hardly need be said that they are not to be given after the midday meal." Unthinkably to the modern reader, there's no discussion of children's distaste for vegetables or advice for hiding them in more appealing foods.

---

* In the puritanical U.S., of course, it's alcohol that's the forbidden fruit, a policy that may or may not produce more binge drinkers. Prohibition seems to have produced more underage ones, in any case; after its passage, hospitals saw the numbers of minors admitted for alcohol poisoning increase dramatically. And Michele Humes blames Prohibition for something even worse: the creation of the children's menu. Trying to make up for the lost revenue of liquor sales, she argues, restaurants tried to attract a whole new junior clientele by making menus just for them ("Feeding the Kiddie," *Slate*, August 7, 2013).

Although the height of virtue now, for centuries vegetables were viewed as little more than a waste of time. (As Bill Bryson writes, "Vegetables were eaten mostly by those who could afford nothing better.") Until vitamins were discovered in the early twentieth century, fruit and vegetables were considered empty calories at best, hazardous filler at worst. It was true that overconsumption, especially of fruit, could cause dangerous diarrhea. Of course, the lack thereof could cause dangerous bowel obstructions. Ann Hulbert would not fail to mark this aside in a letter from the fruit-phobic Luther Emmett Holt's wife to their son Emmett, Jr.: "Father encloses pills for constipation." Well, thank goodness for that.

THERE WERE NOT, however, pills for the problem that would start to develop shortly thereafter: pickiness. Over the next several decades we start to hear more and more about children who will not eat what they're served. Given the diet Holt prescribed, it's hard not to blame them. It's also hard not to blame Holt and his like-minded colleagues, at least in part. To be fair, picky eaters certainly existed before Holt, as did unappealing foods. But it does seem notable that immediately after Holt's reign as the premier expert on children's diets, we suddenly start hearing from mothers worried about their self-starving kids. Before long, this will become an actual clinical condition doctors will call anorexia. (Note that this is not the anorexia that would launch a thousand after-school specials. The Latin means "lack of appetite," and in the early twentieth century, it was essentially the technical term for very picky eaters.)

If nothing else, Holt and his colleagues helped make children's food, previously a fairly straightforward subject, a matter of great anxiety. By 1916 Lena and William Sadler, the physician authors of *The Mother and Her Child*, were reporting that feeding children had become such a fraught activity it was leading to divorce. "The children were constantly cross, and so much of the mother's time was consumed in caring for these irritable, half-fed babies, that the home was disheveled, the meals never ready, the husband's home-coming was a dreaded occurrence, and he, endeavoring to seek rest and relaxation, usually sought for it in the poolroom or saloon, with the usual climax which never fails to bring the time-honored results of debauch—despair and desertion." Mothers did not know what or how to feed their children, and the children apparently did not like what they came up with. In a 1930 address to the American Pediatric Society, Dr. Joseph Brennemann suggested that the cure was actually the cause. In trying to get children to eat better, we created children who didn't want to eat at all:

> Probably no department of medicine has been more diligently and more fruitfully investigated than that of infant and child hygiene and nutrition, and in none has there been more salutary progress. Through innumerable agencies this information has been broadcast to the laity as well as to physicians. Intelligent mothers everywhere have eagerly sought this information and have as eagerly and intelligently sought to apply it in the light of their instructions. A nutritional millennium seemed at hand. And then a strange thing happened. The child refused to eat. I know of no stranger paradox than this: The better intentioned the home, the better the food, the more precise the application of feeding rules and regulations, the more stubborn the refusal.

If Brennemann's anecdotal evidence is to be believed, picky eating quickly became epidemic. He continues, using *anorexia* in its nineteenth-century sense: "Now anorexia is not an occasional occurrence, an isolated phenomenon in childhood; it is the rule in that very stratum of society in which mothers are lying awake nights planning a Gospel diet and the most effective way of administering it. The lowest estimate of its incidence in private practice that I know of is 50 per cent. A scientific survey in a university neighborhood and a pediatrician with a large office practice in a prosperous suburb have placed it at 80 and 85 per cent, respectively. A prominent pediatrist recently said that he had 'paid for his house with anorexia!'" Interestingly, the problem seemed to affect only the well-off. As Brennemann points out, it was almost never seen in orphanages, where the food presumably was even worse.

Doctors scrambled to find solutions. In his bestselling book *The Normal Child: Its Care and Feeding*, prominent Canadian pediatrician Alan

Brown urged parents to stop feeding picky eaters altogether, starving them until they were hungry enough to eat what they were served.

Others took a more child-directed approach. The most notable of these was another Canadian pediatrician, Clara Davis, who conducted an astounding experiment to see what would happen if small children were allowed to choose everything they ate.

Because this was in 1926 and largely unregulated scientists still could do whatever they wanted, she acquired infants aged six to eleven months (two of whom she would later adopt) from indigent teen moms and widows. The children were housed in the ward of a Cleveland hospital (the study later moved to Chicago), where they were regularly offered selections from a list of thirty-four items that included milk, fruit, vegetables, and whole grains, as well as brains, bone jelly, bone marrow, and beef, the latter two served both cooked and raw. Nurses were instructed to help the babies eat the food they chose, but not to steer or deter them in any way.

The children made some rather eccentric choices. As Davis reported, "they tried not only foods but chewed hopefully the clean spoon, dishes, the edge of the tray, or a piece of paper on it." They repeatedly helped themselves to fistfuls of salt. Many went on "jags" where they ate a single food over and over before moving on to something else. Sometimes they ate little, and sometimes, more than an adult (notably, six hard-boiled eggs on top of a full meal; or five bananas in a single sitting). One boy seems to have been particularly fond of orange sections, once eating a daily total of 800 grams (nearly two pounds).

Over the course of the study, however, their idiosyncrasies evened out. The children all chose different things (though brains and bone marrow were apparently popular with most), but each child, on the whole, ended up with a balanced and complete diet. Sickly and scrawny on arrival, the children quickly became healthy and well nourished, relying on what Davis termed "body wisdom" to choose the foods their bodies needed.

For decades, the study was used to prove the argument that left to their own devices, children will naturally eat a healthy and balanced diet. More recent criticism has pointed out that what it actually proves is that children will naturally eat a healthy and balanced diet when they're *provided* only healthy and balanced foods. Davis's study excluded processed foods, refined flours, and sugar. She'd planned to conduct a follow-up experiment to see what would happen if children could choose from processed foods as well, but the Depression got in the way, and the study was never done.

Not in a clinical setting, anyway. In an uncontrolled and undocumented way the study has been ongoing for the past ninety years. This massive accidental experiment has shown that given a little bit of choice, children are no more likely to eat what their bodies need than I am, which is not at all, unless my body actually does require Diet Mountain Dew and candy corn. As Davis's own study proved, small children often try to eat things that aren't even *food*—for instance, serving utensils, for which we have no nutritional requirements. My own children did this a lot. Though picky now, my son was quite indiscriminating as an infant, prone to experimentally cramming new items in his mouth; rocks were particularly tempting. He was also partial to things that were once food but were now toxins, like the cup of juice abandoned behind an armchair weeks earlier that had since turned into a substance that is known in prison as toilet wine.

Spock discusses Davis's study at length in *Baby and Child Care*, using her findings to encourage parents to take a more relaxed approach to feeding. It was normal and okay for kids to balk at vegetables and other new foods. The best way to deal with it was not to deal with it at all. By getting worked up about it, he wrote, you could turn a minor, temporary issue into a lifelong one.

THIS IS INDEED what happened over the next half-century, as children grew fussier and fussier, though whether this was because parents ignored Spock's advice or followed it is unclear and probably beside the point. Kids started wanting specific foods because there were now foods marketed specifically to them.

For the connoisseur of processed foods, this was the Renaissance. The phrase *junk food* was coined, as was the cuisine itself in a million delicious forms, including new imports like pizza. The major fast-food chains all emerged in the 1950s, as did ranch dressing and ranch dressing's best friend, Tater Tots. Despite the name, these were not originally developed as a way to get children to eat more frozen shredded, fried potatoes, but as a way to use up potato shavings left over from the manufacture of other products. But kids loved them, as did pretty much anyone with a mouth.

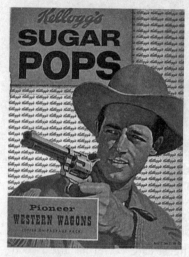

Sugar Pops, now fortified with firearms
*(Courtesy theimaginaryworld.com)*

Kids also loved cereal, and in the 1950s it took off in a big way. Previously targeted at health nuts, after World War II it was aggressively marketed to children using cartoon characters and sugar. The 1950s saw the introduction of Sugar Smacks, Sugar Smiles, Sugar Rice Krinkles, Sugar Crisp, Sugar Pops, Sugar Jets, Sugar Stars, Sugar Frosted Flakes, and Corn-Fetti, "a new kind of corn flakes with the magic sugar coat!"[*] Trix, which we all know is for kids, came on the market containing 46 percent sugar. Sugar Smacks clocked in at 55 percent.

Sugar was the magic fairy dust of the age. Though most of the really great candy bars had been invented between the two world wars, these were rationed, and fully half went to soldiers. But by the fifties, rationing was over, freeing up a lot of sugar that could go directly into kids' mouths. Food scientists came up with ingenious new ways to deliver the product. The decade's innovations included refrigerated cookie dough, instant frosting, Peeps, and candy necklaces. The fifties also saw the invention of Pixy Stix, the most efficient sugar delivery system short of an IV line. For kids who actually wanted to

---

[*] You've probably eaten most of these. In the 1980s cereal companies started replacing the sugar in the title, while keeping it in the actual cereal. Sugar Smacks became Honey Smacks; Sugar Crisp became Golden Crisp; Sugar Pops became Corn Pops; and Sugar Frosted Flakes became plain old Frosted Flakes, and formed the basis of my diet in college.

In the 1960s, Post replaced its utterly terrifying clown mascot with an utterly racist one named So-Hi, which I'm guessing amused '60s teenage potsmokers no end. *(Courtesy theimaginaryworld.com)*

smoke or shoot their sugar, there were candy cigarettes and, by the 1960s, a candy-filled PEZ gun. And for the youngest eaters, Gerber and Beech-Nut offered full lines of baby desserts including Blueberry Buckle and Strained Caramel Cream Pudding.

Interestingly, it was around the time that the marketing of children's food went into overdrive that the timeline to start eating solids accelerated drastically. Until the end of the nineteenth century, babies generally didn't begin eating solids until nine months or a year. But the start date rolled back as more prepared foods became available. By 1954, four to six weeks was becoming standard. Two-thirds of doctors advised mothers to start solids before two months, and a full 90 percent advised it by three.

One doctor in particular recommended getting things going ASAP. This was Walter Sackett, whose 1962 book *Bringing Up Babies* advocated a drastically shortened timeline for a number of milestones, including the resumption of intercourse after birth, which, he says, may occur on the new mother's first night home from the hospital. Hopefully she gets some shut-eye afterward, because the next morning she'll be feeding her neonate choking hazards. Sackett recommends starting infants on solid foods while still in the hospital nursery, with cereal twice daily starting on day 2. By day 10, they may eat strained vegetables; by two weeks, strained meat. Day 17 brings a meat/soup combo, permitting children to enjoy minestrone before they're three weeks old. Tomato juice is allowed at three weeks, and by nine weeks, they should be eating bacon and eggs, "just like dad." And though Wasp babies are best off avoiding highly spiced foods, Sackett reports that Italian American babies take to pizza and spaghetti "like ducks to water."

Pasta puttanesca is fine, then, so long as it's not washed down with a cup of milk. Because *that* is unhealthy; it is too high in fat, and should be avoided once the child turns one. Sackett devotes an entire chapter to the subject, titling it "Milk, the World's Most Overrated Food." A far healthier alternative, he writes, is coffee, though uptight parents may, if they insist, substitute decaf.

Parents proved pretty uptight. Sackett reported that this was what he received the most complaints about, but nonetheless, he doubled down. "Don't scream when you find me recommending tea and coffee for babies. Yes, I know they contain caffeine, and that caffeine is a drug. The same drug is in the cola drinks, which many mothers give their children, and I much prefer the caffeine of coffee and tea to the combination of drugs and sugar found in the carbonated beverages." Coffee and tea, served black, were best. "These 'grown-up' beverages can be offered occasionally, and in small quantities at first, beginning at six or seven months of age."

As for dealing with picky eaters, Sackett recommends the child be served the food he refused to eat at the last meal before he's allowed to eat anything else, even if it's a "wilted and unappetizing" salad. Sackett has no patience for Spocky laid-backness, which he blames for communism. "Increasingly, we are substituting dependency for initiative, which if not checked, will eventually lead to socialism. . . . This all has its beginnings, in my mind, in the demand philosophy of infant feeding, to which I am therefore unalterably opposed."

In a democracy, you eat what you get and YOU LIKE IT. Sackett believes that authoritarian feeding methods are necessary to produce democratic babies, and feeding on demand is a one-way ticket to Red Square. The responsible mother won't even feed *herself* on demand, and must take care to limit pregnancy weight gain to fourteen to twenty-two pounds. For this reason, Sackett discourages the expectant mother from drinking; the alcohol isn't bad for the baby, he says, but it packs on pounds for the mom.[*]

His advice is, of course, nuts, but like a sippy cup of hot java, Sackett goes down easy. Though he disagrees with Spock on nearly every practical point, what Sackett *does* take from Spock is an engaging, encouraging, you-can-do-this tone. His book is so readable and reassuring that I couldn't help but find myself thinking, Yes, I *can* feed my newborn buffalo wings. Double espressos for my toddler? Why the hell not! Sackett sounds weirdly reasonable even when he's suggesting things we now know to be insane.

IT WAS AN INSANE-MAKING TIME. By the sixties kids were getting pickier and pickier, as reflected by one of the decade's bestsellers, *Green Eggs and Ham*. The book was not actually written to encourage fussy eaters to eat, but to make Seuss's editor Bennett Cerf eat his words. (Cerf had bet Seuss he couldn't write a book using fifty words or less.) *Green Eggs and Ham* hit it on the nail, and Geisel won fifty dollars, or would have, but Cerf never paid. Presumably, the royalties from the book made up for it. *Green Eggs and Ham* became the fourth-bestselling children's hardcover of all time and was translated into many languages, including Hebrew, where it's called *Lo Ra'ev Velo Ohev* (I'm not hungry and I don't like it) and the green meat is never specified.

*Green Eggs and Ham*'s success was due in no small part to the fact that so very many children could identify with a protagonist who didn't want to try something new. Within ten years, the phrase *picky eater* would enter

---

* To be fair to Sackett, these guidelines were pretty standard for the time. I was born during this era, and my mother's OB-GYN was so strict about weight gain that she always went for a haircut before her checkups, hoping it would shave off a few ounces at weigh-in. For the same reason she continued to smoke throughout my gestation, a feat she's still proud of as, she tells me, it was really hard to fit in a full pack a day what with all the nausea. The cigarettes kept down both her weight and mine, and my mother often recommended it as an excellent method for producing easy-to-deliver babies.

the lexicon, and we would all know someone who, like Mikey, won't eat it because he hates everything.*

Those kids were eating *something*, however. Oddly enough, from the 1970s through the 1990s—the period when the concept of picky eating became mainstream—kids were actually eating *more*, consuming a couple of hundred additional calories a day than children previously did.† They were also eating far more often. Victorians may have consumed twice as many calories as we do, but they ate less frequently, usually going six to seven hours between meals. By 1977, children were eating every four hours; by 2006, they were eating every three.

Which may be partly responsible for the untouched plates at dinner. Meanwhile, the numbers seem to be increasing: today a full 50 percent of parents claim their children are picky eaters. My son is one of these children, and coincidentally, he bears the same name as one of *Green Eggs and Ham*'s main characters. Sam will not eat green foods of any kind, eggs in any form, or any food that is not one of the ten or so things he likes. He will not eat them here or there; he will not eat them anywhere. His pickiness is so extreme that, two years ago, his pediatrician referred us to an occupational therapist to address it. There we learned there is little consensus regarding treatment for pickiness, or even whether it should be treated at all. Some argue for intervention, while others stress ignoring the behavior; some recommend carrot, while others insist on stick. We tried all the methods, but none of them got Sam to eat carrots or anything else. His list of favored foods has only shrunk, and we're just grateful things aren't worse. Children with the most severe form of picky eating—known as avoidant/restrictive food intake disorder, or ARFID—often require a feeding tube.

Sam has a milder form we call BARFID: when he tries new foods, he vomits. This routine means we almost never eat out, and when we do, we

---

* Make what you will of the (untrue) urban myth that the actor who played Mikey died from eating something he shouldn't (Pop Rocks and Coca-Cola).

† The trend then reversed. Between 1999 and 2010, children's average daily caloric intake went down by a similar amount (R. Bethene Ervin and Cynthia L. Ogden, "Trends in Intake of Energy and Macronutrients in Children and Adolescents from 1999–2000 Through 2009–2010," *NCHS Data Brief* no. 113 [February 2013]: 1–8).

must leave very, very large tips. It also means we've pretty much given up on introducing new things.

The vomiting is Sam's special twist, but refusing new foods is common enough to have a name. Called neophobia, most children have it to a degree, and it tends to decrease with age. The exceptions are a small window around four to seven months, and another period around age two, when a child is actually *more* likely to try new foods. If that happened in Sam's case, I was too busy cleaning up vomit to notice. Meanwhile, Sam continues to survive mostly on pizza, the one food eaten by people who'll only eat one food. The first time Sam ate pizza, it was a where-have-you-been-all-my-life experience. It is his favorite food, and often his only food, even though its primary ingredients—bread, cheese, and tomatoes—he will eat in no other form.

Sam will also eat just about any kind of candy, no matter how revolting. Revolting candy is in fact an entire industry, with products including sour farts; gummi pimples; candy scabs; candy earwax; candy crime-scene samples of blood, saliva, and urine; chocolate poop; chocolate-covered Dingle Bearies; Sour Flush toilet candy (with candy plunger); and candy snot, available in at least three different forms (solid, liquid, and jelly bean), which makes one more form than *actual* snot comes in. As far as my son is concerned, all of these monstrosities are wonderful. Rice, however, makes him gag.

Clearly, Sam's definition of disgusting is different than mine. Because I like only delicious foods, I'd expected my children to share my tastes. In fact, they're primed to: amniotic fluid is flavored by the mother's diet, and infants usually express a preference for these familiar tastes. Once they can make their own choices, however, they invariably order off menu. The correlation between what parents and children (even grown children) like to eat is very, very low. As a daughter, I know this—I do not share my parents' taste for mushrooms and mayonnaise (which are objectively disgusting). But as a mother, I don't understand how Sam can dislike tacos (objectively delicious).

In any case, it's what he finds disgusting that matters more. As food historian Bee Wilson argues, it's not desire that drives children's food choices so much as disgust. Their need to avoid something gross (which apparently does not include chocolate poop) is stronger than their hope to eat something good. If they miss out on something delicious, they don't particularly care, because they literally do not know what they're missing. It's a built-in evolutionary response. We're wired to like sweet and familiar (even a candy toilet), and to fear bitter and new. This is the body's way of avoiding poison. I suppose it made sense a million years ago, but it makes less sense now that it's the reason my son won't eat corn.

Wilson also points to another poison-protection system that psychologist Paul Rozin calls the contagion of disgust—our tendency to avoid not only whatever caused the nausea, but whatever came in contact with it.[*] A brief list of things ruined by their association with the continuous nausea I felt in early pregnancy: the Costco snack bar, the theme songs of all Disney Junior cartoons, maternity jeans, East Texas, and fall. I still avoid the co-op I shopped at in my first trimester, because its smell of brewer's yeast instantly brings it all back.

Associations cling to food. This is why Victorians wouldn't eat fruit, why the ancients demanded virtuous wet nurses. It may also be why Sam likes pizza and hates cucumbers, besides the obvious fact that pizza is amazing and cucumbers are, at best, so-so. When pizza entered his life, it was brought to our house by someone who *rang the bell*, a rare occurrence that's as thrilling for toddlers as it is for dogs. No one yelled at him to eat it; he got to enjoy it in front of the TV; and it probably came with brownies. Cucumbers, however, are served garnished with desperate threats.

It has, I suppose, left a bad taste in his mouth. The question is whether this is metaphorical or literal. Because an alternate theory is that things just taste different to Sam. Children have many more taste buds than adults do.[†] Sam may have even more than most, if he, like me, is a genetic

---

[*] Nausea is an incredibly powerful deterrent; the very thought inspires dread. My cousin once told me about a study that showed that people with seasickness, a condition that is never fatal, had much higher levels of suicidal ideation than people with *terminal illnesses*, because nausea is just that unbearable. I never managed to track the study down, so I don't know if it's true, but anecdotally, the one time I felt ready and willing to die was while sailing to Catalina.

[†] Newborns' sense of taste may carry even more associations. Research done by Daphne Maurer and Catherine J. Mondloch suggests that children are born synesthetes, with intermingled senses that don't get sorted out until the brain develops a

supertaster, one of the 25 percent of people who can taste bitter compounds others can't. Or he may, like his father, be an undertaster who misses many flavors entirely, his sense of taste dulled by chronic hay fever.

Or he may just be giving me the business. Children learn very early on that food is one area in which they can wield some agency. Long before they can control what comes out of their bodies, they're controlling what goes into them. If this is Sam's power play, it's one I probably have coming, having used food as a cudgel for most of my adolescence. I put my parents through a good ten years of mealtime torture, becoming kosher, then anorexic, then vegetarian, then going on a series of increasingly baroque fad diets. I'm now getting a taste of my own medicine, and it doesn't taste good to me either.

When your child will eat candy acne but not a piece of toast, it's hard not to feel like you've failed, and my only comfort is that we appear to be in good company. In the four decades since *Green Eggs and Ham* came out, books about picky eaters and how to deal with them have become a small industry, ranging from *Picky Micky: The Boy Who Thought New Food Was Icky Icky* to the more pointed *You Have to F*****ing Eat.*

The books addressed to kids always end, like *Green Eggs and Ham*, with the child discovering that the suspect food actually *is* delicious. And while I hope our story ends that way, too, that doesn't seem likely right now. We've tried everything, and there's nothing new to try. Picky eating is a recent phenomenon, and the research on it has barely begun. We don't know what causes it or how common it is. And we certainly don't know how to fix it.

---

bit more. Which would mean they hear, see, smell, and feel flavors as well as taste them, in which case I would want to stick to plain milk, too (Daphne Maurer and Catherine Mondloch, "Synesthesia: A Stage of Normal Infancy?" in S. Masib, ed., *Proceedings of the 12th Meeting of the International Society for Psychophysics*, [Padua, October 1996]: 107–112; Daphne Maurer and Catherine J. Mondloch, "Neonatal Synesthesia: A Re-evaluation," in Lynn Robertson and Noam Sagiv, eds., *Synesthesia: Perspectives from Cognitive Neuroscience* [New York: Oxford University Press, 2005], 193–213; Daphne Maurer and Catherine J. Mondloch, "The Infant as Synesthete?" in Yuko Munakata and Mark Johnson, eds., *Processes of Change in Brain and Cognitive Development: Attention & Performance XXI* [New York: Oxford University Press, 2006], 447–69).

What ends up working in *Green Eggs and Ham*, ultimately, is doing nothing at all. "Sam! If you will let me be, I will try them. You will see," the protagonist promises, and then he does. I'll do nothing whenever I can, and I'm starting to think it's the most effective response to the battles over eating. We've come to believe that's the best thing to do with our foods, leaving them largely unprocessed and whole; perhaps that's also the best thing to do with our children's tastes. It's what Spock urged seventy years ago, and what Brennemann urged fifteen years before that. Ignorance seems to have worked for the last few thousand years; and intervention, for the last hundred, rather poorly. Devoting more attention to the issue has only made it worse. We've made a meal of it, and I wonder if it's time to stop.

This suits Sam just fine, who would rather make a meal, as he did today, out of four Danimals and a Popsicle. Maybe he'll broaden his palate, achieve full adult height, and hang on to his teeth; maybe he won't and will turn out just fine anyway, happy and oblivious, because that's who he is. If we let him be, he might try it, we will see. He could do this or that, here or there, anywhere. He would, he could, our Sam-I-Am.

# 6

# All the World's a Stage
## Acting Your Age

Perhaps because spit-up and suede doublets are such a bad combination, we don't often think of Shakespeare as a father. It seems likely he didn't either. He rarely saw his three children, and if they were ever on his mind, you wouldn't know it. He left close to a million words, but very few of them address children in general, and almost none address his own.[*] I suppose he had better things to do. In any case, it's tough to picture Shakespeare bathing a toddler or waiting up for a teenager to come home. And in fact he couldn't have, if for no other reason than toddler and teenager were categories that simply didn't exist at the time.

We think of life stages as universal and inevitable, but they aren't at all. Toddlers, tweens, and teens are modern categories; other eras had entirely different stages and different expectations. Even when they used the same words, they often meant something else. In medieval times *child* meant fetus and *baby* meant a child of any age; in the nineteenth century, *toddler*

---

[*] This may have less to do with neglect than the fact that Shakespeare's children were likely illiterate, as was his wife. But we don't really know. Shakespeare coined the phrases *flesh and blood* and *mum's the word,* but on his own flesh and blood he's just that: mum.

meant an old person. The child we'd call a toddler today used to be called a *run-about,* which now means a motorized scooter advertised on daytime TV. *Infant* could refer to a child too young to talk (it literally means "without speech") or to a child as old as seven. As a modern legal term, infant applies until age eighteen, and thus to my burly neighborhood frat boys. Given that they, like my infant son, occasionally discard bottles and pants in my front yard, this makes a kind of sense.

Both the frat boys and my young son are acting their age, in that every age is, to a certain extent, an act. Even in Shakespeare's time, *stage* referred both to the theater and to a phase of life; thus "All the world's a stage" was a deliberate play on words.[*] Stages are less biological than cultural; they are rehearsed and performed, complete with pageantry and set pieces: *Act 1, scene 7: Preschool Graduation. Interior. Day.* Begin scene.

Although I'm allergic to live theater, I've found this idea tremendously comforting. So much of childhood seems biologically preordained. It's been nice to think we can take some dramatic license with it, skipping the boring parts, toning down the conflict, maybe adding a dance number or two. Sometimes my cast cooperates (we did not have terrible twos); and sometimes they don't (we did have terrible threes). I'm not sure what they've got planned for the next few years, but I'm hoping we can skip the rebellious adolescence altogether, perhaps by moving someplace where troubled teens haven't been invented yet.

If all the world's a stage, every corner of the world views those stages differently. Few languages have a word for toddler or preschooler; many languages, especially older ones, don't have one for fetus. In ancient Latin, *fetus* can apply to the child both in utero and after it's emerged. Ancient Hebrew doesn't really have a word for fetus at all, though it once used the rather surprising term *golem* (literally, "unformed substance").[†] The Chinese word for fetus is similar; it can mean "stuffing," "padding," or "wadding." The French word for toddler, *bambin,* can apply to a child

---

[*] This phrase seems to have held particular meaning for Shakespeare. The Latin version, *Totus mundus agit histrionem,* was the motto of his Globe Theatre.

[†] For etymology nerds, the modern Hebrew word for fetus is *ubar,* and comes from the root word meaning "to pass over," the same root from which the word *Hebrew* itself derives (in that case, meaning "someone from the other shore").

anywhere from ages two to ten.* English doesn't have any special terms for a boy or girl circling puberty, but Talmudic Hebrew has several. Ancient Greek had a specific name for the age at which a boy was expected to start dating older men. The cues vary by audience, by scenery; stage is sometimes determined not by age but location, changing as you move from East to West, or from inside to out. An eight-month-old is a fetus if it's in the womb, but a newborn if it's outside of it.†

Even when we're just dealing with numbers, the numbers can mean different things. In the United States, a child who's been out of the womb 366 days is one, but in countries that use East Asian age reckoning, which counts from conception, he's two. Some cultures add a year on your birthday, and some on the calendar new year. Even the length of the year can vary, with the lunar calendar clocking in eleven days shorter than the Gregorian. Were I to fly to Shanghai, I would find myself twelve hours ahead and two full years older.

On some level, any parent knows how mutable age categories can be, especially when tickets are involved and rounding down means free admission. Still, the ones we have feel so natural and eternal that it's hard to believe there was a time when there weren't terrible twos or goth teens. The lack of black lipstick in the historical record, however, suggests that these are unique to us. So, too, are baby showers, kindergarten graduations, and the mortifications of middle school. The rites of passage that mark our life stages would dumbfound any seventeenth-century time traveler, whose own watershed moments, like breeching—when a school-age boy got his first pair of pants in a ceremony that included both guests and refreshments—no longer exist. My own son got his first pair of pants a few days after he was born. I remember nothing about it, but if it was like every other event that week, he marked the occasion with spit-up so copious it soaked through three layers.

In Shakespeare's time, breeching was observed with a bit more deco-

---

* *Le Bambin* denotes the infant Jesus. I think we can agree a straight English translation—The Toddler—lacks solemnity.
† Because we watched a lot of *The Wire* during my first pregnancy, we used a variant metaphor, describing the birth as coming out of solitary and joining gen pop.

rum, and the stages of life were more concise. Today we parent children through a bewildering parade of micro-categories from the "fourth trimester" of the first three months through the "emerging adulthood" of the early twenties, but for Shakespeare there were only seven stages from birth to death. He lists them in the famous "All the world's a stage" speech, starting with the puking infant and ending with the toothless relic. Shakespeare invents the word *puking* here—nice one—but the idea of seven stages is borrowed from Ptolemy. Ptolemy's own seven ages of man were based on astrology and are thus essentially horoscopes. (Or so I imagine. "Mercury, ages four through fourteen: These next ten years are going to be exciting for you! If you live past age eight—unlikely—expect to be sold into slavery or prostitution. Watch out for Mercury retrograde, which brings bad luck and Huns.")

XXXVII.
The Seven Ages of Man.

Septem Ætates Hominis.
A *Man* is first an *Infant*, 1. | *Homo* est primum *Infans*, 1.

The seven ages of man as depicted by Comenius, from "Infant" to "decrepid old Man"

Over the next millennium, the stages of life would prove a popular topic for philosophers and physicians, who tended to break them down into either three Aristotelian categories, seven Ptolemaic ones, or four, guided by the four seasons or the four humors. In the latter formula childhood is ruled by phlegm, which the parent of any small child can confirm is accurate. Rousseau settled on five, but they applied only to males, and given how he depicts women, I'm guessing it was because he thought girls couldn't count that high. Piaget assigned both sexes four stages, and Erik Erikson doubled that with eight. Now we've got at least ten, and more are invented whenever a new target market is required.

**THE HISTORY OF LIFE STAGES** is a complicated and messy business, and we can't begin at the beginning, because no one concurs on when the staging should start. Even among scientists, there's little agreement on when a clump of cells becomes a life, and culturally and historically, there's been even less. Life and its succession of stages might begin at conception, or in the first trimester or the second. It might happen when the baby is born or when it takes its first breath. Beng babies are considered living humans when their umbilical stump falls off. Aboriginal Anbarra babies remain classified as fetuses until they smile the first time. For Balinese Hindus, babies don't become fully human until the 105th day after birth; before that, they belong to the spirit world, and are considered so holy their feet aren't permitted to touch the ground. The Namibian Himba people believe a baby is alive before it's even conceived, backdating its existence to the time it first came to its mother as a thought.

For hundreds of years in the West, life was said to begin the first time the mother felt the fetus move, an event known as the *quickening* (*quick* is an old synonym for "alive"). According to Aristotle—the first to discuss quickening—it was the point when the fetus acquired a human soul (previously, he wrote, it had the soul of a vegetable or an animal), and it celebrated this event by punching its mother from the inside. Apparently, boys were quicker to quicken than girls; Aristotle said the change takes place around forty days (for a male) or eighty days (for a female).

This is not true, and there's no test for the presence of a soul besides crying at *Toy Story 3*. But before home pregnancy tests or sonograms, quickening was as reliable as it got for confirming a pregnancy and establishing its viability, and the occasion was sometimes marked with festivities, particularly if the fetus in question was heir to a throne. In the seventeenth century, Londoners held thanksgiving celebrations when Charles II quickened on Henrietta Maria, and when Prince James quickened on Mary of Modena. When Henry VIII's wife Jane Seymour announced the quickening of the future Edward VI, people lost their minds. Lord Sandys declared it "the most joyful news ever sent me." It was celebrated with assemblies, orations, choral performances, gun salutes, bonfires, and "a hogshead of wine at everye fyer for poore people to drinke as longe as yt woulde laste."

In England, most dynastic pregnancies received similar treatment, which could be awkward when it turned out the kicking sensation was caused not by a baby but some bad mutton. This was the case with Queen Mary I, whose psychosomatic pregnancy symptoms included weight gain, morning sickness, lactation, amenorrhea, and apparently, the flutters of a phantom fetus, whose quickening was widely celebrated in November 1554. By the following July—the eleventh month of her pregnancy— people were starting to think Mary might have just had gas; the Venetian ambassador wrote that the pregnancy was more apt to "end in wind than anything else."[*]

A commoner's quickening didn't merit the same attention, but the event was still meaningful, and especially so if the commoner was charged with a capital crime; condemned women could request their death sentence be delayed until after the baby's birth. Now that it's largely stripped of its legal and spiritual import, quickening is noted quietly if at all. I don't even remember it with my second pregnancy, and with my first, only that I was in Target at the time, and if it was like all other pregnancy trips to Target, I marked it by frantically inhaling a jar of cocktail olives in the parking lot like the sweatpants-wearing princess I am.

At quickening, the fetus is the size not of an olive but of an avocado, a fact I knew because a weekly email service kept me updated on my child's size relative to produce. For whatever reason, we now rely on fruit to describe gestational stages, which is strange but not entirely new; humans have been comparing fetuses to fruit for millennia. Stranger still, however, is the staging system that became popular about a hundred years ago, which looked not to fruit but to our evolutionary forebears. This was recapitulation, Ernst Haeckel's 1866 theory that posits everyone passes

---

[*] In 1558, when Mary was forty-two, she went into confinement for yet another phantom pregnancy. Mary died later that year, possibly from a tumor, which would explain some of the pregnancy symptoms. If it weren't for the fact that she had 280 people burned at the stake for heresy, you'd almost feel sorry for her.

through each stage of evolution personally. Preschoolers are developmentally primates, elementary students are Neanderthals, and adolescents are stuck in their own personal Bronze Age.

Recapitulation is an interesting idea, and you can see why it might take. Human embryos do, in fact, feature fishlike gill slits, and my son, at four, had the table manners of a howler monkey. But the theory is also simply and demonstrably wrong. We are born *Homo sapiens* and stay *Homo sapiens,* without ever passing through a Neolithic or Cro-Magnon period.

Babies do have at least one thing in common with our primitive forebears, however: their stench. The character and duration of the baby stage has varied throughout history, but its stink was fairly consistent, at least as long as head-to-toe swaddling was the norm, as it was for hundreds of years. Swaddled babies were often allowed to stew in their own filth for twenty-four hours at a stretch. As a result, most babies smelled like, and I'm just guessing here, the reptile house at the zoo. So it's not entirely surprising that for much of history the baby stage was not considered a cute idyll to be savored. Babies had their fans, of course, but plenty of diary entries describe them as unpleasant little creatures whose helplessness made them loathsome. Montaigne put matters bluntly: "I cannot abide that passion for caressing new-born children, which have neither mental activities nor recognizable bodily shape by which to make themselves lovable." Montaigne did not have to abide it long; five of his six daughters died in infancy.

Many shared Montaigne's view, and except for a phase among Rousseauian hipsters, little attention was paid to babyhood or any other developmental stages for the next three hundred years. It was Rousseau, in fact, who introduced the idea of developmental stages, but he didn't develop them much; his first stage, infancy, lasted from zero to five. Now we break these years up into newborn, infant, toddler, preschooler, and child, but for several hundred years they were seen as an undifferentiated stretch of neediness that could last until six or seven.

**THIS DIDN'T CHANGE** until the turn of the twentieth century. The new era was declared the Century of the Child, in reformer Ellen Key's book of the same name, which called for a world devoted to the well-being of children and to the study of their development. Methodical research would be brought to bear in the pursuit of ideal outcomes. Science was transforming so many disciplines at the time; why shouldn't it transform child-rearing?

It did. Within a couple of decades, child development would become a discipline, and childhood stages from birth to adulthood would be codified and canonized. This was in large part the doing of Arnold Gesell, the Yale psychologist whose theories shaped our understanding of early childhood and remain mostly in place today. Gesell more or less originated the terms *toddler* and *preschooler.*[*] He also invented the concept of terrible twos, after observing how rigid and difficult his subjects seemed to become right around the time they turned two and a half.

Like Darwin, Freud, and Piaget, Gesell was a proponent and pioneer of stage theory, the idea that children pass through predictable developmental phases on their way to adulthood. (His particular take on it is known as Gesell's Maturational Theory.) Though stage theory seems old hat and obvious to us, it was pretty novel at the time, the science of stages not having progressed much past Ptolemy and humorism. Gesell advanced it exponentially, establishing minute stages for every skill and timetables for acquiring them. By which I mean he really went to town. He found fifty-three developmental stages in the act of holding a rattle alone.

Gesell also had the innovative idea of linking stages with ages. We group by age so routinely that it's hard to remember there was a time when age did not signify a whole lot. This was true even in schools, where a single class would include students of all different ages, many of whom probably didn't even know what age they were. Until recently, grouping by age would have seemed as arbitrary as, say, grouping by first initial, hair color, or hat size.[†]

---

[*]  Gesell didn't invent these terms, but he did popularize them. *Toddler* had been around for a while, but was rarely used. In the early 1800s, it could also apply to the elderly. The more common term for young children, which Gesell also uses, was *run-about*. Having parented two of them, I think *run-about* is the more apt term.

[†]  Or, say, grouping by body type. This, in fact, is what Gesell's collaborators Frances Ilg and Louise Bates Ames did in works published after Gesell's retirement. Supporters of William Sheldon's debunked theory of constitutional psychology, Ilg and

In all levels of society, adults and children mixed fairly freely, and the idea of something being age appropriate wouldn't have made sense to anyone before the twentieth century. The phrase itself only dates to 1950.

For Gesell it became gospel. The Gesell Institute went so far as to give age-appropriate birthday-party-planning advice to *Life* magazine in the 1950s, and later published *The Gesell Institute Party Book*. I have a copy, and its suggestions are mostly fairly sensible and realistic, though I will note that the proposed schedules fail to include a thirty-minute segment for the birthday boy to lose his shit, an event that will, in my experience, inevitably occur.

Gesell's science, though pioneering, wasn't perfect. The main problem was his sample size: it was small and extremely homogeneous, consisting almost exclusively of white middle-class New Haven kids. The academic term for this demographic is WEIRD (Western, Educated, Industrialized, Rich, Democratic). And it is indeed weird in how little it reflects the rest of the world, and how hugely middle-class Americans, at least, extrapolate from it. From Gesell's little cohort emerged just about every expectation of early childhood stages we have.

Gesell's group was even weirder than WEIRD. Instead of being fairly representative of most Western babies, they were representative of only a very specific subset of them. Gesell did a lot of his research on the sixty children attending Yale's on-campus preschool.* Most were children of faculty. Which means, in essence, that much of what we think we know about young children was based on the 1920s equivalent of my children and their college town friends. Were the study repeated today, we'd all believe, as my kids do, that bedtimes should be peer-reviewed, and that the empirical evidence against the nutritional value of Sour Patch Kids is weak at best.

To say the least, it's a skewed sample, and probably the reason Gesell concluded two-year-olds are so tough. Faculty kids, like their parents, do

---

Ames tailored their advice to endomorphs, mesomorphs, and ectomorphs. Endomorphs were warned to go easy on the snacks.

\* Note that it was sixty children at a given time; over the years, Gesell observed thousands. But still!

not lack confidence in their opinions, nor do they hesitate to express them. What they may lack in articulateness, they make up in volume. Margaret Mead, the daughter of two academics, was typical of the tribe: curious, voluble, and given to tantrums when her stubbornness was not indulged.* (Margaret's father wished she might express that confidence at a lower pitch, begging her to speak more softly.) Having faculty kids of my own, I'm not a bit surprised that the two-year-olds in Gesell's sample were rigid and headstrong. But I'm pretty sure that they were just as rigid and headstrong at twenty, thirty, and forty-five. Perhaps it wasn't the twos that were terrible; it was the kids themselves.

And by terrible, of course, I mean charming and lively and I love them very much. Gesell, for the record, didn't call twos terrible (though he and his coauthors did say that two and a half is "the most exasperating age in the preschool period"). The term itself actually came from an episode of a 1950s Canadian documentary show called *The Family Circle*. Given Canada's national reputation for quiet good manners, the terrible twos are pretty much the last thing you'd expect it to export. It's especially strange that this came from Canadian TV, a medium more typically devoted to the minor upsets of middle school and the norms of polite society. There's an episode of *Caillou* that does nothing but answer the question of how to behave at a brunch buffet. Like all things, I suppose, terrible must be relative.

*The Family Circle* originated a number of other alliterative ages (trusting threes, frustrating fours, fascinating fives, sociable sixes, and noisy nines), but for whatever reason, none of these stuck. Only the terrible twos took off, entering mainstream parlance in the 1970s. Putting aside the fact that this is exactly when I was two, and terrible, I'm not sure why it happened then. I doubt two-year-olds suddenly became worse.

They weren't that bad to begin with. The truth is twos aren't really so terrible at all, at least not any worse than ones or threes or fours. One-year-olds and two-year-olds average the same number of tantrums per month

---

* Perhaps unsurprisingly, as an adult, Mead was a fan of Gesell's. She brought her assistants to the Gesell Institute for training, and used the institute's methods in the field (Jane Howard, *Margaret Mead: A Life* [New York: Simon & Schuster, 1984], 254–99).

(eight). At four minutes each, the two-year-olds' tantrums are twice as long as the one-year-olds', but are still shorter than the five-year-olds'. Another study showed that only 20 percent of families reported regular conflict with their two-year-olds, and in a very non-Gesellian take on things, blamed the way parents handled tantrums rather than innate two-year-old behavior. Terrible twoness does not appear to be intrinsic, nor is it universal. Most other cultures don't have a term like *terrible twos* at all, or any perception that this is a particularly difficult or stubborn time. In modern Hebrew, in fact, it's called "the soft age."

THOUGH HE PARSED early childhood exhaustively, Gesell didn't have much to say about later childhood development. He wrote just one book on ages five through ten, its four hundred pages dwarfed by the thousands and thousands of pages he devoted to the years before. Holding a rattle merits fifty-three stages, apparently, but the entire seventh year gets one measly chapter, thirty-two pages long. To be fair, Gesell's focus was on early childhood; ages five through ten weren't really his thing. But it's telling that ages five through ten don't seem to be anyone's thing. As far as child development studies go, early childhood and adolescence receive the bulk of the attention.

In the academic literature, ages five through ten (or sometimes seven through eleven) are known as middle childhood, which seems apt. It is indeed the middle child, the dull Jan between the impish Cindy of the early years and the cool Marcia of adolescence. Most developmental psychologists haven't paid it much attention, and even those who did, like Piaget, didn't seem too excited about it. Freud and Piaget considered the stage a plateau—Freud called the period *latency*—where children consolidate what they've already learned and catch their breath before adolescence begins. Erikson thought it was a little more exciting than that, a stage in which they learn to navigate the wider social world and learn cooperation, but he still called it the "lull before the storm of puberty."

Outside the professional literature we don't have any special terms for this time of life; few if any cultures do. We have to make do with *kid, youth,* or *child* to describe anyone between five and ten, though there's an awfully big difference between the two ends. The idea that middle child-hood is a distinct stage at all is fairly recent. For hundreds of years, infancy slid right into adulthood. In the past few years we've added yet another age, tweens, though whether this is actually a developmental stage or a target market is debatable. For what it's worth, *tweens* was coined not by Nickelodeon executives but by J. R. R. Tolkien, who used it to describe the reckless twentysomething period in the life of a Hobbit. Given that they're short and sprout hair in unexpected places, that is, I suppose, essentially what twelve-year-old kids are.[*]

And when that happens, it becomes pretty hard not to notice the child is entering a new developmental stage. You can't really pretend your darling baby is still an infant when he has stubble and bacne. Clearly, a new age has dawned.

Historically, this has called for a rite of passage. In ancient Sparta, adolescence was celebrated with a sort of Hunger Games called the Krypteia, in which conscripts were dispatched naked into the bush with only a knife and permission to rob and kill as many slaves as possible.[†] An equally trying ceremony was performed by the seventeenth-century Algonquin Indians, who gave chosen adolescent boys wysoccan, a powerful hallucinogen, then left them in a cage in the woods for a month. During this time, they were supposed to forget everything about their life before. This sometimes included the names of their family members as well as their entire vocabulary. Initiates who remembered their childhood had better pretend they didn't, or they'd have to go through the ritual again.

Some Australian aboriginal tribes also put boys through a rebirth ritual, but theirs involves fewer drugs and more Fight Club. To start, the boy

---

[*] As G. Stanley Hall observed in volume 1 of *Adolescence*, "Puberty literally means becoming hairy." The word derives from the Latin *pubes*, whose Latin meaning is exactly the same as its English one. As for the hormone that gets puberty going, it's got a pretty terrific name, too: it's kisspeptin, named for Hershey, Pennsylvania, where it was discovered.

[†] Or something like that. The nature of the Krypteia, which translates to "secret" or "hidden things," remains mysterious. It may have functioned as a sort of elite force or secret police. Also, according to Plutarch, you were allowed to take a little food with you.

is seized and circumcised on a human table in front of an audience of a hundred onlookers or so. For the following six to eight weeks, the boy is not permitted to speak, as he is supposed to be symbolically dead. (Also, I presume, because it's the first rule of Fight Club.) Following that, the boy has his nasal septum pierced with a spear, then filled with the wing bone of an eagle hawk. A few months later he undergoes a large-bore penile sub-incision that will render him unable to stand while peeing. At no point is he given anesthetics, but he is allowed to bite down on a boomerang. That might hurt, though, too, because some aboriginal tribes also mark boys' rite of passage by knocking out their front incisors with rocks. Boys of the Amazonian Sateré-Mawé tribe are put through a slightly easier though still agonizing rite of pain in which they are made to perform an unflinch-ing ten-minute dance while wearing what are essentially oven mitts lined with enraged bullet ants, whose stings are unimaginably painful and can cause daylong paralysis. All of which really puts the crucible of middle school into perspective.

IN THE MODERN WEST, we mark the transition from child to adult with the less violent if more prolonged rite of passage known as adoles-cence. Though it seems eternal, adolescence is in fact quite new. Like the terrible twos, it's a stage that didn't occur until the early twentieth century. Before then, there was childhood and adulthood and no stage in between. Even today, many cultures, including the majority of preindus-trial societies, have no word for adolescence, because the category doesn't exist.

The invention of adolescence is credited to psychologist G. Stanley Hall, who named and defined it in a seminal 1904 two-volume work. Hall's book was intended for academics, but proved popular with mainstream audiences, in no small part because it was seminal in another way: there was an awful lot of semen in it. As critics were quick to note, Hall tends to foam on about sex, twice using the rather colorful metaphor of "ripple marks" on an ancient "pubic beach." As one colleague wrote, the text was "chock full of errors, masturbation, and Jesus. He is a mad man."

If Hall was a little eccentric, you could hardly blame him. Early in his career he had suffered his own Shakespearean tragedy when, while he was away recuperating from diphtheria, a leaking gas pipe asphyxiated his wife and eight-year-old daughter (a son survived). Hall floundered for some time after that, finally finding his purpose again in studying children and then teens. By that time he had a teen of his own. Hall's relationship with his son tended to be somewhat testy and rocky, so it's no surprise that this is how Hall defines adolescence in general, describing it as a time of "storm and stress," of "mental and moral inebriation," of experimentation and rebellion that endures from fourteen to twenty-four.

Ten years is a very, very long time. Now that puberty tends to begin earlier, adolescence lasts even longer. For the thousands of years when it didn't technically exist, when childhood ran into adulthood, adulthood could come on quite suddenly, at least according to law. In Shakespeare's time, for instance, you became an adult almost literally overnight, as adulthood was conferred upon marriage.* This event often happened later than you'd expect, especially given the comparatively short life-spans. Being familiar with Romeo and Juliet, I thought middle school marriages were common in Shakespeare's time, but it turns out that's not true at all, at least not in England: the mean age for a first-time groom was twenty-six, and the age of majority was twenty-one, in an average life-span of forty-two. Shakespeare himself married at eighteen; his bride was eight years older and several months pregnant. He needed special permission from his parents to do so. By law, Shakespeare was still a child, even if he fit the definition of the rebellious adolescent Hall would set down a few centuries later.

As Shakespeare proves, there were certainly stormy and stressed Hallian teenagers before 1904. Of course there were; there just was no name or category for them. Hall himself makes this point, devoting a chapter

---

* By law, anyway. In practice, most teens spent a few years transitioning to adulthood living away from home as apprentices. In the Middle Ages, some spent those years training to be a knight, as did, I will note, my D&D-playing nerd friends seven hundred years later. But the difference was that my friends and I weren't spending all our time with adults. Until the twentieth century, teens lived very much in the adult world as they trained and worked. They didn't have the opportunity to develop their own unique identity and culture. By the twentieth century, they did. Adolescence was born, and D&D quickly followed.

to troubled teens in history and literature (he references 139 "interesting" adolescents in Shakespeare's works alone). But as Hall observed, by the turn of the twentieth century, something had changed. Several things, actually. One was that teenagers were less likely to work and more likely to attend school. The number of high schools in the United States increased more than sevenfold between 1880 and 1900 (though by 1920, still only one in six Americans would actually graduate). Suddenly a lot of young people were in the same place at the same time without a lot of responsibilities. They spent this free time exactly as you'd think they would, finding dumb hobbies and acting up, which in the literature is called "incubating a youth culture" and "testing boundaries." Adolescence was born, and Hall was there to give it a name and definition.

Hall argued that adolescence was a very American development, and he had a point. Compared to Europe, America had been Teen Town from the beginning.* By 1730, preacher Jonathan Edwards was complaining, "There were many of them very much addicted to night-walking, and frequenting the tavern, and lewd practices, wherein some, by their example exceedingly corrupted others." What Hall would call a natural disposition to risk-taking and rebellion would prove useful in a country trying to emancipate itself from its controlling colonial parent. By 1776, half the American population was under sixteen, and teenagers played major roles in the revolution. Though we call them founding fathers, many of them were essentially still kids.† It didn't hurt that Americans were much bigger than their European counterparts, too, three inches taller on average.

Taller they were, but not necessarily higher-minded. Besides taxation without representation, colonial American teens also rioted over things like the quality of dorm food. In 1766 Harvard students (who could be as young as twelve)—incensed because, they claimed, the school's butter

---

* As for the term *teen-ager,* it was first used in a 1941 *Popular Science* article, hardly a hotbed of youth culture. Still, the term quickly took off, losing its hyphen along the way. For a while, the term *teener* was also used.

† It's pretty extraordinary how young many of the key players were in 1776. James Monroe and Lafayette were both eighteen; Aaron Burr, twenty; Alexander Hamilton, twenty-one; Betsy Ross, twenty-four. Even fuddy-duddy King George was only thirty-eight.

"stinketh"—began a riot that became known as the "Great Butter Rebellion." It ended with the suspension of half the student body. A "Rotten Cabbage Rebellion" followed in 1807.

For Hall, adolescence wasn't the product of American sociocultural conditions so much as American gene-blending. He wrote, "We Americans are a mixed race. This makes the period of adolescence in America unique. Where nature is kept pure this period of ferment is accomplished quickly and with little trouble, as among the Jews and the Germans. The period of adolescence is prolonged in America because of mixture of blood, and if we survive the trials and dangers of this period, we will make the grandest men and women the world has ever known."

Here it must be noted that Hall did not always have the most enlightened ideas on race and gender, having based his work on Ernst Haeckel's racist and sexist recapitulation theory.* Haeckel put the different races and sexes on completely different developmental timelines, declaring that white male babies were more or less the developmental equal of adult white women or adult black men. As the adult white mother of a white male baby, I can assure you that this is not the case. When he was an infant, only one of us was continent and a licensed driver, and it certainly wasn't him.

Unsurprisingly, Haeckel's theories were popular with the Nazis, race "scientists," and eugenicists. Far more disturbing is the fact that they were also popular with Hall, as he was the preeminent American psychologist of his time, the first American to earn a psychology Ph.D., and the first president of the American Psychological Association. He was also the dude who said things like "Most savages in most respects are children, or, because of sexual maturity, more properly adolescents of adult size." And "We should strive sedulously to keep the mental back . . . especially in females, and not 'spoil a good mother to make a grammarian.'"†

---

\* Haeckel made a number of cultural contributions besides racist pseudoscience. Like L. Ron Hubbard, he was a crackpot with funny ideas about evolution and religion who formed a quasi-cult, the Monist League. And like Shakespeare, he was a gifted neologian. The terms he coined include *ecology, stem cell, phylum*, and *World War I*, which had previously been known as the Great War.

† Hall apparently did his part; he denied a female chemist access to a university lab, and argued against admitting women to the psychology graduate program on the grounds that they would "crowd out the best men" (Estelle B. Freedman, *Maternal*

Hall was not the worst racist or misogynist of his time, and by the standards of his day, in some areas he was almost progressive. He argued against colonization and for African education and self-rule, and wrote admiringly of Booker T. Washington (though he couldn't keep from observing that Washington was not like "typical negroes"). Still, it's hard not to cringe and seethe when he describes the eight-to-twelve-year-old child's stage as "pygmoid," and claims African American intellect remains stunted at puberty. Or when he argues that women's retarded evolutionary development makes them more likely to kill themselves, a supposition so "absurd" it prompts Stephen Jay Gould to remind readers in wonderment that Hall is "again, not a crackpot, but America's premier psychologist."

In Hall's formulation, "savages" are adolescents and adolescents are savages, feral creatures with no impulse control and a primal urge to rebel. But, like recapitulation theory itself, this is just wrong. That adolescence is inevitably a time of rebellion is simply not true. In much of the world, teenagers are not expected to rebel, and for the most part, they don't. In China and India, the two countries that have more teens than any other, adolescent rebellion is a much smaller deal. Chinese teens often demonstrate independence by doing things *for* their parents, rather than to *spite* their parents.

Even in Hall's own time, his characterization of adolescence as a wild and reactionary stage struck some colleagues as improbable. Before long, other scholars set out to disprove him, most famously Margaret Mead—hooray for stubborn faculty kids!—who in 1926 went off to Samoa with that explicit goal in mind. She succeeded, sort of, though her work was famously flawed and problematic in its own right. But later studies confirmed that the stormy adolescence of Hall's creation is by no means universal. Particularly in preindustrial societies, adolescent antisocial behavior is extremely rare. Where it does exist, it seems to be an American export: it shows up only after the arrival of Western TV and movies.*

---

*Justice: Miriam Van Waters and the Female Reform Tradition* [Chicago: University of Chicago Press, 1996], 36–37).

\* One example from the Inuit of Victoria Island: Teen delinquency was rare until the eighties, when TV was first introduced. But by 1988 it had become such a problem it necessitated the creation of a police station. First the terrible twos,

In the United States teen rebellion is considered standard, putting the American adolescent in the awkward position of having to rebel in order to conform to societal expectations. For an obedient rule-following teen like I was, this is utterly flummoxing. My solution was to rebel by introducing a whole new set of rules: I became an unhinged anorexic Orthodox Jew, to my parents' great annoyance and horror. In my case, there was OCD involved, making the whole debacle somewhat inevitable and undeniably pathological, but still, it would have been nice to know that the rebellion part of it, at least, was optional.

It certainly appears to be. Even in the United States, despite the stereotype, teens aren't actually all that difficult. The last few decades of research show that the overwhelming majority of parent-teen relationships are good the overwhelming majority of the time; only 5 to 15 percent are fractious. And the most troubled parent-teen relationships are troubled long before adolescence begins. In general, however, teens and parents have good relationships.

So why do we think all teens are brawling delinquents? There are probably a few reasons, but the first is some bad science with a long cultural shelf life. As Laurence Steinberg has pointed out, influential studies conducted in the 1950s and '60s that portrayed teens as leather-jacket-wearing rebels looking for a cause were seriously flawed, grossly oversampling problem teens. They were conducted on kids who were already in therapeutic settings, who were already so unruly intervention had become necessary. When researchers began looking at larger populations in the seventies, studies showed that 75 percent of teens got along with their parents just fine.

The last thirty years of research have said they get along even better. So why do we still consider teens to be tough? I suspect it's because—and this is science—even perfectly nice teens will work your last nerve

---

now teen rebellion—who knew Canadian television was responsible for so much turmoil (Pierre Dasen, "Rapid Social Change and the Turmoil of Adolescence: A Cross-Cultural Perspective," *International Journal of Group Tensions* 29, no. 1–2 [June 2000]): 17–49)?

until it is a raw pulpy blob.* This is, in fact, confirmed by the research. Parents report that the teen years are the hardest phase of raising children (though it's worth noting that this is reported by parents currently parenting teenagers; I suspect the parents of infants and toddlers would differ). In any case, while major conflict is uncommon, bickering is persistent. Unfortunately, it appears this is a good thing. Teenagers who experience moderate conflict with their parents tend to be the best adjusted, more even-keeled than those who have little conflict with their parents, or, obviously, a lot.

Teens, then, may not be universally rebellious, but I'm pretty sure they're universally *annoying*.† As Thomas Hine notes, "the segregation of young people from the rest of society was observed by researchers in Africa even before it became commonplace in the United States." In some Spanish-speaking countries, adolescence is known as *la edad difícil,* and in Hebrew, it's called *tipesh-esreh*—literally, "stupidteens." If developmental stages are in part performance, the teenage years are the play you cringe watching: the script is facile, the direction's ham-fisted, the drama's overwrought, and the actors are chewing the scenery.

In all likelihood, this is how teens have always been, even before adolescence was a distinct, defined age. Researchers studying Pleistocene cave paintings were able to deduce from hand size that the majority were done by adolescent boys, but they could have figured it out from the content alone: a lot of gory hunting scenes and obscene doodles. The women—and there are lots of them—are grossly overendowed, and not one of them is wearing clothes. It's the first art we have, and it amounts to prehistoric *Playboy* cartoons.

Unfortunately, this aspect of adolescent development does seem to be both inevitable and universal. The adolescent brain is very different from both the child's brain and the adult's brain in ways that tend to

---

* Also, they always have. As their writings make clear, teen students often irritated the hell out of both Socrates and Aristotle (Judith Rich Harris, *The Nurture Assumption*, rev. ed. [New York: Free Press, 2009], 275).

† In archaic English the word *teen* actually meant "irritation." This is sheer linguistic coincidence, but I think we can agree that it's fitting all the same.

make the owner do stupid and irritating things. The limbic system, which governs emotion and our more primal urges, is going full throttle, while the prefrontal cortex, which would normally put the brakes on some of these shenanigans, is far from fully developed. All of which makes teenagers more prone to risk-taking and overdramatic behavior. As Shakespeare himself observed four hundred years ago, "I would there were no age between ten and three-and-twenty, or that youth would sleep out the rest; for there is nothing in the between but getting wenches with child, wronging the ancientry, stealing, fighting."

The brain doesn't reach full maturity until the mid-twenties. Neurobiologists are confirming what culture at large has known for ages: we don't grow up until long after we're grown-ups. This, of course, is several years after the law and our community assume. Having gained the rights and responsibilities of adulthood without the sense to handle them, we stagger into maturity with bad credit, an STD, or an ankle monitor; some ancient wrongs we need to right; or a wench whose company we no longer enjoy.

Perhaps that's what happened in Shakespeare's case, though who can say. He wrote as little about his wife as he did about his children—which is not at all—so we're left to infer from the little we know, like the fact that they spent most of their marriage living a hundred miles and a few days' journey apart, or that Shakespeare's only bequest to his widow was the rather stingy gift of his "second-best bed." And maybe he was speaking from personal experience when he wrote: "A young man married is a man that's marred."

That line is from *All's Well That Ends Well*, and the optimist in me likes to think the title is the truer statement. All's well that ends, whether it's an unhappy marriage or an awkward adolescence, and one way or another, both will. That's the upside of stages: eventually they all segue into the next. Infants become toddlers, adolescents become adults, and while those terms may mean different things, the terms are always finite. So there's really no sense in worrying about the helpless months of infancy, the tantrum-filled preschool years, or the sulking teens. All stages, by definition, end.

This includes the stage of Shakespeare's own Globe Theatre, which burned down in 1613. By then Shakespeare had retired to Stratford-upon-

Avon, possibly to spend time with one of the daughters he'd seen so little of, and Elizabeth, the only grandchild he'd live to see. He would die three years later, after the Globe was rebuilt and before it was razed to make room for tenements and the families that filled them. There, puking infants would become whining schoolboys, then soldiers, then seniors. And the show, as always, would go on.

# 7

# I Know You Are but What Am I?

## *Sibling Conflict*

I f our home resembles a war zone, the bedroom our children share is its steaming Antietam, a field of war littered with the detritus of their daily skirmishes. The fight might be over the last fruit strip or the TV or the best chair in front of the TV; it doesn't really matter. Like the Civil War, their conflict has many causes but only one true one: in this case, that they are siblings, and that's what siblings do. The war between brothers is eternal, each generation renewing the hostilities that have defined sibling relations since humanity began. In the most extreme forms, this leads to death; in the mildest, to a nose blown into a sister's pillowcase. Sibship might be war, but it's certainly not civil.

A veteran myself, I should have expected this. My own sister and I fought constantly until our late teens. As a toddler I made frequent and genuine attempts to smother her by sitting on her face; she survived and repaid me with regular kicks and scratches. When we outgrew physical fights but not our resentment, we sabotaged each other's things. The toilet's proximity to the cat litter proved too tempting for both of us, and we routinely dipped each other's possessions through the former before breading them in the latter.

Our nonstop squabbling tortured our mother, who was very close with her own two sisters. This often prompted her to hope darkly that we'd have children who fought as much as we did. Now, of course, her curse comes true daily as Sherman's March roars through my home, leaving a scorched earth of broken toys and crumpled keep-out signs. It is the part of parenting I hate most, which is saying something, given that parenting is a job that also requires cleaning diarrhea out of neck folds.

Many families have it worse. Although it seems like my children never give it a rest, in fact they fight far less than the average. Statistically they should be arguing 3.5 times per hour, a number researchers landed on not by interviewing children or parents but by installing microphones in the subjects' homes. Younger children fight even more—six times each hour. This means they have a fight—a real fight, not just cross words—every nine minutes.

It is very disturbing when the people you love most in the world turn savagely on each other, and from the parents' perspective, it makes no sense. They're fighting for the affection, attention, and material goods their parents supply, all of which said parents are in no mood to hand over after a few hours of constant bickering. From the combatants' point of view, however, the conflict is unavoidable. Children fight because they're wired to. Sibling rivalry is an evolutionary imperative, an innate impulse. We're programmed to turn on the usurpers who compete with us for precious resources like food and parental attention, and we begin early. By six months, infants get upset when their mother pays attention to a baby doll. By sixteen months, they know what bothers their siblings and will annoy them on purpose.

Siblings are literally, biologically, under your skin from birth. Because some fetal cells stay in the mother's body and are then passed along to further offspring, you're born with genetic material from your older siblings *in your body*. It, and they, will probably stay with you until you die. Our relationships with our siblings are often the most profound relationships in our lives, more important and influential than the ones we have with our parents. They are in fact often the only relationship we *have* for life, with someone who's around from the beginning until the end. Humans generally maintain lifelong sibling relationships; we're the only species that does. Which gives us a long, long time to hold a grudge.

It was ever thus. Nearly two thousand years ago, St. Augustine described a baby who "could not yet speak and, pale with jealousy and bitterness, glared at his brother sharing his mother's milk. Who is unaware of this fact of experience?" Certainly not Sir George Baker, physician to George III—that's the crazy one they made the movie about who also has three solos in *Hamilton*—who observed, "Even at the tenderest age, in the very cradle, unmistakeable signs of jealousy may be seen. . . . It is possible to see an infant weaken and languish most wretchedly from this emotion as from wasting disease. The child is not to be freed from this grave illness by any art or physician's help unless the rival infant is taken from his sight." In Ghana this is an actual illness, *kwashiorkor* ("disease of the deposed child"), and is caused not by heartbreak but by severe protein deficiency when the eldest loses his place at the breast.

Sibling conflict is not unique to humans, and humans are nowhere near as bad as some animals are. Animal siblings actually kill each other, often while the parents look on blithely. In certain bird species, sibling murder is so common it's known as obligate siblicide. Black eagles are particularly vicious. In one of the few observed accounts, the slightly older chick attacked its slightly younger sibling thirty-eight different times over the younger's three-day life-span, delivering 1,569 blows with its sharply hooked beak. There was, by the way, more than enough food for both.

Sand tiger sharks commit sibling murder on a far greater scale, beginning before they're even born. They play an in utero version of Hungry Hungry Hippos, using their nascent teeth to chomp up all the sibling embryos they can.* The shark that's eventually born is just the last one standing. How did researchers figure this out? A biologist dissecting a pregnant shark was bitten by an embryo, still swimming around in the uterus, still

---

* Interestingly, they play as teams. A tiger shark litter can include pups by several different fathers. Pups from the same father will first consume pups from a different one. When the dominant shark spares a littermate to be born with, it's a full sibling.

looking for siblings to eat. Pigs are vicious, too, born with eyeteeth that are angled to gash littermates while they nurse.

Sibling rivalry is common to all living things, even plants, which will chemically poison competing offspring to divert resources to themselves. Even *bacteria* fight with their bacterial siblings, resorting, like sharks, to cannibalism and fratricide.

Human siblings rarely resort to murder, and even more rarely to cannibalism, but they certainly scrap. For most of history, however, sibling conflict wasn't subject to much examination and even less concern. Given how incredibly annoying it is, it seems surprising that there's so little complaining in the historical record. I can only assume that parents either didn't see it as a problem or didn't see it as *their* problem.

If they had the means, it wasn't. One of the few books to address sibling conflict, 1798's *Practical Education,* directs its advice on the subject to tutors, not to parents.* Even parents who couldn't afford help probably heard less fighting than we do. They were less likely to be around their children, and their children were less likely to be around each other, given that they were either working or dead. Watching my children fight over a tire swing is, in comparison, a literal day in the park. I know that it's a fairly ridiculous luxury that sibling fighting is my very least favorite part of parenting. For millennia, I imagine, parents' least favorite part of parenting was, say, watching their children starve and die.

Those kids still managed to fight, though. Because even sick and frail and overworked children will find time to argue, and indeed they did. There's little recorded evidence of parents trying to stop sibling conflict, but there's plenty of evidence the conflict occurred. Both myth and history are full of examples, with the Bible alone providing a good half-dozen case studies. Sibling conflict shows up in twenty-five of the fifty chapters in Genesis. The very first homicide occurs between the very first brothers, Cain and Abel, and the succeeding generations don't learn much from

---

* *Practical Education* also suggests that sibling conflict is not just the staff's responsibility, but the staff's fault. Children fight, the authors argue, because they're pitted against each other by their maids, each of whom wants her charge to be judged the best (122), making me picture a Regency version of *Toddlers & Tiaras.*

their example, each scrapping just as much as the last. Esau and Jacob, like sand sharks, begin fighting while still in the womb. After swindling Esau out of his birthright, Jacob goes on to marry a pair of sisters who will compete for his affection. He then favors his own son Joseph so blatantly that Joseph's jealous siblings throw him into a well and sell him into slavery.

Sibling rivalry occurs in a lot of religious traditions and ancient mythologies. It informs both the Book of Mormon (the scripture) and the *Book of Mormon* (the musical). In the Hindu epic the Mahabharata, Arjuna kills his brother Karna, and in the Norse sagas, brothers are forever fighting and killing one another off. Romulus whacks Remus after they bicker over a *wall*. Zeus gets along with his siblings a bit better, marrying two of them (gross) and teaming up with the rest to fight his father in the War of the Titans. Once the war is over, however, the siblings go back to intra-familial turf wars and squabbling.

IN THE BIBLE, the fights are often over parental affection, which is what psychology generally blamed for sibling rivalry, when it considered it at all. But recent studies indicate siblings are actually fighting over something more simple than that: toys. Eighty percent of sibling fights are over possessions. Parental affection comes in last as something worth fighting over, at a dismal 9 percent.

Nine percent of the time, my children are fighting over their parents' attention. My lap is occasionally a war zone, as is my hearing. Once, when both of them were shouting to have their needs met, I complained that I couldn't listen to them both. To which Rachel responded, "You've got two ears. Listen to each of us with one of them."

Most of the time, of course, the shouting is about stuff. In our house this has meant a Noah's Ark shopping strategy in which we get two of everything, which is why my two-year-old son had a flowered one-piece swimsuit. Naturally, it didn't work. Sam invariably preferred the flowered one-piece swimsuit his sister had. I don't understand why, but I suppose I once did, fighting tooth and nail to play with my sister's Cheryl Ladd

*Charlie's Angels* action figure, even though it was identical to my own. It was somehow better, and thus rightfully mine.

When the toys are things like fortunes and empires, the stakes are raised immeasurably, and the players tend to mark their territory with scimitars, declaring "MINE" in blood. Would-be rulers have often turned to fratricide to secure the throne. In 626 CE, Emperor Taizong mowed down two brothers to get to the crown; several centuries earlier, King Jehoram took out six. Sisters are little better. Queen Eliza-

Children fighting over a pet in *"L'Enfance no. 2,"* Recueil de Grimaces, Louis-Léopold Boilly, 1823 *(Courtesy Graphic Arts Collection, Department of Rare Books and Special Collections, Princeton University Library)*

beth I had her sister killed, as did Cleopatra, who also arranged the death of the brother to whom she was married (gross). And she was indirectly responsible for the death of another brother—to whom she was *also* married (I MEAN, REALLY)—when he died battling her for the throne.[*]

Legend holds that Indian emperor Ashoka killed all but one of his hundred brothers, knocking off the legitimate heir by luring him into a pit full of burning coals. When sixteenth-century Incan princes Atahualpa and Huáscar butted heads over their father's kingdom it escalated into the War of Two Brothers, an ugly years-long conflict whose highlights include Atahualpa drinking out of the skull of his brother's slain general. An entirely different War of Two Brothers was fought in Portugal three hundred years later.

---

[*] Though gross—GROSS—to us, sibling marriages were common among Egyptian royals, who used them to preserve the divine purity of the family bloodline and produced some pretty inbred invalids as a result. And traditional Balinese culture has condoned—in fact, required—marriage between brothers and sisters provided they were high-caste twins. Sibling incest is also common in several V. C. Andrews books, of which I'm a big fan. This may be the reason my own children were under the impression that they *had* to marry each other, and were quite relieved to learn that, in fact, their sibling was pretty much the only person in the world they *couldn't* wed.

Under the principle of fighting fire with fire, fratricide was sometimes used to *prevent* civil war.* This became standard practice in the Ottoman Empire after Mehmed II instituted a policy he hoped would circumvent the savage battles that had nearly destroyed the kingdom in the past. Upon taking the throne, a new sultan would imprison all his brothers until he produced his first male heir, at which point the brothers would be strangled with a silk cord by a deaf courtier, a detail I cannot explain but find interesting. The practice culminated in the murders of Mehmed III's nineteen brothers. After that, his successor Ahmed I banned it, though it continued unofficially.

Those of us who don't have the power of a sultanate behind us must resort to other methods to ease the rivalry and stop the fighting, but until quite recently, it appears that few parents bothered. Until about 1920, parenting manuals almost never mention sibling conflict as a problem to be addressed, and the few that do only give it a couple of pages. Locke probably gives the matter the most attention, but doesn't distinguish between siblings and, say, roommates. Locke notes that "Children who live together, often strive for mastery," but this should not be indulged; "they should be taught to have all the deference, complaisance, and civility one for the other imaginable."

Locke also recognized that children are continually provoking, attacking, and tattling on one another, which should not be tolerated, lest it make them cowardly and, apparently, feminine. "The complaints of children one against another, which is usually but the desiring of the assistance of another to revenge them, should not be favourably received, nor hearken'd to: It weakens and effeminates their minds to suffer them to complain."

Insightfully, Locke clued into the fact that the cause of the rivalry was usually toys, and encouraged parents to teach their children to share. "This I imagine will make brothers and sisters kinder and civiller to one another, and consequently to others, than twenty rules about good manners, with which children are ordinarily perplex'd and cumber'd." Kind of missing the point, he goes on to suggest parents make sharing itself

---

* In modern military terminology, *fratricide* is another term for friendly fire.

competitive: "Make this a contest among children, who shall out-do one another this way: and by this means, by a constant practice, children having made it easy to themselves to part with what they have, good nature may be settled in them into an habit, and they may take pleasure, and pique themselves in being kind, liberal and civil, to others."

Until the mid-twentieth century, most other authors offered no advice at all. Given that sibling conflict is the preoccupation of much of the parental literature today, the omission is surprising. Perhaps children of previous generations simply fought less. There tends to be less conflict when children are spread out in age as well as in space, with the younger ones housed with the wet nurse, the older with the apprentice master. Also, there was just less stuff to fight for, and none of it was a cable remote offering access to thousands of channels of dazzling entertainment. What little stuff they had was not really worth the cost of a rift, a sibling being more fun to play with than, say, a cow patty and a handful of feathers.

On the other hand, Cain and Abel managed to start fighting before the invention of *everything*, so it seems safe to assume that while siblings might not have fought *as much*, they still fought *enough*.

USUALLY, THE WINNER was the eldest. Transhistorically and cross-culturally, the firstborn has almost always come out ahead (except, strangely, in Genesis). Firstborns get the full prize package: a minimum of nine months of the parents' solo attention, the inheritance, the title, the ability to boss around all who follow. Under primogeniture, which has been practiced since ancient times and still persists in parts of the world and on *Game of Thrones*, such favoritism is the law of the land.* This is not always such a good idea, as it favors the first over the fittest. Thus big brother King Dipshit gets the throne while Prince Smarter Younger

---

* There's also something called *ultimogeniture*—favoring of the youngest. It was practiced in parts of England during the Middle Ages, though quite rarely, perhaps because it gave smarter older siblings a realllllly good reason to let the youngest have an "accident" (Michael Mitterauer and Reinhard Sieder, *The European Family* [Chicago: University of Chicago Press, 1982], 55–56).

Brother gets the shaft. Darwin himself called primogeniture a "scheme" for "destroying natural selection."*

Darwin wasn't totally right—there are, in fact, some evolutionary reasons for favoring the first. The firstborn has been around longer, and you've already sunk more resources into him; best to guard the investment. The firstborn also tends to have a very small IQ advantage over his siblings, each of whom is slightly dumber than the last, because, it's theorized, each succeeding child gets that much less parental attention.

The brilliant and successful Darwin was the fifth child of six, which should suggest that the math on birth order just doesn't add up, besides the obvious formula: the more births, the less order. While not everyone agrees—it's a rather contentious issue—the current consensus is that birth order matters only within the family, and not within society at large. At home, older siblings may be more likely to be bossy, but in the world, they're not more likely to be boss. Besides that minuscule IQ difference, there's no measurable difference at all. Birth order, then, is about as scientifically predictive as astrological signs, which is to say not at all, except in the case of Scorpios.

That science devoted any resources at all to investigating the effects of birth order (and, in fact, devoted a surprising amount) is largely the fault of Darwin's cousin, a nineteenth-century polymath named Francis Galton, who made some of the first inquiries into the subject. Like many nineteenth-century polymaths, Galton was often brilliant, occasionally crazy, and pretty consistently racist. Galton was also an inventor, though his inventions tended to be of limited use. Worried that his brain might overheat, Galton invented a top hat with a hinged lid that opened to allow cooler air in.

The hat was a dumb idea, but his brain was indeed working pretty hard. Galton made major breakthroughs in the fields of meteorology (inventing

---

* It certainly privileged King Dipshit's subpar genes, at least in theory: primogeniture required younger brothers to keep it in their pants. They were supposed to remain celibate and single, as there would be no inheritance to feed any offspring. And while this did encourage many younger brothers to enter the clergy, many others just went ahead and had their children out of wedlock.

the weather map and identifying the high pressure system), statistics (discovering the cornerstone concepts of correlation and regression toward the mean), psychology (coming up with differential psychology and discovering synesthesia), and forensics (innovating the science of fingerprinting). He pioneered the study of genetics, and, less nobly, eugenics, a term he coined. Galton explored the subject at length in his unpublished novel *Kantsaywhere*, an Ayn Randian picaresque set in a eugenic utopia in which "well-built," "thoroughly virile" men and busty women advance the race through some mortifying sex scenes, while the genetically inferior are sent to labor camps.

In his more sober volume *Hereditary Genius,* Galton explored eugenics with less sex, more science, and just as much racism, claiming that the "African negro" race has a lot of "half-witted men." (Elsewhere, he wrote that Jews are "specialized for a parasitic existence.") Rare is the eugenicist who does not rank his own race at the top, and this first eugenicist would be no exception. Like Ernst Haeckel, Galton concluded that his own tribe—in this case, the British—was the most advanced. But, he concedes, it wasn't always. The Greeks, he wrote, had previously held the title, but lost their rank due to breeding with inferiors. Lest the Greeks feel like losers, they could comfort themselves with the fact that Galton now ranked them first among the world's liars.*

Galton became interested in birth order while conducting a survey of the high-achieving Fellows of the Royal Society, when he noticed that many of its members were firstborns. Which was true, but before we draw any larger conclusions we should remember that Galton was working with a very small and skewed sample of people one presumes were as odd as he

---

* Galton quantified everything. His motto was "Whenever you can, count," and he did. He documented the fidgets of audience members to gauge their interest in a presentation, and conducted painstaking scientific trials on the best ways to brew tea and slice cake. In his later years he spent hours walking the streets of the UK with a contraption concealed in his pocket that he termed a *pricker* (and yes, I hear it, too), consisting of a pin and a scorecard that he used to surreptitiously rate the attractiveness of women he passed. He then compiled the data into a "beauty map" that ranked average female beauty by area (London came in first, Aberdeen last). Galton, who joined the Anti-Suffrage Society, did not quantify his own misogyny, but we can guess it was pretty high.

was. They were certainly as white. Galton notes that 75 percent are English, and of these, 50 percent are pure English, 10 percent Anglo-Welsh, 10 percent Anglo-Irish, 10 percent Anglo-Scotch, 10 percent Scotch-Irish, and 10 percent pure Scotch, pure Irish, or pure Welsh. The remainder, he observes, are of "extremely mixed origin": "One is in about equal degrees English, Irish, French, and German; another is English, Scotch-Creole, and Dutch; another English, Dutch, Creole, and Swedish; and so on." As for that Creole, Galton writes, "I trust the reader knows what 'Creoles' are—namely, the descendants of white families long settled in a tropical colony; and that he does not confound the term with 'mulattoes.'" In other words, their extremely mixed origins included white, pasty white, and snow-blindingly white. Galton was going to study brothers, not *brothers*. And not sisters either. His subjects were, of course, all male.

Galton, who coined the phrase *nature versus nurture*, concluded that the latter was largely responsible for the firstborns' success. They had the advantage of being the heir to the family fortune, as well as a tenure as the sole recipient of the parents' attention. Later scientists would show that it's a lot more complicated than that; and that the misogynist and eugenicist stuff was utter bullshit. Galton was right about one thing, however, which is that there's a lot of quantification involved in sibling relations. Besides the fractional sharing of cupcakes, screen time, and parental affection, there is an actual formula that predicts how nicely siblings will treat each other. Called Hamilton's rule, it quantifies altruism as a function of genetic relatedness, in which $r$ (relatedness) $\times B$ (reproductive benefit of doing something nice) $> C$ (reproductive cost of doing something nice). If it's a closish relative, and it's going to benefit them more than it will cost you, you'll do it; if not, you won't. Hamilton's rule, then, explains why my son will intercede when another child tries to steal his sister's granola bar, but will also try to steal her granola bar for himself.

MOSTLY, THOUGH, he's in it for himself. My children share little besides genetic material, and they don't share all that much of that. Siblings are not, in fact, that similar. My husband and I produced one cautious and thoughtful girl, and two years later rolled out our second model, a whirling tornado. I really don't know what we were thinking putting them in the same bedroom. Although they agreed to the arrangement—provided we divide the space down the middle—it's a little bit like cohousing Alan Dershowitz and Torquemada. They just see the world differently, and neither one shies away from battle. Of course they're going to fight.

For some reason, this comes as a shock. Parents are always surprised when their children turn out to be nothing alike, I suppose because in every other instance, when we put the same ingredients together, we end up with the same product. Though we could not believe how different our children are, we should have seen it coming. Siblings share 50 percent of their genes, but those genes don't manifest in the same ways. In genetic terms, this is called recombination. Geneticist David Lykken likens the process to scrambling a telephone number: arrange the digits in a different order, and you get someone else entirely. Physically, siblings share few characteristics. Only 20 percent share an eye color; only 10 percent have the same complexion or hair. They're dissimilar in temperament, too. Siblings test as having only 15 percent in common personality-wise, making them only slightly more alike than two unrelated people raised in two completely different homes. Weirdly, siblings grow less alike the longer they live together.

Even identical twins don't share all their genes. Although they come from a single genome, they have different individual mutations: 359, on average. In mirror twins, these differences manifest in rather freaky and amazing ways, making the siblings mirror images of each other.[*] If one is right-handed, the other is left. Moles and hair whorls will present on opposite sides. In rare cases, they're mirror images internally, too: one twin will have his organs in the usual place; in the other, they'll be reversed. Skeletal features and teeth may be opposite as well.[†]

---

[*] It is hard not to geek out about the unusual but possible freak genetic occurrences in twins. In extremely rare cases involving an extra X chromosome, identical twins will share a genome but not a gender, with one ending up female, the other male. And when identical twins reproduce with another pair of identical twins—which, by the way, has happened—genetically, their children aren't cousins but full siblings.

[†] All of which makes for fascinating National Geographic specials. In real life, however, multiple births can lead to some rather darker outcomes due to perceived bad

Mirror twins develop when the egg splits late. When it splits *really* late, the twins are typically conjoined. Which I guess means they'd have to stay together their entire lives, but even then, those lives won't be the same.

This is even more true for children who don't share a liver. Being raised in the same home, it turns out, doesn't count for much. Siblings can experience it so differently, each growing up in what researchers describe as their unique microenvironment. No wonder siblings can remember the same event in entirely different ways. Even concrete facts become subjective. One study found that 53 percent disagree on their father's level of education, 46 percent on their mother's. They don't even agree on their parents' *ages*, differing a full 25 percent of the time.

It's as if they had different parents, because essentially, they did. Parents almost invariably treat their children differently, even if they try not to. Previous generations were more obvious about it, but we still do it in a thousand ways, sometimes consciously, sometimes not, responding to each child's gender, age, mood, and—even though we shouldn't—likability. Modern parents haven't stopped playing favorites; they've just stopped doing it *openly*.

Though few parents today will admit they have a favorite child, studies indicate that about two-thirds of parents do. In one small but astounding survey, 80 percent of mothers acknowledged favoring one child over the others. This was no secret to their children, 80 percent of whom agreed. Interestingly, however, when they were asked which child their mother loved most, they almost always got it wrong. Similar results are borne out in larger studies—two-thirds of children accurately perceive their parents'

---

juju. In the Middle Ages, twins were sometimes seen as proof of adultery, leading mothers to abandon them (Shahar, *Childhood in the Middle Ages*, 122). In traditional Balinese culture and mythology, twins are associated with incest, as it's assumed that opposite-sex twins were doing it in the womb. This is good luck if said twins are high-caste (in fact, they'll be encouraged to marry), but horrible luck if they're low-caste. In that case, the family will be banished to live someplace impure—typically, in the graveyard—for forty-two days, and the whole village will undergo extensive purification rituals (Yvonne Lefèber and Henk W. A. Voorhoeve, *Indigenous Customs in Childbirth and Child Care* [Assen, Netherlands: Van Gorcum, 1998], 54). The parents may be encouraged to give one child up for adoption so the twins may be raised apart.

favoritism, but less than half get the favorite right. Presumably, this gave them yet one more thing to fight about.

THE IDEA THAT you're supposed to treat your children equally is recent, and it's still not the norm in much of the world, where different siblings may have different roles and even different titles. In English we refer to both younger and older siblings as sister or brother, but Chinese has entirely separate terms for each. A *ge ge* (older brother) has different rights and responsibilities than a younger one (*di di*), as does a *jie jie* (big sister) and *mei mei* (little sister). In Japan the slang term for the second son is "Master Cold Rice," because historically he ate only after the firstborn, who I'll call Master Hot Lunch, got his. Even the definitions of seemingly straightforward terms like *brother* and *sister* vary from culture to culture. In some, these apply only to full siblings; in others, they include cousins.

In Balinese families, sibling order is so important that it dictates proper names as well. Whether male or female, firstborns are typically named Wayan (literally, "oldest"). The second-born is Made ("middle"), and the third—three-child families being considered ideal—is Nyoman ("last"). Should a fourth child be born, it receives the wonderful name of "little banana" (Ketut). The fifth is a terse Wayan Balik (Wayan Again).*

Treating all your children the same isn't the norm globally, and it's certainly not the norm historically. Playing favorites is called *parental differential treatment*, and it was standard practice until fairly recently. Treating all your children the same would be as ridiculous as, say, treating your husband and the doorman the same because they're both men, greeting them both with kisses and giving both tips for bringing up the mail. The two just play different roles, and there are different expectations for each.

---

* English and Scottish parents sometimes showed even less creativity by giving all their children the same first name. The practice died out in the UK by the nineteenth century, but continues in the family of George Foreman, whose children include George Jr., George III, George IV, George V, George VI, and Georgetta (Chris Galley, Eilidh Garrett, Ros Davies, and Alice Reid, "Living Same-Name Siblings and British Historical Demography," *Local Population Studies* 86 [Spring 2011]: 15–36).

As seventeenth-century poet Anne Bradstreet insisted: "Diverse children have their different natures; some are like flesh which nothing but salt will keep from putrefaction; some again like tender fruits that are best preserved with sugar; those parents are wise that can fit their nurture according to their Nature."

This was especially true in the large families of previous generations, where you might have a dozen children spaced out over twenty-five years. With so many kids, favoring one wasn't such a big deal; if you weren't the darling, you were in excellent company. And even if parents wanted to treat all the children equally, they just couldn't. It's one thing to divide a cupcake into perfect halves, quite another into perfect twelfths.

A few experts thought parents should at least *try*. In 1600, William Vaughan urged, "parents must ordinarily use equality among their children so neere as they may, and not shew more affection to one then to another, least thereby they provoke them to anger and desperation." In his 1622 book *Of Domesticall Duties,* William Gouge addressed the subject at greater length, counseling parents to treat their children equally in a passage that sounds a lot more like a legal contract than a philosophy of love: "The parties to whom parents are to perform all the forenamed duties are expressed under this word (Children) which hath not any speciall respect to prioritie of birth, to constitution of body, to affection of parent, or any such thing, as if first borne, proper, beautifull, darling, or the like children were only meant, but all that are begotten and borne of parents, all their children are meant. Whence I observe, that *Parents ought to have an impartiall respect to all their children,* and performe dutie indifferently and equally to all."*

Given the high frequency of fatal childhood accidents, I think it's safe to say parents certainly performed their duties indifferently. As to equally, well, it's important to remember that the seventeenth-century definition of *equal* is a lot different from ours. Gouge, for instance, says it's fine to favor one child over another if the favored child is *good* and

---

* Gouge also argues that you should treat your children the same because they come from the same place: "our own substance and bowels." And many parents did, in fact, treat all their children like crap.

the unfavored bad: "It is no partialitie to like grace and goodnesse in a childe, and for grace and goodnesse sake to love his childe so much the more, as also for impietie and obstinacy in rebellion to have his heart the more alienated from his childe: this is rather a vertue in a parent. Partialitie is when on by and undue respects one childe is preferred before another." And while he urges parents to distribute their affection and attention equally, the property should not be. The loot, he says, should go largely to the eldest, for several reasons: scripture says so; it's the law of the land; it keeps the estate intact; and firstborns are generally just more awesome than the rest.

Here I should point out that *Of Domesticall Duties* is a Puritan work whose primary reference is the Bible, which is not exactly a handbook for treating your children fairly. While we frantically strive to keep sibling conflict to a low simmer, biblical parents tend to stir the pot with many-colored coats and schemes to divert birthrights. Though they don't agree on much, this is something both the Bible and evolutionary theory endorse. Evolutionary biologists have argued that parents are incentivized to encourage sibling conflict as a way of sussing out the strongest child, the one who's most likely to survive and therefore best to invest resources in. Unsurprisingly, the losing children tend not to agree. In the Bible, as in life, this typically leads to conflict, at which point you root for the one you like best and maybe arm him with a slingshot, like any loving parent would.

Sibling fighting passed nearly unremarked until about a hundred years ago. For the first time in history, parents wanted to do something about it rather than, you know, make it worse with blatant favoritism. For the first time in *ever*, this was actually possible. Western parents had more time and attention to give now that families were smaller, decreasing from an average of seven kids in 1800 to 3.56 a hundred years later.* Child mortality had decreased, permitting parents to focus on the less pressing issues. Also, now that parents were encouraged to do the child-rearing themselves, they

---

* Nineteenth-century families didn't necessarily stay that large, however, due to higher mortality rates. Parents might *have* seven children, on average, but only four were likely to make it to adulthood. So although families were bigger, they weren't, like, reality-show bigger.

discovered how contentious the children actually are, and set about trying to find ways to ameliorate it.

They did, however, take their time. Like sibling resentments themselves, interest in sibling conflict simmered along for a couple of decades before finally hitting a boil. Even when the arrival of scientific parenting subjected all other areas of childhood to intense scrutiny, sibling relationships were ignored to a fairly remarkable degree. Arnold Gesell dismisses the matter in a single paragraph. Luther Emmett Holt doesn't mention the issue at all. Sadist and future APA president John Watson discusses the matter only briefly, and his take is as terrifying as you'd expect: he laments that science has not yet devised a way to make toys safe only for their rightful owner, so that Jimmy might get electrocuted when he tries to play with Billy's things, and thus learn to keep his hands to himself. That not being an option, Watson urges mothers who don't want to listen to fighting to simply buy two of everything. Roger that.

As for G. Stanley Hall, his only concern about siblings is to insist that children *have* them, famously declaring that "being an only child is a disease in itself." Parents of onlies don't need me to tell them that he was perfectly wrong. As study after study has shown, only children are no more narcissistic or maladjusted than children with siblings. Because they model their behavior on their parents, they're actually more likely to share. In fact, if there's any difference between only children and children with siblings, it's that only children are somewhat *better* adjusted, reporting higher levels of self-esteem and motivation.

SIBLING CONFLICT got a bit more attention once Freud started toying with the idea, declaring it a corollary of the Oedipus complex. His estranged disciple Alfred Adler investigated the matter further, focusing on birth order and the "dethronement" an older child experiences when replaced by a newer, cuter model. Adler also discusses the rivalry that results when a younger child feels he will never be as good as his older sibling and turns to cocaine as a result, thus predicting Roger Clinton's arrest sixty years before it happened.

It wasn't until the 1930s, however, that the concept really caught on, when David M. Levy coined the term *sibling rivalry* and published a book on the subject.[*] *Rivalry*, however, is a pretty mild description for what Levy observed when he presented his patients with celluloid dolls that were supposed to represent their younger siblings. The patients promptly destroyed and dismembered the dolls in a massacre so wide-scale Levy had to switch from celluloid to a more durable clay. And it wasn't just spoiled American brats who did this; Levy's experiments with the Kekchi Indians in Guatemala produced the same results.

By the mid-1940s the term, and the concept, began to enter the public consciousness, with more and more books and magazine articles addressing the issue. No surprise: parenting had become child-centered. What happened when child turned into children and there wasn't room in the center for both? It was as if the messiah got a brother, and parents didn't know what to do.

As usual, Dr. Spock set the tone. In *The Pocket Book of Baby and Child Care,* he discusses the matter at length, focusing on the primal drama of the second child's arrival. Spock has been credited with introducing the enduring analogy of the new baby as a mistress or second wife: a cute, unemployed drinker the current wife is not so thrilled to greet. And indeed, his advice is to treat the new baby as such, waiting until you're alone to hold her and playing it cool. "Treat her casually. Don't act excited about her. Don't gloat over her. Don't talk a lot about her. As far as possible, take care of her while the older one is not around."

Over the next several decades Spock's chapter would become an industry. Now hospitals and Lamaze centers offer classes to prepare the big sibling-to-be and minimize the trauma of dethronement. There's an infinite number of products for big brothers and big sisters, including capes, jew-

---

[*] Levy's other major contribution to the field of psychology was the introduction of the Rorschach test to America. According to Rorschach expert Z. A. Piotrowski, sibling rivalry is indicated in patients who see teeth in the inkblots. Note, however, that this also indicates chronic masturbation (Piotrowski, *Perceptanalysis: The Rorschach Method Fundamentally Reworked, Expanded, and Systematized* [New York: Routledge, 1957]).

elry, and should their duties include assisting in the birth, surgical scrubs. There are "Big Brother" bandannas for jealous *dogs*. And then there are all the children's books about the arrival of a new baby, currently numbering over two hundred. When I became pregnant with our second, we bought one for Rachel, though I'm not sure if it helped. Because we chose the Berenstain Bears version, it's possible we led her to expect not a baby but a cub.

As is true of most of his work, Spock's take is informed by Freud, but he never mentions Freud by name, and doesn't even use the still-unfamiliar term *sibling rivalry* for fear that it would alienate readers. (Instead of *rivalry*, then, it's *jealousy*, and even *sibling* remained so rare for so long that Fitzhugh Dodson felt the need to define the term in his 1970 book *How to Parent.*) Did Spock's approach work? Probably not; as he laments in his 1985 edition—emphasis his—"Jealous quarreling among brothers and sisters has been tolerated *much more* recently than it was in previous generations."

Still, there weren't a lot of better ideas. Some were strange: according to a 1979 *New York Times* article, in Mexico, sibling rivalry was treated with garlic, though the article didn't specify how. Other experts mostly just elaborated on Spock's approach, in terms that can't help but rattle the modern ear. Writing in 1970, Fitzhugh Dodson notes that the arrival of a younger sibling may make children feel "gypped" (!) and prompt them to regress, as his own daughter did when she asked that her Coke (!) be served in a baby bottle. Dodson complied.

Then there's Rudolf Dreikurs, whose philosophies my own mother turned to when her daughters' constant bickering drove her to enroll in a night-school class called Discipline Without Tears. The thinking, I suppose, was that the class would give her the tools to deal with us, or, at the very least, get her away from our shouting every Tuesday and Thursday from seven to eight.

A disciple of Alfred Adler, Dreikurs advocated individuality and family democracy, and his technique for dealing with sibling conflict was enormously simple. He wrote an entire chapter on the subject, but everything you need to know is in the title: "STAY OUT OF FIGHTS!" By refereeing, he argued, you just prolong the conflict and encourage it to happen again. Fairy tales, at least, back him up. Hansel and Gretel's parents ignored them completely, and they got along *great*.

More recently, research has backed Dreikurs up, too. As multiple studies have shown, siblings fight more when a parent is present. When parents routinely intervene, the fights are more savage and last longer. Which suggests that the historical record's neglect of the issue was perhaps the right way to deal with it.

When Spock observed that children were fighting "*much more*," maybe it wasn't because his methods didn't work, but because he had methods in the first place, because we were talking about it at all, because we were devoting chapters and books and therapy sessions to it. Sibling conflict interventions have become an industry, but the industry hasn't minimized the conflict so much as multiplied it. As psychologist Laurie Kramer has pointed out, the countless cartoons and books that are supposed to teach squabbling siblings to reconcile actually *increase* the squabbling, by modeling fights and giving siblings new ideas for torturing one another. The best advice, perhaps, is what my parents routinely told my sister and me when we were irritating each other: "If you ignore her, she'll stop." We ignored the advice then; I still do. It can be awfully hard to stay out of sibling fights, and most parents don't. We've made it our problem, and now it is.

I've read many thousands of pages on managing sibling conflict, and Dreikurs's method is the one I've come to favor, though I'm not sure if it's because it works, because it's what my parents did, or because it literally requires me to do nothing. I usually fail, however, because doing nothing is often the hardest thing to do. It is very, very difficult to listen to two screaming children and think, Carry on; and it is very, very easy to scream yourself.

ALTHOUGH DOING NOTHING is the method my mother eventually settled on herself, it was not, in fact, the technique she learned in her Discipline Without Tears class of 1977. What she learned there was role-play. When the children play each other, the thinking went, they come to see a different perspective and learn to resolve their conflict. I don't know where the idea came from, but it certainly wasn't from Dreikurs. I can only guess it was a bit of improv from the instructor, who I'll further guess had no children of his own.

We used the method exactly once. As I recall, the disagreement was over whose turn it was to pick the after-school TV viewing, with me favoring *The Brady Bunch* and Vicky voting for *The Brady Bunch* cartoon. It was an insurmountable divide and we dealt with it in our normal way, screaming and pulling hair, until our mother interrupted and asked us to switch roles.

This went just as you would expect it to. Told she should pretend to be me, Vicky announced, "I'm Jenny and I think I'm *so great*"; told I should pretend to be her, I stuck a finger up my nose, crossed my eyes, and banged my head on wood paneling. This immediately led to physical violence, at which point our mother banished us to our room until we could act like decent human beings.

Once we were confined to a stuffy, TV-less room, the role-play exercise did in fact stop our fighting by uniting us against our mother. With a single enemy to direct our resentment toward, Vicky and I found common ground. Within twenty minutes we'd forgotten all about the fight, and by evening we were the best of friends, at least until eight, when it was time to pick the prime-time show, and the fighting would start again.

Because it proved such a disaster, that was the last time Vicky and I would play each other, but we'd continue playing ourselves for quite some time, wearing grooves in the boards where we hit our marks, again and again. Dreikurs says that children fight in an effort to establish their role in the family. My sister and I had decided our roles early on: she would be Trouble, and I would be Troubled. I would go on to be pathologically good, and she'd cover bad. She would break curfew, and I would break down.

The psychological term for this is *sibling deidentification*, coined by psychologist Frances Schachter in the 1970s, exactly when Vicky and I were becoming a textbook case. When genes alone don't make siblings different enough, the siblings will differentiate themselves in other ways. Schachter argues that it's actually a strategy to reduce rivalry, allowing each sibling to find her own niche. (Refusing to deidentify is pretty much the best way to enrage your sibling, as in the perennial favorite car game, Stop Copying Me.) Vicky and I deidentified constantly, sometimes unconsciously and sometimes explicitly, as when she forbade me to do art (her thing) or be well liked and popular (also her thing). We may not have respected each other, but we always respected these limits.

We needed these boundaries, a Mason-Dixon Line, masking tape down a bedroom floor. It made life easier for us and everyone else when we stayed in our own lane. We looked nothing alike, but we were both girls, and fourteen months apart, and we got confused all the time. I got called by her name as much as I did by my own. It's hard enough to figure out who you are when you don't have a sibling. When you do, you pretty much have to make them your foil, a south for your north: I know you are but what am I?

As a child, the constant effort to Not Be Vicky felt natural and self-directed. Now that I'm a parent, I wonder how much our roles were cast. Children compare themselves constantly, and it's just so much easier if they're not competing in the same category. Thus we've decided that Rachel is tidy and bookish (when in fact she likes TV as much as her brother and her side of the room is just as messy as his), and Sam is a wild beast (when he's not really any louder or sloppier than his sister, though admittedly far more likely to leave the house without pants).

The hope, I suppose, is that creating a little space now will bring them closer as adults. Because this is what happened with my sister and me, I'm relying on the methods my parents used, staying out of it when I can, and providing a common enemy when I can't.

It is a role I am happy to play. Their fighting is the part of parenting I hate most; watching them together is the part I love best. I know it will be only a few years before they refuse to share a space, but for now I can still send them together to their room. I am the evil stepmother, my husband the neglectful father. They are Hansel and Gretel heading off to the woods, hand in hand, laying down the bread-crumb trail that will bring them back together. I am the evil witch. They are the best of friends until it's time to split the last candy cane, when the fight will begin, once again.

# 8

# Kids Today

## *On Discipline*

Because I was a bossy child who appreciated rules, I would not have predicted that I would be as lax a parent as I am, though I probably should have seen it coming. My previous experience being in charge involved stuffed animals, and these were far more compliant than my children turned out to be. When put in a time-out, a plush hippo tends to sit quietly. A four-year-old, however, will kick holes in the drywall, and discipline quickly starts to feel like more trouble than it's worth.

It also seems like something you shouldn't have to do. I understand that this is not how DNA works, but I still can't help but wonder why my children didn't genetically download some basic manners and self-control along with my eczema and short stature. It seems equally unfair that these traits didn't transfer automatically from child to child, like pinkeye or pinworms. It was bad enough that we had to go through the sleep training, the time-outs, the swim lessons, and the learning to read once, but expecting us to go through it all over again for every single child seems like asking a bit much.

The problem, of course, is that you're always starting from zero. Children have not been given a copy of the social contract. They don't know that we've all agreed that a sock is not a Kleenex, and more dangerously, that the phone charger is not a current-conducting bendy straw. Keeping them from killing themselves or anyone else is an endless chore, and to add manners, literacy, a modicum of self-control, and basic human decency to the mix seems like an impossible task. Press-ganging your children into civility and discipline is a yeoman's job.

There's just so much to learn. And although children have an amazing capacity for creating taxonomies (Foods to Eat/Foods to Throw; People Who Give Presents/Other People; Shirt I'm Willing to Wear/All Other Shirts), they are overwhelmed by the sheer volume of things they need to absorb and distinctions that seem completely arbitrary. We expect them to know, for instance, that the hot dog is the main dish, and not the ketchup, though these are served side by side. Water receptacles turn out to be remarkably complicated when you can't distinguish the ones you drink out of from the ones you urinate in. Tubes of diaper cream and toothpaste are nearly identical but are applied to very different body parts (once necessitating, in our home, a call to poison control). And it takes a bit to learn that while their mother may use the F-word, they themselves may not. It's understandable that they'd be confused; and that their parents, cat-herding them through socialization that seems endless, would be exhausted and irritable and prone to use the F-word far more than they should.

All of which slightly undermines the main thing we're trying to teach them, which is how to behave like a decent person in the world. And this, too, turns out to be a complicated and mutable concept. What constitutes good behavior has varied quite a bit throughout history. While I lose my mind when my son eats the aforementioned ketchup with his fingers (or, in one instance, with an unwashed bath toy), in the Middle Ages eating sauce with your hands was perfectly acceptable, so long as you didn't dig in past the first knuckle. Today a seventh grader would be expelled for smoking, but several hundred years ago Eton students were whipped if they failed to light up (tobacco was thought to prevent the plague). For generations, parents obsessed about their children's posture, but now we truly don't seem to care. Diction has become so unimportant that I'm honestly not sure what it means. We've also pretty much given up on honorifics, which my own children use only with animals, which is why they'll call a random rodent "Mr. Squirrel," but the chair of their father's department "Chuck."*

The disciplinary methods used to instill the desirable behavior are enormously variable, too. Over the centuries, parents have flogged their children and refused to touch them entirely; starved and force-fed them; sent them to bed and kept them up; locked them in and locked them out. I would be jailed for disciplining my children with methods that were considered normal less than a century ago, and the punishments we use now would look to seventeenth-century parents like rewards. Even today, there are huge variations from family to family or even from parent to parent, which is why my children ask me for snacks (I generally say yes) and their father for toys (so does he).

Although divergent parenting styles have existed for some time, they wouldn't be defined until developmental psychologist Diana Baumrind took them on in the 1960s. Baumrind divided parenting styles into three Goldilocks-like categories: authoritarian (too hard), permissive (too soft), and authoritative (just right). Later, Eleanor Maccoby and John Martin would add a fourth category, neglectful, to describe parents much like Goldilocks's own, who don't appear at all.

I suspect my husband and I are more like the porridge, the chair, or the bed than the parents: we're *there*, but we don't necessarily do a whole lot. Discipline is easily the part of parenting I shirk the most. It's just so much work and so little fun: it hurts me more than it hurts you. I would rather hide in the kitchen watching Netflix than monitor a time-out or cancel the playdate I desperately need my children to go on. And while we often threaten repercussions, we almost never see them through. When Rob says, "*That's* it," that is, literally, it.

Given my family's lenience, and a universal tendency toward entropy, I'd thought that, as a rule, each generation is more permissive than the

---

* Which drives both my husband and me crazy. Though middle-aged ourselves, we will always call our friends' parents and parents' friends Dr., Mr., Mrs., or Ms., because that's who they are. As an antidote to the casual forms of address used today, Rob is now encouraging the children to address his colleagues with the full Teutonic title of Herr/Frau Doktor Professor.

previous one. This is not true at all. What does seem to be true, however, is that each generation *thinks* it's more permissive than the previous one. Kids today are always worse than kids yesterday, and we've been complaining about their (and our) shortcomings for thousands of years. Kenneth J. Freeman summarized the ancient Greek take on things: "Children began to be the tyrants, not the slaves, of their households. They no longer rose from their seats when an elder entered the room; they contradicted their parents, chattered before company, gobbled up the dainties at table, and committed various offences against Hellenic tastes, such as crossing their legs. They tyrannised over the paidagogoi and schoolmasters." As far back as 20 BCE, Horace wrote, "Our sires' age was worse than our grandsires'. We, their sons, are more worthless than they; so in our turn we shall give the world a progeny yet more corrupt."

BY THIS LOGIC, the best parents and children were the first ones. This may or may not be true. It's hard to tell from the archaeological record alone how our oldest forebears disciplined their children and how said children behaved, but skeletal remains make clear they were not beaten excessively. I'd assumed that early human parents went heavy on the corporal punishment, given that we call prehistory things like the Stone Age and Iron Age and not, say, the Marshmallow Cupcake Age. But researchers believe early parents actually did a lot more hugging than hitting, and say Paleolithic parents didn't spank at all.*

At some point, however, a prehistoric toddler found his parents' last nerve, and physical punishment began. By biblical times it was fairly common, though perhaps not as a parenting technique. Although the Bible is usually cited as justification by parents who spank, most biblical examples

---

* Here is where I admit I do not understand *how* they know this, because evolutionary and adaptive psychology can get kind of hard to follow and I can get kind of distracted. But I believe it's based on the evolved structure of our brains *now* rather than actual physical evidence from the Paleolithic age. Smarter people who are wondering if I got that right may turn to Darcia Narvaez, Jaak Panksepp, Allan N. Schore, and Tracy R. Gleason, eds. *Evolution, Early Experience and Human Development: From Research to Practice and Policy* (New York: Oxford University Press, 2013).

of corporal discipline are directed at adults, who can earn punishments like forty lashes (for losing a court case) or a severed hand (for the rather specific offense of grabbing the testicles of the man your husband is fighting). What little intrafamilial beating there is occurs almost entirely in Proverbs, which recommends the practice for use on children as well as on horses, donkeys, bondsmen, and "fools."*

Corporal punishment of children was used throughout the ancient world. It was especially popular in Sparta, where they probably took things too far, starting with the mandatory boot camp that began at age seven. A student who answered a question wrong got not a swat but a *bite*.† The severe discipline that defined Spartan childhood culminated in a bloody ritual known as the *diamastigosis*, in which boys were flogged, sometimes to death, in front of a cheering crowd that included their parents. This spectacle eventually grew so popular with tourists that an amphitheater was built to host it. An earlier, stranger iteration of the event included piles of cheese guarded by heavily armed adults (the boys were supposed to try to steal it, and were whipped when they did).

The amphitheater that hosted the *diamastigosis*
(Courtesy Pausanias Project)

---

* Elsewhere, the Bible also allows that a son may be stoned to death—a pretty literal version of "grounding"—for being "stubborn and rebellious . . . a glutton and a drunkard" or for cursing his parents. This punishment would be meted out by the community rather than mom and mad, and seems not to have happened much, if ever.

† On the thumb. Which is a little less horrifying but still really, really odd.

In Sparta, child abuse was a privilege exercised not just by parents; any adult was permitted to deliver a beating to any child.[*] In most of the ancient (and much of the modern) world, the adult in question was usually the child's teacher, and surviving literature is full of references to teachers just whaling on their pupils. Corporal punishment at school was common throughout Sumeria, India, China, and Egypt, where one teacher complained, "But though I beat you with every kind of stick, you do not listen." In Greek schools, corporal punishment was so widespread that the symbol used to represent education was the rod.[†]

In Rome, too, discipline and education were basically synonymous (our word *discipline* derives from the Latin word for instruction[‡]). Roman teachers deployed a whole arsenal of weapons on their students, including the *virga* (birch switch), *flagellum* (whip), *scutia* (leather strap), and *ferula* (rod). Still, not everyone was on board. Quintilian disapproved of it on class grounds, arguing that beating was for *slaves*, not well-off kids, and also that it didn't work.

He was right about that, but the data was a couple of thousand years off. In the meantime, physical discipline grew even more common. It's unclear exactly how widespread it was by the Middle Ages, but the equipment developed around this time suggests that it was both ubiquitous and elaborate. Medieval sadists invented ever more specific tools to keep kids in line. These included the goad (a small knife for poking), the flapper (featuring a hole designed to produce blisters), iron rods, canes, shovels, the cat-o'-nine-tails, bunches of sticks, and the rather obviously named "discipline" (a whip made of chains).

Beatings were common in school and at home, which posed a particular problem when the child in question was an English prince. Only kings

---

* Not just in Sparta. According to Plato, in Greece all free men were allowed to punish any deserving children and their tutors (Benjamin Jowett, trans., *The Dialogues*, vol. 5 (*The Laws*), third ed. [London: Clarendon Press, 1892], 190).

† Similarly, the fourteenth-century Chinese pictograph for *teach* shows a hand wielding a whip (A. R. Colón with P. A. Colón, *A History of Children* [Westport, CT: Greenwood, 2001], 59). All of which makes our current symbol of the apple feel kind of wimpy.

‡ In Old French, fittingly, it meant "martyrdom" or "suffering."

were allowed to whip the royal bottom, leaving harried tutors and nurses in the lurch. In the late Middle Ages this led to the designation of the whipping boy, a proxy who received disciplinary beatings in the prince's place. Typically a commoner, the whipping boy was raised as a close friend of the prince, to assure that the prince would at least feel bad *emotionally*.

Over the next few hundred years the thrashings continued, especially at the hands of teachers. Though the English and French were no slouches, Germans deserve special mention both for quantity and enthusiasm. One German schoolmaster reckoned that in fifty-one years of teaching he had given 124,000 lashes with a whip, 136,715 slaps with the hand, 911,527 blows with a stick, and 1,115,800 boxes on the ear. Coming later, Beethoven was more reserved but weirder; when his students displeased him, he rapped them with a metal knitting needle, pinched them, and bit them on the shoulder.* German theologian Barthélemy Batt urged restraint, recommending that children be beaten on their sides with a rod, "that they not die thereof." But his advice that parents not "strike and buffet their children about the face and head, and to lace upon them like malt sacks with cudgels, staves, fork or fire shovel," suggests that many parents in fact did.

Though the brutality was at times excessive, it was considered necessary. Parents and teachers were trying to instill obedience not just to their elders but to the entire host of heaven. Disobedience didn't mean a bad reputation; it meant eternal hellfire. With their souls on the line, it was better to err on the side of raised welts. As Cotton Mather would write some time later, "Better whip't than damned."†

But the Middle Ages weren't all catherine wheels and anguish pears.

---

* Still, they got off easier than Beethoven's cook, at whom he threw eggs. As for the biting: this turns out to be more common than I ever would have expected, often but not always a response to biting from children. At one time, it was fairly standard discipline for adults to bite back, to teach children not to bite again, though in fact it does the opposite. Nonetheless, the practice persists, and my daughter informs me she saw one of her caregivers do it.

† In actuality, Mather himself was, literally, all talk. Despite this threat, he disciplined his own children with long discussions, stern looks, and the occasional withholding of candy, eschewing corporal punishment altogether (Elizabeth Pleck, *Domestic Tyranny*, 45).

Toward the end of the era, people began to focus on more genteel mat-ters like the social niceties. For the first time, one of the things you were trying to beat into your children was *manners*. I have to admire the effort, having made far less progress in this department under far less challeng-ing circumstances, as evidenced by a recent dinner in which my son stuck his bare foot in a tub of butter, then grabbed a spoonful of hummus and proceeded to smear it up and down his sweatpants.

In any case, medieval parents began to focus a bit less on heaven and hell and a little more on please and thank you. This was the dawn of courtesy, and it was not just fish forks (forks not having really been in-vented yet) so much as an overall ethos. A number of courtesy books were published to help the uncouth. Though some were directed specifically to children, many were written for a more general audience, as medieval adults' manners weren't much better than my son's.

In England, the first of these was the thirteenth-century *Book of the Civilized Man* by Daniel of Beccles, which laid down the niceties of civil society in Latin verse. It has still not been fully translated into English, but many of the best bits made it into the vernacular, like "In front of grandees, do not openly excavate your nostril by twisting your fingers" and "Do not attack your enemy while he is squatting to defecate." His other tips include a warning not to be a "nose-blower at dinner nor a spitter"; should you need to belch, you should do so while looking up at the ceiling, and you should refrain from picking fleas off your arms or bosom. After the meal, he advises, only the host may urinate in the hall; all others will need to find a more appropriate venue. As for advice directed at children specifically, the author seems to have regarded them as hopeless ("They cover their clothes with ashes, they make them dirty, they dribble on them; they wipe their noses flowing with filth on their sleeves") and recommends parents keep them out of sight when company is present.

Once people began caring about appearances, parents and teachers could rely on another useful disciplinary tool in the form of shame. This was the method preferred by Locke as well as most American and En-glish schoolmasters, though the latter's methods were a good deal more severe than the former's. Locke recommended parents "praise in public, blame in private," while for the schoolmasters, the spectacle was the whole point, a practice that would eventually culminate in the use of the dunce cap. (Interestingly, the cap itself, invented by thirteenth-century Scottish theologian John Duns Scotus,* was originally conceived of as more of a thinking cap, and became associated with stupidity only when Scotus's philosophies fell out of theological favor.) In Europe, students were also made to wear donkey ears.

Shame headgear has been discontinued, as has shame discipline of most kinds, at least in the United States and Europe. However, it continues today in other parts of the world as well as on the Internet, where its subjects are usually guilty-looking dogs photographed with signs they cannot read attesting to their crimes.

BY THE EIGHTEENTH and nineteenth centuries fear was joining shame in the parents' discipline arsenal, and it was becoming more common to keep children in line with psychological torments rather than physical ones, locking them in dark closets or even drawers. In this respect, bogeymen proved enormously useful, if not entirely new.

Though the phrase itself would not appear until the late nineteenth century, mythical creatures who punish children for bad behavior—often by eating them—have been around since ancient times. I'm not entirely sure why so many bogeymen were on strict naughty-child diets, but it's been true from the beginning. Lilith, Lamia, Empusa, Sybaris, and the strixes all had a taste for kids (as did Mormo, who merely bit them).[†] Later bogeymen would follow their lead, eventually culminating in the

---

* Not to be confused with the ninth-century theologian also named John Scotus, whose classroom discipline methods failed entirely when his students apparently stabbed him to death *with their pens* for "trying to get them to think" (Charles Warren Hollister, Joe W. Leedom, and Marc A. Meyer, *Medieval Europe* [New York: McGraw-Hill, 2002], 117).

† Though he wasn't a bogeyman figure, Kronos famously craved kids as well, eating five of his children. The sixth eventually tricked him into vomiting his siblings back up. *Parents!*

horrifying Filipino iteration, Pugot Mamu, who, lacking a mouth—he beheaded himself—eats children through a hole in his throat. There are also a number of bogeymen who eat children for *not* eating, an admirably literal carrying out of just deserts (or desserts).

Though it seems unimaginable now, at one time being eaten was a credible threat. A few hundred years ago hunger, desperation, and insufficient supervision were daily realities, and as children's literature expert Jack Zipes points out in his analysis of Little Red Riding Hood, children *were* eaten with some frequency by animals both wild and domestic. To propose that they might be eaten by supernatural creatures as well wasn't such a big leap. And to then suppose that supernatural creatures might lurk in the neighborhood was hardly a leap at all. Which partly explains what Zipes describes as "the virtual epidemic of trials against men accused of being werewolves" in the sixteenth and seventeenth century, of which there were "literally thousands if not hundreds of thousands." When half your neighbors have been convicted of lycanthropy, you're probably going to take your parents' warning to be home before dark a lot more seriously. Also, you'll probably never leave the house again.

In any case, as scary as bogeyman stories were, they weren't anywhere near as scary as wandering off in the night to be eaten by the family pig, an outcome that the use of bogeymen was supposed to prevent. Bogeymen are a preemptive discipline strategy, designed to prevent misbehavior rather than punish it. Deployed properly, they could make a parent's job a lot easier, it being far simpler to psychically scar your child into being home before dark than to go out chasing after him every night.

Anything that kept children safer and parents saner was a win, and the strategy was widely used. Of course, the use of bogeymen probably caused untold lifelong psychological damage, but people wouldn't start worrying about that until the late nineteenth century or so. Bogeymen would in part be what prompted that worry, when Freud's fascination with Hoffmann's Sandman would inform his work on the uncanny. After that, their use tapered off.

Until then, though, things got pretty wild. In the Middle Ages, parents relied on bogeymen like witches, demons, hobgoblins, and the bugbear from which the bogeyman's name evolved, as did, regrettably and indirectly, that of Booger from *Revenge of the Nerds*.[*] Probably because *B* is just a scary sound (see: *boo!*), the bogeyman has a similar name in much of Europe: there's Boeman (Netherlands), Busemann (Norway), Buhmann (Germany), Bogle (Scotland), Bua (Georgia), Baboulas (Greece), Babaroga (Yugoslavia), Baba Yaga (Russia), Babau (Italy and Romania), Babay (Ukraine), Bubák (Czech Republic), and Babadook (arthouse cinemas).

In many Spanish- and Portuguese-speaking countries he's known as El Cuco or El Coco, a hairy, ghostly beast that also lent its name to the coconut, when Portuguese sailors saw its resemblance in the shaggy brown fruit. Spain has a number of other bogeymen, including El Ogro (the ogre) and El Sacamantecas, who is perhaps the strangest of all: his name is essentially the Liposuctioner (literally, "fat extractor"), and he kills people to steal their flab.[†]

Sweden doesn't have any names for the bogeyman because they don't have a bogeyman because they are better than we are.

In addition to mythical beasts like *penjamun*, for the Punan Bah in rural Malaysia bogeymen included "Europeans bearing injections." Parents could make threats a little more threatening when they invoked real-life figures, and over the years they've made bogeymen out of Oliver Cromwell, Prince Menshikov, and Otto von Bismarck, as well as countless Jews

---

[*] The ultimate root is probably the Scottish *bogle* or the Middle English *bugge*, both of which essentially mean "ghost." The golf term *bogey* is related, but *boogie* probably is not, and *bogart* isn't at all, the original Dutch meaning "orchard keeper" and the current English, "joint hogger."

[†] *Horrifyingly*, this character seems to have originated with the real-life case of nineteenth-century serial killer Manuel Blanco Romasanta, a Spanish Tyler Durden who supposedly sold soap made from his victims (or, perhaps, just sold the fat unprocessed). There is really too much weird stuff in this story to pack into a single footnote, like the fact that Romasanta was raised as a girl for the first six years of his life. Or the fact that, at his trial, his defense was that he suffered from lycanthropy. Or the fact that Queen Isabella commuted his death sentence so doctors could study this entirely made-up condition. Or the fact that there actually was a market for human fat in Europe at the time; apothecaries used it in mixtures to treat gout, bone pain, TB, rheumatoid arthritis, and toothache, and a number of people were arrested in trafficking in the stuff. Or the fact that there was yet another later real-life Spanish serial killer who was also called El Sacamantecas. Or the fact that there's yet another fat-stealing Spanish bogeyman called the Mantequero (the fat seller). All of which makes me glad I'm not a nineteenth-century Spanish child.

and Gypsies.* In the nineteenth century, Napoleon served as bogeyman in a popular English lullaby:

> Baby, baby, naughty baby,
> Hush, you squalling thing, I say.
> Peace this moment, peace, or maybe,
> Bonaparte will pass this way.

Because kids are gullible enough to believe that dictators and warlords somehow find the time in their schedule to torment children who stay up past their bedtime, warnings like this were not uncommon. Albanian children were threatened with visits from real-life occupying forces like Katallani (the Catalan) and Gogoli (the Mongol). During the Thirty Years' War, German parents sent their children to bed with a lullaby warning them, "The Swede will be here in the morning / Oxenstierna will be here in the morning." A few hundred years later, the enemy was closer to home, and in some German families misbehaving children were brought in line with the threat of a visit from the Social Democrats.

Though bogeymen could traumatize children for life, they were often invoked to ensure that life would be long, warning kids away from particular dangers. Water bogeymen were especially common, like the Scandinavian† Näcken and Brunnsgubben and the Sicilian Marabbecca, which were meant to scare children away from wells and hazardous water. In Japan, *kappa* are still used to warn children from swimming without supervision. Other creatures, like the Latin American Robaniños (Kidsnapper), La Llorona (Weeping Woman), and Chupacabra (Goat-sucker), were a reminder not to go out alone, especially at night.

Because going out alone was exactly what their *caregivers* wanted to

---

* When my parents failed to do this, I did it myself, making a bogeyman out of gun-toting Patty Hearst, abducted not far from my hometown and on the news constantly when I was four. I remained faintly terrified of her until I was eight or nine, though am now a big fan of her work with John Waters.

† Okay, Swedish. While the concept of the bogeyman is more or less nonexistent in Sweden now, they did have these guys a few centuries back. Note, however, that, like all Swedes, these bogeymen worked for the greater common good.

do, a great number of bogeymen were employed to ensure the kids got in bed on time and stayed there. Although I can think of no worse way to lull a child into slumber than with threats of abduction and torture, bedtime bogeymen have been used around the world for hundreds of years. The most famous of these is probably the Sandman. Though decidedly malicious in earlier iterations (see page 279), he eventually morphed into a more banal figure who sprinkles magic sand in children's eyes to bestow good dreams. After an unfortunate incident between my son and a playmate, I can report that this does not work with regular sand, and will instead result in an eyewash performed by an ER doc.

In Quebec, the bedtime bogey was known as the Bonhomme Sept-Heures (Seven O'Clock Fellow), who dropped by at dusk to carry off any children still awake in a big brown sack. His name is likely a fanciful adaptation of the English term *bonesetter*, a folk healer whose house calls tended to provoke a great deal of screaming, making children especially susceptible to the suggestion they be in bed before he arrived.

The Bonhomme and Sandman had colleagues around the world. In Haiti children seem to have had a later bedtime, and were threatened with Mètminwi (Master Midnight). In Congo the position was held by Dongola Miso (Scary-eyed Creature); and in Belgium by Oude Rode Ogen (Old Red Eyes). In Brazil children were frightened into bed by Bicho Papão (Eating Beast); in Yukon Territory by Quankus; and in the Bahamas by the Small Man. In Denmark Bussemanden lived under the bed, ready to pounce on any children who remained awake.

At some point, however, parents realized that the bogeymen that are supposed to make children sleep tend to have the opposite effect. Unfortunately, their friends and siblings realized the same thing. Children, prone to fear the dark, were easily led into fearing the various monsters and ghosts described by their peers, who continue to share these stories today, forcing parents to invent things like anti-monster spray rather than the monsters themselves.

Twenty-first-century bogeymen are a decidedly tamer lot. We still use them to compel good behavior, but now, instead of abducting and eating children, the worst that they do is withhold presents. The threat of being put on a naughty list is far less motivating than, say, the threat of being eaten alive through a hole in the throat of a headless monster. The Tooth Fairy and Santa have their uses, but as bogeymen go, they've been defanged.

Several hundred years ago, however, Santa's threats could be a little more pointed. From 1200 to 1500, St. Nicholas functioned much as the gift-giver he does today but following the Protestant Reformation, like most saints, he was out of a job. After a brief and unpopular period of no presents, he was replaced by bogeymanish proto-Santas whose duties included whipping and kidnapping naughty children. They might also give gifts to the deserving, and to lug these around, acquired the sack that is factory standard for bogeymen around the world.

The proto-Santas were a pretty unsavory lot, and were often based on local superstition as well as abject racism. Besides Ru-Klaus (Rough Nicholas) and Père Foue-ttard (Father Whipper), there was Aschenklas (Ashy Nicholas), Zwarte Piet (Black Peter), Schmutz-li (Dirty), and the dark and hairy Krampus. After Santa became the kindly Santa we know today, these figures stuck around as sidekicks and enforcers. At which point it becomes a little hard not to notice the contrast between snowy white Santa and his darker-complected, not-so-nice friends.

Greetings from Krampus!

Bogeymen have, in fact, long been a projection of a culture's most racist beliefs and anxieties. They've offered a way for parents to teach not just discipline but xenophobia and prejudice. Besides the Jews and Gypsies that have often been pressed into bogeyman service, there's a long list of menacing dark-skinned figures, from Italy's L'uomo Nero to Germany's der schwarze Mann to Poland's Czarny Lud. In other words, there aren't a whole lot of bogeymen who are strawberry blonds. The actual St. Nicholas, by the way, was Mediterranean and lived in Turkey.

**BY THE NINETEENTH CENTURY** or so parents were finding other ways to transmit their racist beliefs as well as their disciplinary ones, and the use of bogeymen gave way to more science-based techniques. For this generation of experts, discipline applied to parents as much as children, and meant "the reasonable regulation and supervision of the fundamental habits of a child throughout all stages of his development and a consistent plan for having the child observe those rules that are laid down." The emphasis was not on punishment but on prevention, on establishing habits that encouraged obedience. Crucial to this was a carved-in-stone routine for every aspect of daily life. As Ada Hart Arlitt argued, a child "will never know that there are laws that govern the universe unless he knows that there are laws that govern the home." Mealtimes, sleep schedules, play, conversation, and even bathroom visits must occur on a regular schedule, and she means *regular*; variations of as little as ten to fifteen minutes a day are too much. With careful and thoughtful planning, you could prevent misbehavior, and actual punishment would rarely be needed. When it was, this, too, should be careful and thoughtful, tailored to both the child and the crime.

Which is wonderful, it really is, but good heavens, what a lot of work. The kids might not have gotten punished, but the parents sure did. No wonder, then, that when Spock came along with alternative methods, parents got right on board. Spock advocated a friendly but firm approach, but it was the former adjective that seemed to stick. Although he was no pushover—he wrote that children should not be given too many choices or explanations, and said the occasional spanking in anger was fine—he was nonetheless perceived as the extremely lenient foil to stricter predecessors.

Spock quickly became synonymous with permissiveness, although he neither advocated nor invented it. Parents had been letting their children do whatever they wanted long before Spock showed up. When families were trying to survive various inquisitions and famines, discipline could take a back seat to the more pressing concerns of basic survival. As far back as 1624, London minister Thomas Barnes was lamenting, "Youth were never more sawcie . . . the ancient are scorned, the honourable are contemned, the magistrate is not dreaded." Robert Russel, meanwhile, fretted over the "lewd and wicked Children" who play in the streets, using swears and—I'm not sure why this was so upsetting—"Nick-names." In the colonies, Reverend Thomas Cobbett found children acting "proudly, disdainfully, and scornfully toward parents." By 1671, Jane Sharp was blaming the parents: "Their children by overcockering, growing so stubborn and unnatural, that they have proved a great grief to their parents."

*Overcockering* meant "spoiling," and the overcockering Sharp has in mind here is the crime of feeding children when they are hungry. Oddly enough, it was this same issue that got Spock into trouble; the perception that he was overly permissive comes from a single misinterpreted passage in which he mentions infant feeding on demand. But on-demand feeding wasn't his idea, and he never took credit for it.* He barely even endorsed it. Nonetheless, Spock became associated with child-led feeding, and then permissiveness, to the degree that he's often credited with originating them as well as all the failings of the feckless no-good generation of baby boomers. By the late sixties, publications like *Newsweek* and *The New York Times Magazine* were running cover stories asking if the counterculture was all Spock's fault.

But kids were kids today long before Spock showed up, especially in America. Perhaps because their youthful tantrum had resulted in full-blown revolution, by the nineteenth century American children had a reputation for being especially rebellious, and their parents, for being especially indulgent. European visitors often wrote, scandalized, about American children's insolence. British-born John Bristed's 1818 book on *America and Her Resources* argued that good parenting was not one of them: "Parents have no command over their children, nor teachers over their scholars. . . . Owing, perhaps, to the very popular nature of our institutions, the American children are seldom taught that profound reverence for, and strict

---

* In the first edition of his book, he claimed it was something people were already doing. Margaret Mead's daughter, whom Spock helped deliver, claimed it was actually Mead who introduced him to on-demand feeding, using it herself after having observed its advantages in her fieldwork.

obedience to, their parents." In 1832 Frances Milton Trollope's *Domestic Manners of the Americans* noted that the country's children seemed to lack manners entirely, describing "the total want of discipline and subjection which I observed universally among children of all ages." J. V. Hecke's 1821 book *Reise durch die Vereinigten Staaten* documented children "in convulsive anger at their parents," arguing with the elderly, and threatening to pelt them with stones. John Oldmixon's 1855 book about his visit to America devotes an entire section to "Spoiled Children," marveling, "Baby citizens are allowed to run wild as the Snake Indians, and do whatever they please; not only mothers take no notice, but fathers are equally deaf and blind."

In this, Americans may have been following the example set by the first family. A number of presidential offspring were notoriously unruly. The Lincolns were considered especially permissive parents, allowing their sons to run wild throughout the White House, once firing a toy cannon (loaded with real gunpowder) at a cabinet meeting. Tad also managed to get his hands on a functioning musket, firing it out a bathroom window and barely missing a washerwoman. Meanwhile, "Lincoln would say nothing, so abstracted was he and so blinded to his children's faults. Had they s—t in Lincoln's hat and rubbed it on his boots, he would have laughed and thought it smart." Theodore Roosevelt's daughter Alice was so demanding that Teddy told a friend, "I can either run the country or I can attend to Alice, but I cannot possibly do both."

Some European visitors viewed this rebelliousness as a good thing. Tocqueville saw American children's independent spirit as proof of an American culture of equality, and Harriet Martineau found their impertinence charming: "For my own part, I delight in the American children; in those who are not overlaid with religious instruction. There are instances, as there are everywhere, of spoiled, pert, and selfish children. Parents' hearts are pierced there, as elsewhere. But the independence and fearlessness of children were a perpetual charm in my eyes." It may have been to their parents as well. Historian Elizabeth Pleck's thorough review of American diaries and letters from 1650 to 1900 notes the absence of discipline in both parents' and children's accounts, which "suggests instead that most parents did not give much thought to the punishment of their children." Lincoln was criticized for actually encouraging his children's antics, going so far as to order (nonfunctioning) weapons from the navy for them. The mechanically adept Tad then figured out how to make them function just fine.

Americans, of course, didn't invent misbehavior, and Spock did not invent the parenting that produced it, as he argued in a 1971 article titled "Don't Blame Me!" He'd never promoted permissiveness in the first place, and he spent much of his career trying to clarify the fact that it was neither what he meant nor what he wrote. Still, it seems to be what parents read. When Spock asked why parents were letting their children hit them, throw food, behave abominably, and stay up all hours, he reports they responded, "But I thought we were meant to do what the baby wanted." Within a year of the book's publication he was writing his publisher that the next edition would "need to monkey around with the topic of *spoiling* which I am afraid is going to become more important as over-enthusiastic parents *take over the idea of flexibility*, hook, line and sinker."

And for this I can hardly blame them. Parenting is so hard; and like our kids, we're all looking for permission to slack off in some areas. Just as when I say "If you tidy up the living room, you can have a snack," and my children hear "Dump Frosted Flakes on the floor and watch cartoons," when Spock said you could feed children when they're hungry, we heard "Fix yourself a drink, your job here is done."

AND THEN WE ALL got sent to our rooms. In the 1960s and '70s figures like Norman Vincent Peale and Spiro Agnew thundered against Spock, and a new crop of advice books urged parents to lay down the law. Forty years later, some of these have not aged well. Besides Walter Sackett's nutty *Bringing Up Babies*—which, you may recall, equates feeding on demand with communism and advocates coffee for babies—there's *You CAN Raise Decent Children* (1971), written by doctors and next-door neighbors Berthold Eric Schwarz and Bartholomew Ruggieri. Schwarz, a psychiatrist, was also a paranormal researcher, and his other books include *Everyday Life: Parent-Child Telepathy, Psychic Nexus*, and *UFO Dynamics*.

*You CAN Raise Decent Children* is largely silent on the paranormal, being too busy spouting what now reads as hate speech. The flap copy frets over the "Spock-marked generation" and asks "Is it possible to raise children who won't turn into hippies, drug freaks, radicals or dropouts?" Yes! say the authors, even "in these days of Women's Liberation and open homosexuality." Readers who flip right to *homosexuality* in the book's index will be directed to see also *perversion* and *transvestism*. Readers looking for advice on more mundane matters, like the pros and cons of spanking, or when and how to suspend privileges, will come up empty, but they will get a lot of Freudian crackpottery and dubious theorizing. Nothing is more dangerous than "modern frankness," maintaining gender norms is paramount, and all child misbehavior is caused by parental neuroses. Regular enemas will lead to glue-sniffing, and asthma may be caused by Oedipal conflicts. Feeding on demand, however, is okay.

The book is also largely silent on the topic of religion, though most of the other disciples of discipline went hard on the subject. Experts like James Dobson, John Rosemond, and Gary and Ann Marie Ezzo emphasized obedience not just to parents but to divine order, in a return to the parenting philosophies that defined the Middle Ages. The neo-disciplinarians also demonstrated a medieval flair for disciplinary creativity, though thankfully involving far fewer spiked maces. Some of the more colorful suggestions can be found in evangelical author/former child star Lisa Whelchel's 2000 book *Creative Correction*. Whelchel's techniques include handcuffing fighting siblings together (with toy restraints), turning off the power to their room, removing their bedroom door, forcing teens to listen to the *Barney* soundtrack, and dosing the offending child with hot sauce. For some reason, it was this last punishment that caused a giant uproar and not the suggestion you burn your child's toys, which Whelchel also recommends as a way to correct budding arsonists.[*]

The straiter-laced found inspiration from the business world, relying on programs like P.E.T. (Parenting Effectiveness Training), which was developed by psychologist Thomas Gordon using methods designed for the workplace. Other programs, like Stephen Covey's *The 7 Habits of Highly Effective Families*, follow the same approach. These appear to be popular,

---

[*] While I would not use many of her techniques myself, and the toy-burning thing is a really bad idea, the book has its good points and I will brook no criticism of Blair Warner. Also, the *Barney* thing is brilliant.

but I'm personally unable to evaluate them, due to my own limited and ignominious history in office settings. Apparently they are useful, though I don't really see how the methods would translate, given that you can't fire your children, and managers, unlike parents, don't have employees openly shitting in the yard.

Still, they are certainly more effective than my current go-to technique, yelling, which research shows pretty clearly to be useless as well as damaging. My sole justification for yelling, besides the fact that my kids can really push it and I can't or don't always control myself, is that my mother did it, too. I tell myself I am reproducing what was overall a very happy childhood, although my children tell me how much they hate it when I yell often enough that it's possible they won't remember things as rosily as I do.

But what else am I supposed to do? (Besides parent calmly and competently, which seems unlikely.) For the last few generations, parents haven't had many options. Thanks to Freud and scientific research, spanking has been falling off, replaced by the few disciplinary techniques that came about during mid-century. There was, for instance, grounding. Originally an aviation term, I'm assuming it was brought home by World War II vets who, a dozen years later, found themselves dealing with adolescent children who could be a great deal more frustrating than flight equipment. At first the term meant the suspension of driving privileges, but it soon came to mean house arrest, a punishment I never really understood, home being the last place you want to be stuck with a difficult teen.

FOR YOUNGER CHILDREN, the mid-century disciplinary technique that caught on is so standard now it's hard to imagine it was invented only recently: the time-out, which was developed by behavioral psychologist Arthur Staats, who used it on his own daughter; apparently well served by the technique, she would go on to become a child psychiatrist herself. As Staats notes, the idea came not from human psychology but from animal training. (The study that first used the term *time-out* was done on pigeons, and the technique was used to train them not to peck at their food levers.) Its success suggests that Staats was onto something, and I have to wonder why animal training techniques have not been applied to children more often.* Anyone who's spent any time with a toddler knows they're basically labradoodles. (Our own toddler son spent so much time chasing squirrels and peeing on trees that the comparison came readily to mind.)

When we were going through a particularly feral period, I asked a friend with well-behaved children what parenting book he'd used. He admitted it was actually a pet training manual: *Don't Shoot the Dog!* by Karen Wylie Pryor.† As Pryor points out, animal training methods apply just as well to spouses, employees, roommates, and children most of all. Others note that said methods are especially effective up to two and a half, at which age children and dogs are apparently intellectual peers.

In its standard form, animal training relies on positive reinforcement, which seems to be ideal for both dogs and small children, neither of whom have the reasoning to understand the process behind negative discipline. Punishment, which typically occurs after the crime has been committed, takes place too late for the child to connect it with the offending behavior. Positive reinforcement, however, is something almost all sentient beings can comprehend. You do something, you get a treat, and you do it again. Who's a good boy?

This is called *operant conditioning*, as coined by Skinner, and although it sounds newfangled, raising children by animal methods has been done for thousands and thousands of years. During their *agoge* training, Spartan boys were raised more or less like goats, living shoeless, unwashed, and minimally clothed in groups known as *agélai* (herds) under the supervision of the *paidonomos* (boyherd). Children needed the firm hand of the barnyard overseer, because, as Plato wrote, "of all the animals the boy is the most unmanageable inasmuch as he has the fountain of reason in him not yet regulated; he is the most insidious, sharp-witted, and insubordinate of animals. Wherefore he must be bound with many bridles."

The historical record also notes a number of children who were raised

---

* Some current parenting experts do recommend techniques that seem to borrow from the animal world, however. In *Dare to Discipline*, for instance, James Dobson recommends you correct a child's misbehavior with a forceful squeeze to the trapezius muscle, which is something I'm pretty sure I've seen Doberman mothers do to their pups.

† This is the daughter of mom-hating author Philip Wylie mentioned in chapter 3.

not just *as* animals but *by* animals.* These are all almost certainly apocryphal or exaggerated, but no parent will be surprised by the presence, in the cultural imagination, of children raised by wolves. These accounts became especially popular in the eighteenth century, with its Rousseauian veneration of nature. Feral children were seen as a throwback to an Edenic past uncorrupted by human interventions.

Those hoping for a missing link, of an example of "natural man," were disappointed. As zoologist Eerhard von Zimmerman wrote in 1777, the case of Peter of Hanover, found in the Hamelin forest by King George's hunting party in 1725, and his fellow feral children "teaches us absolutely nothing about man's natural state, since they were never in it. That would be like studying physiology through the observation of a man attacked by the most violent of diseases." Peter likewise disappointed the society ladies who'd been hoping to see virility in its natural, uncivilized state when he failed to make passes at them; he mostly ignored women entirely.

In all likelihood, most of these little Adams and Eves were children with neurocognitive deficits, abandoned or lost by their families, who survived in rural and forested areas for a period of years before being captured and returned to society. (Linnaeus surmised they were "Most probably idiots who had strayed from their friends, and who resembled the above animals only in imitating their voices.") Some of the stories ended more happily, and some less, but none offered any proof that the natural kingdom and its animal inhabitants do a better job raising human children than human parents do.

One of the most famous stories was that of the above-mentioned Peter of Hanover. After he was discovered in 1725, Peter was brought to the royal court, where, a contemporary reported, "He had no notion of behavior, or manners, but greedily took with his hands out of the dishes, whatever he liked best, such as asparagus, or other garden-things, and

---

* There were also reports of children who were *sired* by animals. As Julia Douthwaite has documented, seventeenth- and eighteenth-century natural histories were fascinated by the idea of women mating with animals, and recorded (certainly false) instances of children born half pig, half wolf, half cow, and half monkey (*The Wild Girl, Natural Man, and the Monster*, 19). In another celebrated case, a woman was reported to have given birth to a litter of rabbits.

after a little time, he was ordered to be taken away, by reason of his daubing indecent behavior."

"Daubing indecent behavior" sounds like eighteenth-century-speak for "vigorous public masturbation," which became even more of a problem with a later wild boy, Victor of Aveyron, found in a French forest in 1800. Discovered on the cusp of puberty, Victor spent hours each day masturbating loudly and openly, a habit his handlers were unable to

Peter playing in *Curiosities of Human Nature* by Samuel G. Goodrich (1843)

break him of. He also showed a disturbing proclivity for public pooping.[*] Eventually he was sent to an institute for the deaf, but his constant masturbation proved too loud even for them, and he was sent to live with a housekeeper.

Despite their poor outcomes, in 1931 these case histories inspired Winthrop Kellogg, an Indiana psychologist, to raise his own child side by side with a chimpanzee. Kellogg and his wife, Luella, treated baby Donald and chimp Gua identically, hypothesizing that the animal would learn to act like the boy. Instead, the opposite happened. Gua tended to acquire skills before Donald did, which Donald would then try to emulate. Monkey see, monkey do, baby do, too. Thus Donald learned to bite the wall and bark when he wanted food. At nineteen months, when he should have had a vocabulary of seventy words, Donald knew only three, and instead had become adept at imitating Gua's noises. Afraid they would end up raising not one but two chimpanzees, the Kelloggs ended the experiment and sent Gua away.

It was an ironic outcome: the human aped the chimp. But that, after all, is what humans do. We ape. Children mirror our worst as much as our best, and they always have. The admonition to "Do as I say, not

---

[*] Reportedly, he did this standing, but squatted to pee.

as I do" dates back to 1654.* We hope our children are watching when we behave with discipline and dignity, when we speak kindly, when we remember to use our inside voices and walking feet, but they also see us when we scream and rage, when we drink from the milk carton and wipe our mouths on our sleeves.

Like all children, mine will inherit my habit of saying one thing and doing another. Like me, they will confiscate their offspring's candy; like me, they will eat it, secretly, themselves. And I will consider myself a success if they do it with their mouths closed. In the meantime I'll keep telling them what to do, and they'll keep ignoring me, behaving like kids today, which is, after all, exactly what they are.

---

* The term first appears in John Selden's 1654 book *Table Talk*, where it refers to pastors, who, like parents, are occasionally noted for their hypocrisy. Interestingly, in late Latin, *hypocrisy* meant "imitation." Do as I say, not as I do.

# 9

# Use Your Words

## *Children's Books*

Because I like to read, friends were surprised, when I had our daughter, that I read so little to *her*. The problem wasn't the reading but the material, which bored both of us. Baby books never involve celebrity biography, and they're almost always set in a barn; the vocabulary is mostly limited to *meow* and *moo*. I could be teaching my child Portuguese—why was I teaching her *cat*? Wouldn't it be far more sensible to teach her things like TV catchphrases and trivia, things that would prove useful for game shows and cocktail parties? Also, wouldn't it be far more entertaining for *me*? For this reason, I began reading to her from *Us* and *Entertainment Weekly*. Her second word, and I'm not making this up, was *Oprah*. Her third was *cake*, and this should give you a pretty good idea of how we spent our time.

Had I stuck to the books children were historically given, however, it could have been far worse. Her first word might have been *moo* or *arf*, or it might have been *castration*, *beheading*, or the N-word. For the history of children's literature is a shocking affair, offering death, murder, abuse, death, racism, death, and damnation. There's *The Tragical History of the Children in the Wood* and *My Mother's Grave*; *Agnes and the Key to Her Little Coffin* and *ABC in Dixie: A Plantation Alphabet* ("C is fer Chawlie

who waits on de table. He's handsome and stylish en his cullah am sable").
Even the books that turn out to be harmless sound like a whole lot of
trouble. For instance: *Ragged Dick*, *Lo cunto de li cunti*, *The Faggot-House*,
and *The Loneliest Ho in the World* (as it turns out, a Christmas story).

Much of it, however, was not harmless. For most of history, authors
have used their words to render children speechless. Some of the books
scarred generations; some merely gave their readers insomnia that would
last until puberty. It's been bad from the beginning, when children's literature was neither for children nor literature, but stories, transmitted orally,
to audiences of adults and kids alike. Because these were, by definition, not
written, we're not sure what they were about, but given universal interests,
it seems safe to assume they consisted mostly of animal fables, gruesome
cautionary tales, and bathroom jokes.

Certainly, that's what we got once people started writing things down.
One of the earliest examples is Aesop, whose fables from the sixth century
BCE formed the backbone of children's literature (and literature in general)
for a thousand-plus years. Aesop left an enormous body of work, much
of which he probably didn't write. In fact, it's possible he didn't actually
exist, his work instead coming from a lot of different sources; and if he
did, it's not at all clear who he was.[*] But most sources claim that he was a
slave with severe physical disabilities. A surviving bust shows a cross-eyed,
bearded face perched atop a sunken chest that's more or less falling into
his penis.

This is not exactly what you'd want to see on the jacket of a children's
book. Then again, Aesop's fables weren't really written for kids—children's
literature and adult literature would not become distinct entities for another two thousand years.[†] They were, however, widely read to and by kids,

---

[*] One very old and very intriguing theory holds that Aesop was from the area
that is now Ethiopia. This, however, is almost certainly wrong, and is based on
a false etymologic link between *Aesop* and *Aethops*, the ancient Greek term for
*Ethiopian*.

[†] Gillian Adams points out that there are only two ancient Greek writers who explicitly address children, and the emphasis is on *explicit*. For these are Sappho, sexy
poet, and Theognis, who's best known for his pederastic elegies. Their works for
children are erotic poems *to* children, and while they're more romantic than porno-
graphic and must be understood in the larger cultural context . . . it's still hard not

and formed the cornerstone of a Greek education, which included a number of topics the modern curriculum doesn't cover. The Aesop's fables we know are the highly sanitized versions that passed through the rinse cycles of the medieval and Victorian eras. But older editions were quite a bit darker and dirtier, featuring a beaver that bites off its own genitals, a pair of hyenas threatening to rape each other, and the edifying tale of "The Camel Who Shat in the River."

Several of Aesop's stories also appear in the *Panchatantra*, a collection of fables and morality tales compiled in India around the third century BCE. The *Panchatantra* doesn't contain anywhere near as much sex as I expected from a book with *tantra* in the title, but that is because I am an idiot: *tantra* is simply the Sanskrit word for "treatise" or "chapter."* That's not to say there's *no* sex, however, and there's plenty of violence, too. Like Aesop, this is a version of children's literature that reads as fairly grown-up. The stories are perfectly charming, but there are several you probably shouldn't read to children unless you're prepared to answer some hard questions about adultery, spousal murder, infanticide, and testicles.

There's not much that *isn't* in the *Panchatantra*. Long and intricately structured, it's essentially a turducken of stories, with a morality tale stuffed inside a fable stuffed inside an epic. And like a turducken, there are a whole lot of animals in it. As in Aesop, most stories involve creatures, setting down what was certainly an already well-established tradition of educating and entertaining children with the antics of animals. Lists of animal sounds, known as *voces variae animantium*, have been used to teach grammar since Roman times. Latin was literally pig Latin, as beginners learned that *porcorum grunnire* (pigs grunt).† Often these lists were part

---

to get the heebie-jeebies (Gillian Adams, "Ancient and Medieval Children's Texts," Peter Hunt, ed., in *International Companion Encyclopedia of Children's Literature*, vol. I [New York: Routledge, 2004], 230).

* Which makes tantric sex sound a lot less interesting but does explain why it takes so long.

† As for the origins of actual pig Latin, they remain ysterious-may, though it's unlikely it dates back much further than the eighteenth century (Thomas Jefferson used it). Over the years it's existed in different forms and under different names, including hog Latin, dog Latin, dog Greek, and pig Greek. It seems worth noting that the name given to the language children use when they don't want adults to

of bestiaries, illustrated guides of all known animals. By the Middle Ages, bestiaries had become a fundamental part of a child's education, despite the fact that they often evidenced a profound misperception of the natural world. Besides including many animals that don't exist (dragons, unicorns, sea pigs), they completely mangled the real ones. You can hardly blame the authors, who'd heard of the animals but never encountered them, for having to make stuff up. Still, they got a little carried away.

Pressing the animals into service as Christian allegorical figures, the authors saddled them with backstories and native habits that, while interesting, were also totally, totally wrong. Elephants are *not* Adam and Eve stand-ins who must eat a small, screaming root-man to reproduce, and they don't live three hundred years. Leopards are *not* the bastard offspring of a lion and a "pard," and they do not live in subterranean caves; panthers are not multicolored Christ figures whose only enemy is the dragon. And if the stories are off, the illustrations are even more so. Crocodiles are depicted as dogs or flying pink creatures. The whale has four feet, scales, multiple eyes, and a ropy tail. The giraffe is a tricolored llama, while the rhino sports the visible ribs and heavy eye makeup of a runway model.

Even animals the authors were

Giraffe: not even close
*(Courtesy Koninklijke Bibliotheek)*

Skinny, smoky-eyed rhino
*(Courtesy Koninklijke Bibliotheek)*

Crocodile as dog
*(Courtesy Kongelige Bibliotek)*

---

understand is, at least in English, usually animal-related. But that's not true everywhere: in Sweden, it's fig Latin (or rather, fig language—Fikonspråket).

familiar with are depicted in bizarre ways. The cat looks like it
does today, but is almost always
shown licking its own anus. Really, you would not believe how
many medieval illustrations there
are of cats up in their business. As
for beavers, they look more or less
like beavers, but as in the Aesop
fable are usually depicted biting
off their genitals.*

Cat up in its business
*(Courtesy Kongelige Bibliotek)*

For several hundred years animals formed not just the subject of
children's reading materials but their *substance* as well. These were
hornbooks, which were made from materials like calfskin and cow horn
mounted on ivory, bone, leather, or wood. Ostensibly produced to teach
children the alphabet and a simple prayer or two, you need only look
at them to figure out how they were *actually* used. For they are shaped
like paddles, and as anyone who's spent any time with children knows,
if you give a child something that looks like a cricket bat, they're not
going to use it to *read*. They are going to use it to deliver beatings, and
that in fact is exactly what medieval children (and their teachers) did.
They also used hornbooks as rackets, which is why they eventually became known by the far more apt name of battledores.†

---

\* Though erroneous, the belief that an endangered beaver self-castrates is a persistent
 one and dates back at least as far as ancient Egypt. Beavers were generally hunted for
 castoreum, a secretion prized as both a scent and a flavoring (it's said to smell like a
 combination of new car and vanilla, and is still used in perfumes and edibles today).
 A clever beaver would thus bite off his castoreum maker and throw it at his pursuer,
 escaping with his life if not his manhood. The castration myth persisted in part
 because of a linguistic coincidence: *castor* and *castration* sound alike, though there's
 no etymological link. Eventually the myth became an allegory for resisting sexual
 temptation. But the myth is exactly that: beavers' testicles aren't, in fact, external,
 and even the cleverest beaver would be unable to bite them off; and the castor sacs
 aren't located there, besides.

† The hornbook was also called the "Christ-cross row," because the alphabet it
 depicted began not with an *A* but with a cross. This, as you probably guessed, is
 where we get the word *crisscross*.

Given this, it's not surprising that when the printing press arrived and books began to be written directly for children, the goal of almost all of these was to get children to *stop* acting like animals. These were courtesy books and etiquette guides, and there were lots of them. Among the first was Erasmus of Rotterdam's 1530 text *A Handbook on Good Manners for Children*, which urged children not to eat like a pig, laugh like a horse, grin like a dog, frown like a bull, speak like an elephant, stand like a stork, flap like a magpie, or, in a simile that doesn't really hold up, wink like a tuna fish.

The rest of the book holds up pretty well, however. Nearly five hundred years after it was written, it remains surprisingly readable, and except for a chapter on bowing, most of his recommendations are still relevant today. He comes down against manspreading ("[s]itting with knees apart . . . is the hallmark of a braggart") and gossiping, reminding readers that what happens at the feudal banquet stays at the feudal banquet. With uncanny frequency he lays out the norms that would show up on *Seinfeld* five centuries later. Besides a lot of advice on how to properly eat soup, he urges readers not to double-dip or be a low-talker, and to keep secrets in the vault.

The book did quite well for an etiquette guide, becoming the bestselling book of the sixteenth century in a crowded field that would only continue to grow. Though the popularity of children's courtesy books might seem strange now, it made perfect sense at the time. Society was changing rapidly, and there was a desperate need for books that would teach children how to navigate a world that suddenly frowned on blowing your nose on your tunic. The books remained popular for several hundred years, with later volumes imparting such good advice as "Belch near no man's face with a corrupt fumosity," "Foul not the tablecloth," "Smell not of thy meat, or put it up to thy nose," and "Spit not in the Room, but in the Corner, and rub it with thy Foot, or rather go out and do it abroad."

Like all classy things, courtesy books originated in France and Italy. Eventually, the books would grow rather lurid, with one of the last and most famous being Lord Chesterfield's *Letters to His Son on the Art of Becoming a Man of the World and a Gentleman*, described by Samuel Johnson as imparting "the morals of a whore and the manners of a dancing-master." Writing to his illegitimate son, Lord Chesterfield argues that dancing is more important than scholarship, endorses dirty talk with "a coquette of fifteen," shares his tips on finding a good mistress (preferably more than one at a time), and suggests his son hook up with Lord Chesterfield's own romantic conquests.

But at the start, courtesy books were quite proper. In England, one of the first was *The Babees Book* (1475), a guide for noble children being sent off to serve as pages for other nobles. At the time, *baby* simply meant "child"; still, to the modern ear, it's disconcerting to find that it's essentially an employee handbook. In a similar vein, John Russell's *Boke of Nurture* teaches children fun and vital lessons like how to fold a towel, polish silverware, pour wine, serve tableside, carve a roast, perform the duties of valet, prepare a medicinal bath, and manage a seating chart.

THANKFULLY, AS TIME WENT ON, people began to consider what children might actually *want* to read. One of the first to do so was John Amos Comenius, a Czech religious and educational reformer who changed everything with the 1658 publication of the first children's picture book, *Orbis Pictus* (*The Visible World*). Widely translated, emulated, plagiarized, and reprinted, the book would go through 244 editions over the next three hundred years, acquiring admirers that included the young Goethe. The book was revolutionary in a number of ways. First, *it had pictures*. Comenius felt the best way to engage children was to appeal to their senses, especially sight, for "it is apparent that Children (even from their infancy almost) are delighted with Pictures, and willingly please their eyes with these sights." Second, it was physically designed for youngsters. Instead of being, say, a doorstop like a folio, or a *weapon*, like a hornbook, it was compact and portable. And finally, it was far more relevant than the dusty Greek and Latin texts that schoolchildren were normally stuck with, written in a language the child actually spoke and depicting the world the child knew and saw every day.

Of course, the world said children knew and saw every day could be disturbing, as Comenius himself was well aware; he'd been orphaned at twelve when his parents and two of his sisters died of the plague, and he'd spent most of his life fleeing war and religious persecution. *Orbis Pictus* is generally sunny and upbeat, but it does include a chapter on "The Tormenting of Malefactors," in which children learn that "Theeves are hanged by the Hangman on a Gallows"; "Whore-masters are beheaded"; "Witches are burnt in a great fire," sometimes after having their tongues, hands, or ears cut off; and "Traytors are pulled in pieces with four Horses." Numbered figures helpfully illustrate these procedures. There is also a rather insensitive chapter on "Monstrous and Deformed People," which introduces children to dwarfism, gigantism, and conjoined twins, as well as more run-of-the-mill oddities, "amongst whom are reckoned, the jolt-headed, the great nosed, the blubber-lipped, the blub-cheeked, the goggle-eyed, the wry-necked, the great-throated, the crumped-backed, the crumple-footed, the steeple-crowned," and perhaps unfairly, "the bald-pated." Pictures of the aging Comenius reveal that he may have had a touch of the last monstrous deformity himself.

Mostly, however, the book focuses on the mundane aspects of life, providing names and descriptions, in both vernacular and Latin, for anything a seventeenth-century child might encounter, from "The Bath" to "The Blacksmith" to "A Burial." There are remarkably accurate chapters on geography and geometry as well as the body and its workings. There's a chapter on wine, and another on beer. Lest you think this inappropriate for children, there's also a chapter on temperance, which warns, "*Revellers* are made drunk (fig. 4), they *stumble* (fig. 5), they *spue* (fig. 6), and *babble* (fig. 7). From *Drunkenness* proceedeth *Lasciviousness*; from this a *lewd Life* amongst *Whoremasters* (fig. 8), and *Whores* (fig. 9) in *kissing, touching, embracing,* and *dancing* (fig. 10)."

Comenius was a bishop as well as an ecumenical pacifist, and while he hoped everyone would see the true Protestant light, he didn't believe in forced conversion. It was best, he felt, to simply present the facts of each religion and let the reader draw the obvious conclusion. In *Orbis Pic-*

*tus* he devotes a chapter each to Christianity, Judaism, "Mahometism," and "Gentilism" (paganism), and with a couple of exceptions ("The Indians, even to this day, worship the Devil") these are remarkably nonjudgmental for the time. The chapter on Judaism—in an era when blood libel rumors were rampant—is surprisingly accurate and accepting.* The chapter on Islam misses the mark a bit more: "*Mahomet*, a warlike Man, invented to himself a new Religion, mixed with *Judaism*, *Christianity* and *Gentilism*, by the advice of a *Jew*, and an *Arian Monk*, named *Sergius*; feigning, whilst he had the *Fit of the Falling-sickness*, that the *Archangel Gabriel* and the *Holy Ghost*, talked with him, using a *Pigeon*, to fetch Meat out of his Ear." Which is all quite *Wrong*, not to mention *Offensive*, though in Comenius's defense, *Orbis Pictus* is just about the only contemporary children's book to mention Islam at all, and a lack of accurate source material is the main reason he got so much incorrect. Elsewhere, he wrote admiringly of Islamic teaching methods and advocated for Christian-Islamic dialogue.

In any case, religion is only a small part of Comenius's book, surprising given the fact that (a) it was written in the 1600s, (b) by a bishop, (c) whose explicit goal was to bring readers closer to faith. It seems that Comenius felt the best way to achieve this was not through preachers but through creatures, for it's again with animals that he really goes all in. There are nearly three times as many chapters on animals as there are on religious matters. The book's epigraph is the biblical passage in which Adam names all the animals, and the first chapter is an animal alphabet that will set the tone for the rest of the book and, frankly, for the next four hundred years. For it's here that Comenius comes up with the formula that will stick to the sole of children's literature like a particularly tenacious cow pie: The sheep says baa. The snake says sssss. The owl says hoot, and the parent says enough.

Though animal voices had been a literary staple for over a thousand years, these *voces variae* had always ended at the verb, telling us only that the cat cries and the dog barks. Comenius goes a step further, telling us

---

* Comenius also played an indirect role in the Jews' readmission to England, after a four-hundred-year ban, when it was brought about in large part through the efforts of John Dury, a Comenian follower.

what they actually say.* It's a small change, but it made a big difference. With the addition of these noises Comenius made a phonological alphabet, thus paving the way for the universal language he believes will produce a universal brotherhood.

The search for a universal language was a preoccupation of the time, and Comenius was one of its leading proponents. He called for "a language absolutely new, absolutely easy, absolutely rational, in brief a pansophic language, the universal carrier of light." What better place to begin than with animal sounds, which are, after all, a sort of universal language of their own? Sure, we like to consider how animal sounds vary from place to place, pointing out how much more sophisticated the French cat's *miaou* is than our own's, but I think we can agree these are small variations in dialect, not different languages.†

By the eighteenth century the search for a universal language had evolved into the search for an Edenic one, the prelapsarian tongue that Adam and Eve themselves had used, and natural philosophers looked to children for clues. If a child grew up in isolation, it was believed, he would naturally begin to speak this language on his own. When children who actually *did* grow up in isolation were discovered, they proved a great disappointment; largely mute, their Edenic language consisted mostly of grunts, shrieks, and burps.

Comenius's dream of a universal language would eventually die out, but his sheep-says-baa formula would prove immortal and inescapable. It would be repeated by storybooks and singers and See 'N Says; it would become an Internet meme. Even Jacques Lacan would tackle it, concluding that the formula provides an opportunity for a child to "raise the sign to the function of the signifier." The cow goes moo; the poststructuralist goes j/e.

A postmodernist feminist pacifist who advocated for marriage counseling, prenatal care, and equal access to education for girls as well as boys

---

* Unfortunately, he did not include the fox on his list, so what that creature says remains, as the song says, an ancient mystery.
† Which makes the differences no less interesting. I was particularly intrigued to learn that cows used to say not *moo* but *boo*, and that this is how booing started. Originally, it was supposed to mimic the lowing of a dissatisfied herd.

and for the poor as well as the rich, Comenius was so incredibly forward-thinking it's hard, if you're me, not to secretly believe that he was delivered to the seventeenth century by time machine to set us all on the right track. If so, the mission largely failed. Sadly, much of the work done by this revolutionary Protestant reformer would be reversed by another group of revolutionary Protestant reformers, the Puritans, who came along like a wet, smallpox-infected blanket to put a damper on all the fun.[*]

THE PURITANS DID NOT disapprove of children's literature; in fact, they more or less invented the genre. They also invented the client base. Puritan children were literate by law: a 1642 statute required that they learn to read.[†] Should a parent fail to teach his offspring to do so, he might find a posting on the meetinghouse door, offering his children as servants to a family that would know what to do with them.

Children had to be literate to read the Bible, but besides the Good Book, there were an awful lot of Bad Books. The Puritans had a very, very different idea of what constitutes proper reading material for children than Comenius did. Gone were the moo-cow and the shining sun; in were the Judgment Day and burning hellfire. Puritan children's books were always and only about religious matters, and they rarely if ever included pictures. A distaste for frivolities like illustrations, coupled with a general unease toward anything that could be construed as a graven image, meant there was not a big emphasis on the visual arts in Puritan publishing or, really, Puritan anything, with one exception. True to form, they really let loose in the graveyard, permitting the elaborately—and literally—graven images that weren't allowed anywhere else.

That the Puritans were inspired by death becomes very, very clear when examining their children's literature. Passages like this one were typical: "Place yourselves frequently on your death beds, in your Coffins, and

---

[*]  Not for nothing did H. L. Mencken define Puritanism as "the haunting fear that someone, somewhere, may be happy."

[†]  Interestingly, they didn't have to know how to *write*, and many children and adults never learned. Which, I suppose, is sort of the ideal condition in a community that wants to limit the back talk.

in your Graves. Act over frequently in your Minds, the Solemnity of your own Funerals; and entertain your Imaginations with all the lively scenes of Mortality; Meditate much upon the places, and upon the Days of Darkness, and upon the fewness of those that shall be saved; and be always with your Hourglass in your hands, measuring out your own little Span and comparing it with the endless Circle of Eternity."[*]

The indoctrination began at infancy. Instead of "The sheep says baa," babies were taught phrases like "Learn to die." There was no escaping it. Even something as benign as the ABCs became a reminder of the ineluctable march toward death. *X-ray* and *yo-yo* wouldn't come along for another couple hundred years, but still, I think *The New England Primer* could have found something a little more upbeat than "*Xerxes* did die, and so must I; While *Youth* do chear, Death may be near." (The authors do a little better in the section on syllables, giving as an example of a four-syllable word "fornication.")

Puritans were responsible for books with sunny, child-friendly titles like *Deaths of Pious Children* and *The Exhortation that a Father Gave to His Children Which he Wrot a Few Dayes Before His Burning*.[†] Even the books that sound painless turn out to be terrifying, like Thomas White's *A Little Book for Little Children*, which opens with a wildly inappropriate this-one-time-at-band-camp story ("When I was at *Oxford* in our Colledge, there were six Scholars who made a drunken match to drink up a barrel of Beer between them; the next day one of them, as he was at Supper, fell

---

[*]  It's hard not to see Puritans as very early goths. Like goths, they had a morbid obsession with death and dark clothes. They were also young—the colonies were full of teenagers—and we all know there's no demographic more drawn to the maudlin than adolescents. In our own age, adolescent literature is the only one that remains somewhat death-obsessed. In the early nineties there was, in fact, a whole YA series devoted to the topic called Sweet Goodbyes. Titles in the series include *My Sister, My Sorrow*; *Good-bye, Best Friend*; *The Dying of the Light*; *Please Don't Go*; *Life Without Alice*; and *Losing David*, a romance featuring not one but two terminally ill characters: a boy with leukemia and a girl with HIV.

[†]  As should be obvious, Puritans were just as good at naming their books as they were at naming their children, with the best being John Cotton's *Spiritual Milk for Boston Babes in Either England. Drawn out of the Breasts of Both Testaments*. It's not nearly as interesting as it sounds, however, unless you're compelled by catechistic drilling about original sin.

down as dead"), then goes on to recount stories of devout children who met martyrs' ends. White is unsparing with the details, which include flaying, disemboweling, burning alive, a tongue cut out and fried in a pan—I mean, it's an Eli Roth movie. The Puritan reluctance to illustrate is surely a blessing here.

More child deaths are chronicled in Thomas Janeway's enormously popular 1671 book, *A Token for Children*, which describes, *in baby talk,* the virtuous lives and early ends of thirteen saintly children. His success inspired death-obsessed drama queen Cotton Mather to write an edition for American children, *A Token for the Children of New England*, which recounted the deaths of children closer to home, *Preserved for the Encouragement of Piety in other Children*.

THINGS LOOSENED UP a bit by the time John Newbery came along in the mid-1700s. Now known mostly for the shiny-stickered award that bears his name, Newbery wrought a sea change in children's publishing. If the Puritans established the genre, Newbery established the industry, becoming wildly successful in the process.

Newbery introduced a number of huge innovations, inventing the model that would inform children's publishing for the rest of history, not to mention the Happy Meal. His big idea was fairly simple: include a bonus gift with your purchase. Buy *A Little Pretty Pocket-Book* and you'd also receive a ball (for a boy) or a pincushion (for a girl), which apparently is what passed for toys in the eighteenth century. In any case, the idea caught on and spread to virtually every other product marketed to children, and is probably the reason there are currently eight boxes of stale cereal in my pantry.* Newbery also established book series so he could sell multiple books instead of one-offs. Prefiguring Columbia Records' famous introductory offer, he offered bonus books for one penny.

Newbery's other major innovation was product placement. Characters in Newbery publications read and tout other Newbery publications

---

* If I'm being fair, it's also the reason for all the trial-sized Clinique products in my medicine cabinet.

shamelessly. In *The Twelfth Day Gift*, characters plug six separate New-bery titles. In *The History of Little Goody Two-Shoes*, Goody stumps for four different Newbery products, going so far as to provide a shopping list and directions to the store: "The books usually read by the scholars of Mrs Two-Shoes are these, and are sold at Mr Newbery's, at the Bible and Sun in St Paul's." The shop gets another big endorsement in *Blossoms of Morality*: "I cannot help pitying those *poor little boys, whose parents are not* in a condition to purchase them such a nice gilded library as that with which you have supplied me from my good friends at the corner of Saint Paul's churchyard. Surely such unhappy boys must be very ignorant for all their lives, for what can they learn without books."

Newbery's books also flogged products from Newbery's other ven-ture, a patent medicine business. A book/drug shop seems a very strange combination now, but it was fairly common at the time, convenient for the mother who needed to buy laudanum and a dictionary in one stop. Newbery sold a line of thirty different nostrums, which were advertised in the backs of his books and promoted within the narratives. Of these, the best known was Dr James's Fever Powder, a blockbuster cure for cataracts, gout, scurvy, and cattle distemper that was even used by King George III. Despite the product's success, it's doubtful it did anyone much good. Its primary ingredient was antimony, a toxin related to arsenic. The powder is likely what killed Newbery author Oliver Goldsmith, himself a medical doctor, who died after taking two or three doses against the urgings of his apothecary. Ironic, then, that the product is promoted in the opening lines of *Goody Two-Shoes*, a book Goldsmith is thought to have written: "Care and Discontent shortened the Days of Little Margery's Father.—He was forced from his Family, and seized with a violent Fever in a Place where Dr James's Powder was not to be had, and where he died miserably." Gold-smith, it seems, died miserably precisely because it *was*.

Newbery's less dangerous tonics included the German Doctor's Diet-Drink (a sugarless root beer), Anderson's Scots Pills (a vigorous purga-tive), and Daffy's Elixir (a boozy laxative fortified with opium). Other concoctions were less appealing. The recipe for Unguents de Cao reads: "Get a good fat young dog alive, and when you are prepared with two gallons of water, or as much is as necessary to cover him, knock him on the head and throw him into it."

Newbery's most interesting product was probably Dr. John Hooper's Female Pills, which remained on the market into the twentieth century. Advertisements claimed, "they are the best medicine ever discovered for YOUNG WOMEN, when afflicted with what is commonly called the IRREGULARITIES. They are excellent for the Green-Sickness,* Palpitations of the Heart, Giddiness, a dejected Countenance & sinking of the Spirits, loathing of Food, a dislike of Exercise & Conversation, & are the best purging Stomatick, & Remedy for the Scurvy." Because pregnant women were warned not to take them, unhappily pregnant women did exactly that. The pills contained cinnamon, myrrh, and iron sulfate—an abortifacient. Ironically, Newbery, then, was selling the very thing that could prevent the production of future customers for his books. Still, it was probably a good business decision, as it ensured more disposable income for the customers he already had.

While it's not really fair or accurate to call Newbery a drug-dealing abortionist, it's probably about right to say he was a good deal more complicated than the "father of children's literature" he was known as, the avuncular man who referred to young readers as "his little friends." He was certainly someone who could be shrewd if not ruthless, as some of his authors had occasion to learn. Washington Irving charged: "He coined the brains of authors in the times of their exigency, and made them pay dear for the plank put out to keep them from drowning. It is not likely his death caused much lamentation among the scribbling tribe." No scribbler came in for more abuse than the poet Christopher Smart. Smart—who was also Newbery's stepson-in-law—ended up doing a seven-year stint in a madhouse after Newbery forcibly committed him for reasons that

---

* Chlorosis or "green sickness" is an all-but-forgotten malady also known as the "disease of the virgins" that plagued young women from the 1500s through the 1930s. Symptoms included pallor, lack of appetite, weakness, pica, and dysmenorrhea. In some cases, it was probably anemia, and in others, maybe anorexia. Presumably, Dr. Hooper's pills had fewer side effects than the treatment for green sickness that doctors usually recommended: a hasty marriage.

remain unclear, but may have included religious mania, bipolar disorder, alcoholism, or simply a power play on Newbery's part.[*]

Newbery sure knew how to put together a kids' book, however. By 1800, children's books had improved enough for an eager reader to produce a needlework sampler proclaiming, "Patty Polk did this and she hated every stitch she did in it. She loves to read much more." Children's books had finally become entertaining. That's not to say the books were necessarily any better for a child's mental health, and in fact they were about to get much worse. For the nineteenth century saw the rise of the Grimm brothers, whose surname, in a kind of perfect linguistic coincidence, exactly describes their material.[†]

IN 1812, Wilhelm and Jacob Grimm published *Nursery and Household Tales*. Despite the title, the book wasn't really intended for children. As their preface makes clear, the brothers viewed it as more of a scholarly work aimed at academics, written in an effort to capture the *Volksmärchen*, the oral tradition of folk tales that was rapidly disappearing from a modernizing Germany. With copious footnotes and no illustrations, the Grimm tales didn't really look like a children's book either. And yet upon its release, readers and reviewers, taking the book at its title, began reading the stories to their kids and freaking the freak out.

It's hard to say which story pushed readers over the edge, because they are all so wildly inappropriate. Take, for instance, "The Juniper Tree," in which a stepmother beheads her stepson and ties his head back on before telling her own daughter to punch him in the head so *she'll* be blamed for his death—then cooks the boy up and feeds him to his father. It ends happily: the boy is magically resurrected and the stepmother is crushed to

---

[*] Interestingly, Newbery was not the only dangerous father-in-law in the children's book business. Cotton Mather prayed for the death of a son-in-law he found particularly hateful, and claimed credit when his prayers were answered (Schiff, *The Witches*, 293).

[†] This is true in both English and old German, in which *grimm* means something closer to "wrath." Weirdly, Grimm was also the surname of the Grimm brothers' adversary, fairy tale author A. L. Grimm (no relation). A. L.'s stories were in fact far *less* grim, and he was highly critical of the brothers' inappropriate material.

death when an avenging bird drops a millstone on her. Even more violent is "The Robber Bridegroom," in which a bride, arriving at her fiancé's house for the first time, learns that he plans to chop her up and boil her. She hides, and instead witnesses the dismemberment of another unlucky young girl who is first forced to drink wine until her heart bursts, then stripped of her clothes. Nursery tales, *mein Arsch*.

Then there are the stories whose titles alone tell you all you need to know: "How Children Played Butcher with Each Other" (aka "The Children Who Played Slaughtering"), "The Murder Castle," "The Hand with the Knife," "The Poor Boy in the Grave," "The Starving Children,"* and "The Story of the Youth Who Went Forth to Learn What Fear Was." "Thousandfurs" sounds like a Bond movie, and reads like a V. C. Andrews book: having promised his dying wife that he'd remarry only someone as beautiful as she, a king becomes so obsessed with marrying his own daughter that she's forced to flee into the forest.

As Grimm scholar Maria Tatar observes, sex and violence are the "major thematic concerns" of the Grimms' tales, and even more disturbing than that is the fact that the sex is so often incest and the violence so often child abuse. This is partly a matter of their cast; despite their name, fairy tales are typically not about fairies but about families, so any sex and violence will probably be directed toward a relation. And whether this says more about the Grimms or the *Volks* who provided the *Märchen* in the first place, I'm not sure.† But I will point out that other folklorists shared versions in which fathers *don't* try to rape their daughters and stepmothers don't turn their stepsons into sausage.

---

\* To juvenile English-speaking ears, the title is more entertaining in the German: "*Die Kinder in Hungersnot.*"

† To be fair, the source material *was* pretty vulgar, and not just in Germany. In the French version of "Little Red Riding Hood," Red escapes when she tricks the wolf into letting her go outside to poop. And the Italian version of "Sleeping Beauty" is heinous: the handsome prince tries to wake her not with a kiss but a rape, followed by a lot more rape. Beauty conceives and gives birth to twins, waking only when one infant suckles the cursed piece of flax out of her finger. She then falls in love with the rapist prince, who, as it turns out, is already married. His jealous wife orders the palace cook to roast the twins and serve them to the prince. Learning of his wife's treachery, the prince orders that *she* be burnt to death instead. The two children are revealed to be alive, and Beauty and rapist live happily ever after.

The Grimms claimed that their primary source was Frau Viehm-ann, a German "peasant woman." In fact, she was neither German nor a peasant, but the Huguenot wife of a tailor. The fact that she was Huguenot—and therefore French—sort of undermines the whole point of the Grimms' project, which was a nationalistic effort to preserve the *echt Deutsch*ness of material the Grimms describe as "purely German in its origins." They promised that the tales were carefully reviewed and purged of "everything that seemed suspicious, namely what might have been of foreign origin." But anyone who'd read Perrault or the *Pentam-erone* knew that wasn't true. These stories had been migrating and mu-tating across Europe for hundreds of years; Cinderella, in fact, originated in China.

Despite the tales' mongrel origins, they came to represent a pure Teu-tonic folk tradition. The Grimms' tales were a favorite of the Nazis and were required reading in German schools. Goebbels even produced a series of twenty-three propaganda films recasting the tales as Aryan allegories. Red Riding Hood, her cloak adorned with a swastika, stood for Germany; the wolf, for vulpine Jews. The handsome prince picks Cinderella for her racial purity, rejecting her mixed-blood stepsisters. Puss in Boots is Hitler himself, and Snow White's[*] father invades Poland.

In some Allied schools and libraries, the Grimms' tales were banned, and it's not hard to see why.[†] Besides the fervent nationalism, the stories could be cheerfully and openly anti-Semitic. "The Jew in the Brambles" is particularly bad: for sport, the hero tortures a Jew by forcing him to dance in a thorn hedge. After the Jew buys his release, the two end up before a judge who doesn't believe the Jew would willingly hand over money, be-cause "No Jew would do that." The Jew admits he's a thief and is hanged. The Jew in "The Good Bargain" gets off relatively easy, receiving several beatings for being a tightwad instead.

---

[*] Disney's *Snow White* was reportedly Hitler's favorite film, and he may have been the artist responsible for some recently discovered paintings of Doc and Bashful done in 1940.

[†] Children in Allied countries could turn instead to *The Allies' Fairy Book*, which was produced as a Grimm alternative during World War I. Arthur Rackham did the illustrations.

Earlier on in the nineteenth century, however, what parents objected to was not the anti-Semitism or the violence but the sex. In the first edition, Rapunzel lets down her guard as well as her hair, and finds herself pregnant. Then there's the tale of Hans Dumm, who can impregnate a girl with a wish. The Grimms, whose own childhood was something of a Cinderella story without the happy ending (after their father's death and a subsequent descent into poverty, the ragged and hungry brothers frequently suffered mistreatment at the hands of better-off peers), were not averse to making edits to improve sales, and in the next edition, the sex was taken out. The violence, however, stayed. As Tatar points out, the Grimms rarely cut violence and often added it.

Why, I have no idea, but it does seem worth noting that the same culture that produced the Grimms' tales (and the Holocaust!) also produced psychoanalysis. Fairy tales were, in fact, one of psychoanalysis's first subjects; both Freud and Jung mined their symbolism for telling nuggets. Psychoanalyst (and Holocaust survivor) Bruno Bettelheim championed the form in *The Uses of Enchantment*, arguing that fairy tales allow children to safely explore and resolve their darker fears. And maybe fairy tales really are good, psychologically healthy reading for developing minds. As the parent of a child for whom a Disney Junior cartoon could cause night terrors, however, I doubt this.

In any case, the tales were certainly part of a larger, tougher German tradition. In 1845, another German psychiatrist, Heinrich Hoffmann, decided to write and illustrate his own children's book after failing to find a suitable one for his three-year-old son. The result was *Funny Stories and Whimsical Pictures with 15 Beautifully Colored Panels for Children Aged 3 to 6*, or, as it's more commonly known, *Der Struwwelpeter* (*Slovenly Peter*).[*] Here's a sampling of what Hoffmann—again, a *psychiatrist*—thought made funny whimsical reading material for preschoolers:

- "The Dreadful Story of Pauline and the Matches," in which a girl fatally burns herself;

---

[*] Like the Grimms' tales, *Der Struwwelpeter* would also get a World War working-over, with the parody *Bombenpeter* appearing in 1915, and *Struwwelhitler* in 1941.

- "The Story of Bad Frederick," about a boy who tears the wings off flies, throws the kitten down the stairs, kills birds, whips his nurse, and savagely beats his dog;

- "The Story of Little Suck-a-Thumb," whose thumb is amputated by a tailor wielding giant scissors when he can't remember to keep it out of his mouth;

- "The Story of the Black Boys," in which Santa dips three boys in ink to teach them not to tease a "black-a-moor";

- "The Story of August Who Would Not Have Any Soup," and promptly starves to death;

- "The Story of Johnny Head-in-Air," in which Johnny nearly drowns because he doesn't watch where he's walking; and

- "The Story of Flying Robert," who is never seen again.

Ha-ha-ha-ha-ha! What whimsy. When Pauline's apron and hair, arms and hands, eyes and nose catch fire, leaving just her little red shoes? The part when her cats scream helplessly? So charming. Ha-ha-ha-ha-ha!

Perhaps because of the material, the book has fallen out of favor, but it was once well known and widely read; Mark Twain translated it into English. It remains culturally relevant in Germany, home of the Struwwelpeter Museum as well as the industrial metal band Rammstein, which made the book the subject of a song.

OVER IN ENGLAND, meanwhile, nineteenth-century authors were beginning to take children's delicate sensibilities into account, editing out big words and troubling themes with expurgated versions of classic texts. Among the first to do so were siblings Charles and Mary Lamb, whose child-friendly adaptation *Tales from Shakespeare* was published just a few years before the Grimms' collection. The book was beautifully done, but the Lambs' own unedited lives were messy and decidedly adult. Charles was a tremendous alcoholic, and both siblings suffered bouts of mental

*Der Struwwelpeter*'s Freddy Krueger–ish title character

Ha-ha! He is bleeding!

illness severe enough to require inpatient stays. Mary's psychotic outbursts got so bad a straitjacket was kept at home to subdue her. This was not enough, however, to keep Mary from stabbing her mother to death with a fork. The writing of the *Tales*, in fact, served as a form of therapy in the aftermath of that event.

By mid-century, things were becoming decidedly didactic. Popular texts included Mary Martha Sherwood's three-volume novel, *History of the Fairchild Family*, whose most salient story was titled "Fatal Effects of

Disobedience to Parents." More interesting was the work of evangelical writer Hesba Stretton (Sarah Smith), who made a cottage industry of books in which desperately poor young girls found faith and inspired all who encountered them. Readers loved the books, in large part because they featured Lifetime movie–style plotlines and a cast of drunks, prostitutes, and plucky waifs. Stretton's 1866 book *Jessica's First Prayer* sold ten times as many copies as *Alice's Adventures in Wonderland*.

One of many female evangelical authors of preachy books, Stretton was also a founding member of the London Society for the Prevention of Cruelty to Children. Ironically, one of her female evangelical author colleagues would become known for producing the cruelest children's books of the nineteenth century, if not all of human history. This was Favell Lee Mortimer, whose books scarred a generation. That she's completely unknown now is surprising, given how widely read she was in her day. Mortimer was the leading expert on children's literacy and religious education, with over a million books in print. Her works were translated into thirty-eight languages, including Ojibwa, Swahili, Yoruba, and Tamil.

I don't know what she sounds like in Tamil, but in her native English, she's straight-up battery acid. Mortimer comes across like Dana Carvey's Church Lady, because that's precisely what she was: an evangelical convert who made it her business to terrify a legion of children into literacy and salvation. Well, isn't that special.

Although Mortimer was the privileged daughter of a cofounder of Barclays Bank, hers was not a happy life, marred by an unrequited love and an abusive marriage, straitened by evangelical fervor, and colored by what looks like a propensity toward sadism. But in her work, at least, she seems to have found satisfaction and success. Mortimer came up with a number of innovations, inventing both the flash card and the title formulation "[Subject] Without Tears." My local library currently offers fifty-three books so titled, including *Maya Hieroglyphs Without Tears*, *Bargaining Theory Without Tears*, *Onions Without Tears* (a cookbook), and *ISO27001 Assessments Without Tears*, but Mortimer's 1857 *Reading Without Tears* was the first.

The book is subtitled *A Pleasant Mode of Learning to Read*. Mortimer must have had a different definition of *pleasant*. There may be no tears in the text, but there's an awful lot of death—as a critic noted, of the book's 129 stories, 41 end in a fatality. This would be high for a horror movie, but for a reading primer, it's extraordinary. Burning alive predominates, but there's also drowning, mauling, blunt-force trauma, gunplay, strangulation, and sundry other household accidents. Here, for instance, is the lesson meant to illustrate the *oy* sound: "What is the mat-ter with that lit-tle boy? He has taken poi-son. He saw a cup of poi-son on the shelf. He said, 'This seems sweet stuff.' So he drank it. Can the doc-tor cure him? No. Will the poi-son de-stroy him? Yes, he must die." *Oy*, indeed.

When my own children were learning to read, we relied on a rather prosaic series in which we read that Mag has a bag and Pat has a cat. In Mortimer's version, Pat has a gun and a careless attitude, with predictable results: "The lit-tle school-fel-low was there. He was a thought-less boy. A gun lay on the ta-ble. The boy did not know it was load-ed. He took it up and point-ed it at Em-ma. 'I will shoot you,' said he. He pull-ed the trig-ger. Em-ma fell down dead on the floor. Oh, what a mel-an-chol-y e-vent!" The point of this lesson, by the way, is not gun safety, but the proper pronunciation of the hard *ch* sound.

Another armed child's story ends with an even higher body count. "Ma-ny chil-dren have been kill-ed by play-ing with gun-pow-der," is the opening, so you pretty much know what to expect when the story's protagonist decides, "I will go in-to the nurs-er-y and fright-en my lit-tle broth-ers and sis-ters." He proceeds to throw "a lit-tle gun-pow-der in-to the fire. And what hap-pens? The flames dart out and catch the pow-der in the can-is-ter. It is blown up with a loud noise. The chil-dren are thrown down—they are in flames—the win-dows are bro-ken—the house is sha-ken! Mis-ter Ben-son hears the noise, and rush-es up stairs. What a sight! His chil-dren ly-ing on the floor burn-ing! The serv-ants help to quench the flames. They go for a cab to take the chil-dren to the hos-pi-tal. The doc-tor says, 'The chil-dren are blind, and they will soon die.' And they died." Well, of course they did. So does Lizzie, in "Lizzie's Last Day," trampled to her own death when she stops to watch a *funeral procession*.

Mortimer was as death-obsessed as a Puritan (as her niece and biographer noted, "Her doctor said she was the only person he ever met who wished to die"), but unlike the Puritans, she doesn't thunder fire and brimstone. Cotton Mather yells; Mortimer coos. With her calm manner and second-person address, it's as if she's whispering in your ear, murmuring that you are going to die, probably soon, and unless you get right you'll suffer fiery torments for all eternity.

She's just got such a nice way of putting it. Mortimer truly is a pleasure to read, which, as Todd Pruzan notes, is a little sickening. Because she says awful, awful things. Besides the nonstop morbidness, there's the matter-of-fact racism ("In sum-mer gip-sies wan-der from place to place, and sleep in tents . . . Some gip-sies have been taught by good peo-ple . . . But most gip-sies are ig-no-rant. Some of them steal and tell lies"). Then

there's the vulgarity. This is unintentional, entirely due to mutations in the meanings of certain words over the last hundred and fifty years. Still, for the modern reader, it's awfully hard to keep a straight face when we read, "Dick has a cock. It can peck." I'll say. When, a few lines later, we read that "Dick is in bed," we're not a bit surprised, though we are taken off guard when she asks, "Did you see Dick leap ov-er the dike?" And while you get used to the all the gay lads and faggots, it's hard not to startle when you read that "The cock is at the top of the heap of coke." What in the world is it doing there?

The Dicks, pricks, and cocks you can chalk up to generational vocabulary shifts, but when Mortimer writes, "Do not pry in-to my press. I have hid-den a gun in it," I mean—you start to wonder if she was maybe a little crazy. In a centenary tribute in the London *Times*, her nephew admits that she could be eccentric, especially where pets and water were involved.

---

126   READING WITHOUT TEARS.

Pack  Neck  Kick  Cock  Duck

ack   eck   ick   ock   uck

back  deck  sick  lock  tuck

Note.—*The Child should not pronounce the c, but say only* "P' a k', Pack."

**Jack has a duck**
**It can swim**
**Dick has a çock**
**It can peck**
**Sam has a nag**
**It can kick**

---

252   READING WITHOUT TEARS.

| Clock | Cloak | grot  | groat |
|-------|-------|-------|-------|
| rod   | rode  | rob   | robe  |
| Tom   | tome  | cock  | coke  |
| con   | cone  | crock | croak |
| John  | Joan  | sock  | soak  |
| cot   | coat  | Moll  | mole  |
| rot   | wrote | Poll  | pole  |
| not   | note  | doll  | dole  |
| got   | goat  | sop   | soap  |
|       |       | mop   | mope  |
|       |       | pop   | pope  |
|       |       | hop   | hope  |

A rob-ber came to rob me of my robe.

The cock is at the top of the heap of coke.

She slept with her parrot, which she forced to lie on its back, using slaps to overrule the animal's every natural impulse to not sleep on its back in a bed. Eventually, she'd kill it by washing it in soap and water and setting it to dry before the fire. When she washed her lamb—in the ocean—she dried it by burying it up to its nose in the sand. She did other odd things, like trying to force a blindfolded donkey to swim; and of course, writing a dozen utterly terrifying books *for children.*

In 1950, after a *New Yorker* contributor complained about the book's menacing subject matter, Mortimer's own grandniece[*] wrote a five-page reply to argue that *Reading Without Tears* wasn't even her nastiest text. "Mrs. Mortimer was the author of another and more famous work," she wrote, "which is one of the most outspokenly sadistic children's books ever written." That book is 1833's *The Peep of Day, or, A Series of the Earliest Religious Instruction the Infant Mind Is Capable of Receiving.* I certainly hope the infant mind would do no such thing. Here is what baby learns in the first chapter:

I hope that your body will not get hurt.

Will your bones break? Yes, they would, if you were to fall down from a high place, or if a cart were to go over them.

If you were to be very sick, your flesh would waste away, and you would have scarcely any thing left but skin and bones.

Did you ever see a child who had been sick a very long while? I have seen a sick babe. It had not round cheeks like yours, and a fat arm like yours. Its flesh was almost gone, and its little bones were only covered with skin. . . .

How easy it would be to hurt your poor little body.

If it were to fall into the fire, it would be burned up. If hot water were to fall upon it, it would be scalded. If it were to fall into deep water, and not be taken out very soon, it would be drowned. If a

---

[*] This was Rosalind Constable, whom Pruzan describes as the "gin-swilling, pill-popping, iconoclastic lesbian daughter of Nazi-sympathizing London aristocrats." Constable was involved with Patricia Highsmith, and ran with a set that included Sylvia Plath, Allen Ginsberg, and Andy Warhol. Mrs. Mortimer, presumably, would not approve.

great knife were run through your body, the blood would come out. If a great box were to fall on your head, your head would be crushed. If you were to fall out of the window, your neck would be broken. If you were not to eat any food for a few days, your little body would be very sick, your breath would stop, and you would grow cold, and you would soon be dead.

The book was a huge seller that inspired two sequels, including the succinctly titled *More About Jesus*, and remains in print today.

Children who preferred travel to evangelical theology or threats of bodily harm could turn to one of Mortimer's three books of geography, which set a new standard for inaccuracy. Mortimer never visited the countries she wrote about, instead relying on outdated source books, common stereotypes, and frank racism for her information.[*] In 2005 writer Todd Pruzan compiled the highlights into a single volume titled *The Clumsiest People in Europe*, and it is well worth a read as a truly stunning compendium of nineteenth-century hate speech. The Italians are "ignorant and wicked"; Sicilians "fierce, violent, and cruel"; the Chinese are "very selfish and unfeeling"; the "Siamese resemble the Burmese in appearance, but they are much worse-looking"; and Polish Jews are "very dirty" with "eyes like the hawk and noses like its beak" who "try in every way to get money." The Turks "are so lazy that, though the land is very fruitful, they do not sow grain enough for their own bread, but send for grain to other countries. They read scarcely anything but the Koran, which they learn by heart. Yet in one respect they are to be praised. It is this. They bear troubles well." The Greeks, however, do not; "when they are unhappy, they scream like babies."

Lisbon is "full of litter and rubbish"; Washington is "one of the most desolate cities in the world"; "Cairo *might* be a beautiful place, with its numerous gardens and magnificent mosques, but it *is* a most odious city"; and as for Amsterdam, "There is no city in which there is so much danger of being drowned." You're better off just staying home, as long as you're

---

[*]   As Todd Pruzan points out, this is understandable when the country in question is, say, Siberia, but less forgivable when it's *Wales*, located just a few miles from Mortimer's own home.

English. Of her own countrymen, Mortimer has this to say: "They are not very pleasant in company, because they do not like strangers, nor taking much trouble . . . They are often in low spirits, and are apt to grumble, and to wish they were richer than they are, and to speak against the rulers of the land. Yet they might be the happiest people in the world, for there is no country in which there are so many Bibles."

Reading the books a pattern quickly emerges: Protestant countries = good; everywhere else = bad; Catholic countries = the worst. Thus we read:

> The Irish say they are Christians, yet most of them will not read the Bible. Is not that strange? Why do they not read it, if they are Christians? Because their ministers tell them not to read it. Why? Because these ministers or priests tell them a great many wrong things, which are not written in the Bible, and they do not want the people to find out the truth.
>
> The religion they teach is called the Roman Catholic religion. It is a kind of Christian religion, but it is a very bad kind.

It's not as though Mortimer goes easy on other faiths ("Mahomet . . . wrote a book called the Koran, and filled it with foolish stories, and absurd laws, and horrible lies"; "The religion of Taou teaches men to act like madmen. The religion of Buddha teaches them to act like idiots"), but it's the Catholics she really has it in for. Here it may be worth pointing out that Mortimer's unrequited love rejected not just her but the Church of England, eventually forsaking Anglicanism to become a Catholic cardinal. Indeed, open hostility toward the Church runs through much of Mortimer's work. The subject heading for her first geography book, *Near Home: The Countries of Europe Described*, is in fact "Anti Catholicism—Juvenile literature." In her *New Yorker* piece, Mortimer's grandniece reports on her mother's visit to "the stern, beshawled old lady," recalling, "upon a table in the musk-scented drawing room lay a book called 'Morning Exercises Against Popery.'" Interested parties can find this text online.*

---

* Interestingly, one of the few contemporary children's writers who was as theologically menacing as Mortimer was the Roman Catholic Reverend John Furniss,

Though she went all-in on the anti-Catholicism, in her xenophobia and racism Mortimer was simply a product of her time. As Pruzan documents, nineteenth-century encyclopedias could be even worse, in one instance likening Malays to apes. Mortimer was in no way alone, and other children's stories were certainly unabashedly racist, too. Among the worst were the popular if unfortunately named series of Dumpy Books for Children, whose titles include the notorious *Story of Little Black Sambo* as well as lesser known disasters including *Ten Little Niggers*, *Little Yellow Wang-Lo*, and *The Tale of Two Japs*.

**MORTIMER, THEN,** was in good bad company, and as far as being the most disturbing Victorian writer goes, she certainly had competition. Enter Charles Dodgson, aka Lewis Carroll, a hyperintelligent Henry Darger whose creepiness remains a matter of hot debate in scholarly circles. Because the mores of the time were so different—and because his family excised the portions of his diary that might have shed light on matters—the creepiness is difficult to quantify. Still, it's hard not to be skeeved out by a few things. Like the fact that he wrote one ten-year-old, "Extra thanks and kisses for the lock of hair. I have kissed it several times—for want of having you to kiss, you know, even hair is better than nothing." Or that he said things like "I am fond of children (except boys)," and wrote things like "I confess I do not admire naked boys in pictures. They always seem . . . to need clothes, whereas one hardly sees why the lovely forms of girls should ever be covered up." Or that Nabokov, such a fan that he agreed to translate *Alice* into Russian for a mere five dollars, observed a "pathetic affinity" between Dodgson and Humbert Humbert.

Most disturbing was Dodgson's MO for meeting young girls, and the fact that he *had* an MO for meeting young girls. He carried toys and

---

author of such passages as this one describing hell: "A little child is in this red-hot oven. Hear how it screams to come out. See how it turns and twists itself about in the fire. It beats its head against the roof of the oven. It stamps its little feet on the floor." Despite their theological differences, you can't help thinking he and Mortimer would have gotten along.

games with him to lure any he might encounter into conversation—trains and beaches were particularly fruitful hunting grounds—and would follow up by sending the girl an autographed first edition of *Alice*. After that came the invitations to visit, preferably without parental chaperone ("And would it be de rigueur that there should be a third to dinner? Tête à tête is so much the nicest"). This was followed by a request to photograph the child, preferably without clothes ("If you should decide on sending over Gertrude and not coming yourself, would you kindly let me know what is the minimum amount of dress in which you are willing to have her taken?") All of which starts to sound an awful lot like an invitation to a pool party at Roman Polanski's.

The photographs are so disturbing now it's hard to imagine there was a time they weren't. But in fact Victorians perceived them entirely differently—nudes of young children were commonly done and viewed as quite innocent, so innocuous that they appeared on Christmas cards. The pictures were part of a larger Victorian cult of the child, which saw children as one of the few acceptable subjects of affection in a deeply repressed age. So while it was perfectly fine to kiss a seven-year-old girl, it was wholly unacceptable to hold the hand of one ten years older, with the dividing line somewhere around the Victorian legal age of consent (a disturbing twelve). Which is why Dodgson was once in the what seems to us very strange position of having to apologize to a mother for kissing her seventeen-year-old daughter by explaining that he thought she was much *younger.*

Some critics have suggested that Dodgson's bad reputation is due to some historical revisionism that inadvertently made him out to be more of a perv than he actually was. Because interactions with very young children were acceptable, but ones with young adults were not, early biographers revised the ages of some of his "friends" downward to make Dodgson appear more saintly, only to make him seem all the more criminal a few generations later. As Karoline Leach points out, a reading of his full diaries reveals a man who thoroughly enjoyed the company of adult women and did not, in fact, express romantic attraction toward his subject, Alice Liddell.

Dodgson was certainly an odd bird (in the Alice books, he is represented by a dodo<sup>*</sup>): tall and ungainly, deaf in one ear, with a stutter and a tendency toward migraines,[†] an Oxford don and professor of mathematics who never married and spent way too much time with little girls for modern sensibilities. But even if Dodgson did have what we would consider highly inappropriate feelings, there's no evidence that he physically acted on them.[‡] He sure expressed affection in writing, however, where young girls often served as muse. His primary muse was Alice,[§] subject of all three Alice books—which he called a "love gift"—and whose full name he spells out in an acrostic poem in *Through the Looking-Glass*. But there were many others, their names spelled out in acrostic poems as well.

In 1863, Dodgson and the Liddell family had some kind of rift, the cause of which remains unknown thanks to those expurgated diaries. Many scenarios, some rather wild, have been suggested: perhaps Dodgson proposed marriage to Alice, then age eleven; perhaps he was simply getting too close to her; perhaps he was getting too close to her governess. Then there's the recent discovery of a full-frontal photo of a girl who may or may not be Alice's pubescent sister, which Dodgson may or may not have taken. In any case, relations eventually resumed, but remained cool.

Dodgson moved on to other girls, sometimes using the Alice books as a calling card. For girls he encountered, then, the books served as a sort of draw. For other readers, however, they were simply a pleasure and breath of fresh air, an entirely new form of children's literature. The books questioned authority, rather than imposed it; they entertained rather than lectured. They ushered in what became known as the golden age of children's literature, and remain classics today. As a child myself I felt like I *should*

---

*  Possibly a self-deprecating reference to his stutter—he is said to have introduced himself as "Do-Do-Dodgson"—though as Douglas-Fairhurst documents, there's scant evidence to support this idea.

†  Which may have been behind the distorted realities in his work. Interestingly, there's a form of migraine now known as Alice in Wonderland syndrome, because sufferers experience the feelings of size distortion that afflict Alice in the book.

‡  Beyond some kisses (normal for the time) and, of course, the child pornography (also normal for the time).

§  Liddell also infatuated John Ruskin, who fell head over heels with other children as well. The Victorian age was a weird, weird time.

like them, because they were classics and I was pretentious, but something about them put me off.

The other golden-age children's book that puts me off is *Peter Pan*, whose author, J. M. Barrie, is in a solid three-way tie with Mortimer and Dodgson for strangest Victorian author. Like Dodgson, Barrie is the subject of much critical controversy, most of it revolving around What Was Up with All the Young Boys. Barrie was certainly odd, in ways that oddly resembled his protagonist. Like Peter Pan, Barrie seems to have never grown up, and there's some suggestion that this was true medically as well as metaphorically. Some have argued that Barrie suffered from psychogenic dwarfism, a condition in which severe stress impedes puberty, preventing normal growth and development. In Barrie's case, it may have been caused by the death of his older brother when Barrie was six; his parents became neglectful and distant, mourning the child who would be a boy forever—and whom Barrie sought to emulate, both consciously and un-.

Whether he actually had the condition, however, is unclear. At five-three, Barrie was short, but not necessarily stunted; he had facial hair, though it's reported it didn't come in until he was twenty-four, and his voice remained high. It seems likely that he was asexual. As his ward told his biographer, "I don't believe that Uncle Jim ever experienced what one might call 'a stirring in the undergrowth' for anyone—man, woman, or child." He married, but the marriage probably wasn't consummated. (Barrie sometimes refused to speak to his wife, and they both showed their dog far more affection than they showed each other. His wife eventually had an affair, and they divorced.)

Surpassing Dodgson, Barrie not only courted his child muses—he gained custody of them. In 1897, after he was already a successful playwright, Barrie met the Llewelyn Davies family on a walk in Kensington Park.* Before long he'd insinuated himself into the family of five boys,

---

* Interestingly, the Llewelyn Davies boys were first cousins of gothic novelist Daphne du Maurier, whose own rather gothic childhood is a story in itself, and the reason du Maurier would not permit the publication of her childhood diaries until fifty years after her death.

charming their mother, Sylvia, if not their father, Arthur, who resented Barrie's constant presence. Arthur had a point. Barrie tended to do things like whisk Sylvia and his then-favorite boy, Michael, off to Paris, leaving both Arthur and Barrie's own wife at home. He also used the boys extensively in his work. *The Little White Bird*, the first book inspired by the Llewelyn Davies boys and the one that introduces Peter Pan, is disturbed and disturbing. It tells the story of a bachelor who becomes obsessed with a very small boy and makes it his "sinister design" to undermine the "culpably obtuse" mother (named Mary, like Barrie's wife): "to expose her to him in all her vagaries, take him utterly from her and make him mine."* At one point, the protagonist actually kidnaps the child in a scene that would give anyone the heebie-jeebies:

> I returned to David, and asked him in a low voice whether he would give me a kiss. He shook his head about six times, and I was in despair. Then the smile came, and I knew that he was teasing me only. He now nodded his head about six times.
>
> This was the prettiest of all his exploits. It was so pretty that, contrary to his rule, he repeated it. I had held out my arms to him, and first he shook his head, and then after a long pause (to frighten me), he nodded it.
>
> But no sooner was he in my arms than I seemed to see Mary and her husband and Irene bearing down upon my chambers to take him from me, and acting under an impulse I whipped him into the perambulator and was off with it without a license down the back staircase.

Parts of this book later became the children's book *Peter Pan in Kensington Gardens*, which Barrie dedicated "To Sylvia and Arthur Llewelyn Davies and their boys (my boys)." It was presumptuous at best, threatening at worst, and weird no matter what.

After both parents died early, awful deaths (Arthur, from a disfiguring cancer of the jaw; Sylvia, from cancer near the heart), Barrie became

---

* Here I will mention that the original title of *Peter Pan* was *The Boy Who Hated Mothers*.

the boys' legal guardian, possibly by extralegal means. He claimed, perhaps untruthfully, that he and Sylvia had been engaged. He may have also forged Sylvia's will, changing the "Jenny" she hoped would serve as guardian to "Jimmy," himself.* In any case, the will was not contested, and the five boys remained in Barrie's charge. It does not appear to have been a healthy arrangement. Peter Llewelyn Davies described the custody situation as "almost unbelievably queer and pathetic and ludicrous and even macabre in a kind of way." Peter would eventually commit suicide by throwing himself under a train. Michael drowned with his companion/lover in what was either a tragic swimming accident or a suicide pact (they were found with their arms around each other), and eldest son George died in World War I. No wonder D. H. Lawrence observed that Barrie "has a fatal effect on those he loves. They die."

At the end of the play *Peter Pan*, Peter muses: "To die would be an awfully big adventure." I don't know about that, but on a meta level *Peter Pan* does suggest why death shows up in so many children's books. Books are like Peter in that they never change; but the children the books are read to are growing up every minute. Every children's book becomes a sort of elegy for the reader's own childhood, whose end inches closer and closer. No wonder children's stories involve so much death and loss. Still: Maybe a nice story about puppies?

**OVER THE NEXT FEW DECADES** the concept of bedtime stories would catch on, and books gradually became less upsetting. They also got much shorter, evolving into picture books that might feature just a few lines of text. Very brief, highly illustrated "toy books" had been around for a while, but by the end of the nineteenth century they were becoming more sturdy, professionally produced affairs, like the Beatrix Potter books that began rolling out in 1902. By the 1940s there were baby books and

---

\* In a bit of karmic payback, Barrie himself was the victim of a deathbed will switcheroo, when his secretary dosed him with heroin (toward the end of his life, he used it daily), then had him sign a new will disinheriting the surviving Llewelyn Davies children and leaving almost everything to her (Dudgeon, *Neverland: J. M. Barrie, the Du Mauriers, and the Dark Side of Peter Pan*, 10).

board books and Little Golden Books, which, with lots of pictures and few words, could make bedtime a ten-minute affair for the bargain price of twenty-five cents a title.

The author who did some of the most interesting work in children's picture books was a piece of work herself. This was Margaret Wise Brown, the striking blond Wasp who served as a one-woman children's book factory and established the format that would dominate the next century. Brown published over a hundred different titles under different names at seven different publishers, with the best known including *Goodnight Moon* and *The Runaway Bunny* (1958's *The Dead Bird* didn't have quite the same sticking power). Almost all the books involve animals, usually alive, but not always; 1946's *Little Fur Family* was bound in actual rabbit fur (for fancy readers, two copies were also bound in mink at fifteen dollars each). I'm guessing this would not sit so well with readers now, nor would Brown's home, which featured a fur couch and fur rugs.[*]

If a stereotype of the children's book author exists, Brown didn't fit it. She admitted, "I don't especially like children," and didn't have any of her own, being far too busy with an adventurous, carefree life. Still, Brown was unusually good at figuring out what children would want to read, and just as important, what their parents would want to read *to* them; Brown typically limited herself to a hundred well-chosen words. Whether with fur, pictures, or words, Brown's books engaged children's senses, and were uniquely successful in doing so. She was a Comenius for a new age: a bisexual socialite guided by whimsy. For babies she invented the "feely" book with *Cottontails*, which was meant to be handled rather than read. Because babies feel with their mouths more than their hands, the book was constructed from nontoxic materials.

---

[*] As might be obvious, Brown's relationship with animals was complicated. Owner of an infinite number of pets, author of a hundred books that almost always featured them, she was also an avid hunter who specialized in the rather bloody form of the sport known as "beagling." (She didn't restrict her prey to animals either, once threatening to shoot a certain publisher with bow and arrow [Marcus, *Margaret Wise Brown: Awakened by the Moon*, 268].) Given her affection for fur, maybe she just liked animals and didn't really care if they were dead or alive. She sold the rights to her book *Baby Animals* for a paltry $150 because she needed the money right away to buy a wolfskin jacket (Handy, *Wild Things*, 6).

Brown had no use for fairy tales and thought the best material for children was what her mentor Lucy Sprague Mitchell called the "here and now," the things in the child's everyday world—room, moon, brush, mush—which Brown catalogs so memorably in 1947's *Goodnight Moon*. The book becomes something entirely new, emphasizing rhythm rather than meaning. The result is a hypnotic singsong story that magically lulls sleepyheads to sleep.* Not everyone got it. Anne Carroll Moore, the highly influential children's librarian at the New York Public Library who also declared war on *Stuart Little*, did not much care for Brown and banned *Goodnight Moon*; it would not be permitted on the shelves until 1973, when it was already well on its way to becoming a cultural icon. Firmly entrenched now, its parodies include *Goodnight Loon* (about Minnesota), *Goodnight Goon* (zombies), *Goodnight Dune* (Frank Herbert's sci-fi novel), *Goodnight Forest Moon* (Star Wars), *Goodnight Brew* (beer), *Goodnight iPad*, *Goodnight Nanny Cam*, *Goodnight Democracy*, *Goodnight Bush*, *Goodnight Keith Moon*, and the more directly titled *Fuck You, Sun*.

Five years after *Goodnight Moon*'s publication, when Brown was forty-two and engaged to a Rockefeller sixteen years her junior, she had an emergency appendectomy while traveling in France. Within a few weeks she would die, literally kicking up her heels: to prove she was fully recovered, Brown did a high kick that dislodged an embolism. She died on the spot.

If Brown had a literary heir, it was probably Dr. Seuss, né Theodor Geisel. Like Brown, Geisel emphasized sound over meaning. He was also ambivalent about children—his second wife reported that they made him nervous—and did not have any of his own.† (He was known for telling parents, "You have 'em, I'll entertain 'em.") And at this, he was very, very good.

---

\* Or terrifies them, if read by the wrong person, as *The Simpsons* notably demonstrated by having Christopher Walken read it to an audience of panicking preschoolers.
† He may have been less (or perhaps more) ambivalent about children if his wife's health problems hadn't prevented them from having any. They did, however conceive an imaginary daughter, whom they'd brag about when friends' boasting about their own children got out of hand. They named her Chrysanthemum-Pearl (*The 500 Hats of Bartholomew Cubbins* is dedicated to her) and reported that she cooked a fine chocolate and oyster stew.

He also didn't have much competition. By the 1940s and '50s, the children's market was dominated by Dick and Jane, and a Houghton Mifflin editor thought their insipid stories were the reason children's literacy rates were tanking. As a cure he invited Geisel to write a story that first graders "would be unable to put down" from a first-grade vocabulary list. Only 236 words long, the final manuscript took Geisel nine months to write, mostly because limiting himself to the list required careful storytelling. Out went Geisel's original plan to write about a feline king and queen—*queen* wasn't on the word list—but *cat* and *hat* were. *The Cat in the Hat* became a massive bestseller, allowing Geisel to quit his day job and start building the Seuss empire. This included not just books but words: a master neologian, he invented the terms *oobleck*, *grinch*, and *nerd*.

Geisel brought in other authors and established an imprint that did phenomenally well, though there were some misfires. *Do You Know What I'm Going to Do Next Saturday?* by Seuss's wife, Helen Palmer Geisel, has aged particularly badly; it features binge eating and, more alarmingly, "Shooting! I'll go shooting with the United States Marines. Big guns! Little guns! I'll shoot every gun that they shoot."

Geisel started out in Paris, where he crossed paths with Hemingway and the Lost Generation (he came up with the idea for his first book, *And to Think I Saw It on Mulberry Street*, while listening to the ship's engines on a transatlantic crossing), and his life was not entirely free of the scandals that marked that group. After he left his cancer-stricken wife Helen for their close friend and neighbor, Helen killed herself, leaving a heartbreaking suicide note that, in very non-Seussian language, made it clear she would not live without him.

Geisel's work never dealt with this particular issue, but it did in fact tackle plenty of other thorny ones in perky rhyme that somewhat obscured the heavy subject matter. Though children probably didn't notice, *Yertle the Tertle* is about Hitler; *The Butter Battle Book*, about nuclear proliferation; and *Marvin K. Mooney Will You Please Go Now!*, about Nixon. *Horton Hears a Who!* represents postwar Japan* (and not, as some have

---

\* This was in part an apology for the work Geisel produced for the U.S. armed forces during World War II. A lot of Geisel's early work (including the propaganda pieces

surmised, abortion, though the book's tag line "a person's a person, no matter how small" was irresistible to pro-life groups; Geisel threatened to sue one that used it on its stationery). *The Lorax* promoted environmental- ism and proved so offensive to the logging industry that it produced its own rebuttal book called *The Truax*. In China, *Green Eggs and Ham* was banned until 1991; officials felt it promoted the wrong brand of Marxism as well as homosexuality. Geisel admitted that his work was "subversive as hell," but still, gay commies is probably reading too much into it.

I DON'T KNOW if most children's authors have complicated and troubled lives, or if we just notice the ones who do. They certainly tend to produce the most notable books, either because they're so very bad (looking at you, Favell Lee Mortimer) or so very good. My own childhood reading was dominated by the latter, and my favorite authors, for the most part, were the ones who'd had a rough time. There was Maurice Sendak, whose childhood was marked by the loss of his extended family to the Holocaust; and Roald Dahl, who lost a daughter to measles and a marriage to being an asshole. ("He left his wife *when she had cancer*," my mother always added, erroneously, as if it were a line in the book.[*]). Even Ludwig Be- melmans's orderly *Madeline* concealed a rough backstory. It was based on the recollections of Bemelmans's mother's childhood in a convent school, which she told to six-year-old Ludwig after they were abandoned by his father for another woman. His mother was pregnant at the time, as was Ludwig's beloved nanny—also by Ludwig's father—who promptly killed herself. This left Ludwig with some issues, and he later shot a waiter at the hotel he worked at. Something is not right, indeed.

Then there's Russell and Lillian Hoban's Frances series, which is al- most unbearably wistful, and no wonder: written just before the Hobans'

---

as well as political cartoons and ad work) features disturbingly racist caricatures. Geisel himself was fairly horrified by it later on, and produced a number of anti- racism works by way of reparation.

[*] In fact, it was a stroke, not cancer, and he left her after, not during. And at least one of his children, whose opinion probably counts more than my mother's, remembers him fondly.

marriage ended, the books seem to document a happy family that was dissolving as they wrote. I suppose it was just the time. In the sixties and seventies, most children's books on offer alloyed sweetness with melancholy. They didn't lull so much as unsettle, and were perhaps the reason I spent the hour after bedtime palpating for tumors. At best, the books were merely poignant, with *Corduroy*, the story of a shopworn teddy bear, being the best example. *Corduroy* would become my favorite, though I'm also partial to the title character's first incarnation, *Corduroy, the Inferior Decorator*. That book was never published, but you can find a recording of Don Freeman reading the text over swinging jazz online for a very sixties experience I highly recommend.

In the years since my own childhood, bedtime books have become less poignant and more pointed. Titles in the last thirty years have included *I Wish Daddy Didn't Drink So Much*; *My Mom Has Hepatitis C*; *My Big Sister Takes Drugs*; *Charlie and the Curious Club: Candy or Medicine?*; *Jimmie Boogie Learns About Smoking*; *Mommy's Black Eye*; *Latawnya, the Naughty Horse, Learns to Say "No" to Drugs*; *My Parents Open Carry*; and—this is not a joke, I checked—*Don't Make Me Go Back, Mommy: A Child's Book About Satanic Ritual Abuse*. "Dad is in prison" has become a whole genre to itself, with lots of picture books addressing the subject, including *A Visit to the Big House* and *The Night Dad Went to Jail*. The more artistically inclined child of an inmate can find the subject represented in coloring books.

*The Night Dad Went to Jail* (2014) is illustrated not with people but puppies (suggesting, I guess, that Dad actually went to the pound). You can understand why—we use these books to address the things that are too hard for us to bring up ourselves, and having them addressed by an adorable beagle makes it easier still. In our house, we've been spared the need for the worst of the issue books, but we still relied on them when we had to tell our children that it was time to stop peeing on our laps, or that they were about to be unseated by the new sibling on its way.

And this, I suppose, is the job of children's books, good or bad. They let us use their words when our own fail us, when we need to teach our children something about life that is just too hard to say or too awful to understand. Maybe it's that people hurt and kill one another; maybe it's that children have terrible accidents, and we don't really know what happens when we die; maybe it's that cats like to lick their rectums. Storytelling began as a way to explain our world, and while the word has changed, the role of stories hasn't. Ancient Greeks had to explain the natural world; medieval serfs, how to behave; Puritans, how to prepare for the afterlife; and us, why our satanic drunk of a father is in the pokey again.

The sweetly poignant books my parents read me prepared me for a world in which both good things and bad things happen, and neither good nor bad lasts forever. I've found this to be true and useful, which is why I've been reading the same books to my own children, even though this is probably a mistake. Books remain the same, but readers don't, and what made sense for one generation will horrify the next. As adults, my children will probably be appalled that I read them books with cisgenderist pronouns; their children will shake their heads at something else. But in the meantime, it's bedtime, and time for a story once again.

So good night, N-word; good night, Nazi Red Riding Hood. Good night, murdering stepmother; good night, castrating beaver; good night, green gay Marxist ham. Good night, good night, good night.

# 10

# Lullaby and Good Night

## *Sleep*

Given that small children do little besides sleep and eat, you would not expect their lives to be as complicated as they are. Single-celled organisms seem to accomplish these basic functions easily, but children require protracted negotiations and a fraught routine delicately held together by naps and yogurt tubes. Invariably the system breaks down and the screaming begins, because no one's slept more than forty-five minutes in a row in the past two years.

If we think parenting is challenging today, sleep is the part that challenges us the most, the issue that parents seek help for more than any other. As it turns out, both the challenge and the way we sleep are fairly new. Sleep training is a recent invention, and as for sleep itself, the full night we expect for our children and ourselves is new, too. What seems like a biological imperative is as much a sociohistorical construct as the disco nap.

The bad news is we may be constructing it to be much harder than it used to be. The historical record offers little advice on getting children to go to bed, which itself is good evidence that it was nowhere near the trial that it is today. Historical child-rearing manuals have plenty to say on the subject of dress, comportment, and *fruit*, but as far as sleep goes, they generally recommend only that children do it, with few specificities on how this might be achieved. Letters and diaries don't record many complaints from sleep-deprived caregivers.[*] Now, of course, there are endless feeds of complaints online and shelves of books to remedy them. All of which results in a routine that gets ever longer as our attempts to make bedtime fast and easy make it ever more hard and complex, and what should take five minutes frequently stretches on for hours.

Going to sleep literally requires children to do nothing, but nothing turns out to be nearly impossible for them to do. They desperately need a glass of water, which inevitably leads to a desperate need for the toilet. They need a tissue, but not *that* tissue: a tissue from the green box with the leaf design on it downstairs. They have a question about the ballpoint pen they saw on the coffee table six hours earlier that cannot wait until morning. They definitely have a fever. They are going to throw up. They *might* not throw up if they're given some graham crackers. They suddenly develop a pressing need to know if that guy, that guy they played with one time? With the blond hair? Jason, maybe? If that guy was six years old or five. Their legs hurt. They need socks. They need to take their socks off. They need another story, but not *that* story, and while you're going downstairs to find the book, maybe bring another tissue?

Kids have always been annoying, both day and night, but the particular intensity of their night routine is new. There are few aspects of parenting that annoy me more. I suspect this is because it comes at the end of a long day with them, when I've already mentally clocked out; now it's cutting into my downtime. It feels like being called in on your day off—to wipe someone.

Children do not care. While we agonize and obsess over their sleep habits, they give zero thought to ours. My kids have woken me up in the

---

[*] Which is not to say none. In his twelfth-century memoir, Guibert of Nogent recalls how the all-night screaming of his adopted baby sister tortured the household. Interestingly, he blames her crying not on biology or temperament but on straight-up demon possession, which, at three A.M., seems as good an explanation as any even today (*A Monk's Confession: The Memoirs of Guibert of Nogent*, trans. Paul J. Archambault [University Park: Pennsylvania State University Press, 1995], 68–69).

middle of the night innumerable times, for reasons ranging from under-standable (they are scared or sick) to the completely infuriating (because they felt like sitting in my lap). My daughter once woke me up to inform me she knows how to fold a plastic bag.

For most of history, sleep was a piece of cake in that it was treated a lot more like eating: something done communally two or three times a day rather than privately in one stretch. Viewed this way, our current sleep habits seem ridiculous. Imagine having to perform an elaborate routine before each meal, in which the child changes her clothes, prepares her body, then is read a series of books, the subject of which is various children and animals who are themselves preparing to eat a meal. At this point the child is dispatched to eat a meal by herself in a separate room, while her parents monitor her with AV equipment. That she should refuse to eat at all and spend the next two hours trying to break out of that room is prob-ably something we should see coming.

Our forebears seem to have managed the whole thing with a great deal less fuss and anxiety, under far less comfortable conditions. For all of prehistory, humans slept on the ground in actual nests. Things im-proved in the cradle of civilization, which offered both civilization and cradles. These cradles often consisted of woven baskets, which served as tiny barges in the origin stories of Moses, Karna, and Sargon. I'm not sure why this trope was so common, but any parent of a small child who refuses to sleep will appreciate the functionality of a cradle that can be set adrift downstream. Ancient infants also co-slept with caregivers in accom-modations that varied according to class and culture. If you were poor, your bed might consist of your day clothes; if you were rich, you could enjoy the fragrant comforts of goat hair bolsters.

In general, the Arabian subcontinent was light-years ahead of the rest of the world as far as sleep goes, using cushions long before they caught on in the West (*mattress* comes from the Arabic word for cushion, "*al-matrah*").* By 3600 BCE, Persians had invented what was essentially a water

---

* The Chinese were also great pioneers, with heated sleeping platforms dating back to the Neolithic period.

bed by filling goatskin bladders with water. When Islam came along, it brought further improvements, including the *qayloulah*, or afternoon nap, which was considered so important it was enshrined as a sunnah.* The Quran discusses sleep at length, and Islamic law offers lots of advice on when and how sleep should take place.

For children over age seven, that means in their own bed, a separation decreed by hadith.† While it was fine and common for younger children to sleep with their parents or siblings, by seven they were supposed to sleep alone. Unlike the dog pile that would become the rule in much of medieval Europe, especially the colder parts, in more temperate parts of the ancient world, communal sleeping was limited. This was also true in Rome. Although Romans practiced communal *pooping*, those who could afford it required a little more privacy in the bedchamber, which was known as the *cubiculum*.‡ Children might sleep in a *cubiculum* of their own, or share one with parents, siblings, or servants. Babies were dispatched to a cradle, called *cunae*, about which I know little except it may be etymologically linked to the C-word. A surviving example from Pompeii features a clean craftsman design that would not look out of place in a Pottery Barn catalog.

In much of Europe, meanwhile, people were sleeping on leaves, and would continue to do so well into the Middle Ages. Though they'd eventually embrace mattresses, after Crusaders brought back the concept, for hundreds of years Europeans slept on what amounts to teeming piles of compost. This, in fact, is where we get the expression "make the bed": people literally made their own beds, stuffing straw or leaves into a sack or covering a heap with a blanket. Making things even less comfortable, they'd likely share this infested pile with two or three or five others, with the whole household sleeping communally in the home's hall. On cold nights, they were joined by the livestock. My kids can't sleep if there's a

---

* Meaning, something Muslims do to imitate the custom of Muhammad. As far as I know, Islam is the only religion that backs up the nap with actual dogma, a very fine thing.

† Also meaning a custom of Muhammad.

‡ From which we get the modern *cubicle*. The name is derived from *cubare*, to lie down (from which we also get *concubine*), and has nothing to do with cubes and even less to do with office work. And while in my experience it's an opinion not always held by management, the proper use of a cubicle *by definition* is for sleep.

cricket within a two-block radius, but medieval children apparently had no problem bedding down with donkeys.

By the Renaissance, younger children were put in cradles and cribs, which were sometimes suspended by ropes from the ceiling like macramé plant holders. These could sway, in a fashion that was supposed to mimic movement inside the womb; in their typically shaky take on anatomy, doctors believed the fetus hung from the umbilical cord like a tire swing.

There was, as it turns out, a surprising amount of ropework involved in Renaissance bedding. Rope was also used in place of slats or bedsprings (and needed frequent tightening, likely inspiring the phrase *sleep tight*). Babies would sleep tightest of all, laced into cradles that had holes or pegs to keep them fastened in place. Until the eighteenth century, these cradles were long and narrow, as this was believed to be necessary to impose an upright human form on their squishy baby bodies. For the same reason, the child would be laid out straight and heaped with blankets; warmth was thought to prevent rickets. By keeping the baby from sun, however, the blankets may have actually contributed to it, while also hampering their acquisition of an attractive tan.

That wasn't the only hazard cradles posed in the days before baby-proofing and recall notices. What made them convenient—their compact portability—also made them dangerous, easy to nudge into the fire or down the stairs. By the middle of the nineteenth century, cradles were seen as backward, old-fashioned contraptions whose "furious rocking . . . seemed to confuse the infant brains of our grandfathers." They were replaced by the fixture that remains the standard today: the freestanding high-barred crib. These were taller and roomier than cradles and were considered healthier, which they might have been had they not been painted with lead. Since lead is sweet, this meant cribs were essentially candy-coated with a delicious flaky toxin that caused anemia and developmental delays.

This wasn't so great, sure, but the crib still offered a number of advantages, the first of which is that it's effectively a baby jail that keeps the child more or less safe and contained. Happy and quiet, however, is another matter, as the societal changes that made the crib a necessity also disrupted the sleep routines that had held peaceful sway for thousands and thousands of years.

UNTIL THEN, even though the environment was much less comfortable, apparently most people conked out just fine. No one got too worked up about the occasional insomnia. No one lost it over the more-than-occasional night feedings, because then, as now, babies didn't sleep through the night. The difference is that no one expected any baby to, or for that matter, any adult to either.

Although it's what we've come to prefer, monophasic sleep—sleeping in one long stretch—is not what we evolved to do, and it's not what humans did until recently. As historian Roger Ekirch famously discovered, until the invention of artificial light in the nineteenth century, sleep occurred in two distinct segments. The initial stretch, from nightfall to the middle of the night, was known as first sleep. At that point, people rose for an hour or two and did whatever it was that people did before the Internet and Nick at Nite. (The historical record indicates they typically spent this time praying, talking, or writing, though go-getters might use it to visit neighbors or commit petty larceny.) They then went back to bed for second sleep, which lasted until morning. In traditional societies without artificial light, people generally maintain this biphasic sleep schedule. Under the right conditions, it's likely we all would. In a study conducted by researcher Thomas Wehr, in which subjects were housed without artificial light, they, too, reverted to biphasic sleep.

Babies' sleep is even more segmented. Like cats, they are polyphasic sleepers who nap around the clock. It takes a while for their circadian rhythms to get going, and for the first couple of months they can't even distinguish night from day. I suppose we should be braced for this, given that they can't really distinguish anything at all: a foot is food; a dog is a pillow. Still, none of these cognitive failings frustrate us as much as their insistence that one A.M. is playtime.

A few hundred years ago, though, they were right. One A.M. *was* a pretty good time to be up, hanging out with the rest of the family in the interval between the two sleeps. Even then, adults and children weren't on the same sleep schedule, but the lack of a medieval Ferber suggests babies' polyphasic pattern matched up better with their biphasic parents' than it does with our own.

Now, however, the mismatch between parent and child is rather stark.

In our house this is most glaring in the mornings. Like all small children, ours came equipped with the factory standard alarm clock that goes off before six A.M., and on birthdays and holidays, at four thirty. Some have theorized that this is an evolutionary leftover: generationally differing sleep schedules ensured someone from the clan was always awake, on watch. So the teenager, whose melatonin kicks in hours after the adults', can take the midnight shift, and the old guy whose prostate gets him up at dawn can take the early one; and the parents of small children will just be awake every minute always. I'm sure this was an advantage ten thousand years ago, but now that we have security systems and alarm clocks, it just makes me want to murder someone.

Technology only made things worse. The electricity that made artificial light possible also enabled other entertainments, all of which encouraged parents to stay up later and send the kids to bed earlier so they could listen to the Charleston without interruptions from junior. Unfortunately, these also made kids a lot less likely to cooperate. Staying up to watch your mother darn socks by candlelight wasn't a big draw, but phonographs, radios, and well-lit entertainments made going to bed a lot less appealing.

This twentieth-century shift was the start of what is known, in the literature, as "bedtime resistance." The few studies that examine it have reported rates in the range of about 20 to 50 percent. I know lots of parents who cope with two hours of this nightly, but in our house bedtime pushback is minimal. I think this is because we're boring, and no kid begs to stay up just to watch Daddy tweet while Mommy darns socks by laptop.

A hundred years ago, however, in more lively homes, little Horace and Estelle might clamor to stay up late and listen to John Philip Sousa's latest track. Thanks to larger houses, they wouldn't get to. Once there was space, parents discovered it was nice to have some adult time awake, and also nice to have it asleep. Given the choice, few of us would choose to sleep with a teenager at the foot of our bed, or a couple of toddlers sprawled across our face. Once parents could make other arrangements, they did so, and for the first time in history, children were dispatched to sleep alone in their own rooms.

A century or so later, it's unclear whether or not this is a good idea. Co-sleeping is still an enormously controversial subject and a really great way to start a fight, especially when the combatants are sleep-deprived and cranky. There are a lot of varying factors involved, and it's hard to say definitively which practice is safest and most effective. At this point, however, it looks like science and safety may be (somewhat) on the side of sleeping alone, while history and global precedent are more on the side of sleeping together. Co-sleeping was the norm for most of history and remains so for the majority of the world's families. Even in the United States, it's nowhere near rare; a full third of families co-sleep. These numbers are up from just a couple of decades ago, when the American co-sleeping rate was less than 1 percent.

It is not entirely clear, however, exactly what co-sleeping means. For some families, it means sharing a bed; for some, a sidecar; for some, just a room. In our own house, it has tended to mean children migrating from their beds to ours with a retinue of accessories, displacing one parent to the cold comforts of a love seat and the other parent to the edge of the mattress for an all-night game of sleep Twister in which every spin directs a child's foot to a parent's groin.

For growing numbers of families, co-sleeping means sharing bed and blankets, beginning when the child is an infant and continuing indefinitely. The increase is due in large part to the Searses, who popularized the idea of the "family bed" in their many books on the subject. The Searses' own embrace of co-sleeping is due in part to Jean Liedloff's 1975 *Continuum Concept*. Having noticed how well it worked for indigenous peoples, she recommended it, even though, as she wrote, "At this moment in history, with our customs as they are, sleeping with one's baby seems a wildly radical thing to advocate." The childless Liedloff practiced co-sleeping herself, though in her case it was with a "two-pound baby woolly monkey."

Liedloff pitched co-sleeping as a return to nature and tradition, but that's not really true. While room-sharing with babies has been near universal in history, bed-sharing has not, and as far as infants are concerned, there have been detractors since ancient times. Soranus was warning against co-sleeping with newborns in the first century. In the Middle Ages, bishops urged mothers to keep children in cribs or cradles until age three, sometimes backing the demand up with religious legislation. Cribs

and cradles were thought to be safer, though these, too, could be dangerous when they were placed too close to the hearth or to the livestock.

In crib, cradle, or craw, the child would be in the company of others
and not, like today, in a room of his own. We're so used to this arrangement that it's hard to imagine how rare it is in much of the world—where
it's considered frankly abusive—and how recent it is for us. Sleeping
communally in the same room, if not the same bed, was the norm for
millennia. Although there were seven billion fewer people in the world a
thousand years ago than there are now, somehow, once the sun set, they
tended to end up in the same space.

Of course they did. It was safer and warmer, and often, there was
nowhere else to go.* If the home had a bedroom at all, it certainly wasn't
designated for the sole use of youngsters. Children were expected to fall
asleep among the clatter of adults, and apparently were able to, since none
of them seem to have died of fatigue. Older children typically slept on
trundles by their parents' bed, up until they left to start families of their
own. When houses grew larger, separate rooms for children were considered neither a priority nor a good idea, as you wouldn't want to leave
a child alone. Instead, they were dispatched to share a room (and often
a bed) with others. Siblings made obvious bunkmates, but some generations felt that it was best to keep children apart, instead pairing them with
adults who might supervise them through the night. Often this meant
the adults who were least well positioned to decline, i.e., the help. George
Washington's stepgrandson shared a bedroom with Washington's (male)
secretary, a scenario that's awfully hard to imagine now.

At a time when there were fewer beds in general and less expectation of
personal space, however, this would have seemed perfectly normal among
all social classes. In both Europe and America, it was not uncommon for
people to share hotel beds with complete strangers. Should you stay at a
friend's house, you might end up sleeping with the husband and wife or

---

* This is something the modern Western family only experiences when staying in
hotels. Since children and parents have different bedtimes, this can result in some
creative arrangements, and in my own family usually means someone ends up sleeping in either the bathroom or the closet. I can attest that the closets at Chicago's
Palmer House are particularly comfortable.

even the whole family. For the sake of propriety, adolescent daughters were placed at one end of the bedding, and guests and passing hoboes at the other.

In one of the weirder arrangements, young people (usually girls) were sometimes bedded with very old people (always men). The practice was, in fact, so established it actually has a name: shunamitism, from the biblical passage in which the elderly King David uses the Shunamite girl Avishag as a human bed warmer.* We're told that David "knew her not," but it's unclear whether later practitioners slept with the girls or *slept* with the girls (or frankly raped them). Shunamitism was also observed in ancient Greece and Rome, where it was called *gerokomy*. Which I guess means it was so established it has two names, which I guess means I'll go throw up now.

Unsurprisingly, old men liked shunamitism, and it continued for hundreds and hundreds of years. In the eighteenth century the pornographer Réstif de la Bretonne devoted a chapter of *Le Palais-Royal* to "Les Sunamites," describing a Parisian brothel, run by Madame Janus, that specialized in providing pairs of young virgins for the service. Clients who tried to do anything more than slumber with these girls were assessed a fine, but this apparently was not an effective enough deterrent, as some of the girls became pregnant. Still, shunamitism continued through the nineteenth century and was recommended by celebrated physicians including Thomas Sydenham and Herman Boerhaave.

Others, presumably including the young girls themselves, thought it was a very bad idea, and several experts condemned it. Dr. B. W. Richardson warned in an 1880 article, "there is no practice more deleterious to [the young] than to sleep with the aged. The vital warmth that is so essential for their growth and development is robbed from them by the aged, and they are enfeebled at a time when they are least able to bear the enfeeblement."

---

* The elderly Gandhi did this, too, as an experiment in *brahmacharya*, a complicated Hindu concept that includes celibacy (also, it seems, he was cold). Disturbingly, all parties were naked; even more disturbingly, his bedmates included two grandnieces. Gandhi seems to have seen nothing wrong with the endeavor, writing about it openly (and "voluminously"); and there's no evidence, or even much suggestion, that it was sexual in any way. Make of it what you will (Vinay Lal, "Nakedness, Nonviolence, and Brahmacharya: Gandhi's Experiments in Celibate Sexuality," *Journal of the History of Sexuality* 9, no. 1–2 [January–April 2000]: 105–36).

In 1719 the physician Edward Baynard made a similar charge in *Health, a Poem*, urging parents not to bed "youth with aged bones," or, for good measure, "the over-fat."

BY THE MID-NINETEENTH CENTURY, people were starting to think it a bad idea for children to share a bed with anyone at all. William Whitty Hall's 1863 book *Sleep* charged, "It seems little short of a murderous process for more than one person to sleep together in a chamber of ordinary size." It was bad enough for adults to sleep together; for children it could be downright fatal.

No surprise that the prudish Victorians would lead the charge for separate beds and separate rooms. Doctors and reformers began pushing for children to have their own chambers, arguing, essentially, that human bodies are disgusting and must be isolated, that their very presence fouls the air.

"Impure air" was something Victorians were fairly obsessed with, especially where children were involved. Though we don't give a lot of thought to it now, it was a serious preoccupation in the eighteenth and nineteenth centuries, in no small part because the air was, in fact, a near-solid property full of contaminants, odors, and disease. The bedroom could be particularly foul. Besides the stink generator that is the human body, bedrooms contained no shortage of smells and pollutants, from chamber pots to animal-hair bedding to the animals themselves. Smoke belched from hearths and from humans, and things were no better outside.* Open the window, and you'd bring in a nice fresh draft of raw sewage and industrial by-products. Carbon emissions from planes and trains and buses would not become a problem for another century or so, but in the meantime the current mode of transportation was taking a dump right there on the sidewalk.

---

* Whether it was healthier to sleep with the window open or closed was the subject of some debate, once tackled by two of the country's most prominent orators: Ben Franklin and John Adams, who had to bunk together on a trip. According to Adams's diary, they spent part of the night arguing the issue, with Franklin calling for fresh air and Adams for closed windows. The debate concluded when both combatants fell asleep (*Diary of John Adams*, vol. 3, Monday, September 9, 1776).

No wonder, as Bill Bryson notes, Victorians came to believe "breathing at night was a degenerate practice." Which is crazy, of course, but they were partly right. What *was* true, in an age of epidemic tuberculosis, was that some really nasty substances could escape from the lungs, and if the random boarder your parent tucked into your bed was up coughing all night, you'd end up not just tired but infected. Unfortunately, it would be a while longer until people understood how the infection actually spreads, and in the meantime believed it arose spontaneously from stuffy rooms.

The fuss about air was, in part, a fuss about putting on airs, driven by class anxiety. Shared beds and bedrooms were for people who couldn't afford better, and airborne diseases were for the poor and undeserving. If you loved your children, you would provide them a large room with ample windows for adequate ventilation. And if you *really* loved them, you would buy a house with a sleeping porch, for, as one home economics book declared, "A sleeping porch is a kind of life insurance."

Failing that, advice books urged mothers to thoroughly air out both the room and the occupant, while magazine writers warned of death from "air-famine." Luther Emmett Holt became a particular proponent of regular airings-out, writing that "it is almost invariably the case that those who sleep out of doors are stronger children," a recommendation that led Dr. Spock's mother to make her son sleep outdoors year-round *in Connecticut*.

The Spock family had a sleep porch for this purpose. Apartment dwellers who wanted to afford their children the same privilege could install a window-mount baby cage that allowed baby to sleep in the open air while acquiring both frostbite and searing acrophobia. These were wire crates, affixed to apartment windows much like air-conditioning units, which were somehow both legal and popular in the 1920s and '30s in the United States and the UK. Eleanor Roosevelt made her own version ahead of the trend in 1906 when she installed a chicken-wire cage outside the window of her East 36th Street townhouse for daughter Anna to nap in. "I thought I was being a very modern mother," Roosevelt recalled, but Anna despised it, crying so forcefully that neighbors threatened to call the Society for the Prevention of Cruelty to Children.

BOGGINS' OPEN-AIR SLEEPING COMPARTMENT
View from the street.

BOGGINS' OPEN-AIR SLEEPING COMPARTMENT
View from the room.

The practice of putting children to sleep in cold storage eventually died out in the United States but remains popular in other parts of the world, especially the more frigid countries of Europe like Finland and Russia, where children are regularly bundled up and set out to nap in the snow.[*]

**AS THE HIGH-RISE** outdoor sleeping pens might indicate, the early twentieth century was a time of growing anxiety over children's sleep and how to improve it. For the first time in ever, parents worried that children were not getting the sleep they needed, a panic fanned by experts and magazines. Luther Emmett Holt declared, "The American child is kept on a starvation ration of sleep." Magazines warned of a new condition, "chronic fatigue," while books like *The Tired Child* explained why it was so dangerous.

It's hard not to notice that reports of children not sleeping enough follow right on the heels of escalating concern about sleep; and also hard not to wonder if, as with picky eating, attempting a cure created a condition. By the early twentieth century, a condition was certainly developing. After several millennia of sleeping restfully in dirty leaf piles, we were now a generation of princesses on beds full of peas.

There were a lot of reasons for this, and one of them was that children

---

[*] Those of us with Russian grandparents can confirm that while cold naps are thought to be healthful, all other cold things are considered suspect, and when left in a Russian's care you will be hothoused in layers of cardigans on even the warmest day. Cold drinks are out of the question, especially cold milk, which you'd no more serve a child than you would a loaded gun.

were now going to bed sober. The soothing syrups and straight gin that had previously smoothed the path to sleepytime were falling out of favor. This was of course a good thing as they were often dangerous. Some were dangerous and ineffective, like "soot tea"—exactly what it sounds like—and concoctions made with camphor or sweetened tobacco water, both of which are in fact stimulants. Opiates and alcohol were reliably effective, but sometimes deadly, so they were out. Which meant baby was now "going to sleep at the top of his voice," as one contemporary magazine described it.

The solution, in this early twentieth-century age of scientific parenting and timetables, was regularity. Baby now had to nap and sleep on a strict schedule. Older children's sleep was equally regimented. Even a variation as small as half an hour, experts warned, "may induce masturbation, surreptitious reading in bed, restlessness, and inability to concentrate in school."

But the strict schedule probably didn't help matters much, and may have made things worse. In response, experts doubled down, assigning more hours of rest. Meanwhile, the standardization of time was resulting in the standardization of sleep times. When it was 7:15 in one place and 7:42 a mile away, consistent and universal sleep schedules were pointless if not impossible. But when children had to be at school at a universally determined 8:00 A.M., they were more likely to be in bed by a universally determined 7:00 P.M. Bedtime became an actual set time.

Bedtime also became a set piece, with a growing number of rituals and accessories, such that, by 1943, *Good Housekeeping* was warning against "elaborate good-night rituals" that stretched on far too long and required too much equipment. *Blankie* entered the lexicon. Night-lights were introduced. Stuffed animals—toys you could take to bed!—proliferated and replaced the louder, smellier, actual animals that had served as bedmates for millennia. These would pave the way for "lovies" and other transitional love objects that would became a standard part of the child development arsenal. Our daughter had a favored doll, but our son pretty much skipped this stage entirely. For a while he did snuggle up with the TV remote, which horrified me until he explained that taking it to bed prevented his sister from picking the cartoon in the morning.

Before we tucked him in, like most modern parents, we read to him.

Given how low-tech bedtime stories are you'd guess they were much older, but they, too, are fairly recent. Until the end of the nineteenth century, the ritual of parents putting children to bed, if it was performed at all, was more likely to involve opiate syrups, neglect, beatings, or threats. It certainly did not involve board books.

Though the publishing industry would eventually nail the formula, early bedtime books left a lot to be desired.* One of the earlier examples, W. P. Garrison's well-reviewed *Good-Night Poetry: A Parent's Assistant in Moral Discipline*, thought the best way to prepare children for sleep was to correct the misdeeds of the day with didactic poems. The index includes such entries as "Blood nobly shed," "Death better than slavery," "Defects happily made known by an enemy," and "War's horrors to no purpose" in what I remind you is a *bedtime book for children.*

Maria Tatar argues that bedtime stories probably evolved from a tradition of recounting all the terrible things that would happen to children who didn't go promptly to bed in the hopes, I suppose, that they would pass out in sheer terror.† The earliest bedtime stories were scarring morality tales, and even lullabies feature children falling out of trees. Wee Willie Winkie chases children; Hans Christian Andersen's Ole Shut-Eye gets children to shut theirs by squirting milk in them. The Sandman is even worse: he puts children to sleep by *throwing sand in their eyes*, something my own children get time-outs for. In E. T. A. Hoffmann's version, he's utterly terrifying: "He's a wicked man who comes to children when they refuse to go to bed and throws handfuls of sand in their eyes till they bleed and pop out of their heads. Then he throws the eyes into a sack and takes them to the half-moon as food for his children, who sit in a nest and have crooked beaks like owls with which they pick up the eyes of human children who have been naughty."

---

* As late as the 1940s, my mother's bedtime "stories" came from *Bartlett's Familiar Quotations*, which was not particularly interesting for a five-year-old, though I imagine fairly effective at boring her to sleep.

† In my own experience, when this has been done entirely accidentally because it turns out your child isn't quite ready for *My Little Pony*, this method does not work. And while the child will eventually sleep, it will be in your bed, upside down, kicking your head all night. You will stay awake.

No wonder children were suffering from "chronic fatigue." By the twentieth century these stories would mellow into cheerful Golden Book tales about puppies and kittens, but children protested more than ever. The parent who wanted to hear their protests from anywhere in the house could buy a baby monitor, invented in 1937, though they wouldn't really catch on for another fifty years. We did not use one and I frankly don't understand why you would want to make your child's crying *louder*. In any case, its invention was inspired not by anxiety over bedtime or even over SIDS deaths—which it does not in fact prevent—but by kidnapping fears after the abduction of Charles Lindbergh's son.*

BUT WHO COULD BLAME the kid who was having trouble falling asleep? Children of all ages were sleeping in an entirely new way: alone, in a single stretch, on a strict schedule. All of which turns out to be something most children don't like until they're taught to, and typically aren't entirely sold on even then.

Thus began the campaign to sell it to them in the form of sleep training. Though it would not become common until the 1980s, the concept had been around for a while. Given national stereotypes, it will surprise no one that the earliest references to the practice of sleep training are German. In his 1799 book *Guter Rath an Mütter* (*Good Advice for Mother*), celebrity physician Christoph Wilhelm Hufeland (who also introduced the concept of macrobiotics) introduced a beta version of sleep training, saying children should sleep in their own beds and parents shouldn't give in to their cries for milk or attention right away.† Over the next century a number of German physicians like Adolph Henke and Hermann Klencke

---

* This was the Radio Nurse, invented by the head of the Zenith Radio Corporation, Eugene McDonald, and designed by Isamu Noguchi. McDonald reportedly wanted to keep an ear on his daughter as she slept on their yacht, pretty much the definition of rich people problems.

† Note that Hufeland thought that while babies should sleep alone, nubile girls should sleep next to very old men. He was an advocate of shunamitism, recommending the practice in *Makrobiotik, or The Art of Prolonging Life*, which, he suggested, was exactly what shunamitism might do (for the old men, anyway; no mention of any benefits for the nubile girls).

would author parenting books that offered similar advice. By the 1930s, "the influence of national socialism is unmistakable" in books that exhort baby to get with the program and praise the "heroic" mother who lets her baby cry.

To be fair, American baby books were saying more or less the same thing.* Catharine Beecher's 1842 *A Treatise on Domestic Economy* advised mothers to put babies to bed awake and alone, tears be damned: "In doing this, a child may cry, at first, a great deal; but for a healthy child, this use of the lungs does no harm, and tends rather to strengthen, than to injure, them. A child who is trained to lie or sit, and amuse itself, is happier than one who is carried and tended a great deal." At the turn of the century, Luther Emmett Holt advocated similar methods, insisting babies be placed in their cribs awake, to learn to fall asleep on their own. If the baby protests, "It should simply be allowed to 'cry it out,'"—the first use of the term, which, it turns out, sounds even worse when the baby is called an "it." Holt then lays down the blueprint for what will eventually become the Ferber method, advising, "This often requires an hour, and in extreme cases, two or three hours. A second struggle will seldom last more than ten or fifteen minutes, and a third will rarely be necessary." However, this is to be done only if you're sure why the baby is crying, and it is because he is a jerk who wants attention, not because he is hungry or cold or otherwise disturbed. Mothers who worry the baby will cry so hard it will cause an abdominal rupture may fit the child with a supportive knitted band. For sweaty children, Holt recommends hair pillows, and of course, ice-cold air.

These were the tenets by which Spock himself was raised, uncomfortably, so you wouldn't blame the man for taking a different tack entirely in his own advice book. And in the first edition, he does, telling mothers to "keep bedtime agreeable and happy," and endorsing the use of stuffed animals, blankets, and night-lights. If you've got a crier, it's fine to sit with the child until he falls asleep, and it's also fine not to; if he should then cry for "five or ten minutes, don't worry too much."

---

\* Especially William and Lena Sadler's 1916 *The Mother and Her Child*, which strongly urged mothers "to stick to the heroic work" of letting their babies cry themselves to sleep (218).

It quickly became clear, however, that parents were worrying plenty. Two years later, Spock would deliver a talk on "Chronic Resistance to Sleep in Infancy," a problem that "was formerly rare but is now becoming more frequent." Spock blamed the uptick on the cultural shift he himself helped drive, and endorsed cry-it-out methods in some cases. By 1957 he was advising parents to deal with resistant sleepers thusly: "put the baby to bed at a reasonable hour, say good night affectionately but firmly, walk out of the room, and don't go back. Most babies who have developed this pattern cry furiously for 20 or 30 minutes the first night, and then when they see that nothing happens, they suddenly fall asleep! The second night the crying is apt to last only 10 minutes. The third night there usually isn't any at all." As for toddlers who won't stay in bed, they may be tied in bed with a badminton net, "cut in half and the two pieces sewed together side by side. Then it can be bound with firm cord to the top rail of the side of the crib next to the wall, and also part way along the top of the head and foot of the crib." Which may be why Joan Crawford thought it was okay to tie her son Chris to the bed with a "sleep safe" harness, designed for toddlers, every night until he was twelve.

Uncharacteristically, the approach of the man Spock described as "very frightening," Bruno Bettelheim, was gentler. He addressed the subject in a thoughtful 1951 article, "Does Your Child Fight Sleep?" assuring parents this was common and normal and offering mostly good advice, except for the strange recommendation to let children essentially eat themselves to sleep. "Anxiety or fears which prevent a child from falling asleep can at least be alleviated by letting the child suck on some hard food or munch a cookie after the lights are turned out," he promises, though this seems like a bad idea for anyone who worries about dental hygiene or, you know, choking to death in your sleep.

OVER THE NEXT couple of decades parents would search for solutions that didn't involve asphyxiation and restraints. In the 1980s, one would finally arrive with Richard Ferber's *Solve Your Child's Sleep Problems*. Ferber canonized the cry-it-out method so successfully that, as Ann Hulbert writes, Ferber "is more than a household name. He is a household verb."

Stricter regimens, like Marc Weissbluth's, would follow, as would dia-metrically different ones, like the Searses'. All have their fans and foes, as you will learn with scalding intensity should you make the mistake of offering an opinion on an Internet message board.

In the literature, cry-it-out programs are called, alarmingly, extinction methods. This sounds extreme, as though smothering may be involved, but in fact *extinction* is simply the behavioral modification term for end-ing undesirable habits. And while Ferber has a reputation for toughness, as Hulbert notes, his advice really isn't much different from Spock's. They share a sensibility, both realizing "that the people who are truly hard to train are parents, not babies."

When my husband and I finally decided some kind of sleep training was called for, we did it not to improve our daughter's sleep but our own. None of us were happy about this. The whole idea seemed faintly ridiculous, as though sleep were something a human would require training in, like cus-tomer service or cultural sensitivity. On the upside, it may be the only sort of training my family would excel in, would in fact Olympic gold medal in, being champion sleepers to such a degree that my cousins think we may all suffer from a mild form of narcolepsy. Family members have been known to conk out while practicing piano or getting dressed to go out, and I myself once fell asleep in the second row at an Iron Maiden concert.

At six months it was not clear whether our daughter had inherited my outstanding sleep genes or my husband's occasional insomniac ones. None of us were sleeping well at the time, due to an overlong bedtime routine and multiple wakings. At a friend's urging we decided to try the Ferber method, modified to accommodate our short attention spans and lack of backbone.

And so it was that we spent an October night listening to her scream while we huddled in our room and tried to block the sounds out with TV. *Rear Window* happened to be on, and it seemed strangely appropriate, Jimmy Stewart helplessly watching a homicide he is unable to stop while we helplessly listened to our child scream bloody murder. It was miserable. But by the time Jimmy Stewart falls asleep, in the film's last scene, our daughter had fallen asleep, too. Within a couple of nights she had adjusted to a new world in which her parents either didn't exist at night or did but didn't love her. Either way, she slept. The whole thing was easy enough that when it came time to sleep-train our son two years later, my husband knocked it out in one night while I was at book club.

As I'd hoped and expected, our children became champion sleepers. They sometimes end up in our bed and get up way too early, but they go to sleep just fine, and leave us alone most nights. Unless we fall down a Netflix rabbit hole, my husband and I get all the sleep we need.

All of which I take as proof not that sleep training works nor that I'm an unusually good parent. It might be genes, but mostly, I think, it's just luck: you win some, you lose some. And when, for a brief period of time, our luck failed, and our children began to have trouble falling asleep, we did what gamblers do and got out our wallets. Tired of an hour or two of post-bedtime requests, we began offering fifty cents each night they stayed in bed after tuck-in. This turned out to be all the incentive they needed, and they'd fall asleep, dreaming, I suppose, of all the things they might buy.

How lucky can you get?

# Second Nature

For a good fifteen years before I had kids I referred to myself as Mama, usually in a statement declaring Mama's urgent requirements. "Mama needs a drink," "Mama needs a nap": two decades later I have no idea what was making Mama so stressed out, as my sole responsibility was monitoring my carbs.

The name, though, was apt. I acted like a mother. Even at twenty-six, I had a purse full of snacks and Kleenex, and my wardrobe consisted largely of housecoats. Actual children were the only accessory I lacked. Naturally, when I got married, it was to someone who already seemed to think of himself as a father, insofar as he referred to our downstairs bathroom as "Daddy's can."

Which was why it was such a surprise, when children came along, to realize we had no idea what we were doing. No natural instincts were kicking in, and we were now entirely responsible for the existence of someone who had zero life skills of her own. We did not have a lot of skills ourselves. The ones from our previous life didn't transfer at all, as our daughter had no need for a light grammatical edit or a Ph.D. adviser.

After a period of bewildered panic, however, we settled in, falling back on the cultural playbook we'd inherited and absorbed without really realizing it. Nine years later, we've more or less gotten the hang of things. I've become a mother in every sense, except for when I visit my own parents and revert to being someone who needs her mother to do everything for her. And while I now know that this work is boring, exhausting, tedious, and thankless, somehow I think *my* mother does it because she both enjoys it and is uniquely qualified for it, a belief in no way undermined by the frequent sighs she issues when confronted with a sink full of my dishes.

In a way, though, this is the reason I'm now generally a capable parent, at least when I choose to be. Being a son or a daughter amounts to a long run as understudy. You finally get pushed onstage and realize you know all the lines. Writing in 1957, Dr. Spock endorsed the process: "This is the way Nature expects human beings to learn child care—from their own childhood." I agree, though I'm not sure Nature has as much to do with it as inertia does. It's simply the path of least resistance, and hence the one most of us end up rolling down.

Then again, if anything is natural, it's inertia. If history is any indication, that's generally a good thing. A lot of parenting's thorniest issues—sleep resistance, picky eating—began when we started trying to fix something that wasn't particularly broken in the first place. This includes, of course, parenting itself. Though we've been worrying about it for less than a hundred years, we've somehow managed to keep the species going without giving it much thought.

Sometimes, of course, this was a bad thing, but as often as not, it worked out. You do less harm when you're doing nothing at all. There is something to be said for letting things take their course. My own particular course seems to be just copying my parents, and since I turned out more or less intact, it's the one I've stuck to: not nature, but second nature, and maybe that's how Mother Nature would have it.

It still startles, though, the way becoming parents makes us become our *own* parents. I've acquired my mother's voice and entire repertoire, down to the exasperated groans. The notes I write my children are in my father's handwriting, and when my daughter "cleans" by hiding old food under the rug, it is his teeth I grit. I do not know if this is an act or natural; if I do it because I saw my parents do it so many times or because it's hardwired into my DNA. It's probably both, but I don't think it matters much; by deed or by blood, these things pass on.

I wonder, sometimes, how far back these traits and tics go. Does my snort echo through the generations, embarrassing the Irish scullery maids and Polish peasants who shared it as much as it does me? Did a Prussian farmer have my husband's sneeze? Did some Mesopotamian forebear make the same face my son does when confronted with olives?

And does it just continue on? Because the logical conclusion, of course, is that our children will turn into us: the role they were born to play. Like a lot of people, I suppose, I think little enough of myself that this seems like a terrible outcome. At five, my daughter would tell me, "I want to grow up to be just like you!" and I would think, But that's exactly what I'm afraid of.

Better she shouldn't get any of my good qualities than also have to take the bad. Fifty years from now, when the child my son claims he'll name Batman graduates from college, let him not be a dick about his parents taking some pictures, as I was and always am. My impatience, my eczema, my inability to let anything go: let these end with me.

Knowing our history does not mean we aren't doomed to repeat it. I've spent the past five years reading nothing *but* parenting histories and I'm still making parenting mistakes every day. I am pretty sure that's okay. If I've learned anything, it's that barring the really awful stuff, things mostly turn out fine, and the ones that don't were beyond our control anyway.

In a sense, all parenting is a history of parenting. We do what our parents did because that's what we know; or sometimes we do what they *didn't* do, because now we know better. Like them and their parents before, we do our best, unless we can pay someone else to do it for us.

Reproduction is exactly that. We reproduce not just our genes, but our childhood experiences. Forty years out, I'm reproducing my childhood down to the Danish modern furniture and the water rings on the Danish modern furniture. Even the parts I swore I wouldn't: those are here, too, though now of course I understand why a parent might yell a little too loudly after a child ruins the finish on a Scandinavian end table.

You win some, you lose some. We ended up with terrible eaters who won't clean their rooms but sleep like champs, who treat everyone but each other kindly and have no serious health problems. They ended up with parents who holler too much but are generally pretty pleasant, and typically let them eat and do what they want. This, apparently, is who we are, be it nature, nurture, or—as I suspect—inertia. Things happen and we roll with it. On and on it goes.

I don't know what the next few years will bring, but if history is any indication, it'll be more of the same: a lot of really boring stretches with some wonderful moments and the occasional permanent marker mishap. That, after all, is how it's gone for untold millennia. Some things are harder now and some things are easier; so much is different, but so much really isn't. Priorities and methods change, but the big stuff stays the same, and the species continues on, another morning and another evening, and back to bed we go.

Because this is the other part of reproduction: the endless repetition of days. Having gotten them bathed, dressed, and fed once, you then have to do it a few thousand more times. Another child comes along and you do it all again, over and over until it becomes a blur, a sped-up filmstrip, and suddenly it's over and the credits are running. Mostly I'm happy that we are done with bottles and diapers, but in sentimental moments there are things I miss: baby pants, their weight in my arms, the wide-eyed delight in discovering something new. It just goes so fast, poof, like the Cheerios they drop and then step on, a crumb trail disappearing as fast as they lay it down.

The food that gets pushed under the carpet, though: that will stay there forever.

The days are long but the years are short, everyone said, and it's true that nine years have flown by in a blink. I shut my eyes for a second and the smiling, crying blobs became real people who do not require constant interventions. I now sometimes go thirty full minutes without being asked for anything. An entire afternoon can pass without a fight or tantrum. They have grown from helpless dependents to good company, and I no longer love them best when they're asleep.

Tonight, as usual, mine are sleeping soundly. Because they don't talk in their sleep I don't know what they're dreaming about, so will have to guess it's about the havoc they'll wreak tomorrow, or their plans for a two A.M. dash to my bed to deliver a mild head injury. At which point I'll wake, briefly, from a dream to a dream come true, and find myself cocooned next to a child with a fruit gummy stuck to his pajamas.

And even if I did not know, when my dearest dreams became manifest, that there'd be so much laundry, I can't help but be grateful for a husband and family I did not know I'd get to have, for the mix of nature, nurture, luck, and laziness that let millennia of ancestors survive so we could be here now. I'll stay up just long enough to appreciate it, before my gratitude mutates into the grievances and worries that preoccupied me through the day. And then I'll fall back asleep to the thought that things will probably work out just fine, as things tend to do.

# Acknowledgments

Thanks to the generous folks who shared their expertise, experience, materials, and time, especially: Paul Anderson, Daniel Archer and Frederic Klein, Jake Bowers and Cara Wong, Milka Eliav, Mary Gallagher, Suzanne Grimshaw (heroic procurer of the rarest of books), Sara Konrath, Trina and Doron Koushmaro, Miriam Meisler, Luke Shaefer, Tiffany Shlain, Joshua Thorp (another heroic procurer of books), David Waldner, Elizabeth Wingrove, and the staff and resources of the University of Michigan library system.

Thanks to family and allofamilies: Judith, Alain, and Victoria Traig; Anita Mickey; Lissos, especially Elizabeth; McGraths, especially Peter; Clabbys, especially Mary Lou; Harwoods; Weidenbaums; Schleichers and Smiths; Julia Smillie; Ryan Gray; Angela Hernandez; Jonathan Zimmerman; Pavaos; Kerners; Nenninger-Hynes; Shaefers; and Uhles, especially Amanda, who provided keen editorial advice as well as friendship and pie.

Thanks, so many thanks, to the wonderful Megan Lynch and Emma Dries, Sara Birmingham, Michelle Crowe, Linda Sawicki, Elissa Cohen, and the good people of Ecco and HarperCollins. Thanks to the kind and capable Emily Forland, and the good people of Brandt & Hochman.

Thanks, finally, to the subject matter: Rob, Rachel, and Sam, without whom, nothing.

# Notes

## Introduction: *Act Natural*

xiii **landmark paper**: Robert L. Trivers, "Parent-Offspring Conflict," *Integrative and Comparative Biology* 14, no. 1 (February 1, 1974): 249–64.

## 1. Look Busy: *On Outsourcing*

2 **early humans were actually pretty good parents**: Darcia Narvaez, Jaak Panksepp, Allan N. Schore, and Tracy R. Gleason, eds., *Evolution, Early Experience and Human Development: From Research to Practice and Policy* (New York: Oxford University Press, 2013).

2 **"Without alloparents"**: Sarah Blaffer Hrdy, *Mothers and Others: The Evolutionary Origins of Mutual Understanding* (Cambridge, MA: Harvard University Press, 2011), 109.

2 **essentially daycare centers**: Susan Allport, *A Natural History of Parenting* (New York: Harmony Books, 1997), 7.

3 **exposing**: For a thorough and fascinating history of the practice, see John Boswell, *The Kindness of Strangers: The Abandonment of Children in Western Europe from Late Antiquity to the Renaissance* (Chicago: University of Chicago Press, 1998).

3 **"If it is a boy"**: Rodney Stark, *The Rise of Christianity: A Sociologist Reconsiders History* (Princeton, NJ: Princeton University Press, 1996), 98.

4 **sexual ones**: Paul Veyne, Arthur Goldhammer, Philippe Ariès, and Georges Duby, eds., *A History of Private Life: From Pagan Rome to Byzantium*, vol. 1 (Cambridge, MA: Harvard University Press, 1992), 79.

6 **To resolve it**: Sarah Blaffer Hrdy, *Mother Nature* (New York: Ballantine Books, 2000), 464–65.

6 **St. Guinefort**: Boswell, *The Kindness of Strangers*, 337.

8 **Justin Martyr**: Ibid., 113.

8 **foundling hospitals**: For a thorough and astounding account, which this chapter draws on, see Hrdy, *Mother Nature*, 288–317.

8 **rose past 40 percent**: Ibid., 304.

8 **had to install a grille**: Ibid.

9 **70 to 90 percent range**: Ibid., 298–304.

9 **"Here children are killed at public expense"**: Quoted in Hrdy, *Mother Nature*, 304.

9 **"safe haven" law**: Jessica Valenti, *Why Have Kids?* (Boston and New York: New Harvest Books, 2012), 95–96.

10 **surnames**: Hrdy, *Mother Nature*, 305; and A. R. Colón with P. A. Colón, *A History of Children: A Socio-Cultural Survey Across Millennia* (Westport, CT: Greenwood, 2001), 366–67.

11 **"Happy is he who has no children"**: Quoted in Shulamith Shahar, *Childhood in the Middle Ages* (New York: Routledge, 1992), 10.

12 **thrown like a football**: Karin Calvert, *Children in the House: The Material Culture of Early Childhood, 1600–1900* (Lebanon, NH: University Press of New England, 1992), 24.

12 **hung from hooks**: Ibid.

12 **Nearly a third**: Paul B. Newman, *Growing Up in the Middle Ages* (Jefferson, NC: McFarland, 2007), 68.

12 **standing stool or walking stool**: For more on these devices, and the dangers they posed, see Calvert, *Children in the House*, 33–36.

13 **wet-nursing network**: For more on this bizarre system, see Hrdy, *Mother Nature*, 351–70, to which my account is especially indebted; Edward Shorter, *The Making of the Modern Family* (New York: Basic Books, 1975), 176–89; and Colón and Colón, *A History of Children*, 326.

14 **Prospective nurses**: Shorter, *The Making of the Modern Family*, 178.

14 **mortality rates doubling**: Ibid., 181.

15 **When parents defaulted**: Hrdy, *Mother Nature*, 369.

16 **"do with their children"**: Quoted in Steven Mintz, *Huck's Raft: A History of Modern Childhood* (Cambridge, MA: Belknap Press, 2006), 12.

16 **"The want of affection"**: Charlotte Augusta Sneyd, trans., *A Relation, or Rather a True Account, of the Island of England* (London: John Bowyer Nichols and Son, 1847), 24–26.

17 **Henry Timbrell**: Joan Lane, *Apprenticeship in England, 1600–1914* (London: UCL Press, 1996), 223–24.

17 **Medieval schoolboys**: Philippe Ariès, *Centuries of Childhood: A Social History of Family Life*, trans. Robert Baldick (New York: Knopf, 1962), 315, 321.

17 **fagging**: Anthony Fletcher, *Growing Up in England: The Experience of Childhood, 1600–1914* (New Haven, CT: Yale University Press, 2008), 198–200.

17 **Mrs. Devis's esteemed London school**: Ibid., 263.

18 **Louis XIII**: Ariès, *Centuries of Childhood*, 100–102.

20 **"strong drink"**: John Locke, *Some Thoughts Concerning Education* (London: A. and J. Churchill, 1693), 19.

20 **Puritan parents**: For more on the Puritan way of parenting, see Mintz, *Huck's Raft*, 7–31, to which my account is indebted.

21 **too important to outsource to the mother**: For more on Puritan fathers' involvement, see the excellent Mary Frances Berry, *The Politics of Parenthood* (New York: Viking, 1993), 42–48.

21 **"Go into the Burying-Place"**: Quoted in Mintz, *Huck's Raft*, 20.

21 **children's play was in fact illegal**: Mary Cable, *The Little Darlings: A History of Child Rearing in America* (New York: Simon & Schuster, 1975), 7.

22 **Edward Bumpus**: John Demos, "Family Life in Plymouth Colony," Paula S. Fass and Mary Ann Mason, eds., in *Childhood in America* (New York: New York University Press, 2000), 204.

23 **Experience Clap**: Judy S. DeLoache and Alma Gottlieb, eds., *A World of Babies: Imagined Childcare Guides for Seven Societies* (Cambridge: Cambridge University Press, 2000), 50.

23 **When Puritan children were abducted**: Mintz, *Huck's Raft*, 7–8.

23 **"the first modern parents"**: C. John Sommerville, *The Rise and Fall of Childhood* (Thousand Oaks, CA: Sage Publications, 1982), 112.

23 **"the first anxious parents"**: David F. Lancy, *The Anthropology of Childhood: Cherubs, Chattel, Changelings* (Cambridge: Cambridge University Press, 2008), 144.

24 **enslaved women**: For more on childcare and childhood under slavery, see Lester Alston, "Children as Chattel," in Elliott West and Paula Petrik, eds., *Small Worlds: Children and Adolescents in America, 1850–1950* (Lawrence: University of Kansas, 1992), 208–31.

24 **"but you"**: Quoted in Marie Jenkins Schwartz, *Born in Bondage: Growing Up Enslaved in the Antebellum South* (Cambridge, MA: Harvard University Press, 2000), 1.

24 **"in which a young child"**: Alston, "Children as Chattel," 225–26.

25 *Little Lord Fauntleroy*: Calvert, *Children in the House*, 102–3.

25 **"economically worthless but emotionally priceless"**: Viviana A. Zelizer, *Pricing the Priceless Child* (Princeton, NJ: Princeton University Press, 1985).

25 **kidnapped for ransom**: Mintz, *Huck's Raft*, 167.

25 **Kidnapping wasn't even criminalized**: Colón and Colón, *A History of Children*, 364.

26 **Dr. Nathan Allen**: "National Degeneracy," *The Medical Times and Gazette*, vol. I (London: J. & A. Churchill, 1871), 341.

26 **"baby farms"**: For more on the subject, see Mintz, *Huck's Raft*, 169.

26 **"concerns by means"**: Ibid.

27 **Charlotte Perkins Gilman**: Charlotte Perkins Gilman, *Concerning Children* (Boston: Small, Maynard & Co., 1900).

27 **"Since the invention"**: J. Herbert Claiborne, Jr., M.D., "Cocaïne," *Babyhood* magazine 1, no. 3 (February 1885): 80–81.

27 **Readers' interest**: "Some Queries Concerning Cocaïne—The Proper Time for Sleep and Food," *Babyhood* magazine 1, no. 6 (May 1885): 190.

28 **detox doctors**: Calvert, *Children in the House*, 123.

28 **no shortage of booze**: Ibid., 124.

29 **"whether there should be"**: John B. Watson, *Psychological Care of Infant and Child* (New York: Norton, 1928), 5–6.

29 **"she must look upon herself"**: Ibid., 149.

29 **"I shall never be satisfied"**: Letter to Johns Hopkins University president Frank J. Goodnow (June 1920), quoted in Joanne Cavanaugh Simpson, "It's All in the Upbringing," *Johns Hopkins Magazine*, April 2000. http://pages .jh.edu/jhumag/0400web/35.html.

29 **Three of Watson's children**: For more on Watson's family, work, and legacy, see Ann Hulbert, *Raising America* (New York: Vintage, 2004), 122–53.

29 **Heir Conditioner**: Ibid., 244.

30 **universal childcare**: For more on the program and the Lanham Act, see Berry, *The Politics of Parenthood*, 105–8, to which my account is indebted.

30 **admitted only whites**: Ibid., 105.

30 **the child was kicked out**: Ibid., 106.

31 **a study showing how much it actually benefited**: Chris M. Herbst, "Universal Child Care, Maternal Employment, and Children's Long-Run Outcomes: Evidence from the US Lanham Act of 1940," *Journal of Labor Economics* 35, no. 2 (April 2017): 519–64.

31 **John Bowlby**: For more on Bowlby and attachment theory, see Judith Warner, *Perfect Madness: Motherhood in the Age of Anxiety* (New York: Riverhead Books, 2006), 91–94; and Hrdy, *Mother Nature*, 383–88.

32 **"straight autobiography"**: Sir Richard Bowlby, *Fifty Years of Attachment Theory: The Donald Winnicott Memorial Lecture* (New York: Routledge, 2004), 16.

32 **"constant attention"**: John Bowlby, *Maternal Care and Mental Health* (Geneva: World Health Organization, 1951), 67.

33 **"I wouldn't send"**: Joseph Schwartz, *Cassandra's Daughter: A History of Psychoanalysis* (New York: Viking, 1999), 225.

33 **"by relieving"**: John Bowlby, *Attachment and Loss*, vol. 2: *Separation, Anxiety, and Anger* (London: Hogarth, 1973), 89.

34 **"[v]ery frightening" figure who "scared the hell"**: Quoted in Hulbert, *Raising America*, 283.

35 **"Some of our psychologists"**: Ibid., 278.

35 **1.6 percent of children**: Statistics from United States Census Bureau, https://www.census.gov/topics/families/child-care/data.html.

35 **Black Panthers**: Berry, *The Politics of Parenthood*, 134. For more on the Black Panthers' Child Development Center and its curriculum focusing on black children's development, see David Hilliard, ed., *The Black Panther Party: Service to the People Programs* (Albuquerque: University of New Mexico Press, 2008), 56–60.

35 **Young Lords**: Berry, *The Politics of Parenthood*, 134–35.

36 **"it is very difficult"**: Quoted in Hrdy, *Mother Nature*, 495–96.

37 **evolved to attract caregivers**: Ibid., 447–49.

37  **"one of the least parented"**: 2004 marketing study quoted in Susan Gregory Thomas, *In Spite of Everything* (New York: Random House, 2011), xiv–xv.

37  **Judith Warner**: Warner, *Perfect Madness*, 93–94.

38  **Their philosophy**: Kate Pickert, "The Man Who Remade Motherhood," *Time*, May 21, 2012, 32–39.

38  **"Reattach your baby"**: Susan Douglas and Meredith Michaels, *The Mommy Myth: The Idealization of Motherhood and How It Has Undermined All Women* (New York: Free Press, 2005), 318.

38  **"If I hadn't worked"**: William Sears, Martha Sears, Robert Sears, and James Sears, *The Baby Book* (New York: Little, Brown, 2003), 410.

39  **2003 Pew poll**: "The 2004 Political Landscape," Pew Research Center (November 5, 2003). http://www.people-press.org/2003/11/05/the-2004-political -landscape.

39  **spending more time**: Suzanne Bianchi, "Family Change and Time Allocation in American Families," *The Annals of the American Academy of Political and Social Science* 638 (2011): 27, 29.

39  **Hrdy points out**: Hrdy, *Mother Nature*, 511.

39  **They also argue**: Anna Rotkirch and Kristiina Janhunen, "Maternal Guilt," *Evolutionary Psychology* 8, no. 1 (January 1, 2010): 90–106.

39  **"important motivator"**: Quoted in Diane Eyer, *Motherguilt: How Our Culture Blames Mothers for What's Wrong in Society* (New York: Crown, 1996), 88.

## 2. The Second Coming: *On Childbirth*

43  For more on the history of childbirth, see Tina Cassidy, *Birth: The Surprising History of How We Are Born* (New York: Atlantic Monthly Press, 2006), and Randi Hutter Epstein, M.D., *Get Me Out: A History of Childbirth from the Garden of Eden to the Sperm Bank* (New York: Norton, 2011), both of which inform this chapter.

44  **"shitting a pumpkin"**: Susan Faludi, "Death of a Revolutionary," *New Yorker*, April 15, 2013.

44  **"like an orange"**: Jessica Mitford, *The American Way of Birth* (New York: Dutton, 1992), 52

44  **"Nature has provided"**: "Reviews," *The American Journal of Obstetrics and Diseases of Women and Children* 73, January–June 1916 (New York: William Wood & Co.), 1135.

44  **The few studies**: Catherine A. Niven and Tricia Murphy-Black, "Memory for Labor Pain: A Review of the Literature," *Birth* 27, no. 4 (December 2000): 244–53; and Ulla Waldenström and Erica Schytt, "A Longitudinal Study of Women's Memory of Labour Pain—from 2 Months to 5 Years After the Birth," *BJOG: An International Journal of Obstetrics & Gynaecology* 116, no. 4 (March 2009): 577–83.

45 **Squirrel monkey**: Wenda R. Trevathan, *Human Birth: An Evolutionary Perspective* (New York: Routledge, 1987), 78.

45 **walk just fine**: Anna G. Warrener, Kristi L. Lewton, Herman Pontzer, and Daniel E. Lieberman, "A Wider Pelvis Does Not Increase Locomotor Cost in Humans, with Implications for the Evolution of Childbirth," *PLoS ONE* (March 11, 2015). https://doi.org/10.1371/journal.pone.0118903.

45 **Holly Dunsworth**: For a great explication of Dunsworth's argument, see Laura Helmuth, "The Disturbing, Shameful History of Childbirth Deaths," *Slate*, September 10, 2013. For the original paper, see Holly M. Dunsworth, Anna G. Warrener, Terrence Deacon, Peter T. Ellison, and Herman Pontzer, "Metabolic Hypothesis for Human Altriciality," *Proceedings of the National Academy of Sciences* 109, no. 38 (September 2012): 15212–16.

45 **pelvises tighter**: Cassidy, *Birth*, 82.

46 **hyena**: Sarah Blaffer Hrdy, *Mother Nature* (New York: Ballantine Books, 2000), 51.

47 **maternal mortality rates**: Roger Schofield, "Did the Mothers Really Die? Three Centuries of Maternal Mortality in 'The World We Have Lost,'" in Lloyd Bonfield, Richard Smith, and Keith Wrightson, eds., *The World We Have Gained: Histories of Population and Social Structure* (Hoboken, NJ: Blackwell, 1986), 231–60; B. M. Willmott Dobbie, "An Attempt to Estimate the True Rate of Maternal Mortality, Sixteenth to Eighteenth Centuries," *Medical History* 26, no. 1 (January 1982): 79–80; and Irvine Loudon, *Death in Childbirth: An International Study of Maternal Care and Maternal Mortality, 1800–1950* (Oxford: Clarendon Press, 1993).

48 **Hospitals didn't begin**: Libby Copeland, "She Thought She Was Irish—Until a DNA Test Opened a 100-Year-Old Mystery," *Washington Post*, July 27, 2017.

48 **rooming-in**: Cassidy, *Birth*, 226.

49 **the odds weren't good**: Loudon, *Death in Childbirth*, 581.

49 **lying-in hospitals**: For a more detailed history, from which I draw, see Lisa Forman Cody, "Living and Dying in Georgian London's Lying-In Hospitals," *Bulletin of the History of Medicine* 78, no. 2 (2004): 309–48; and Richard W. Wertz and Dorothy C. Wertz, *Lying-In: A History of Childbirth in America*, expanded ed. (New Haven, CT: Yale University Press, 1989).

50 **"a despised subject"**: For more on the deplorable early history of obstetric education, on which this paragraph draws, see Loudon, *Death in Childbirth*, 173.

50 **witness any at all**: Wertz and Wertz, *Lying-In*, 85.

50 **James Platt White**: Oliver P. Jones, Ph.D., M.D., "Our First Professor of Obstetrics, James Platt White (1811–1881)," *The Buffalo Physician* (Spring 1974): 42–47; Mary Roach, *Bonk: The Curious Coupling of Science and Sex* (New York: Norton, 2008), 13–14.

50  **required incoming students**: Gary Taubes, *The Case Against Sugar* (New York: Knopf, 2017), 88.

50  **"a system"**: Loudon, *Death in Childbirth*, 297, 295.

51  **Alexander Gordon**: For more, see Sherwin B. Nuland, *The Doctor's Plague* (New York: Norton, 2003), 44–48, from which my account is sourced.

51  **"so excruciating"**: Alexander Gordon, *A Treatise on the Epidemic of Puerperal Fever of Aberdeen* (London: C. C. and J. Robinson, 1795), 6.

51  **believed to be caused by**: Loudon, *Death in Childbirth*, 58.

51  **Their shame and anxiety**: Wertz and Wertz, *Lying-In*, 125.

51  **1843 paper**: Oliver Wendell Holmes, "The Contagiousness of Puerperal Fever," *New England Quarterly Journal of Medical Surgery* 1 (1843): 503–30.

52  **"has a head"**: Charles Meigs, *Females and Their Diseases: A Series of Letters to His Class* (Philadelphia: Lea and Blanchard, 1848), 47.

52  **"Divinity has ordained"**: Charles Meigs, *Obstetrics: The Science and the Art* (Philadelphia: Blanchard and Lea, 1852), 368.

52  **"What sufficient motive"**: Charles Meigs, "Dr. Meigs' Reply to Professor Simpson's Letter," *Buffalo Medical Journal and Monthly Review of Medical and Surgical Science* 3 (1848): 677.

52  **"a gentleman's hands are clean"**: Charles Meigs, *On the Nature, Signs, and Treatment of Childbed Fevers* (Philadelphia: Blanchard and Lea, 1854), 104.

52  **"What is the use"**: Quoted in Loudon, *Death in Childbirth*, 289.

53  **autopsies were required**: Cassidy, *Birth*, 57.

53  **"The same evening"**: William Campbell, "On Puerperal Fever," *Medical Gazette* 9 (1831), 354.

53  **Ignaz Semmelweis**: For more, see Nuland, *The Doctors' Plague*, to which my account is indebted.

53  **most didn't**: Loudon, *Death in Childbirth*, 82.

53  **Instead of washing**: Wertz and Wertz, *Lying-In*, 127.

54  **a 1917 study**: Described in Loudon, *Death in Childbirth*, 37, 279–80.

54  **Virginia Apgar**: For more on Apgar's legacy, see Melinda Beck, "How's Your Baby? Recalling the Apgar Score's Namesake," *Wall Street Journal*, May 26, 2009; and Atul Gawande, "The Score," *New Yorker*, October 9, 2006, both of which inform my account.

54  **"Please Bus Your Trays"**: Beck, "How's Your Baby?"

56  **barber-surgeons**: Cassidy, *Birth*, 131.

56  **Wertt**: Ibid., 200.

57  **Ambroise Paré**: Ibid., 132–33.

58  **Marie Antoinette's first child**: Antonia Fraser, *Marie Antoinette: The Journey* (New York: Anchor Books, 2002), 166–68.

58  **Chamberlens**: For more on the Chamberlens and their forceps, see Cassidy, *Birth*, 165–67; Epstein, *Get Me Out*, 23–29; and Gawande, "The Score," all of which inform my account here.

59   **1.5 percent of mothers**: Jean Towler and Joan Bramall, *Midwives in History and Society* (London: Croom Hall, 1986).

59   **fees were astronomical**: Cassidy, *Birth*, 166.

59   **William Smellie**: For more on Smellie, see Wertz and Wertz, *Lying-In*, 39–43; and Robert Woods and Chris Galley, *Mrs Stone & Dr Smellie: Eighteenth-Century Midwives and Their Patients* (Liverpool: Liverpool University Press, 2015), to which my account is indebted.

60   **"the delicate fist"**: Elizabeth Nihell, *A Treatise on the Art of Midwifery* (London, 1760), 325.

60   **"raw-bon'd"**: Quoted in Woods and Galley, *Mrs Stone & Dr Smellie*, 189.

61   **three guineas**: Geoffrey Chamberlain, *From Witchcraft to Wisdom: A History of Obstetrics and Gynaecology in the British Isles* (London: RCOG Press, 2007), 75.

61   **"more men-Midwives"**: Woods and Galley, *Mrs Stone & Dr Smellie*, 189.

61   **the student could perform**: Chamberlain, *From Witchcraft to Wisdom*, 75.

61   **in one instance, in 1748**: Woods and Galley, *Mrs Stone & Dr Smellie*, 210–11.

61   **2010 journal article**: Don Shelton, "The Emperor's New Clothes," *Journal of the Royal Society of Medicine* 103, no. 2 (February 1, 2010): 46–50.

62   **"You wouldn't want to watch"**: Judith Walzer Leavitt, *Make Room for Daddy: The Journey from Waiting Room to Birthing Room* (Chapel Hill: University of North Carolina Press, 2009), 225.

62   *Come Gently, Sweet Lucina*: I'm extremely grateful to Randi Hutter Epstein's *Get Me Out* for introducing me to this amazing work, 174–77. For a longer account of Carter's legacy, see Rixa Ann Spencer Freeze, *Born Free: Unassisted Childbirth in North America*, Ph.D. diss., University of Iowa, 2008. Abstract at http://ir.uiowa.edu/etd/202/.

63   **In a mix-up**: Patricia Carter, *Come Gently, Sweet Lucina* (Titusville, FL: Patricia Cloyd Carter, 1957), 302.

66   **Ancient Israelite women**: Joe Zias, "Cannabis Sativa (Hashish) as an Effective Medication in Antiquity" in Stuart Campbell and Anthony Green, eds., *The Archaeology of Death in the Ancient Near East* (Oxford: Oxbow Books, 1995), 232–34.

66   **Ancient Greek women**: Nancy Demand, *Birth, Death, and Motherhood in Classical Greece* (Baltimore: Johns Hopkins University Press, 1994), 20; and Helen King, *Hippocrates' Woman: Reading the Female Body in Ancient Greece* (New York: Routledge, 2002), 126.

67   **hen parties**: For more on birthing parties, see A. Lynn Martin, *Alcohol, Sex, and Gender in Late Medieval and Early Modern Europe* (New York: Palgrave Macmillan, 2001), 25–27, to which my account is indebted.

67   **Eufame MacLayne**: For more, see Cassidy, *Birth*, 84–85; and Donald T. Atkinson, *Magic, Myth and Medicine* (New York: World Publishing Company, 1956).

68   **Dr. Viethes**: Atkinson, *Magic, Myth and Medicine*, 271–72.

68 **"A more easy labor I never witnessed . . . !"**: Cassidy, *Birth*, 78.

68 **"like aqua vitae with a midwife"**: Martin, *Alcohol, Sex, and Gender in Late Medieval and Early Modern Europe*, 27.

68 **practical reasons**: Donald Caton, *What a Blessing She Had Chloroform: The Medical and Social Response to the Pain of Childbirth from 1800 to the Present* (New Haven, CT: Yale University Press, 1999), 75. See same for more on the history of pain relief in childbirth in general, which informs my account here.

69 **named the baby Anaesthesia**: Jessica Mitford, *The American Way of Birth* (New York: Dutton, 1992), 41.

69 **fears that chloroformed mothers**: Caton, *What a Blessing She Had Chloroform*; G. T. Gream, *The Misapplication of Anaesthesia in Childbirth, Exemplified by Facts* (London: John Churchill, 1848).

70 **Queen Victoria**: David H. Chestnut et al., *Chestnut's Obstetric Anesthesia: Principles and Practice* (Philadelphia: Elsevier Saunders, 2014), 4–5.

70 **123 deaths**: Mitford, *The American Way of Birth*, 45.

70 **sleepy babies**: Caton, *What a Blessing She Had Chloroform*, 72–73.

70 **twilight sleep**: See Cassidy, *Birth*, 91–94, for a full discussion of the twilight sleep phenomenon, to which my account is indebted.

71 **Karl August Bier**: Cassidy, *Birth*, 99–100.

72 **"we proceeded"**: For an English translation of Bier's report, see Hinnerk F. W. Wulf, M.D., "The Centennial of Spinal Anesthesia," *Anesthesiology* 89, no. 8 (1998): 500–506.

72 **John Bonica**: "John J. Bonica, Pioneer in Anesthesia, Dies at 77," *New York Times*, August 20, 1994.

72 **Grantly Dick-Read**: For more on Dick-Read, see Cassidy, *Birth*, 95; and Amy Tuteur, *Push Back: Guilt in the Age of Natural Parenting* (New York: Dey Street Books, 2016).

73 **1950 *JAMA* article**: Duncan E. Reid and Mandel E. Cohen, "Evaluation of Present Day Trends in Obstetrics," *JAMA* 142, no. 9 (1950): 615–23.

73 **Fernand Lamaze**: For more on Lamaze, see Cassidy, *Birth*, 148–55, to which my account is indebted.

74 **"a case of syphilis"**: Caroline Gutmann, *The Legacy of Dr. Lamaze*, trans. Bruce Benderson (New York: St. Martin's Press, 2001), 133–34, 188; my account of Lamaze is partially sourced from this text.

75 **Many involved food**: Cassidy, *Birth*, 175.

75 **labor induction methods**: Ibid., 175–76.

75 **one of the stranger instances**: Kenneth Jon Rose, *The Body in Time* (New York: Wiley, 1988), 102.

76 **because the baby was already dead**: Cassidy, *Birth*, 174.

76 **Emanuel Friedman**: See Cassidy, *Birth*, 155–58.

76 **initial study**: Emanuel A. Friedman, "Graphic Analysis of Labor," *American Journal of Obstetrics and Gynecology* 68, no. 6 (December 1954): 1568–75; and Emanuel Friedman, "Primagravid Labor: A Graphicostatistical Analysis,"

*Obstetrics and Gynecology* 6, no. 6 (December 1955): 567–83. The first paper reported on one hundred women; the second expanded to five hundred.

76  **All were white Jews**: Elaine K. Diegmann, Clare M. Andrews, and Carol A. Niemczura, "The Length of the Second Stage of Labor in Uncomplicated, Nulliparous African American and Puerto Rican Women," *Journal of Midwifery and Women's Health* 45, no. 1 (January–February 2000): 67–71.

77  **recent studies**: Diegmann et al., "The Length of the Second Stage of Labor in Uncomplicated, Nulliparous African American and Puerto Rican Women."

77  **the first successful C-section**: Cassidy, *Birth,* 112–14.

77  **In the British empire**: Ibid.

78  **halo effect**: Niven and Murphy-Black, "Memory for Labor Pain: A Review of the Literature."


### 3. You're Doing It Wrong: *Advice Manuals Through the Ages*

81  For more on advice manuals, see Ann Hulbert's astoundingly thorough and entertaining *Raising America* (New York: Knopf, 2003); Julia Grant's *Raising Baby by the Book* (New Haven, CT: Yale University Press, 1998); Christina Hardyment's *Dream Babies* (New York: Harper and Row, 1983); and Daniel Beekman's *The Mechanical Baby* (Westport, CT: Lawrence Hill & Co., 1977), all of which inform this chapter.

83  **olive oil or honey**: *Soranus's Gynecology* (Baltimore: Johns Hopkins University Press, 1956), 83.

83  **though they do both**: Ibid., 116.

83  **"Among the Germans"**: Robert Montraville Green, *A Translation of Galen's Hygiene (De Sanitate Tuenda)* (Springfield, IL: Charles C. Thomas, 1951), 32 (6:51).

85  **Giovanni Dominici**: For more on Dominici, see Nirit Ben-Aryeh Debby, "Political Views in the Preaching of Giovanni Dominici in Renaissance Florence, 1400–1406," *Renaissance Quarterly* 55, no. 1 (Spring 2002): 19–48.

85  **"the son of a peasant"**: Giovanni Dominici, *Regola del governo di cura familiare*, part four (On the Education of Children), trans. Arthur Basic Coté (Washington, D.C.: The Catholic University of America, 1927), 67.

86  **"It will not be amiss"**: Ibid., 34.

86  **Dominici reminds his female reader**: Giovanni Dominici, *Regola del governo di cura familiare,* vol. I (Florence: Angiolo Garinei Libraio, 1860).

86  **"lest they may"**: Ibid., 41.

86  **"Many such have aroused"**: Ibid.

86  **Claude Quillet**: For more on Quillet and his work, see Beekman, *The Mechanical Baby*, 10–15, from which my account is sourced.

87  **"A female child"**: Claude Quillet, *Callipaedia* (Philadelphia: American Antiquarian Publishing Co., 1872), 48.

87  **"From a Left Womb"**: Ibid., 50.

87  **"What shall we here"**: Ibid.

87  **"like beast or male"**: Giovanni Dominici, *Regola del governo di cura familiare*, vol. I, 88.

87  **Following Galen**: Randi Hutter Epstein, M.D., *Get Me Out: A History of Childbirth from the Garden of Eden to the Sperm Bank* (New York: Norton, 2011), 11.

90  **did not record their birth dates**: William Kessen, "Rousseau's Children," *Daedalus* 107, no. 3 (Summer 1978): 155–66.

90  **potty training**: John Locke, *Some Thoughts Concerning Education* (London: A. and J. Churchill, 1693), 29.

90  **"drinking cold drink"**: Ibid., 9.

91  **exactly what some parents did**: My account of parents' fervor for Rousseau is indebted to Wendy Moore, *How to Create the Perfect Wife* (New York: Basic Books, 2013).

91  **"I cannot believe"**: Quoted in Moore, *How to Create the Perfect Wife*, 44.

91  **let them come inside**: Ibid., 39.

92  **"killed all the rest"**: Ibid., 120.

92  **"a little emaciated figure"**: Quoted in Hardyment, *Dream Babies*, 19.

93  **"in all cases of dwarfishness"**: William Buchan, *Advice to Mothers* (Philadelphia: John Bioren, 1804), 195.

93  **"No subsequent endeavours"**: Ibid., 2.

93  **"the father, from his education"**: William P. Dewees, *Treatise on the Physical and Medical Treatment of Children* (Philadelphia: H. C. Carey and I. Lea, 1826), xiii.

94  **"These gentlemen"**: An American Matron, *The Maternal Physician* (New York: Isaac Riley, 1811), 7.

94  **"Infants should be kissed"**: Luther Emmett Holt, *The Care and Feeding of Children*, 5th ed. (New York: D. Appleton and Co., 1910), 168.

94  **"never be played with"**: Ibid., 165.

95  **John Watson**: For more on Watson, see Hulbert, *Raising America*, 122–53; Beekman, *The Mechanical Baby*, 145–53; and Kerry Buckley, *Mechanical Man: John Broadus Watson and the Beginnings of Behaviorism* (New York: Guilford Press, 1989), all of which inform this account.

95  **"There is a sensible way"**: John B. Watson, *Psychological Care of Infant and Child* (New York: Norton, 1928), 87.

95  **"Give me a dozen"**: John B. Watson, *Behaviorism* (New York: Norton, 1924).

96  **"Would it not be possible"**: Quoted in Hulbert, *Raising America*, 153.

96  **As for Watson's other studies**: Ibid., 133.

97  **"Parents today"**: John B. Watson, "If You're a Failure—Change Your Personality," *NEA Magazine*, November 3–4, 1928.

97  **"Won't you then remember"**: Watson, *Psychological Care of Infant and Child*, 87.

97  **"sharpening her brains"**: Quoted in Buckley, *Mechanical Man*, 163.

97  **"would not hesitate"**: Ibid., 165.

97  **H. L. Mencken**: Hulbert, *Raising America*, 139–40.

97  **pay them any mind**: Buckley, *Mechanical Man*, 63.

98  *larynx*: Ibid., 118.

98  **Benjamin Spock himself**: Barbara Ehrenreich and Deirdre English, *For Her Own Good: Two Centuries of the Experts' Advice to Women* (New York: Anchor, 2005), 211.

98  **pretended to hit her**: Buckley, *Mechanical Man*, 180.

98  **"talk it out club"**: Hulbert, *Raising America*, 152.

98  **doing everything wrong**: Ibid., 199.

99  **Benjamin Spock**: For more on Spock, see Hulbert, *Raising America*, 225–55; and Thomas Maier, *Dr. Spock: An American Life* (Boston: Houghton Mifflin Harcourt, 1998), both of which inform this account.

99  **a long and thorough index**: Beekman, *The Mechanical Baby*, 196–97.

100  **"The women strain toward him"**: Martha Weinman, "Now 'Dr. Spock' Goes to the White House," *New York Times Magazine* 109 (December 4, 1960), 121.

100  **"he doesn't know what's good for him"**: Quoted in Hulbert, *Raising America*, 252.

100  **"filiarchy"**: Jennifer Senior, *All Joy and No Fun: The Paradox of Modern Parenthood* (New York: Ecco, 2014), 128.

100  **"The fact is"**: Quoted in Ibid., 32.

102  **"you are not attractive looking"**: Elizabeth Mehren, "The Personal Spock: The Controversial Doctor Recalls His Childhood, Which Was Influenced by a Domineering Mother," *Los Angeles Times*, November 3, 1989.

102  **found the book "sensible"**: Ibid.

102  **Spock's wife, Jane**: Hulbert, *Raising America*, 242.

102  **"got Spocked"**: Quoted in Maier, *Dr. Spock: An American Life*, 321.

102  **"If we teach"**: Walter Sackett, Jr., *Bringing Up Babies* (New York and Evanston, IL: Harper & Row, 1962), xviii.

103  **"Some of you may have heard"**: Fitzhugh Dodson, *How to Parent* (Los Angeles: Nash Publishing, 1970), 226.

103  **"The main purpose"**: Ibid., 227.

104  **a couple of hours**: Lynn Neary, "Love It or Hate It, the Pregnancy 'Bible' Has a Lot to Say," *All Things Considered*, July 6, 2011.

104  **93 percent**: Hulbert, *Raising America*, 361.

### 4. Nasty, Brutish, and Short: *The First Three Years*

107  For more on developmental stages, see Nicholas Day's fascinating *Baby Meets World* (New York: St. Martin's Griffin, 2014), to which this chapter is indebted.

108  **acquiring human form**: Karin Calvert, *Children in the House: The Material Culture of Early Childhood, 1600–1900* (Lebanon, NH: University Press of New England, 1992), 19–20.

109  **As for sitting, standing, and walking**: *Soranus's Gynecology* (Baltimore: Johns Hopkins University Press, 1956), 116.

109  **frequently neglected**: Calvert, *Children in the House*, 20–21.

110  WELCOME LITTLE STRANGER: Ibid., 98.

111  **Teething**: Colin Heywood, *A History of Childhood: Children and Childhood in the West from Medieval to Modern Times* (Cambridge: Polity, 2001), 90.

111  **John Arbuthnot**: William Buchan, *Domestic Medicine*, 10th ed. (London: A. Strahan, 1788), 618.

111  **Marion Thrasher**: Marion Thrasher, "Dentition and Some of Its Diseases," in Edward C. Kirk., ed., *The Dental Cosmos: A Monthly Record of Dental Science* 36 (Philadelphia: S. S. White Dental Manufacturing Co., 1894), 238.

111  **To ward off the danger**: Gabrielle Hatfield, *Encyclopedia of Folk Medicine: Old World and New World Traditions* (Santa Barbara, CA: ABC-Clio, 2004), 337–38.

113  **Steven Pinker**: Steven Pinker, *The Language Instinct* (New York: Harper Perennial, 2007), 28.

113  **Anthropologists have even hypothesized**: Dean Falk, "Prelinguistic Evolution in Early Hominins: Whence Motherese?" *Behavioral and Brain Sciences* 27, no. 4 (2004): 491–541.

114  **awful experiments**: J. P. Davidson, *Planet Word* (London: Michael Joseph, 2011).

115  **Beng**: Judy DeLoache and Alma Gottlieb, eds., *A World of Babies: Imagined Childcare Guides for Seven Societies* (Cambridge: Cambridge University Press, 2000), 2.

116  **All animals walk**: Martin Garwicz, Maria Christensson, and Elia Psouni, "A Unifying Model for Timing of Walking Onset in Humans and Other Mammals," *Proceedings of the National Academy of Science USA* 51 (December 22, 2009): 21889–93.

117  **We think of crawling**: For more on the history, science, and sociology of crawling, see Nicholas Day's *Baby Meets World*. For history, Karin Calvert's *Children in the House* is another great resource. Both inform my account here.

117  **"[T]he bottom layer"**: Desiderius Erasmus, Letter to John Francis (1524) in *The Correspondence of Erasmus*, Letters 1356 to 1534, trans. R. A. B. Mynors and Alexander Dalzell (Toronto: University of Toronto Press, 1992), 471.

119  **"the development of locomotion"**: Day, *Baby Meets World*, 268.

119  **"bear-walking"**: Nicholas Day, "Meet the Family That Never Learned to Walk on Two Legs," *Slate*, May 2, 2013.

120  **Doman and Delacato**: For more on Doman and Delacato, see Day, *Baby Meets World*, 246–47, which informs my account here.

120    **recapitulation theory**: For more, see Stephen Jay Gould, *Ontogeny and Phylogeny* (Cambridge, MA: Belknap Press, 1977), which informs my description here.

120    **"possibly the most absurd"**: Russell Miller, *The Bare-Faced Messiah: The True Story of L. Ron Hubbard* (London: Silvertail Books, 2015; original ed., 1987), 204.

120    **weirdly obsessed**: L. Ron Hubbard's borrowing of Haeckel's recapitulation theory was first noted by evolutionary biologist P. Z. Myers, who treats readers to a pretty wonderful—and hilarious—analysis of Hubbard's *A History of Man* with special attention to the clam issue on *The Underground Bunker* website: http://tonyortega.org/2013/08/09/pz-myers-helps-us-plunder-the-riches-of-l-ron-hubbards-book-of-scientology-evolution/.

120    **"These lower races"**: Ernst Haeckel, *The Wonders of Life: A Popular Study of Biological Philosophy*, trans. Joseph McCabe (London: Watts & Co., 1904), 406.

120    **Other Doman-Delacato interventions**: see D. N. Mackay, J. Gollogly, and G. McDonald, "The Doman-Delacato Treatment Methods, I: Principles of Neurological Organization," *British Journal of Mental Subnormality* 32, no. 62 (1983): 3–19; and Terence M. Hines, "The Doman-Delacato Patterning Treatment for Brain Damage," *Scientific Review of Alternative Medicine* 5, no. 2 (2001): 80–89.

121    **Arnold Gesell**: For more on Gesell, see Ann Hulbert, *Raising America* (New York: Knopf, 2003), 154–87, which informs my account here.

121    **As Nicholas Day has cleverly pointed out**: Day, *Baby Meets World*, 234–35.

121    **six different time zones**: Vanessa Ogle, *The Global Transformation of Time: 1870–1950* (Cambridge, MA: Harvard University Press, 2015), 25.

123    **"the Rodney Dangerfield of motor milestones"**: Karen E. Adolph, Sarah E. Berger, and Andrew J. Leo, "Developmental Continuity? Crawling, Cruising, and Walking," *Developmental Science* 14, no. 2 (March 2011), 306–18.

124    **African Infant Precocity Syndrome**: Karen E. Adolph, Lana B. Karasik, and Catherine S. Tamis-LeMonda, "Motor Skill," in Marc H. Bornstein, ed., *Handbook of Cultural Developmental Science* (New York: Psychology Press, 2010), 61–88; Lana B. Karasik, Karen E. Adolph, Catherine S. Tamis-LeMonda, and Marc H. Bornstein, "WEIRD Walking: Cross-Cultural Research on Motor Development," *Behavioral Brain Science* 33, no. 2–3 (June 2010): 95–96.

124    **"the age of concussion"**: Heywood, *A History of Childhood*, 97.

124    *puddinhead*: Calvert, *Children in the House*, 35.

126    **occasionally become synonymous**: Lloyd deMause, "The Evolution of Childhood," in Lloyd deMause, ed., *The History of Childhood* (Lanham, MD: Rowman & Littlefield, 1995), 39.

126    **"the receptacle of all"**: Turneau de la Morandière, quoted in Rose George, *The Big Necessity: The Unmentionable World of Human Waste and Why It Matters* (New York: Picador, 2014), 23. George's description of French and British sanitation history informs my account here.

127  **as critics have noted**: Philip Mitsis, "Locke's Offices," in Jon Miller and Brad Inwood, eds., *Hellenistic and Early Modern Philosophy* (Cambridge: Cambridge University Press, 2003), 45.

128  **"overwhelming brutality"**: Quoted in Peter Mandler, *Return from the Natives: How Margaret Mead Won the Second World War and Lost the Cold War* (New Haven, CT: Yale University Press, 2013), 134.

128  **"'Early and severe'"**: Ibid.

128  **bathroom habits**: For more on toilet training and national character, see Katie Engelhart, "The Powerful History of Potty Training," *Atlantic Monthly*, June 20, 2014; and Marvin Harris, *The Rise of Anthropological Theory* (Lanham, MD: AltaMira Press, 2001), 443–44.

128  **Hitler**: For more on Hitler's toilet training, see Walter Langer and David Webb, *A Psychological Analysis of Adolf Hitler* (CreateSpace Independent Publishing Platform, 2012), 168.

128  **botched toilet training**: Mortimer Ostrow, *Myth and Madness* (New Brunswick, NJ: Transaction Publishers, 1996).

128  **neo-Nazism**: Christian Pfeiffer, *Der Spiegel* no. 12 (March 22, 1999), 60–66.

129  **Beng babies receive their first enema**: DeLoache and Gottlieb, *A World of Babies*.

## 5. Tooth and Nail: *Feeding and Fighting*

131  For more on children and food, see Bee Wilson, *First Bite* (New York: Basic Books, 2015), to which this chapter is indebted.

132  **breast milk was menstrual blood**: Helen King, *Hippocrates' Woman: Reading the Female Body in Ancient Greece* (New York: Routledge, 1998), 143.

132  **"unnatural, imperfect"**: John C. Rolfe, trans., *Gellius: Attic Nights*, vol. 2, book XII, Loeb Classical Library no. 200 (Cambridge, MA: Harvard University Press, 1927), 355–59.

132  **premature aging**: *Soranus's Gynecology* (Baltimore: Johns Hopkins University Press, 1956), 90.

132  **mistook the antibody-rich colostrum**: Ibid., 89.

133  **alcohol passes through breast milk**: Ibid., 93.

133  **poured over bread**: Ibid., 117.

133  **baby bottle prototypes**: For more, see Ian G. Wickes, "A History of Infant Feeding," Parts I–IV, *Archives of Disease in Childhood* 28 (1953); and Samuel X. Radbill, M.D., "Infant Feeding Through the Ages," *Clinical Pediatrics* 20, no. 10 (October 1, 1981): 613–21, both of which inform my history of bottles and formulas here.

133  **serve animal milk straight**: For more on the history of animal wet nurses, see Deborah Valenze, *Milk: A Local and Global History* (New Haven, CT: Yale University Press, 2011), 158–59; and Nicholas Day, *Baby Meets World*

(New York: St. Martin's Griffin, 2014), 49–51, both of which inform my account here.

135 **The missing essentials**: Radbill, "Infant Feeding Through the Ages."

135 **cod liver oil**: Rima D. Apple, *Mothers and Medicine: A Social History of Infant Feeding 1890–1950* (Madison: University of Wisconsin Press, 1987), 39–41.

135 **twenty-seven infant formulas**: Felisa J. Bracken, "Infant Feeding in the American Colonies," *Journal of the American Dietetic Association* 29, no. 4 (1953): 349–58.

135 **corn syrup**: Apple, *Mothers and Medicine*, 44.

135 **only 25 percent did**: Charles Hirschman and Marilyn Butler, "Trends and Differentials in Breast Feeding: An Update," *Demography* 18, no. 1 (1981): 39–54.

135 **many would follow**: For a wonderful history of prepared baby foods, see Amy Bentley, *Inventing Baby Food: Taste, Health, and the Industrialization of the American Diet* (Berkeley: University of California Press, 2014).

137 **"serv'd out of every dish"**: John Locke, *Some Thoughts Concerning Education* (London: A. and J. Churchill, 1693), 39.

137 **"Children in general"**: William Buchan, *Advice to Mothers* (Philadelphia: John Bioren, 1804), 303.

137 **"leading error"**: Andrew Combe, *The Physiology of Digestion* (Edinburgh: MacLachlan & Stewart, 1836), 259.

137 **"Most diseases"**: S. O. Johnson, "The Health of Our Daughters," *The Mother's Magazine* 38 (1870), 99.

137 **Victorians typically ate**: Paul Clayton and Judith Rowbotham, "How the Mid-Victorians Worked, Ate and Died," *International Journal of Environmental Research and Public Health* 6, no. 3 (March 2009): 1235–53.

137 **Increasingly sedentary**: Abigail Carroll, *Three Squares: The Invention of the American Meal* (New York: Basic Books, 2013), 137–39.

137 **"The ill-shaped"**: Johnson, "The Health of Our Daughters."

137 **"The foundation of the habit"**: *Babyhood: A Monthly Magazine for Mothers*, vol. 6 (New York and London: Babyhood Publishing Co., 1890), 165.

138 **"Children will eat anything"**: Thomas Dutton, *The Rearing and Feeding of Children* (London: Henry Kimpton, 1895), 55.

138 **"Nothing can well be worse"**: Leroy Yale, "Vegetables as Food for Young Children," *Babyhood*, vol. 6, 359–61.

138 **"it ought never be forgotten"**: T. H. Gallaudet, "Domestic Education at the Table—Continued," *The Mother's Magazine* 7 (1839), 171.

138 **"As soon as he can sit at the table"**: Quoted in George R. Clay, "Children of the Young Republic," *American Heritage* 11, no. 3 (April 1960), 46.

138 **"do not die of clarified molasses"**: John Oldmixon, *Transatlantic Wanderings: or, a Last Look at the United States* (London: Routledge, 1855), 47.

139 **"A young lady"**: "The Little Glutton," in *The Girl's Birthday Book* (London: Houlston and Wright, 1860), 315.

139 **"Children, too, should early be accustomed"**: Gallaudet, "Domestic Education at the Table—Continued," 171.

140 **nursery foods**: For more on the abysmal history of nursery foods, see Bee Wilson, *First Bite*.

140 **1937 book**: Mary E. Sweeny and Doris Curts Blick, *How to Feed Young Children in the Home* (Detroit: The Merrill-Palmer School, 1937).

140 **"most omelets are objectionable"**: Luther Emmett Holt, *The Care and Feeding of Children*, 10th ed. (New York: D. Appleton and Co., 1921), 153.

140 **gave bananas the okay**: Ann Hulbert, *Raising America* (New York: Knopf, 2003), 125.

141 **"Fruit makes one of the most difficult chapters"**: Locke, *Some Thoughts Concerning Education*, 19–20.

141 **"I think children should be wholly kept from"**: Ibid., 20.

141 **began to fall out of favor**: Tom Standage, *A History of the World in 6 Glasses* (Toronto: Random House of Canada, 2006), 135–36.

142 **"regarded fruit in a child's stomach"**: J. Wellington Byers, M.D., "Fruit for Children," *Babyhood*, vol. 6, 231.

142 **"fruits are always 'golden'"**: Ibid., 234.

142 **"death by fruit"**: Siân Pooley cited in Wilson, *First Bite*, 76.

142 **lengthy 1890 article**: Leroy Yale, "Vegetables as Food for Young Children," *Babyhood*, vol. 6, 359–61.

143 **"Vegetables were eaten mostly"**: Bill Bryson, *Shakespeare: The World as Stage* (New York: Harper Perennial, 2008), 55.

143 **"Father encloses pills"**: Quoted in Hulbert, *Raising America*, 77.

143 **"The children were constantly cross"**: William Sadler and Lena Sadler, *The Mother and Her Child* (Chicago: A. C. McClurg & Co., 1916), 177.

144 **"Probably no department of medicine"**: Joseph Brennemann, "*Vis Medicatrix Naturae* in Pediatrics," *American Journal of Diseases of Children* 40, no. 1 (July 1930): 6.

144 **"Now anorexia is not"**: Ibid.

145 **urged parents to stop feeding picky eaters**: Alan Brown, *The Normal Child: Its Care and Feeding* (Toronto: McClelland and Stewart, 1926), ix.

145 **Clara Davis**: For more on Clara Davis's study and its impact, see Wilson, *First Bite*, 5–10; and Stephen Strauss, "Clara M. Davis and the Wisdom of Letting Children Choose Their Own Diets," *Canadian Medical Association Journal* 175, no. 10 (2006): 1199–201, both of which inform my account here.

145 **regularly offered selections**: Clara M. Davis, "Self-Selection of Diet by Newly Weaned Infants," *American Journal of Diseases of Children* 36 (October 1928): 651–79; Clara M. Davis, "Results of the Self-Selection of Diets by Young Children," *Canadian Medical Association Journal* 41 (September 1939): 257–61.

145 **"they tried not only"**: Davis, "Results of the Self-Selection of Diets by Young Children," 260.

146  **the study was never done**: Wilson, *First Bite*, 9.

146  **Spock discusses Davis's study**: Benjamin Spock, *The Pocket Book of Baby and Child Care* (New York: Pocket Books, 1946), 207–8, 222, 234.

147  **Trix**: Andrew F. Smith, *Food and Drink in American History*, vol. 1 (Santa Barbara, CA: ABC-Clio, 2013), 163.

147  **went to soldiers**: For more on military sugar consumption, see Gary Taubes, *The Case Against Sugar* (New York: Knopf, 2017), 75–76.

148  **Two-thirds of doctors**: Bentley, *Inventing Baby Food*, 59, 61.

148  **intercourse after birth**: Walter Sackett, Jr., *Bringing Up Babies* (New York and Evanston, IL: Harper & Row, 1962), 43.

148  **Sackett recommends starting infants**: Ibid., 35.

149  **"just like dad"**: Ibid., 64.

149  **"like ducks to water"**: Ibid., 65.

149  **substitute decaf**: Ibid., 52.

149  **"Don't scream"**: Ibid., 51.

149  **"Increasingly, we are substituting"**: Ibid., xviii.

150  **fourteen to twenty-two pounds**: Ibid., 12.

150  **alcohol isn't bad for the baby**: Ibid., 13.

151  **kids were actually eating *more***: Sibylle Kranz, Anna Maria Siega-Riz, and Amy Herring, "Changes in Diet Quality of American Preschoolers Between 1977 and 1998," *American Journal of Public Health* 94, no. 9 (September 2004): 1525–30; and Cecilia Wilkinson Enns, Sharon J. Mickle, and Joseph D. Goldman, "Trends in Food and Nutrient Intakes by Adolescents in the United States," *Family Economics and Nutrition Review* 15, no. 2 (2003): 15–27.

151  **eating every three**: Wilson, *First Bite*, 175.

152  **likely to try new foods**: Wilson, *First Bite,* 24–26; Patricia Pliner and Sarah-Jeanne Salvy, "Food Neophobia in Humans," in Richard Shepherd and Monique Raats, eds., *The Psychology of Food Choice* (Wallingford, UK: CAB International, 2006), 84.

152  **The correlation**: Paul Rozin, "Family Resemblance in Food and Other Domains: The Family Paradox and the Role of Parental Congruence." *Appetite* 16, no. 2 (April 1991): 93–102.

153  **it's not desire**: Wilson, *First Bite*, 13.

153  **contagion of disgust**: Ibid., 14.

## 6. All the World's a Stage: *Acting Your Age*

161  *quickening*: For more on the history of quickening, see Ruth Graham, "He Took It into His Head to Frisk a Little," *Slate*, May 29, 2015.

162  **"a hogshead of wine"**: Quoted in Elizabeth Norton, *Jane Seymour: King Henry VIII's True Love* (Stroud, Gloucestershire: Amberley, 2009), 138.

162  **Queen Mary I**: See Anna Whitelock, *Mary Tudor: England's First Queen* (London: Bloomsbury, 2009).

162  **recapitulation**: For more on Ernst Haeckel and his theory, see Stephen Jay Gould, *Ontogeny and Phylogeny* (Cambridge, MA: Belknap Press, 1977).

163  **unpleasant little creatures**: Karin Calvert, *Children in the House: The Material Culture of Early Childhood, 1600–1900* (Lebanon, NH: University Press of New England, 1992), 72–73.

163  **"I cannot abide"**: Quoted in Philippe Ariès, *Centuries of Childhood*, trans. Robert Baldick (New York: Knopf, 1962), 130.

164  **Arnold Gesell**: For more on Gesell's contributions, see Nicholas Day, *Baby Meets World* (New York: St. Martin's Griffin, 2014), 229–48; and Ann Hulbert, *Raising America* (New York: Vintage, 2004), 154–87, both of which inform my account here.

165  **Most were children of faculty**: Alice Boardman Smuts, *Science in the Service of Children, 1893–1935* (New Haven, CT: Yale University Press, 2008), 181; Evelyn Goodenough Pitcher and Louse Bates Ames, *The Guidance Nursery School: A Gesell Institute Book for Teachers and Parents*, rev. ed. (New York: Harper & Row, 1975).

167  **still shorter than the five-year-olds'**: Michael Potegal and Richard J. Davidson, "Temper Tantrums in Young Children: 1. Behavioral Composition," *Journal of Developmental & Behavioral Pediatrics* 24, no. 3 (2003): 140–47.

167  **Another study**: Jay Belsky, Sharon Woodworth, and Keith Crnic, "Troubled Family Interaction During Toddlerhood," *Development and Psychopathology* 8, no. 3 (Summer 1996): 477–95.

167  **"lull before the storm of puberty"**: Erik Erikson, *Identity and the Life Cycle* (New York: Norton, 1980), 93.

168  **Krypteia**: John Van Antwerp Fine, *The Ancient Greeks: A Critical History* (Cambridge, MA: Belknap Press, 1983), 164.

168  **wysoccan**: "Huskanawing Ceremony of the Virginia Indians," in *Annual Report to the Board of Regents of the Smithsonian Institution*, 1920 (Washington, D.C.: Government Printing Office, 1922), 558–59.

168  **Australian aboriginal tribes**: Robert Tonkinson, *The Mardu Aborigines: Living the Dream in Australia's Desert*, 2nd ed. (New York: Holt, Rinehart and Winston, 1991), 87–95.

169  **Sateré-Mawé**: Victoria Williams, *Celebrating Life Customs Around the World*, vol. 1 (Santa Barbara, CA: ABC-CLIO, 2017), 41–43.

169  **G. Stanley Hall**: For a fun overview of Hall and his work, see Jill Lepore, *The Mansion of Happiness: A History of Life and Death* (New York: Vintage, 2013), 137–51. I'm also indebted to Ann Hulbert's account in *Raising America* (41–62).

169  **"chock full of errors"**: Quoted in Dorothy Ross, *G. Stanley Hall: The Psychologist as Prophet* (Chicago: University of Chicago Press, 1972), 385.

171  **Several things, actually**: For more on the evolution of the teenager, see Thomas Hine, *The Rise and Fall of the American Teenager* (New York: Harper Perennial, 2000), and Jon Savage, *Teenage: The Prehistory of Youth Culture:*

*1875–1945* (New York: Viking, 2007), both of which inform my account here.

171 **"There were many of them"**: Jonathan Edwards, *The Works of Jonathan Edwards*, vols. I–II, Anthony Uyl, ed. (Woodstock, Ontario: Devoted Publishing, 2017), 409.

171 **half the American population**: Thomas Hine, "The Rise and Decline of the Teenager," *American Heritage* 50, no. 5 (September 1999), 71–80.

171 **three inches taller**: "American Men of 1776 Said to Have Stood Tall," *New York Times*, April 15, 1982.

172 **"Great Butter Rebellion"**: "Riot and Rebellion," *Harvard Crimson*, May 3, 1963.

172 **"We Americans"**: Quoted in Savage, *Teenage*, 70.

172 **Haeckel's racist and sexist recapitulation theory**: For more on Haeckel's racist formulations, see Stephen Jay Gould's *Ontogeny and Phylogeny*, especially 132, and *The Mismeasure of Man* (New York: Norton, 1996), 144–47.

172 **"Most savages"**: G. Stanley Hall, *Adolescence*, vol. II (New York: D. Appleton, 1904), 649.

172 **"We should strive sedulously"**: Ibid., 573.

173 **"typical negroes"**: G. Stanley Hall, "The Negro in Africa and America," *Pedagogical Seminary* 12, no. 3 (1905): 361.

173 **"pygmoid"**: G. Stanley Hall, *Youth: Its Education, Regimen, and Hygiene* (New York: D. Appleton and Co., 1908), 1.

173 **"again, not a crackpot"**: Gould, *The Mismeasure of Man*, 147.

173 **Chinese teens**: Eva Pomerantz interviewed in Christine Gross-Loh, *Parenting Without Borders* (New York: Avery, 2014), 186–87.

173 **that explicit goal in mind**: Hine, *Rise and Fall of the American Teenager*, 54.

174 **the most troubled parent-teen relationships**: Judith G. Smetana, Nicole Campione-Barr, and Aaron Metzger, "Adolescent Developments in Interpersonal and Societal Contexts," *Annual Review of Psychology* 57 (2006): 255–84.

174 **75 percent of teens**: Laurence Steinberg, "We Know Some Things: Parent-Adolescent Relationships in Retrospect and Prospect," *Journal of Research on Adolescence* 11, no. 1 (2001): 1–19. See also Po Bronson and Ashley Merryman, *NurtureShock: New Thinking About Children* (New York: Twelve Books, 2009), for its helpful chapter on "The Science of Teen Rebellion."

175 **Parents report**: Christy Miller Buchanan, Jacquelynne S. Eccles, Constance Flanagan, Carol Midgley, Harriet Feldlaufer, and Rena D. Harold, "Parents' and Teachers' Beliefs about Adolescence: Effects of Sex and Experience," *Journal of Youth and Adolescence* 19, no. 4 (1990): 363–94.

175 **Teenagers who experience moderate conflict**: Smetana, Campione-Barr, and Metzger, "Adolescent Developments in Interpersonal and Societal Contexts," 259–60.

175   **"the segregation of young people"**: Hine, *Rise and Fall of the American Teenager*, 45.

## 7. I Know You Are but What Am I?: *Sibling Conflict*

179   For more on sibling relationships and conflict, see Po Bronson and Ashley Merriman, *NurtureShock* (New York: Twelve Books, 2009), 115–30; George Howe Colt, *Brothers: On His Brothers and Brothers in History* (New York: Scribner, 2012); and Jeffrey Kluger, *The Sibling Effect: What the Bonds Among Brothers and Sisters Reveal About Us* (New York: Riverhead, 2011), all of which inform my account here.

180   **3.5 times per hour**: Laurie Kramer, Lisa A. Perozynski, and Tsai-Yen Chung, "Parental Responses to Sibling Conflict: The Effects of Development and Parent Gender," Child Development 70, no. 6 (November–December 1999): 1401–14.

180   **Younger children fight even more**: Hildy S. Ross, Rebecca E. Filyer, Susan P. Lollis, Michal Perlman, and Jacqueline L. Martin, "Administering Justice in the Family," *Journal of Family Psychology* 8, no. 3 (1994): 254–73.

180   **By six months**: Sybil Hart and Heather Carrington, "Jealousy in Six-Month-Old Infants," *Infancy* 3, no. 3 (2012), 395–402.

180   **By sixteen months**: Judy Dunn, *Sisters and Brothers* (Cambridge, MA: Harvard University Press, 1985), 24.

180   **you're born with genetic material**: Amy M. Boddy, Angela Fortunato, Melissa Wilson Sayres, and Athena Aktipis, "Fetal Microchimerism and Maternal Health: A Review and Evolutionary Analysis of Cooperation and Conflict Beyond the Womb," *BioEssays* 37 (2015): 1106–18

181   **lifelong sibling relationships**: Catherine Salmon and Todd K. Shackelford, eds., *Oxford Handbook of Evolutionary Family Psychology* (New York: Oxford University Press, 2011), 16.

181   **"could not yet speak"**: Saint Augustine, *Confessions*, trans. Henry Chadwick (New York: Oxford University Press, 1991), 10.

181   **"Even at the tenderest age"**: Sir George Baker, *De affectibus animi et morbis inde oriundis* (Cantabrigiae: J. Bentham, 1755), quoted and translated in Richard Hunter and Ida Macalpine, *Three Hundred Years of Psychiatry, 1535–1860* (New York: Oxford University Press, 1963), 401.

181   ***kwashiorkor***: David F. Lancy, *The Anthropology of Childhood: Cherubs, Chattel, Changelings* (Cambridge: Cambridge University Press, 2008), 54.

181   **one of the few observed accounts**: Douglas Mock, *More Than Kin and Less Than Kind* (Cambridge, MA: Belknap Press, 2006), 51.

181   **Sand tiger sharks**: Ibid., 25.

182   **even plants**: Douglas W. Mock and Geoffrey A. Parker, *The Evolution of Sibling Rivalry* (New York: Oxford University Press, 1997), 373–410.

182 **Even *bacteria***: Jean-Pierre Claverys and Leiv S. Håvarstein, "Cannibalism and Fratricide: Mechanisms and Raisons d'Être," *Nature Reviews Microbiology* 5, no. 3 (March 2007): 219–29.

182 ***Practical Education***: Maria Edgeworth and Richard Lovell Edgeworth, *Practical Education* (London: J. Johnson, 1798), 275.

183 **Eighty percent of sibling fights**: Bronson and Merryman, *NurtureShock,* 127.

185 **Ottoman Empire**: For more on Ottoman fratricide, see Caroline Finkel, *Osman's Dream: The History of the Ottoman Empire* (New York: Basic Books, 2006), 71.

185 **"strive for mastery"**: John Locke, *Some Thoughts Concerning Education* (London: A. and J. Churchill, 1693), 120.

185 **"The complaints of children"**: Ibid., 121.

185 **"This I imagine"**: Ibid., 122.

186 **"Make this a contest"**: Ibid., 123.

187 **a "scheme"**: Quoted in Sarah Blaffer Hrdy and Debra Judge, "Darwin and the Puzzle of Primogeniture: An Essay on Biases in Parental Investment after Death," *Human Nature* 4, no. 1 (March 1993): 2.

187 **evolutionary reasons for favoring the first**: Ibid., 3.

187 **birth order**: For more on this controversial subject, see Judith Rich Harris, *The Nurture Assumption* (New York: Free Press, 2009); Frank Sulloway, *Born to Rebel: Birth Order, Family Dynamics, and Creative Lives* (New York: Pantheon, 1996); Dalton Conley, *The Pecking Order: Which Siblings Succeed and Why* (New York: Pantheon, 2004); and Colt, *Brothers*, all of which inform my account here.

187 **Francis Galton**: For more on Galton, see Martin Brookes, *Extreme Measures: The Dark Visions and Bright Ideas of Francis Galton* (New York: Bloomsbury, 2004), to which my account is indebted.

188 **"half-witted men"**: Francis Galton, *Hereditary Genius* (London: Macmillan, 1869), 339.

188 **"specialized for a parasitic existence"**: Quoted in William H. Tucker, *The Science and Politics of Racial Research* (Champaign: University of Illinois Press, 1996), 125.

188 **The Greeks**: Galton, *Hereditary Genius*, 343.

189 **"extremely mixed origin"**: Francis Galton, *English Men of Science: Their Nature and Nurture* (New York: D. Appleton, 1875), 12.

190 **scrambling a telephone number**: Cited in Colt, *Brothers*, 31.

190 **siblings share few characteristics**: Judy Dunn and Robert Plomin, *Separate Lives: Why Siblings Are So Different* (New York: Basic Books, 1990), 20.

190 **siblings grow less alike**: Colt, *Brothers*, 30–31.

190 **Although they come from a single genome**: Rui Li et al., "Somatic Point Mutations Occurring Early in Development: A Monozygotic Twin Study," *Journal of Medical Genetics* 51, no. 1 (January 2014): 28–34.

191 **They don't even agree**: Conley, *The Pecking Order*, 10.

191 **studies indicate that about two-thirds of parents do**: Studies cited in Colt, *Brothers*, 42.

191 **Similar results are borne out**: J. Jill Suitor, Jori Secrist, Michael Steinhour, and Karl Pillemer, "'I'm Sure She Chose Me!' Consistency in Intergenerational Reports of Mothers' Favoritism in Later Life Families," *Family Relations* 55, no. 5 (December 2006): 526–38.

193 **"Diverse children"**: Luther Caldwell, ed., *An Account of Anne Bradstreet* (Boston: Damrell & Upham, 1898), 59.

193 **"parents must"**: William Vaughan, *The Golden-grove, Moralized in Three Books* (London: E. Stafford, 1600), book 2, chapter 11.

193 **"The parties to whom"**: William Gouge, *Of Domesticall Duties* (London: John Haviland for William Bladen, 1622), 575.

194 **"It is no partialitie"**: Ibid., 576.

194 **Evolutionary biologists have argued**: Scott Forbes, *A Natural History of Families* (Princeton, NJ: Princeton University Press, 2007), 4.

195 **buy two of everything**: John B. Watson, *Psychological Care of Infant and Child* (New York: Norton, 1928), 88–90.

195 **"being an only child is a disease in itself"**: Quoted in Lauren Sandler, *One and Only: The Freedom of Having an Only Child, and the Joy of Being One* (New York: Simon & Schuster, 2014), 3.

195 **only children are somewhat *better* adjusted**: Sandler, *One and Only*, 59–63.

195 **"dethronement"**: *The Collected Clinical Works of Alfred Adler*, vol. 1 (New York: Alfred Adler Institute, 2005), 112–13, 224.

195 **cocaine**: Ibid., 113.

196 **The patients promptly destroyed**: Colt, *Brothers*, 109.

196 **"Treat her casually"**: Benjamin Spock, *The Pocket Book of Baby and Child Care* (New York: Pocket Books, 1946), 261.

197 **alienate readers**: Thomas Maier, *Dr. Spock: An American Life* (Boston: Houghton Mifflin Harcourt, 1998), 210.

197 **"Jealous quarreling"**: Benjamin Spock, *Dr. Spock's Baby and Child Care* (New York: Dutton, 1985), 14.

197 **garlic**: Jean Strouse, "The World According to Garlic," *New York Times*, December 9, 1979.

197 **Fitzhugh Dodson**: Fitzhugh Dodson, *How to Parent* (Los Angeles: Nash Publishing, 1970), 129–32.

198 **more savage and last longer**: Hildy S. Ross, Rebecca E. Filyer, Susan P. Lollis, Michal Perlman, and Jacqueline L. Martin, "Administering Justice in the Family," *Journal of Family Psychology* 8, no. 3 (September 1994): 254–73.

198 **Laurie Kramer**: For more on Laurie Kramer's work and effective interventions for sibling fighting, see the excellent chapter on the subject in Po Bronson and Merriman, *NurtureShock*, 115–30.

199 *sibling deidentification*: Frances Schacter, Ellen Shore, Susan Feldman-Rotman, Ruth E. Marquis, and Susan Campbell, "Sibling Deidentification," *Developmental Psychology* 12, no. 5 (1976): 418–27.

## 8. Kids Today: On Discipline

202 **Eton students were whipped**: Bill Bryson, *Shakespeare: The World as Stage* (New York: Harper Perennial, 2008), 56.

204 **"Children began to be the tyrants"**: Kenneth J. Freeman, *Schools of Hellas: An Essay on the Practice and Theory of Ancient Greek Education from 600 to 300 B.C.* (London: Macmillan and Co., 1907), 74.

204 **"Our sires' age"**: E. C. Wickham, trans., *Odes*, Book III.vi, in *Horace for English Readers* (Oxford, UK: Clarendon Press, 1903), 89.

204 **Paleolithic parents didn't spank**: Darcia Narvaez, quoted in "Why Cavemen Were Better Parents Than We Are Today," *Daily Mail*, September 23, 2010.

205 *diamastigosis*: Paul Cartledge, *Spartan Reflections* (Berkeley: University of California Press, 2003), 172.

206 **"But though I beat you"**: Quoted in Miriam Lichtheim, *Ancient Egyptian Literature,* vol. II (Berkeley: University of California Press, 2006), 169.

206 **Medieval sadists**: Lloyd deMause, "The Evolution of Childhood," in Lloyd deMause, ed., *The History of Childhood* (Lanham, MD: Rowman & Littlefield, 1995), 41.

207 **whipping boy**: Jasper Ridley, *A Brief History of the Tudor Age* (London: Constable and Co., 1998).

207 **One German schoolmaster**: Reserved Smith, *A History of Modern Culture*, vol. 2 (London: Routledge, 1934), 423.

207 **Beethoven**: Editha Sterber and Richard F. Sterber, *Beethoven and His Nephew: A Psychoanalytic Study of Their Relationship* (New York: Pantheon, 1954), 89.

207 **"they not die thereof"**: Bartholomew Batty, *The Christian Man's Closet*, trans. William Lowth (London: Thomas Dawson, 1581), 14–26.

207 **"Better whip't than damned"**: Quoted in Elizabeth Pleck, *Domestic Tyranny: The Making of American Social Policy Against Family Violence from Colonial Times to the Present* (Urbana and Chicago: University of Illinois Press, 2004), 45.

208 **"In front of grandees"**: I am grateful for the English translations offered by Humphrey Clarke at *Quodlibeta*, http://bedejournal.blogspot.com/2009/04/urbanus-magnus-civilised-man.html.

209 **"praise in public, blame in private"**: John Locke, *Some Thoughts Concerning Education* (London: C. J. Clay and Sons, 1892), 37.

209 **psychological torments rather than physical ones**: DeMause, "The Evolution of Childhood," 45.

209 **Lilith, Lamia, Empusa, Sybaris**: Ibid., 11.

210  **"virtual epidemic of trials"**: Jack Zipes, *The Trials and Tribulations of Little Red Riding Hood* (New York: Routledge, 1993), 19–23.

210  **Freud's fascination**: Marina Warner, *No Go the Bogeyman: Scaring, Lulling, and Making Mock* (New York: Farrar, Straus and Giroux, 1999), 32.

211  **"Europeans bearing injections"**: David F. Lancy, *The Anthropology of Childhood: Cherubs, Chattel, Changelings* (Cambridge: Cambridge University Press, 2008), 178.

211  **Oliver Cromwell**: Chris Roberts, *Heavy Words Lightly Thrown: The Reason Behind the Rhyme* (New York: Gotham, 2005).

212  **"Baby, baby, naughty baby"**: Iona and Peter Opie, eds., *The Oxford Dictionary of Nursery Rhymes* (New York: Oxford University Press, 1997), 59; Warner, *No Go the Bogeyman*, 218.

212  **"The Swede"**: Colin Heywood, *A History of Childhood: Children and Childhood in the West from Medieval to Modern Times* (Cambridge: Polity, 2001), 90.

212  **Social Democrats**: Ibid., 97.

213  **bogeymen were employed**: DeMause, "The Evolution of Childhood," 12.

214  **St. Nicholas**: For more on the subject, see Gerry Bowler, *Santa Claus: A Biography* (Toronto: McLelland & Stewart, 2005).

215  **"the reasonable regulation"**: William E. Blatz and Helen Bott, *Parents and the Pre-school Child* (New York: W. Morrow, 1929), 280.

215  **"will never know"**: Ada Hart Arlitt, *The Child from One to Six* (New York: McGraw-Hill, 1930), 2.

216  **"Youth were never more sawcie"**: Thomas Barnes, *The Wise-Mans Forecast Against the Evill Time* (London, 1624).

216  **"lewd and wicked Children"**: Robert Russel, *A Little Book for Children and Youth: Being Good Counsel and Instructions for Your Children, Earnestly Exhorting Them to Resist the Temptation of the Devil* (London, 1695).

216  **"proudly, disdainfully, and scornfully"**: Quoted in Steven Mintz, *Huck's Raft: A History of Modern Childhood* (Cambridge, MA: Belknap Press, 2006), 19.

216  **"Their children by overcockering"**: Jane Sharp, *The Midwives Book*, ed. Elaine Hobby (reprint ed., New York: Oxford University Press, 1999), 269.

216  **Spock**: For more on Spock, self-demand feeding, and permissiveness, see Ann Hulbert, *Raising America* (New York: Vintage, 2004), 242–55.

216  **"Parents have no command"**: John Bristed, *America and Her Resources* (London: Henry Colburn, 1818), 458–59.

217  **"the total want of discipline"**: Frances Milton Trollope, *Domestic Manners of the Americans*, vol. 1 (London: Whittaker, Treacher and Co., 1832), 298.

217  **"in convulsive anger"**: Quoted in George R. Clay, "Children of the Young Republic," *American Heritage* 11, no. 3 (April 1960), 46.

217  **"Baby citizens are allowed"**: John Oldmixon, *Transatlantic Wanderings: or, a Last Look at the United States* (London: Routledge, 1855), 47.

217 **functioning musket**: Stephen A. Wynalda, *366 Days in Abraham Lincoln's Presidency* (New York: Skyhorse Publishing, 2010), 211. The musket incident occurred at the home of the boys' babysitter. Apparently, in the nineteenth century, leaving functioning muskets in your bathroom was not a fireable offense.

217 **"Lincoln would say nothing"**: William Herndon, *Herndon on Lincoln: Letters*, eds. Douglas L. Wilson and Rodney O. Davis (Urbana: University of Illinois Press, 2017), 237.

217 **"I can either run the country"**: Quoted in Stacy A. Cordery, *Alice* (New York: Penguin, 2008), 79.

217 **"For my own part"**: Harriet Martineau, *Society in America*, vol. II (New York: Saunders and Otley, 1837), 271.

217 **"suggests instead"**: Pleck, *Domestic Tyranny*, 44.

218 **going so far as to order**: Wynalda, *366 Days in Abraham Lincoln's Presidency*, 211.

218 **Spock did not invent**: For a fuller discussion of Spock's unearned reputation for permissiveness, see Thomas Maier, *Dr. Spock: An American Life* (Boston: Houghton Mifflin Harcourt, 1998), 206–9, which informs my account here.

220 **useless as well as damaging**: Ming-Te Wang and Sarah Kenny, "Longitudinal Links Between Fathers' and Mothers' Harsh Verbal Discipline and Adolescents' Conduct Problems and Depressive Symptoms," *Child Development* 85, no. 3 (May 2014): 908–23.

220 **done on pigeons**: John Joseph Donvan and Caren Brenda Zucker, *In a Different Key: The Story of Autism* (New York: Broadway Books, 2016), 209.

221 **Spartan boys**: Mark Golden, "Childhood in Ancient Greece," in Jenifer Neils and John H. Oakley, *Coming of Age in Ancient Greece: Images of Childhood from the Classical Past* (New Haven, CT: Yale University Press, 2003), 19.

221 **"of all the animals"**: Benjamin Jowett, trans., Plato, *The Dialogues*, vol. 5 (*The Laws*), third ed. (London: Clarendon Press, 1892), 190.

222 **Feral children**: For more on the history of feral children, see Julia Douthwaite, *The Wild Girl, Natural Man, and the Monster* (Chicago: Chicago University Press, 2002); and Michael Newton, *Savage Girls and Wild Boys* (New York: Thomas Dunne Books, 2003), both of which inform my account here.

222 **"teaches us absolutely nothing"**: Quoted in Douthwaite, *The Wild Girl, Natural Man, and the Monster*, 47–48.

222 **Peter likewise**: Ibid., 22–23.

222 **"Most probably idiots"**: Quoted in Newton, *Savage Girls and Wild Boys*, 38.

222 **"He had no notion of behavior"**: Ibid., 18.

223 **Victor of Aveyron**: For more on Victor, see Douthwaite, *The Wild Girl, Natural Man, and the Monster*, and Newton, *Savage Girls and Wild Boys*, both of which inform my account here.

223 **Winthrop Kellogg**: For more on the Kelloggs' experiment, see Judith Rich Harris, *The Nurture Assumption: Why Children Turn Out the Way They Do*, rev. updated ed. (New York: Free Press, 2009), 92–94, which informs my account here.

## 9. Use Your Words: Children's Books

226 **Aesop**: Grammatiki A. Karla, *"Life of Aesop*: Fictional Biography as Popular Literature?" in Koen De Temmerman and Kristoffel Demoen, eds., *Writing Biography in Greece and Rome: Narrative Technique and Fictionalization* (Cambridge: Cambridge University Press, 2016), 47–64.

229 **hornbooks**: For more on hornbooks, see Andrew W. Tuer, *History of the Horn-book* (New York: C. Scribner's Sons, 1896), and Beulah Folmsbee, *A Little History of the Horn-book* (Boston: The Horn Book, Inc., 1942).

230 **"[s]itting with knees apart"**: Erika Rummel, ed., *The Erasmus Reader* (Toronto: University of Toronto Press, 1990), 107.

230 **"Belch near no man's face"**: Frederick J. Furnivall, ed., *The Boke of Nurture by Hugh Rhodes, A.D. 1577* (Bungay, Suffolk: John Childs and Son, 1867), 19.

230 **"Foul not the tablecloth," "Smell not of thy meat"**: Quoted in Mary Cable, *The Little Darlings: A History of Child Rearing in America* (New York: Simon & Schuster, 1975), 8.

230 **"Spit not in the Room"**: *A Little Pretty Pocket-book* (Worcester, MA: Isaiah Thomas, 1787), 107.

231 **Lord Chesterfield**: For more on Lord Chesterfield, see Lorinda B. R. Goodwin, *An Archaeology of Manners* (New York: Kluwer Academic Publishers, 2002).

231 **John Amos Comenius**: For more on Comenius and *Orbis Pictus*, see C. John Sommerville, *The Rise and Fall of Childhood* (Thousand Oaks, CA: Sage Publications, 1982), 116–18; Seth Lerer, *Children's Literature: A Reader's History from Aesop to Harry Potter* (Chicago: University of Chicago Press, 2009), 84; and Patricia Crain, *The Story of A: The Alphabetization of America from The New England Primer to The Scarlet Letter* (Stanford: Stanford University Press, 2002), 30.

231 **"it is apparent"**: John Amos Comenius, *The Orbis Pictus of John Amos Comenius* (Syracuse, NY: C. W. Bardeen, 1887), xv.

234 **With the addition of these noises**: Crain, *The Story of A*, 33; and Murray Cohen, *Sensible Words: Linguistic Practice in England 1640–1785* (Baltimore: Johns Hopkins University Press, 1977), 19.

234 **"a language absolutely new"**: John Amos Comenius, *The Way of Light*, trans. E. T. Campagnac (London: Hodder & Stoughton, 1938), 4.

234 **their Edenic language**: For more on the interest in feral children's language development, see Julia Douthwaite, *The Wild Girl, Natural Man, and the Monster* (Chicago: Chicago University Press, 2002); and Michael

Newton, *Savage Girls and Wild Boys* (New York: Thomas Dunne Books, 2003).

235   **Should a parent fail to teach**: Stacy Schiff, *The Witches* (New York: Little, Brown, 2015), 43.

235   **"Place yourselves frequently"**: John Norris, *Spiritual Counsel: A Father's Advice to His Children* (London: S. Manship, 1694).

236   **Puritans were responsible**: For more on Puritan children's literature, see C. John Sommerville, *The Discovery of Childhood in Puritan England* (Athens: University of Georgia Press, 1992).

236   **"When I was at *Oxford* in our Colledge"**: Thomas White, *A Little Book for Little Children* (Boston: T. Green, 1702), 4–5.

237   *in baby talk*: Sommerville, *The Discovery of Childhood in Puritan England*, 31.

237   **John Newbery**: For more on Newbery, see Shirley Granahan, *John Newbery: Father of Children's Literature* (Edina, MN: ABDO, 2010), and Charles Welsh, *A Bookseller of the Last Century* (New York: E. P. Dutton and Co., 1885), which inform my account here.

237   **inventing the model**: Nicholas Mason, *Literary Advertising and the Shaping of British Romanticism* (Baltimore: Johns Hopkins University Press, 2013).

238   **The powder is likely what killed**: Joseph M. Miller, "Poisoning by Antimony: A Case Report," *Southern Medical Journal* 5, no. 75 (May 1982): 592.

238   **Unguents de Cao**: Welsh, *A Bookseller of the Last Century*, 36.

239   **Dr. John Hooper's Female Pills**: Ibid., 22; and Geoffrey R. Stone, *Sex and the Constitution: Sex, Religion, and Law from America's Origins to the Twenty-First Century* (New York: Liveright, 2017), 52–53.

239   **as some of his authors**: For more on Newbery's ruthlessness, see Chris Mounsey, *Christopher Smart: Clown of God* (Lewisburg, PA: Bucknell University Press, 2001); and Lori Branch, *Rituals of Spontaneity: Sentiment and Secularism from Free Prayer to Wordsworth* (Waco, TX: Baylor University Press, 2006).

239   **"He coined the brains"**: Welsh, *A Bookseller of the Last Century*, 79.

239   **Newbery forcibly committed him**: Mounsey, *Christopher Smart*, 147.

240   **"Patty Polk did this"**: Ethel Stanwood Bolton and Eva Johnston Coe, *American Samplers* (Boston: Massachusetts Society of the Colonial Dames of America, 1921), 96.

240   **Wilhelm and Jacob Grimm**: For more on the Grimm brothers, see Maria Tatar, *The Hard Facts of the Grimms' Fairy Tales* (Princeton, NJ: Princeton University Press, 1987); Jack Zipes, *The Brothers Grimm: From Enchanted Forests to the Modern World* (Basingstroke: Palgrave Macmillan, 2002); and Joan Acocella, "Once Upon a Time," *New Yorker*, July 23, 2012, 73–78, all of which inform my account here.

241   **sex is so often incest**: Tatar, *The Hard Facts of the Grimms' Fairy Tales*, 10.

242   **Huguenot**: Acocella, "Once Upon a Time."

242 **Nazis**: For more on the Grimms' Nazi popularity, see Zipes, *The Brothers Grimm*.

242 **propaganda films**: Allan Hall, "Nazi Fairy Tales Paint Hitler as Little Red Riding Hood's Savior," *Telegraph*, April 15, 2010.

242 **In some Allied schools**: Kate Connolly, "Grimm's Fairy Tales: 200th Year Triggers a Celebration," *Guardian*, December 20, 2012.

243 **the sex was taken out**: Tatar, *The Hard Facts of the Grimms' Fairy Tales*, 7–8.

243 **and often added it**: Ibid., 5.

244 **Charles and Mary Lamb**: For more on the Lambs, see Sarah Burton, *A Double Life: A Biography of Charles and Mary Lamb* (New York: Penguin, 2004).

246 **Hesba Stretton**: For more on Stretton and other didactic writers, see Kimberly Reynolds, *Children's Literature: From the Fin de Siècle to the New Millennium* (London: Northcote House, 2012).

246 **Favell Lee Mortimer**: For more on the very strange Mortimer, see Todd Pruzan's very wonderful *The Clumsiest People in Europe* (New York: Bloomsbury, 2008), to which I'm indebted both for my account here and for its general delightfulness.

247 **41 end in a fatality**: Hazel Hawthorne, "Reading Without Tears," *New Yorker*, December 31, 1949, 44–47.

247 **"Her doctor said"**: F. B. Meyer, *The Author of the Peep of Day: Being the Life Story of Mrs. Mortimer, by Her Niece Mrs. Meyer* (London: Religious Tract Society, 1901).

248 **her nephew admits**: Quoted in Pruzan, *The Clumsiest People in Europe*, 15.

249 **"most outspokenly sadistic children's books ever written"**: Rosalind Constable, "Dept. of Amplification," *New Yorker*, March 4, 1950, 79.

251 **The subject heading for her first geography book**: Megan Norcia, *X Marks the Spot: Women Writers Map the Empire for British Children, 1790–1895* (Athens: Ohio University Press, 2010), 71.

251 **"the stern, beshawled old lady"**: Constable, "Dept. of Amplification."

252 **Lewis Carroll**: For more on Carroll/Dodgson, see Robert Douglas-Fairhurst's wonderful *The Story of Alice* (Cambridge, MA: Belknap Press, 2015); Morton N. Cohen, *Lewis Carroll: A Biography* (New York: Vintage, 1996); and Karoline Leach, *In the Shadow of the Dream Child: The Myth and Reality of Lewis Carroll* (London: Peter Owen Publishers, 2015), all of which inform my account here.

252 **"Extra thanks and kisses"**: Quoted in Cohen, *Lewis Carroll*, 186.

252 **"I am fond of children"**: Ibid., 182.

252 **"I confess I do not admire"**: Ibid., 229.

252 **Nabokov**: Douglas-Fairhurst, *The Story of Alice*, 390.

252 **MO for meeting young girls**: For more on Dodgson's pickup routine, see Ibid., 237–38.

253 **"And would it be de rigueur"**: Quoted in Cohen, *Lewis Carroll*, 184.

253 **"If you should decide on sending over Gertrude"**: Quoted in Michael Bakewell, *Lewis Carroll: A Biography* (London: Heinemann, 1996), 218.

253 **nudes of young children were commonly done**: Douglas-Fairhurst, *The Story of Alice*, 252.

253 **he thought she was much *younger***: Ibid., 265.

253 **early biographers revised**: Leach, *In the Shadow of the Dream Child*, 45, 74.

253 **a reading of his full diaries**: Ibid., 107–9.

254 **recent discovery**: Hannah Furness, "BBC Investigates Whether Lewis Carroll Was 'Repressed Paedophile' After Nude Photo Discovery," *Telegraph*, January 26, 2015.

255 **J. M. Barrie**: For more on Barrie, see Andrew Birkin, *J. M. Barrie and the Lost Boys: The Real Story Behind Peter Pan* (New Haven, CT: Yale University Press, 2003); Lisa Chaney, *Hide and Seek with the Angels: A Life of J. M. Barrie* (New York: St. Martin's, 2006); and Piers Dudgeon, *Neverland: J. M. Barrie, the Du Mauriers, and the Dark Side of Peter Pan* (New York: Pegasus Books, 2011), all of which inform my account here.

255 **psychogenic dwarfism**: "J. M. Barrie: Stuck in Neverland," *The Scotsman*, December 13, 2009.

255 **"I don't believe"**: Birkin, *J. M. Barrie and the Lost Boys*.

257 **may have also forged Sylvia's will**: Dudgeon, *Neverland*, 196.

257 **"almost unbelievably queer"**: Quoted in Ibid., 194.

258 **Margaret Wise Brown**: For more on Brown and her work, see Leonard S. Marcus, *Margaret Wise Brown: Awakened by the Moon* (Boston: Beacon Press, 1992); Amy Gary, *In the Great Green Room: The Brilliant and Bold Life of Margaret Wise Brown* (New York: Flatiron Books, 2017); and Bruce Handy, *Wild Things: The Joy of Reading Children's Literature as an Adult* (New York: Simon & Schuster, 2017), which inform my account here.

259 **Dr. Seuss**: For more on Dr. Seuss/Theodor Geisel, see Donald E. Pease, *Theodor Seuss Geisel: A Portrait of the Man Who Became Dr. Seuss* (New York: Oxford University Press, 2010), and Thomas Fensch, *The Man Who Was Dr. Seuss: The Life and Work of Theodor Geisel* (The Woodlands, TX: New Century Books, 2000), which inform my account here.

259 **"You have 'em, I'll entertain 'em!"**: Michael J. Bandler, "Wearing the Hat," *Chicago Tribune*, November 20, 1994.

260 **"would be unable to put down"**: Pease, *Theodor Seuss Geisel*, 101.

260 **crossed paths with Hemingway and the Lost Generation**: Heinz-Dietrich Fischer and Erika J. Fischer, *Complete Biographical Encyclopedia of Pulitzer Prize Winners, 1917–2000*, vol. 16 (Munich: K. G. Saur, 2002), 81.

261 **"subversive as hell"**: Fensch, *The Man Who Was Dr. Seuss*.

261 **Ludwig Bemelmans**: Greg Cook, "How a Jilted Mom, a Former Nun, and a Shattered Childhood Inspired 'Madeline,'" WBUR, February 17, 2015.

261 **Frances**: For more on the Hobans and their books, see Kate Moses, "Ode to Frances," *Salon*, April 17, 2001.

## 10. Lullaby and Good Night: *Sleep*

265  For a general overview of sleep and its history, see A. Roger Ekirch, *At Day's Close: Night in Times Past* (New York: Norton, 2005); David K. Randall, *Dreamland: Adventures in the Strange Science of Sleep* (New York: Norton, 2012); and Benjamin Reiss, *Wild Nights: How Taming Sleep Created Our Restless World* (New York: Basic Books, 2017).

265  **the issue that parents seek help for**: Sara Harkness, Constance H. Keefer, Natalie van Tijen, and Ellen van der Vlugt, "Cultural Influences on Sleep Patterns in Infancy and Early Childhood," paper presented at the meeting of the American Association for the Advancement of Science, Symposium on Ethnopediatrics: Cultural Factors in Child Survival and Growth, Atlanta, GA, February 1995.

267  **something done communally two or three times a day**: For a compelling discussion of the way modern sleep has been privatized, see Benjamin Reiss, *Wild Nights*.

268  **The Quran**: Ahmed S. BaHammam, "Sleep from an Islamic Perspective," *Annals of Thoracic Medicine* 6, no. 4, (October–December 2011): 187–92.

268  **made their own beds**: Lawrence Wright, *Warm & Snug: The History of the Bed* (London: Routledge & Kegan Paul, 1962), 18.

268  **joined by the livestock**: Ekirch, *At Day's Close*, 279.

269  **Babies would sleep tightest of all**: Karin Calvert, *Children in the House: The Material Culture of Early Childhood, 1600–1900* (Lebanon, NH: University Press of New England, 1992), 28–29.

269  **"furious rocking"**: "The Crib and the Cradle," *Godey's* 52 (May 1856), 478, quoted in Calvert, *Children in the House*, which documents the rise of the crib; see 132–35.

270  **monophasic sleep**: Roger Ekirch's discoveries are shared in his wonderful book *At Day's Close*. David K. Randall shares Ekirch's work and Thomas Wehr's scientific corroboration of it in the fascinating *Dreamland: Adventures in the Strange Science of Sleep*.

270  **in traditional societies**: A. Roger Ekirch, "Segmented Sleep in Preindustrial Societies," *Sleep* 39, no. 3 (March 1, 2016): 715–16.

270  **reverted to biphasic sleep**: Thomas A. Wehr, "A 'Clock for All Seasons' in the Human Brain," in R. M. Buijs et al., eds., *Progress in Brain Research* 111 (1996): 321–42; and Thomas A. Wehr, "The Impact of Changes in Nightlength (Scotoperiod) on Human Sleep," in F. W. Turek and P. C. Zee, eds., *Neurobiology of Sleep and Circadian Rhythms* (New York: Marcel Dekker, 1999), 263–85.

270  **Babies' sleep is even more segmented**: Randall, *Dreamland*, 71–73.

271  **generationally differing sleep schedules**: David Samson, Alyssa Crittenden, Ibrahim Mabulla, Audax Mabulla, and Charles Nunn, "Chronotype Variation Drives Night-time Sentinel-Like Behaviour in Hunter-Gatherers," *Proceedings of the Royal Society B* 284, no. 1858 (July 12, 2017).

271 **The few studies that examine it**: Anne Conway, Alison L. Miller, and Anahid Modrek, "Testing Reciprocal Links Between Trouble Getting to Sleep and Internalizing Behavior Problems, and Bedtime Resistance and Externalizing Behavior Problems in Toddlers," *Child Psychiatry & Human Development* 48, no. 4 (August 2017): 678–89; and Maggie Koerth-Baker, "Don't Tell the Kids, But Bedtime Is a Social Construct," *FiveThirtyEight*, July 12, 2017.

272 **Co-sleeping was the norm**: John Seabrook, "Sleeping with the Baby," *New Yorker*, November 8, 1999, 56–66.

272 **These numbers are up**: Randall, *Dreamland*, 70.

272 **"two-pound baby woolly monkey"**: Jean Liedloff, *The Continuum Concept* (reprint ed., Da Capo Press, 1986), 158.

272 **Soranus was warning**: *Soranus's Gynecology* (Baltimore: Johns Hopkins University Press, 1956), 110.

272 **backing the demand up**: Mary Martin McLaughlin, "Survivors and Surrogates: Children and Parents from the Ninth to Thirteenth Centuries," in Carol Neel, ed., *Medieval Families: Perspectives on Marriage, Household and Children* (Toronto: University of Toronto Press, 2004), 20–124.

273 **It was safer and warmer**: For more on the history of communal sleeping, see Ekirch, *At Day's Close*, 278–84.

274 **For the sake of propriety**: Ibid., 278–79.

274 **shunamitism**: For a thorough discussion of shunamitism, see Danielle Gourevitch, "On the Medical Tradition of Shunamitism," *Koroth* 9 (1988): 49–61.

274 **"there is no practice"**: B. W. Richardson, M.D., "Health at Home (Part Second)," *Appleton's Journal* (January–June 1880), 525.

275 **"a murderous process"**: William Whitty Hall, *Sleep* (New York: W. W. Hall, 1863), 47.

276 **"a degenerate practice"**: Bill Bryson, *At Home: A Short History of Private Life* (New York: Doubleday, 2009), 320–21.

276 **class anxiety**: Randall, *Dreamland*, 78; and Peter N. Stearns, Perrin Rowland, and Lori Giarnella, "Children's Sleep: Sketching Historical Change," *Journal of Social History* 30, no. 2 (Winter 1996): 345–66.

276 **a kind of life insurance**: Helen Kinne and Anna Maria Cooley, *The Home and the Family: An Elementary Textbook of Home Making* (New York: Macmillan Company, 1910), 218.

276 **"almost invariably the case"**: Luther Emmett Holt, *The Care and Feeding of Children*, 10th ed. (New York: D. Appleton and Co., 1921), 29.

276 **Eleanor Roosevelt**: Jean Edward Smith, *FDR* (New York: Random House Trade Paperbacks, 2008), 57.

277 **a time of growing anxiety**: Stearns et al., "Children's Sleep: Sketching Historical Change."

278 **"soot tea"**: Karin Calvert, *Children in the House: The Material Culture of*

*Early Childhood, 1600–1900* (Lebanon, NH: University Press of New England, 1992), 77.

278 **"at the top of his voice"**: *Babyhood*, vol. 6 (New York and London: Babyhood Publishing Company, December 1889–November 1890), 249.

278 **"may induce"**: Quoted in Stearns et al., "Children's Sleep: Sketching Historical Change," 353.

278 **may have made things worse**: Ibid., 353.

278 **"elaborate good-night rituals"**: Grace Langdon, "Training a Baby to Sleep," *Good Housekeeping*, February 1943, 19, 40, 44.

279 **early bedtime books**: Maria Tatar, *Enchanted Hunters: The Power of Stories in Childhood* (New York: Norton, 2009), 34–67.

279 **bedtime stories probably evolved**: Ibid., 44.

279 **"He's a wicked man"**: Quoted in Ibid., 46.

281 **"the influence of national socialism"**: For a fascinating discussion of the origins of sleep training in Germany, see Karen Bergstermann, *"Seit wann müssen Kinder schlafen lernen?"* (Since when do children have to learn to sleep?), *Deutschen Hebammen Zeitschrift*, August 2010. For a summary in English with useful commentary, see http://www.phdinparenting.com/blog/2011/5/9/the-history-of-sleep-training-in-germany.html.

281 **"In doing this"**: Catharine E. Beecher, *A Treatise on Domestic Economy* (New York: Harper & Brothers, 1848 reprint), 219–20.

282 **Spock would deliver a talk**: Benjamin Spock, "Chronic Resistance to Sleep in Infancy," read at the regional meeting of the American Academy of Pediatrics, Milwaukee, WI, June 28–30, 1948, published in *Pediatrics* 4, no. 1 (July 1949): 89–93.

282 **badminton net**: Benjamin Spock. *The Common Sense Book of Baby and Child Care* (New York: Duell, Sloan and Pearce, 1957), 392.

282 **Joan Crawford**: Jerry Parker, "Like Daughter, Like Son Chris," *Los Angeles Times*, October 29, 1978.

282 **"letting the child suck"**: Bruno Bettelheim, "Does Your Child Fight Sleep?" *Parents' Magazine* 10 (1951): 26, 54–55, 83–84, 86, 88, 90, 92, 94.

282 **"more than a household name"**: Ann Hulbert, "The Dr. Spock of Sleep," *Slate*, May 31, 2006.

283 **"the people who are truly hard to train"**: Ibid.

# Index

Page numbers in *italic* type indicate illustrations. Page numbers followed by *n* indicate footnotes.